2014 MINUTES OF THE GENERAL ASSEMBLY CUMBERLAND PRESBYTERIAN CHURCH

Office of the General Assembly

Cumberland Presbyterian Church

August 2014

**8207 Traditional Place
Cordova (Memphis), Tennessee 38016**

©2014 Office of the General Assembly, CPC

All Rights Reserved. No part of this book may be reproduced or transmitted in any form or by any means, electronic or mechanical, including photocopying, recording, or by any information storage or retrieval system, without permission in writing from the publisher. For information address Office of the General Assembly, Cumberland Presbyterian Center, 8207 Traditional Place, Cordova (Memphis), Tennessee, 38016-7414.

Published and distributed by The Discipleship Ministry Team, CPC
Memphis, Tennessee

The Discipleship Ministry Team of the Ministry Council of the Cumberland Presbyterian Church is the successor organization to the Board of Christian Education of the Cumberland Presbyterian Church.

Funded, in part, by your contributions to Our United Outreach.

First Edition 2014

ISBN-13: 978-0692274934
ISBN-10: 0692274936

OUR UNITED OUTREACH
Made Possible In Part By Your Tithe To Our United Outreach

2014 MINUTES

General Assembly
Cumberland Presbyterian Church

ONE HUNDRED EIGHTY-FOURTH MEETING

CHATTANOOGA, TENNESSEE

****

NEXT MEETING - CALI, COLOMBIA

JUNE 19-26, 2015

****

Vision of Ministry

Biblically-based and Christ-centered
    born out of a specific sense of mission,
    the Cumberland Presbyterian Church strives to be true to its heritage:
    to be open to God's reforming spirit,
    to work cooperatively with the larger Body of Christ,
    and to nurture the connectional bonds that make us one.
The Cumberland Presbyterian Church seeks—to be the hands and feet of Christ in witness and service to the world and, above all, the Cumberland Presbyterian Church lives out the love of God to the glory of Jesus Christ.

THE CUMBERLAND PRESBYTERIAN CHURCH
TABLE OF CONTENTS

Vision of Ministry and Priority Goals 2
Program 4
Commissioners 6
Youth Advisory Delegates 7
Committees and Abbreviations 7
Committee Meeting Rooms 7
Committee Assignments 8
Assembly Meetings and Officers 9
By Laws of General Assembly Corporation 12
Memorial Roll of Ministers 22
Living General Assembly Moderators 23
Membership of Boards and Agencies 24

Reports
    Moderator 32
    Stated Clerk 34
    Ministry Council Report One 40
    Ministry Council Report Two 57
    Board of Stewardship, Foundation and Benefits 59
    Board of the Historical Foundation 71
    Board of Trustees of Memphis Theological Seminary 81
    OUO Committee 96
    Commission on Chaplains and Military Personnel 98
    Permanent Judiciary Committee 100
    Nominating Committee 102
    Place of Meeting Committee 104
    Unified Committee on Theology and Social Concerns 106
    Unification Task Force 108
    Board of Trustees of Bethel University 115
    Board of Trustees of the Cumberland Presbyterian Children's Home 116

Agency Budgets 121

Audits 130

General Assembly Minutes 266

Appendices 275

Church Calendar 293

PROGRAM SCHEDULE

Assembly Meetings:	Chattanooga Choo Choo Hotel & Convention Space
General Assembly Office:	Director's Room in the Terminal Station
Women's Ministry Office:	Gallery C in the Centennial Center
Retiring Moderator:	The Reverend Forest Prosser, Tennessee-Georgia Presbytery
Host:	Tennessee-Georgia Presbytery
Pastor Host:	The Reverend Jennifer Newell, Tennessee-Georgia Presbytery
Worship Director	The Reverend Abby Cole Keller, Presbytery of East Tennessee
Music Director:	Mr. Gerald Peel, First CPC Chattanooga, Tennessee, Tennessee-Georgia Presbytery

SUNDAY, JUNE 15, 2014

Location	Time	Event	
Terminal Station	3:00 p.m.	Registration	**Main Lobby**
Terminal Station	3:00 p.m.	Orientation for Commissioners & Youth Advisory Delegates	**Roosevelt Room**
		Orientation for Committee Chairs and Co-Chairs	
		(Commissioner/YAD packets may be picked up before or after the orientation session.)	
Centennial Center	3:00 p.m.	Setup displays	**Hallways & Track 29**
Centennial Center	7:00 p.m	Praise Gathering/Singing	**Imperial Ballroom**

FIRST DAY - MONDAY, JUNE 16, 2014

Centennial Center	8:00 a.m.	CPCA Opening Worship	**Imperial Ballroom**
Terminal Station	8:30 a.m.	Registration for Commissioners and Youth Advisory Delegates	
		(for those who did not register on Sunday)	**Main Lobby**
Terminal Station	9:00 a.m.	Women's Ministry Registration (open until 5:00 p.m.)	**Main Lobby**
	10:15 a.m.	Break	
Various Locations	10:30 a.m.	Pre-Assembly Workshops	**TBA**
Terminal Station	12:00 p.m.	CPCA National Sunday School Convention Luncheon	**Roosevelt Room**
Centennial Center	2:00 p.m.	CPC Opening Worship	**Imperial Ballroom**
		The Retiring Moderator: The Reverend Forest Prosser,	
		Tennessee-Georgia Presbytery	
		Worship Director: The Reverend Abby Cole Keller, Presbytery of East Tennessee	
	3:00 p.m.	Break for Commissioners and YADs to move to Commissioners	
		Section for business session	
	3:15 p.m.	Constitution of the General Assembly	
		Adoption of the Agenda	
		Report of the Credentials Committee	
		Election of Moderator	
		Election of Vice-Moderator	
		Presentation by the Stated Clerk, Mike Sharpe	
		Presentation by Children's Home	
		Communications	
		Corrections to preliminary minutes	
		Committee Appointments and Referrals to Committees	
		Welcome, Pastor Host, Local Officials	
		Introduction of Board and Agency Representatives	
Various Locations	4:00 p.m.	General Assembly Committees meet	**See Bottom of Page 7**
Terminal Station	4:30 p.m.	Women's Ministry Regional Council Meeting and Dinner	**Roosevelt Room**
	5:30 p.m.	Break for Dinner	

EVENING PROGRAM

First CPC	7:00 p.m.	Joint Communion Service (CPC/CPCA)	**Sanctuary**
First CPC	8:30 p.m.	Joint Moderator's Reception honoring the Moderator and	**Fellowship Hall**
		Vice-Moderator of the General Assembly,	
		the Immediate Past Moderator, the President-Elect and	
		the President of the Cumberland Presbyterian Women's Ministry	

SECOND DAY - TUESDAY, JUNE 17, 2014

Centennial Center	8:30 a.m. Joint Devotional led by Global Community	**Imperial Ballroom**
	9:00 a.m. Unification Task Force Update	**Imperial Ballroom**
	10:30 a.m. Break	
Terminal Station	10:45 a.m. Women's Ministry Convention	**Roosevelt Room**
Centennial Center	10:45 a.m. CPC General Assembly business session Resolutions by Commissioners Adjourn for Committee Meetings	**Centennial Theatre**
Various Locations	11:15 a.m. Committee Meetings	**See Bottom of Page 7**
Centennial Center	12:30 p.m. CPCA National Missionary Society Luncheon	**Imperial Ballroom**
	1:30 p.m. Committee Meetings (see meeting room list above)	
	2:00 p.m. Joint Women's Ministry Meeting	**Imperial Ballroom**
Terminal Station	5:30 p.m. Bethel University Dinner	**Roosevelt Room**

EVENING PROGRAM

Track 29	7:00 p.m. Joint Worship sponsored by CPC/CPCA Youth	Track 29
Track 29	8:00 p.m. Fun Night for Everyone	Track 29

THIRD DAY - WEDNESDAY, JUNE 18, 2014

Centennial Center	8:30 a.m. Joint Devotional led by Women Ministries	**Imperial Ballroom**
Various Locations	9:30 a.m. Committee Meetings	**See Bottom of Page 7**
Centennial Center	9:30 a.m. Women's Ministry Convention Reconvenes	**Imperial Ballroom**
Track 29	12:00 p.m. Memphis Theological Seminary and the Program of Alternate Studies Luncheon	**Track 29**
Centennial Center	12:00 p.m. Women's Ministry Field Trip plus Workshops (2-4:00 p.m.)	**TBA**
	5:00 p.m. Conclusion of Committee Meetings	
Terminal Station	5:30 p.m. Cumberland Presbyterian Children's Home Dinner	**Roosevelt Room**

EVENING PROGRAM

Centennial Center	7:00 p.m. Joint Louisa Woosley Celebration	**Imperial Ballroom**
Terminal Station	8:30 p.m. Joint Reception Honoring Women in Ministry (Reception to begin following worship service)	

FOURTH DAY - THURSDAY, JUNE 19, 2014

Centennial Center	8:30 a.m. Joint Devotional led by Children's Ministries	**Centennial Theatre**
	9:00 a.m. General Assembly Business	
Terminal Station	9:00 a.m. Women's Ministry Convention Reconvenes	**Roosevelt Room**
	12:00 p.m. Lunch Break	
Centennial Center	12:00 p.m. Cumberland Presbyterian Women's Ministry Luncheon	**Imperial Ballroom**
	2:00 p.m. General Assembly Business	**Centennial Theatre**
	5:00 p.m. Dinner Break Take Down Displays	

EVENING PROGRAM

Centennial Center	7:00 p.m. General Assembly Business	**Centennial Theatre**

Closing Worship: The Reverend Jennifer Newell, Tennessee-Georgia Presbytery

(In the event that business is not concluded on Thursday,
the closing worship will be at the conclusion of business on Friday morning.)

COMMISSIONERS
to the
ONE HUNDRED EIGHTY-FOURTH GENERAL ASSEMBLY

PRESBYTERY	MINISTER	COMMITTEE	ELDER	COMMITTEE
Andes (1)	Juan Blandon	C/M/P		
Arkansas (2)	Gordon Warren	C/M/P	Robert Clement	HE
	Jo Warren	TSC	James Strickland	MC/C/D
Cauca Valley (2)	Fabiola Ariza	C/M/P		
Choctaw (1)	Nathan Scott	S/E	Pat Espinoza	J
Columbia (2)	Terry Peery	J	Joyce Jeffries	MC/C/D
	Kirk Smith	HE	Mike McCord	J
Covenant (3)	Randy Lowe	MC/C/D	Darl Henley	MC/C/D
	R. B. Mays	C/M/P	Ron Peebels	J
			Kenny Quinton	CPCH/HF
Cumberland (3)	Bill Macy	C/M/P	Marlene Darland	CPCH/HF
	Frank McCallum	S/E	Kathy McGrew	TSC
	Jeff McMichael	J	Steve Shaw	MC/C/D
Cumberland East Coast (1)	Douglas Park	CPCH/HF		
Del Cristo (2)	Gerald Hagelin	HE	Cindy Chitwood	C/M/P
	Cynthia Maddux	TSC	Tom McWilliams	CPCH/HF
East Tennessee (3)	Gary Hartman	HE	Cliff Fluharty	TSC
	Abby Keller	J	Rebecca Miller	HE
	Bill Middleton	TSC	Dianne Pipkin	C/M/P
Grace (3)	Mindy Acton	S/E	Tommy Neel	C/M/P
	Scott Fowler	J	Ann St. John	TSC
	Sherrlyn Frost	MC/C/D	Debbie Silva	S/E
Hong Kong (1)				
Hope (1)	Terry Herston	HE		
Japan (1)	Takehiko Miyai	C/M/P	Hiroshi Yoshizuki	C/M/P
Missouri (1)	Richard Plachte	MC/C/D	Lana Moore	HE
Murfreesboro (4)	Mark Barron	C/M/P	Peggy Foster	S/E
	William James	S/E	Linda Ingram	TSC
	James McGill	CPCH/HF	Robert Joins	HE
	Richard Morgan	TSC	Maria Mott	CPCH/HF
Nashville (4)	Paula Louder	S/E	Herb Dewees	TSC
	Stewart Salyer	HE	Randy Gannon	C/M/P
	John Smith	HE		
	Susan Varner	MC/C/D		
North Central (2)	James Messer	C/M/P	Victory Moore	C/M/P
	Kevin Vanderlaan	MC/C/D	Priscilla Wilson	J
Red River (3)	Chuck Brown	TSC	Judy Franco	HE
	Barney Hudson	C/M/P	Erin Smith	CPCH/HF
	Allan Mink	CPCH/HF		
Robert Donnell (1)	Darren Kennemer	TSC	Tyrone Harris	HE
Tenn./Georgia (3)	Rhonda McGowan	CPCH/HF	Diane Bunch	CPCH/HF
	Forest Prosser	J	Michael McCormack	J
	Kevin Wilson	MC/C/D	Pat Varnell	S/E
Trinity (2)	Don Nunn	TSC	Ladd Daniel	J
	Sam Wayman	HE	Randy Kennedy	S/E
West Tennessee (5)	Lisa Anderson	CPCH/HF	Jerry Covington	C/M/P
	Larry Blakeburn	J	Cynthia Creyssels	TSC
	Clinton Buck	J	Cheryl Leslie	S/E
	Mitch Boulton	CPCH/HF	Linda Spaulding	HE
	Paul Criss	S/E		

YOUTH ADVISORY DELEGATES
to the
ONE HUNDRED EIGHTY-FOURTH GENERAL ASSEMBLY

(Each Presbytery is eligible to send two Youth Advisory Delegates)

PRESBYTERY	DELEGATE	COMMITTEE
Arkansas	Mandy Jones	MC/C/D
	Mindy Jones	S/E
Choctaw	A'an Parra	J
Columbia	McKenzie Bybee	TSC
	Conner Upshaw	MC/C/D
Covenant	Haley Russell	TSC
	Dylan Weaver	J
Cumberland	(no youth)	
del Cristo	(no youth)	
East Tennessee	Kaylah Mullins	MC/C/D
	Pryor Summitt	J
Grace	Craig Barkley	CPCH/HF
	Brady Thrash	C/M/P
Hope	(no youth)	
Japan	(no youth)	
Missouri	Mariah Jones	J
Murfreesboro	Justin Dillard	HE
	Jay Truitt	C/M/P
Nashville	Seth Langley	HE
	Allie Vaughn	CPCH/HF
North Central	Madison Ulrich	HE
	Dakota Young	C/M/P
Red River	Nicole Franco	CPCH/HF
	Kennedy McKeaigg	S/E
Robert Donnell	Dakota Harris	S/E
Tennessee Georgia		
Trinity	Luke House	HE
	Davis Webb	TSC
West Tennessee	Michael Keenan	CPCH/HF
	Rachel Starks	C/M/P

COMMITTEES ABBREVIATIONS AND MEETING ROOMS

Chattanooga Choo Choo Hotel & Conference Center

ABBREV.	COMMITTEE	MEETING ROOMS
C/M/P	Chaplains/Missions/Pastoral Development	Hotel Bldg 1, Norfolk Rm 150
CPCH/HF	Children's Home/Historical Foundation	Hotel Bldg 3, Suite 1008
HE	Higher Education	Hotel Bldg 3, Suite 1017
J	Judiciary	Formal Garden Area, American Railcar
MC/C/D	Ministry Council/Communications/Discipleship	Hotel Bldg 1, Southern Rm 150
S/E	Stewardship/Elected Officers	Centennial Theatre Lobby
TSC	Theology/Social Concerns	Centennial Theatre

COMMITTEE ASSIGNMENTS

1. **CHAPLAINS/MISSIONS/PASTORAL DEVELOPMENT**
   Chair: Rev. James Messer   **Co-Chair:** Rev. Barney Hudson
   Ministers: Fabiola Ariza, Mark Barron, Juan Blandon, Bill Macy, R.B. Mays, Takehiko Miyai Gordon Warren
   Elders: Cindy Chitwood, Jerry Covington, Randy Gannon, Victory Moore, Tommy Neel, Dianne Pipkin Hiroshi Yoshizuki
   Youth Advisory Delegates: Rachel Starks, Brady Thrash, Jay Truitt, Dakota Young

2. **CHILDREN'S HOME/HISTORICAL FOUNDATION**
   Chair: Rev. Lisa Anderson   **Co-Chair:** Rev. Rhonda McGowan
   Ministers: Mitch Boulton, James McGill, Allan Mink, Douglas Park
   Elders: Diane Bunch, Marlene Darland, Maria Mott, Tom McWilliams, Kenny Quinton, Erin Smith
   Youth Advisory Delegates: Craig Barkley, Nicole Franco, Michael Keenan, Allie Vaughn

3. **HIGHER EDUCATION**
   Chair: Rev. Sam Wayman   **Co-Chair:** Elder Judy Franco
   Ministers: Gerald Hagelin, Gary Hartman, Terry Herston, Stewart Salyer, John Smith, Kirk Smith
   Elders: Robert Clement, Tyrone Harris, Robert Joins, Rebecca Miller, Lana Moore, Linda Spaulding
   Youth Advisory Delegates: Justin Dillard, Luke House, Seth Langley, Madison Ulrich

4. **JUDICIARY**
   Chair: Elder Ladd Daniel   **Co-Chair:** Rev. Larry Blakeburn
   Ministers: Clinton Buck, Scott Fowler, Abby Keller, Jeff McMichael, Terry Peery, Forest Prosser
   Elders: Pat Espinoza, Mike McCord, Michael McCormack, Ron Peebels, Priscilla Wilson
   Youth Advisory Delegates: Mariah Jones, A'an Para, Pryor Summit, Dylan Weaver

5. **MINISTRY COUNCIL/COMMUNICATIONS/DISCIPLESHIP**
   Chair: Rev. Sherrlyn Frost   **Co-Chair:** Rev. Kevin Wilson
   Ministers: Randy Lowe, Richard Plachte, Kevin Vanderlaan, Susan Varner
   Elders: Darl Henley, Joyce Jeffries, Doris Shipp, James Strickland
   Youth Advisory Delegates: Mandy Jones, Kaylah Mullins, Conner Upshaw

6. **STEWARDSHIP/ELECTED OFFICERS**
   Chair: Rev. Mindy Acton   **Co-Chair:** Rev. Paul Criss
   Ministers: William James, Paula Louder, Frank McCallum, Nathan Scott
   Elders: Peggy Foster, Randy Kennedy, Cheryl Leslie, Debbie Silva, Pat Varnell
   Youth Advisory Delegates: Dakota Harris, Mindy Jones, Kennedy McKreaigg

7. **THEOLOGY/SOCIAL CONCERNS**
   Chair: Rev. Darren Kennemer   **Co-Chair:** Rev. Cynthia Maddux
   Ministers: Chuck Brown, Bill Middleton, Richard Morgan, Donn Nunn, Jo Warren
   Elders: Cynthia Creyssels, Herb Dewees, Cliff Fluharty, Linda Ingram, Ann St. John
   Youth Advisory Delegates: McKenzie Bybee, Hailey Russell, Davis Webb

8. **CREDENTIALS:**
   Chair: Reverend Bill Middleton
   Members: Reverend Wendell Ordway, Elder Lana Moore
   Youth Advisory Delegate: Mandy Jones

ASSEMBLY MEETINGS AND OFFICERS

Historical Review of the Stated Meetings and Officers of:

THE CUMBERLAND PRESBYTERY, 1810-1813

Date	Place	Moderator	Clerk	Members
1810, February	Sam McAdow's House, Dickson Co., TN	Samuel McAdow	Young Ewing	3
1810, March 20	Ridge Meeting-House, Sumner Co., TN.	Samuel McAdow	Young Ewing	14
1810, October 23	Lebanon Meeting-House	Finis Ewing	Young Ewing	16
1811, March 19	Big Spring, Wilson Co., TN	Robert Bell	Young Ewing	19
1811, October 9	Ridge Meeting-House	Thomas Calhoun	David Foster	23
1812, April 7	Suggs Creek Meeting-House	Hugh Kirkpatrick	James B. Porter	28
1812, November 3	Lebanon, KY	Finis Ewing	Hugh Kirkpatrick	22
1813, April 6	Beech Meeting-House, Sumner Co. TN	Robert Bell	James B. Porter	34

THE CUMBERLAND SYNOD, 1813-1828

Date	Place	Moderator	Clerk	Members
1813, October 5	Beech Meeting-House	William McGee	Finis Ewing	13
1814, April 5	Suggs Creek	David Foster	James B. Porter	27
1815, October 17	Beech Meeting-House	William Barnett	David Foster	15
1816, October 15	Free Meeting-House, TN	Thomas Calhoun	David Foster	22
1817, October 21	Mt. Moriah, KY	Robert Donnell	Hugh Kirkpatrick	27
1818, October 20	Big Spring, TN	Finis Ewing	Robert Bell	27
1819, October 19	Suggs Creek, TN	Samuel King	William Barnett	24
1820, October 17	Russellville, KY	Thomas Calhoun	William Moore	30
1821, Third Tues. in Oct.	Russellville, KY	Minutes not recorded		
1822, October 15	Beech Meeting-House	James B. Porter	David Foster	47
1823, October 21	Russellville, KY	John Barnett	Aaron Alexander	48
1824, October 19	Cane Creek, TN	Samuel King	William Moore	68
1825, October 18	Princeton, KY	William Barnett	Hiram McDaniel	76
1826, Third Tues. in Oct.	Russellville, KY	Minutes not recorded		
1827, November 20	Russellville, KY	James S. Guthrie	Laban Jones	63
1828, October 21	Franklin, TN	Hiram A. Hunter	Richard Beard	94

THE GENERAL ASSEMBLY, 1829-

Date	Place	Moderator	Clerk	Members
1829, May 19	Princeton, KY	Thomas Calhoun	F. R. Cossitt	26
1830, May 18	Princeton, KY	James B. Porter	F. R. Cossitt	36
1831, May 17	Princeton, KY	Alex Chapman	F. R. Cossitt	34
1832, May 15	Nashville, TN	F. R. Cossitt	F. R. Cossitt	36
1833, May 21	Nashville, TN	Samuel King	F. R. Cossitt	35
1834, May 20	Nashville, TN	Thomas Calhoun	James Smith	48
1835, May 19	Princeton, KY	Sam King	James Smith	42
1836, May 17	Nashville, TN	Reuben Burrow	James Smith	43
1837, May 16	Lebanon, TN	Robert Donnell	James Smith	49
1838, May 15	Princeton, KY	Hiram A. Hunter	James Smith	47
1840, May 19	Elkton, KY	Reuben Burrow	James Smith	55
1841, May 18	Owensboro, KY	William Ralston	C. G. McPherson	56
1842, May 17	Owensboro, KY	Milton Bird	C. G. McPherson	57
1843, May 16	Owensboro, KY	A. M. Bryan	C. G. McPherson	68
1845, May 20	Lebanon, TN	Richard Beard	C. G. McPherson	95
1846, May 19	Owensboro, KY	M. H. Bone	C. G. McPherson	86
1847, May 18	Lebanon, Ohio	Hiram A. Hunter	C. G. McPherson	71
1848, May 16	Memphis, TN	Milton Bird	C. G. McPherson	100
1849, May 16	Princeton, KY	John L. Smith	C. G. McPherson	75
1850, May 21	Clarksville, TN	Reuben Burrow	Milton Bird	102
1851, May 20	Pittsburgh, PA	Milton Bird	Milton Bird	71
1852, May 18	Nashville, TN	David Lowry	Milton Bird	107
1853, May 17	Princeton, KY	H. S. Porter	Milton Bird	108
1854, May 16	Memphis, TN	Isaac Shook	Milton Bird	112
1855, May 15	Lebanon, TN	M. H. Bone	Milton Bird	101
1856, May 15	Louisville, KY	Milton Bird	Milton Bird	99
1857, May 21	Lexington, MO	Carson P. Reed	Milton Bird	106
1858, May 20	Huntsville, AL	Felix Johnson	Milton Bird	124
1859, May 19	Evansville, IN	T. B. Wilson	Milton Bird	131
1860, May 17	Nashville, TN	S. G. Burney	Milton Bird	168
1861, May 16	St. Louis, MO	A. E. Cooper	Milton Bird	51
1862, May 15	Owensboro, KY	P. G. Rea	Milton Bird	58
1863, May 21	Alton, IL	Milton Bird	Milton Bird	73
1864, May 19	Lebanon, OH	Jesse Anderson	Milton Bird	65
1865, May 18	Evansville, IN	Hiram Douglas	Milton Bird	78
1866, May 17	Owensboro, KY	Richard Beard	Milton Bird	155
1867, May 16	Memphis, TN	J. B. Mitchell	Milton Bird	176
1868, May 21	Lincoln, IL	G. W. Mitchell	Milton Bird	184
1869, May 20	Murfreesboro, TN	S. T. Anderson	Milton Bird	173
1870, May 19	Warrensburg, MO	J. C. Provine	Milton Bird	167

Date	Place	Moderator	Clerk	Members
1871, May 18	Nashville, TN	J. B. Logan	Milton Bird	173
1872, May 16	Evansville, IN	C. H. Bell	Milton Bird	182
1873, May 15	Huntsville, AL	J. W. Poindexter	John Frizzell	165
1874, May 21	Springfield, MO	T. C. Blake	John Frizzell	185
1875, May 20	Jefferson, TX	W. S. Campbell	John Frizzell	169
1876, May 18	Bowling Green, KY	J. M. Gill	John Frizzell	184
1877, May 17	Lincoln, IL	A. B. Miller	John Frizzell	171
1878, May 16	Lebanon, TN	D. E. Bushnell	John Frizzell	205
1879, May 15	Memphis, TN	J. S. Grider	John Frizzell	143
1880, May 20	Evansville, IN	A. Templeton	John Frizzell	194
1881, May 19	Austin, TX	W. J. Darby	John Frizzell	187
1882, May 18	Huntsville, AL	S. H. Buchanan	John Frizzell	188
1883, May 17	Nashville, TN	A. J. McGlumphey	T. C. Blake	204
1884, May 15	McKeesport, PA	John Frizzell	T. C. Blake	148
1885, May 21	Bentonville, AR	G. T. Stainback	T. C. Blake	185
1886, May 20	Sedalia, MO	E. B. Crisman	T. C. Blake	193
1887, May 19	Covington, OH	Nathan Green	T. C. Blake	187
1888, May 17	Waco, TX	W. H. Black	T. C. Blake	217
1889, May 16	Kansas City, MO	J. M. Hubbert	T. C. Blake	217
1890, May 15	Union City, TN	E. G. McLean	T. C. Blake	220
1891, May 21	Owensboro, KY	E. F. Beard	T. C. Blake	213
1892, May 19	Memphis, TN	W. T. Danley	T. C. Blake	229
1893, May 18	Little Rock, AR	W. S. Ferguson	T. C. Blake	226
1894, May 17	Eugene, OR	F. R. Earle	T. C. Blake	167
1895, May 16	Meridian, MS	M. B. DeWitt	T. C. Blake	208
1896, May 21	Birmingham, AL	A. W. Hawkins	J. M. Hubbert	200
1897, May 20	Chicago, IL	H. S. Williams	J. M. Hubbert	224
1898, May 19	Marshall, MO	H. H. Norman	J. M. Hubbert	221
1899, May 18	Denver, CO	J. M. Halsell	J. M. Hubbert	181
1900, May 17	Chattanooga, TN	H. C. Bird	J. M. Hubbert	230
1901, May 16	West Point, MS	E. E. Morris	J. M. Hubbert	226
1902, May 15	Springfield, MO	S. M. Templeton	J. M. Hubbert	255
1903, May 21	Nashville, TN	R. M. Tinnon	J. M. Hubbert	247
1904, May 19	Dallas, TX	W. E. Settle	J. M. Hubbert	251
1905, May 18	Fresno, CA	J. B. Hail	J. M. Hubbert	249
1906, May 17	Decatur, IL	Ira Landrith	J. M. Hubbert	279
1906, May 24	Decatur, IL	J. L. Hudgins	T. H. Padgett	106
1907, May 17	Dickson, TN	A. N. Eshman	J. L. Goodknight	140
1908, May 21	Corsicana, TX	F. H. Prendergast	J. L. Goodknight	136
1909, May 20	Bentonville, AR	J. T. Barbee	J. L. Goodknight	142
1910, May 19	Dickson, TN	J. H. Fussell	J. L. Goodknight	144
1911, May 18	Evansville, IN	J. W. Duvall	J. L. Goodknight	109
1912, May 16	Warrensburg, MO	J. D. Lewis	J. L. Goodknight	119
1913, May 15	Bowling Green, KY	J. H. Milholland	J. L. Goodknight	112
1914, May 21	Wagoner, OK	F. A. Brown	J. L. Goodknight	105
1915, May 20	Memphis, TN	William Clark	D. W. Fooks	116
1916, May 18	Birmingham, AL	J. L. Price	D. W. Fooks	125
1917, May 17	Lincoln, IL	F. A. Seagle	D. W. Fooks	102
1918, May 16	Dallas, TX	C. H. Walton	D. W. Fooks	117
1919, May 15	Fayetteville, AR	J. H. Zwingle	D. W. Fooks	101
1920, May 15	McKenzie, TN	J. E. Cortner	D. W. Fooks	123
1921, May 19	Greenfield, MO	Judge John B. Tally	D. W. Fooks	108
1922, May 18	Greeneville, TN	Hugh S. McCord	D. W. Fooks	102
1923, May 17	Fairfield, IL	P. F. Johnson, D. D.	D. W. Fooks	105
1924, May 15	Austin, TX	D. M. McAnulty	D. W. Fooks	93
1925, May 21	Nashville, TN	W. E. Morrow	D. W. Fooks	114
1926, May 20	Columbus, MS	I. K. Floyd	D. W. Fooks	111
1927, May 19	Lakeland, FL	T. A. DeVore	D. W. Fooks	97
1928, May 21	Jackson, TN	J. L. Hudgins	D. W. Fooks	97
1929, May 16	Princeton, KY	H. C. Walton	D. W. Fooks	98
1930, May 15	Olney, TX	O. A. Barbee	D. W. Fooks	92
1931, May 21	Evansville, IN	J. L. Elliot	D. W. Fooks	98
1932, May 19	Chattanooga, TN	G. G. Halliburton	D. W. Fooks	104
1933, June 14	Memphis, TN	W. B. Cunningham	D. W. Fooks	94
1934, June 14	Springfield, MO	A. C. DeForest	D. W. Fooks	103
1935, June 13	McKenzie, TN	C. A. Davis	D. W. Fooks	104
1936, June 18	San Antonio, TX	E. K. Reagin	D. W. Fooks	100
1937, June 16	Knoxville, TN	George E. Coleman	D. W. Fooks	109
1938, June 16	Russellville, AR	D. D. Dowell	D. W. Fooks	117
1939, June 15	Marshall, MO	E. R. Ramer	D. W. Fooks	126
1940, June 13	Cookeville, TN	Keith T. Postlethwaite	D. W. Fooks	116
1941, June 19	Denton, TX	L. L. Thomas	D. W. Fooks	120
1942, June 18	McKenzie, TN	George W. Burroughs	D. W. Fooks	108
1943, June 17	Paducah, KY	A. A. Collins	D. W. Fooks	94
1944, June 15	Bowling Green, KY	I. M. Vaughn	D. W. Fooks	94
1945, May 31	Lewisburg, TN	S. T. Byars	Wayne Wiman	103
1946, June 13	Birmingham, AL	C. R. Matlock	Wayne Wiman	105
1947, June 12	Knoxville, TN	Morris Pepper	Wayne Wiman	108

Date	Place	Moderator	Clerk	Members
1948, June 17	Nashville, TN	Paul F. Brown	Wayne Wiman	105
1949, June 16	Muskogee, OK	Blake Warren	Wayne Wiman	109
1950, June 15	Los Angeles, CA	L. P. Turnbow	Wayne Wiman	98
1951, June 14	Longview, TX	John E. Gardner	Wayne Wiman	105
1952, June 12	Memphis, TN	Emery A. Newman	Wayne Wiman	120
1953, June 18	Gadsden, AL	Charles L. Lehning, Jr.	Wayne Wiman	107
1954, June 17	Dyersburg, TN	John S. Smith	Wayne Wiman	124
1955, June 16	Lubbock, TX	Ernest C. Cross	Shaw Scates	118
1956, June 21	Cookeville, TN	Hubert Morrow	Shaw Scates	118
1957, June 21	Evansville, IN	William T. Ingram, Jr.	Shaw Scates	119
1958, June 18	Birmingham, AL	Wayne Wiman	Shaw Scates	116
1959, June 17	Springfield, MO	Virgil T. Weeks	Shaw Scates	120
1960, June 15	Nashville, TN	Arleigh G. Matlock	Shaw Scates	130
1961, June 21	Florence, AL	Ollie W. McClung	Shaw Scates	126
1962, June 20	Little Rock, AR	Eugene L. Warren	Shaw Scates	126
1963, June 19	Austin, TX	Franklin Chesnut	Shaw Scates	117
1964, June 17	Chattanooga, TN	Vaughn Fults	Shaw Scates	123
1965, June 16	San Francisco, CA	Thomas Forester	Shaw Scates	114
1966, June 15	Memphis, TN	John W. Sparks	Shaw Scates	124
1967, June 21	Paducah, KY	Raymon Burroughs	Shaw Scates	123
1968, June 19	Oklahoma City, OK	Loyce S. Estes	Shaw Scates	115
1969, June 18	San Antonio, TX	J. David Hester	Shaw Scates	116
1970, June 17	Knoxville, TN	L. C. Waddle	Shaw Scates	116
1971, June 16	Jackson, TN	E. Thach Shauf	Shaw Scates	116
1972, June 19	Kansas City, MO	Claude D. Gilbert	Shaw Scates	110
1973, June 18	Ft. Worth, TX	Thomas H. Campbell	Shaw Scates	101
1974, June 17	Bowling Green, KY	David A. Brown	Shaw Scates	116
1975, June 16	McKenzie, TN	Roy E. Blakeburn	Shaw Scates	120
1976, June 21	Tulsa, OK	Hubert W. Covington	T. V. Warnick	115
1977, June 30	Tampa, FL	Fred W. Bryson	T. V. Warnick	122
1978, June 19	McKenzie, TN	Jose Fajardo	T. V. Warnick	120
1979, June 18	Albuquerque, NM	James C. Gilbert	T. V. Warnick	126
1980, June 16	Evansville, IN	Robert L. Hull	T. V. Warnick	126
1981, June 15	Denton, TX	W. Jean Richardson	T. V. Warnick	126
1982, June 21	Owensboro, KY	W. A. Rawlins	T. V. Warnick	124
1983, June 20	Birmingham, AL	Robert G. Forester	T. V. Warnick	127
1984, June 11	Chattanooga, TN	C. Ray Dobbins	T. V. Warnick	125
1985, June 17	Lexington, KY	Virgil H. Todd	Roy E. Blakeburn	125
1986, June 23	Odessa, TX	James W. Knight	Roy E. Blakeburn	125
1987, June 15	Louisville, KY	Wilbur S. Wood	Roy E. Blakeburn	125
1988, June 6	Tulsa, OK	Beverly St. John	Robert Prosser	119
1989, June 12	Knoxville, TN	William Rustenhaven, Jr.	Robert Prosser	96
1990, June 25	Ft. Worth, TX	Thomas D. Campbell	Robert Prosser	88
1991, June 24	Paducah, KY	Floyd T. Hensley, Jr.	Robert Prosser	106
1992, June 22	Jackson, TN	John David Hall	Robert Prosser	102
1993, June 21	Little Rock, AR	Robert M. Shelton	Robert Prosser	100
1994, June 20	Albuquerque, NM	Donald C. Alexander	Robert Prosser	100
1995, June 19	Nashville, TN	Clinton O. Buck	Robert Prosser	102
1996, June 17	Huntsville, AL	Merlyn A. Alexander	Robert Prosser	95
1997, April 11	Nashville, TN	Merlyn A. Alexander	Robert Prosser	80
1997, June 16	Louisville, KY	W. Lewis Wynn	Robert Prosser	95
1998, June 15	Chattanooga, TN	Masaharu Asayama	Robert Prosser	97
1999, June 21	Memphis, TN	Gwendolyn Roddye	Marjorie Shannon	96
2000, June 19	Bowling Green, KY	Bob G. Roberts	Robert D. Rush	96
2001, June 18	Odessa, TX	Randolph Jacob	Robert D. Rush	88
2002, June 17	Paducah, KY	Bert L. Owen	Robert D. Rush	95
2003, June 23	Knoxville, TN	Charles McCaskey	Robert D. Rush	96
2004, June 21	Irving, TX	Edward G. Sims	Robert D. Rush	87
2005, June 27	Franklin, TN	Linda H. Glenn	Robert D. Rush	91
2006, June 18	Birmingham, AL	Donald Hubbard	Robert D. Rush	87
2007, June 18	Hot Springs, AR	Frank Ward	Robert D. Rush	84
2007, December 7	Nashville, TN	Frank Ward	Robert D. Rush	62
2008, June 7	Japan	Jonathan Clark	Robert D. Rush	82
2009, June 15	Memphis, TN	Sam Suddarth	Robert D. Rush	86
2010, June 13	Dickson, TN	Boyce Wallace	Robert D. Rush	88
2011, June 20	Springfield, MO	Don M. Tabor	Michael Sharpe	82
2012, June 18	Florence, AL	Robert D. Rush	Michael Sharpe	90
2013, June 17	Murfreesboro, TN	Forest Prosser	Michael Sharpe	93
2014, June 16	Chattanooga, TN	Lisa Anderson	Michael Sharpe	86

BYLAWS

Bylaws of the Cumberland Presbyterian Church General Assembly Corporation
A Non-profit Religious Corporation Organized and Existing
Under the Laws of the State of Tennessee

ARTICLE 1-RELIGIOUS CORPORATION

1.01 Purpose. The Cumberland Presbyterian Church is a spiritual body comprised of a portion of the universal body of believers confessing Jesus Christ as Lord and Savior. As an ecclesiastical body, the Cumberland Presbyterian Church is a connectional Church which includes all of the judicatories of the Church. The highest judicatory of this ecclesiastical body is the General Assembly of the Cumberland Presbyterian Church (referred to in these Bylaws as "the Church"). This corporation has been formed to serve and support the Church by holding real and personal property of the Church, employing staff to serve the Church, and performing other secular and legal functions.

1.02 Ecclesiastical Authority Not Limited by Corporate Powers. The enumeration in state statutes or these Bylaws of specific powers which may be exercised by the Commissioners, Board of Directors, or the officers of the corporation when acting in their corporate capacity shall not limit their authority when acting in their ecclesiastical capacity for the Church.

1.03 Church Authorities. The doctrine of the Cumberland Presbyterian Church, expressed in the Confession of Faith, Constitution, Rules of Discipline, and Rules of Order of the Cumberland Presbyterian Church, shall have precedence over any inconsistent provision of these Bylaws.

ARTICLE 2-TERMINOLOGY

2.01 Delegates. The corporation's delegates shall be called "Commissioners."
2.02 General Assembly. A meeting of the Commissioners shall be called a "General Assembly."
2.03 President. The corporation's president shall be called the "Stated Clerk."
2.04 Ecumenical Representative. A person who is not a member of a Cumberland Presbyterian Chuch or presbytery but who supports the mission of a denominational entity and is elected to a term of service on that entity shall be called an "Ecumenical Representative."

ARTICLE 3-OFFICES

3.01 Location. The principal office of the corporation in the State of Tennessee shall be located in Shelby County, Tennessee. The corporation may have such other offices, either within or outside the State of Tennessee, as the General Assembly or the Board of Directors may direct from time to time.

ARTICLE 4–COMMISSIONERS

4.01 Commissioners. The Commissioners shall have the powers and authority described in the corporation's charter and these Bylaws. Included among them are the power to:

   a. Elect the elected members of the Board of Directors.
   b. Approve any amendment to the corporation's charter except an amendment to delete the names of the original directors; to change the name of the registered agent, or to change the address of the registered office;
   c. Elect and remove the Moderator, Stated Clerk, and the Engrossing Clerk.
   d. Fill vacancies on the corporation's various boards, agencies and committees, and on the boards of any subsidiaries;
   e. Approve the merger or dissolution of the corporation, or the sale of substantially all of the corporation's assets; and
   f. Transact such other business of the corporation as may properly come before any meeting of the Commissioners.

4.02 Selection of Commissioners: Number and Qualifications. Commissioners shall be selected by the presbyteries. A presbytery shall be entitled to send one minister and one elder for each 1,000, or fraction thereof, active members (including ordained clergy) in the presbytery. Each elder selected as a

Commissioner must be serving as a member of a session at the time of the General Assembly at which he or she will serve. A Commissioner shall continue to serve until no longer qualified or until his or her successor is selected and qualified. The clerk of each presbytery shall certify the presbytery's duly elected commissioners, youth advisory delegates, and alternates to the Stated Clerk in a manner provided by the Stated Clerk.

4.03 Youth Advisory Delegates. Each presbytery may select not more than two youth advisory delegates who should be from 15 through 19 years of age. Advisory delegates may serve as members with full rights on General Assembly committees, but shall not vote as Commissioners.

4.04 Annual Meeting and Notice. The Commissioners shall meet annually at a date and time established by the General Assembly. The meeting shall be continued from day to day until adjournment. Written notice of the meeting shall be mailed to the stated clerks of all presbyteries and published in the Cumberland Presbyterian at least sixty (60) days prior to the proposed meeting.

4.05 Special Meetings and Notice. The Moderator, or in case of the Moderator's absence, death, or inability to act, the Stated Clerk, may with the written concurrence or at the written request of twenty Commissioners, ten of whom shall be ministers and ten elders, representing at least five presbyteries, call a special meeting of the Commissioners. If warranted by a change of circumstances, a called special meeting may be cancelled by the Moderator, or in case of the Moderator's absence, death, or inability to act, the Stated Clerk, with the written concurrence of at least ten of the Commissioners who requested or concurred in the call of the special meeting. Written notice of any special meeting shall be mailed to the stated clerks of all presbyteries, to all Commissioners, and to their alternates at least sixty (60) days prior to the meeting. The notice shall specify the particular business of the special meeting, and no other business shall be transacted.

4.06 Place of Meeting. The General Assembly may designate any place within or outside the state of Tennessee as the place for an annual meeting. If the Commissioners fail to designate a place for an annual meeting, or if an emergency requires the place to be changed, the Board of Directors may designate a place for the annual meeting. The Moderator or the Stated Clerk, as the case may be, when calling a special meeting shall designate the time and place of the meeting in the notice of the meeting.

4.07 Quorum. Any twenty or more Commissioners, of whom at least ten are ministers and ten elders, entitled to vote shall constitute a quorum at any General Assembly. When a quorum is once present to organize a meeting, business may continue to be conducted and votes taken despite the subsequent withdrawal of any Commissioner. A meeting may be adjourned despite the absence of a quorum.

4.08 Voting. Every Commissioner shall be entitled to one vote, which must be cast by the Commissioner in person; no proxies are permitted. All corporate actions shall be taken by majority vote except as otherwise provided by the corporation's parliamentary authority. Voting for members of the Board of Directors shall be non-cumulative.

ARTICLE 5-BOARD OF DIRECTORS

5.01 Authority. The Board of Directors shall manage the business and affairs of the corporation except for any power or authority which is reserved to the Commissioners or delegated to any other agency of the corporation. The Board of Directors is authorized to amend the corporation's charter only to delete the names of the original directors; to change the name of the registered agent; or to change the address of the registered office.

5.02 Composition of the Board of Directors. The Board of Directors shall consist of seven (7) members, who shall be the directors of the corporation. Six (6) members shall be elected by the Commissioners and the Stated Clerk shall serve by virtue of office. All members, whether elected or ex officio, shall have all of the privileges of office.

5.03 Qualification for Election. Each person elected to the Board of Directors shall be a natural person who is a person in good standing of a presbytery or local Cumberland Presbyterian Church. No two directors shall be from the same presbytery, provided, however, that a director who moves from one presbytery to another may continue to serve until the expiration of his or her term of office.

5.04 Election and Tenure. The elected members of the Board of Directors shall serve terms of three (3) years each. The terms shall be staggered so that two (2) directors shall be elected each year. Each person elected shall serve until his or her successor has been elected and qualified.

5.05 Action of Board in Emergency or By Default. If, for any reason, the General Assembly fails to fill a vacancy on the Board of Directors at the next General Assembly, then the Board of Directors may fill the vacancy by majority vote of the members then in office.

5.06 Meetings. The Board of Directors shall meet annually or more often at such time and place as it may set. Special meetings may be called by or at the request of the Stated Clerk or any three directors at any place, either within or outside the state of Tennessee.

5.07 Notice. Notice of any meeting shall be given at least five (5) days before the date of the meeting, except that notice by mail shall be given at least ten (10) days before the date of the meeting. Notice may be communicated in person; by telephone, fax, or electronic mail; or by first class mail or courier. Except as specifically provided by these Bylaws, neither the business to be transacted at nor the purpose of any special or regular meeting of the Board of Directors need be specified in the notice of the meeting.

5.08 Notice of Special Actions. Any meeting of the Board of Directors at which one or more of the following actions shall be considered must be preceded by seven (7) days written notice to each member that the matter will be voted upon, unless notice has been waived. Actions requiring such notice are: amendment or restatement of the corporate charter; approval of a plan of merger for the corporation; sale of all or substantially all of the corporation's assets; and dissolution of the corporation.

5.09 Officers of the Board of Directors. The Board of Directors may have such officers of the board as it may deem appropriate.

5.10 Quorum and Voting. A majority of the members shall constitute a quorum for the transaction of business at any meeting of the Board of Directors. When a quorum is once present to organize a meeting, it is not broken by the subsequent withdrawal of any of those present. A meeting may be adjourned despite the lack of a quorum. The vote of a majority of the members present at a meeting at which a quorum is present shall be the act of the Board of Directors unless a greater vote is specifically required by the Charter or the Bylaws.

5.11 Conference Meetings. Any or all the members of the Board of Directors or any committee designated by it may meet by means of conference telephone or similar communications equipment which permits all persons participating in the meeting to hear each other simultaneously. A member who participates in a meeting by such means is deemed to be present in person at the meeting.

5.12 Action by Written Consent. Whenever the members of the Board of Directors are required or permitted to take any action by vote, such action may be taken without a meeting on written consent, setting forth the action so taken and signed by all of the members entitled to vote,

5.13 Emergency Actions. If the Board of Directors determines by a vote of three-fourths of all its members that an emergency exists of such magnitude as to threaten the work of the whole Church, or of all boards and other agencies of the Church, and that the emergency requires action before the next meeting of the General Assembly, then the Board of Directors shall exercise the powers of the Commissioners in such emergency.

5.14 Compensation. Members of the Board of Directors shall receive no compensation in their capacity as members of the Board of Directors. Members may be paid their expenses, if any, of attendance at each meeting of the Board of Directors.

5.15 Removal of Directors. An elected member of the Board of Directors may be removed by the Commissioners for misfeasance or if he or she is no longer qualified to be elected to the Board of Directors.

ARTICLE 6-WAIVER OF NOTICE

6.01 Written Waiver. Any notice required to be given to any member of the Board of Directors or a Commissioner under these Bylaws, the Charter, or the laws of Tennessee may be waived. The waiver shall be in writing, signed (either before or after the event requiring notice) by the person entitled to the notice, and delivered to the corporation.

6.02 Waiver by Attendance. The attendance of a member of the Board of Directors or a Commissioner at any meeting shall constitute a waiver of notice of the meeting, unless the person attends a meeting for the express purpose of objecting to the transaction of any business because the meeting was not properly called or convened.

ARTICLE 7-MODERATOR AND VICE-MODERATOR

7.01 Nomination and Election. At the beginning of each annual meeting the General Assembly shall elect a Commissioner to serve as Moderator until the next annual meeting. Nominations for Moderator shall come from the floor. One nominating speech, not to exceed ten minutes, shall be permitted on behalf of each nominee. If there is more than one nominee, the election shall be conducted by written ballot. A committee appointed and supervised by the Stated Clerk shall receive the ballots, count them, and certify the election. If no nominee receives a majority of the votes cast, a run-off election shall be conducted. Only those leading nominees who together received a majority of the votes cast on the preceding ballot shall be included in the run-off election.

7.02 Nature of Office. The Moderator of the General Assembly is the ecclesiastical head of the Cumberland Presbyterian Church during the tenure of the office and a spiritual representative of the Cumberland Presbyterian Church wherever God leads. The Moderator receives a precious gift and great opportunity for service in the Church: the freedom to go anywhere and to listen to the mind, heart and spirit of the denomination and to speak with and to the Church. The office of Moderator has great honor and respect, and the person elected to the Office is a priest, prophet, and pastor of the Church at large. The Moderator prays with and for the work of the Spirit of God in the life of the denomination at every opportunity. The Moderator participates in the life and work of the Church as far as possible, and pays particular attention to ecumenical relations, especially with the Cumberland Presbyterian Church in America. Judicatories, congregations, and others are urged to invite the Moderator, and the Moderator is encouraged to attend meetings of Church entities and judicatories to observe the life and work of the Church at every level.

7.03 Duties and Privileges of Office.
    a. The Moderator shall preside at all meetings of the General Assembly.
    b. The Moderator shall appoint, with the consent of the General Assembly, such special committees as are needed;
    c. The Moderator shall serve as chairperson of the General Assembly Program Committee and as a member of the Place of Meeting Committee;
    d. The Moderator shall perform such other duties as may be assigned by the General Assembly.
    e. The Moderator shall serve as an advisory member of the Ministry Council during tenure in office and for the year following tenure.
    f. The Moderator shall observe the places and times God is calling the Church to service, assess the need for a Denominational response to God's call, and report items that concern the General Assembly.
    g. The Moderator shall wear the official cross and stoles of office during the term of office.

7.04 Expenses of Office. Any allowance budgeted by the General Assembly to offset the expenses of the Moderator shall be administered by the Stated Clerk. Persons issuing an invitation to the Moderator are encouraged to agree in advance on arrangements for the payment of travel expenses. Upon the Moderator's retirement from office, a gavel and a replica of the Moderator's cross shall be presented to the Moderator.

7.05 Vice-Moderator. The General Assembly shall elect a Vice-Moderator in like manner. The Vice-Moderator shall perform such duties as may be assigned by the Moderator of the General Assembly and perform the duties of the Moderator in the event of the Moderator's disability or absence from office for any reason.

7.06 Removal. The Moderator or Vice-Moderator may be removed by the General Assembly whenever in its judgment the removal would serve the best interests of the corporation.

ARTICLE 8-STATED CLERK

8.01 President. The Stated Clerk is the principal executive officer of the corporation and shall also have the titles of "president" and "treasurer".

8.02 Nomination and Election. The Nominating Committee may nominate the serving Stated Clerk for re-election. If the Nominating Committee declines to nominate the serving Stated Clerk for re-election, or if the Stated Clerk has vacated the office, resigned, or declined to be re-nominated, then the Corporate Board shall conduct a search for and nominate a candidate to the General Assembly. In either event, further nominations may be made by the Commissioners. The Commissioners shall elect the Stated Clerk by majority vote.

8.03 Term of Office. The Stated Clerk shall be elected to a term of four (4) years. The regular term of office begins on January 1 and ends on December 31. There is no limit on the number of terms which may be served by an individual Stated Clerk.

8.04 Duties. The Stated Clerk shall be concerned with the spiritual life of the Church and with maintaining and strengthening a united witness for the Church. The Stated Clerk shall also generally supervise and control the business affairs of the corporation and see that all orders and resolutions of the General Assembly are carried into effect. In fulfillment of these duties, the Stated Clerk shall:
    01. Have responsibility to provide for the orderly governance of the Church in accordance with the Constitution, Rules of Order and Rules of Discipline.

02. Maintain records of the corporation and respond to requests for official records of General Assembly actions and interpretations of its actions.
03. Represent the Church when an official of the General Assembly is needed.
04. Represent the Cumberland Presbyterian Church in establishing and maintaining relations with other Churches, particulary those of the Presbyterian and Reformed tradition, and in addressing common concerns.
05. Sign all documents on behalf of the corporation or the Cumberland Presbyterian Church.
06. Represent the corporation or the Church in litigation or other legal matters affecting the Cumberland Presbyterian Church, including the selection and employment of legal counsel.
07. Make suitable arrangements for General Assembly meetings, including researching possible meeting sites, contracting for facilities, and arranging space for committee meetings and sessions of the General Assembly;
08. Provide for printing and other communication needs of the General Assembly while in session.
09. Call meetings of the Place of Meeting Committee and the Program Committee.
10. Prepare and distribute an information form to be completed by Commissioners for the Moderator's use in making committee appointments.
11. Advise the Moderator in the appointment of committees.
12. In consultation with the Moderator, refer all matters to come before the next General Assembly; and provide copies of all such referrals to the Commissioners and advisory delegates before the General Assembly convenes.
13. Prepare and distribute preliminary minutes and an agenda for General Assembly meetings which shall provide time for the consideration of any appropriate business, including memorials from a judicatory or denominational entity delivered to the Stated Clerk in writing by April 30.
14. Supervise the recording and publication of minutes and a summary of actions taken by each General Assembly.
15. Make copies of General Assembly minutes available to ordained ministers, licentiates, candidates, commissioners, clerks of sessions, members of denominational entities, schools of the Church, synod, and presbytery clerks, to the Stated Clerk's exchanges and other interested persons in order to encourage lower judicatories and persons in the Church to implement the actions of the General Assembly.
16. File the minutes of each General Assembly with the Historical Foundation as a permanent record.
17. Maintain and update annually the Digest of the General Assembly actions.
18. Represent the Church at large on the Ministry Council.
19. Provide support services for the Moderator and all denominational entities.
20. Receive and make any appropriate response to communications to the Cumberland Presbyterian Church or General Assembly.
21. Maintain a name and address file on congregations, session clerks, pastors, and other leadership of congregations with statistical information about congregations, presbyteries, and synods.
22. Solicit, receive, publish, and disseminate annual reports from churches.
23. Review reports by denominational entities and assist them in complying with correct reporting and budgeting procedures and in avoiding duplication of work.
24. Hold, report annually, and distribute as authorized by the General Assembly or the Ministry Council the Contingency Fund and all other General Assembly Funds not entrusted to the care of a denominational entity.
25. Call the Judiciary Committee into session or by other means secure the advice of the committee on appropriate matters.
26. Communicate with presbyteries and synods on behalf of the General Assembly and attend their meetings from time to time.
27. Provide training for presbytery and synod clerks and orientations for General Assembly commissioners.
28. Generally perform duties as are prescribed in the Constitution or directed by the General Assembly.

8.05 Removal. The Stated Clerk may be removed by the General Assembly whenever in its judgment the removal would serve the best interests of the corporation.

ARTICLE 9-OTHER OFFICERS

9.01 Secretary. The chief executive officer of the Ministry Council shall, by virtue of office, be the secretary of the corporation, and shall in general perform all duties incident to the office of secretary.

9.02 Engrossing Clerk. The Engrossing Clerk shall be elected by the General Assembly to a term of four (4) years. The regular term of office begins on January 1 and ends on December 31. There is no limit on the number of terms which may be served by an individual Engrossing Clerk. The Engrossing Clerk shall serve as Stated Clerk pro tempore during the meeting of the General Assembly in the event the Stated Clerk is absent or unable to serve. The Engrossing Clerk shall perform such other duties as may from time to time be prescribed by the Board of Directors or the General Assembly.

9.03 Additional Officers. The corporation may have such additional officers as it may from time to time find necessary or appropriate.

ARTICLE 10-ORGANIZATION AND RELATIONSHIPS

10.01 Generally. The following are denominational entities related to the Cumberland Presbyterian Church:

01. Subsidiary corporations: Board of Stewardship, Foundation and Benefits of the Cumberland Presbyterian Church; Memphis Theological Seminary of the Cumberland Presbyterian Church; Ministry Council of the Cumberland Presbyterian Church.
02. Related corporations: Bethel University; Cumberland Presbyterian Children's Home; Historical Foundation of the Cumberland Presbyterian Church and the Cumberland Presbyterian Church in America.
03. Commissions: Chaplains and Military Personnel.
04. Committees: Committee on Nominations; Joint Committee on Amendments; Judiciary, Our United Outreach; Place of Meeting Committee; Program Committee; Unified Committee on Theology and Social Concerns.

10.02 Election and Tenure. The following qualifications and rules relate to service on any denominational entity.

01. Unless elected as an Ecumenical Representative, no person shall be qualified to serve except a member in good standing in a presbytery or local congregation of the Cumberland Presbyterian Church.
02. No person who is employed in an executive capacity including Chief Executive, Vice-President, Team Leader, Director, or equivalent in the Cumberland Presbyterian Church is eligible to serve on a denominational entity. No employee of a denominational entity is eligible for service on the same denominational entity.
03. Each person shall be elected for a term of three years unless elected to fill the remainder of an unexpired term. However, if a person elected to serve on a denominational entity where residence in a particular synod is a qualification for election shall move to another synod while in office, the term to which he or she was elected shall terminate at the close of the next meeting of the General Assembly.
04. Members of the Committee on Nominations may not be elected to a consecutive term. All other persons may serve up to three consecutive terms for a total not to exceed nine years in office.
05. A Cumberland Presbyterian who has served on any entity is not eligible to serve on the same entity (except for an authorized consecutive term) until at least two (2) years have elapsed since the conclusion of the previous service.
06. A Cumberland Presbyterian who is serving on any entity is not eligible to serve on another entity until at least one (1) year has elapsed since the conclusion of the previous service.
07. An Ecumenical Representative who is serving or has served on any entity is not eligible to serve on any other entity (except for an authorized consecutive term on the same entity) until at least one (1) year has elapsed since the conclusion of the previous service.

10.03 Resignation or Removal.
01. Any person serving on a denominational entity who is no longer qualified or eligible to serve shall be deemed to have resigned.
02. Any person serving on an incorporated denominational entity may resign by delivering written notice of resignation to the secretary or an executive officer of the denominational entity, who shall promptly report the resignation to the Stated Clerk. Any person serving on an unincorporated denominational entity may resign by delivering written notice of resignation to the Stated Clerk. A resignation is effective when delivered unless some other effective date is specified in the written resignation.
03. No member who continues to meet the standard requirements for election or appointment to any denominational entity shall be removed from office except for misfeasance. Removal of a person elected by the General Assembly shall be by vote of the General Assembly.

10.04 Board of Stewardship, Foundation and Benefits. The corporation shall elect the eleven (11) directors of the Board of Stewardship as provided in its charter.

10.05 Cumberland Presbyterian Children's Home. The corporation shall elect the fifteen (15) directors of Children's Home as provided in its corporate articles. The corporation shall elect the directors in such a manner that, immediately following any election, there shall be at least six (6) directors who are members of ecumenical partners of the Children's Home.

10.06 Historical Foundation. The corporation shall elect six (6) of the twelve (12) directors of the Historical Foundation as provided in its charter. The corporation shall elect the directors of the Historical Foundation in such a manner that, immediately following any election, there shall be at least one (1) member from each synod and no person shall be elected if the election would cause two directors from the same presbytery to be serving simultaneously. The remaining six (6) directors shall be elected by the Cumberland Presbyterian Church in America.

10.07 Memphis Theological Seminary. The corporation shall elect the twenty-four (24) directors of Memphis Theological Seminary as provided in its charter. The corporation shall elect the directors in such a manner that, immediately following any election, there shall be at least eleven (11) directors who are members of ecumenical partners of the Seminary.

10.08 Ministry Council.
01. The corporation shall elect the fifteen (15) directors of the Ministry Council as provided in its charter.
02. The corporation shall elect the directors of the Ministry Council in such a manner that immediately following any election, there shall be three (3) directors from each synod; at least six (6) but no more than nine (9) directors who are ordained clergy; and no more than nine (9) directors of the same gender.
03. The Stated Clerk, Moderator, and Immediate Past Moderator shall be designated as Advisory Members to the board of directors of the Ministry Council. In addition, the corporation shall elect three (3) Youth Advisory Members who shall be between the ages of 15 – 17 be elected for 1-year terms, with eligibility for re-election for one additional term.

10.09 Commission on Chaplains and Military Personnel. The commission shall consist of three (3) members elected by the corporation.

ARTICLE 11-COMMITTEES

11.01 General. The corporation shall have the committees provided for in these Bylaws and such other standing or special committees as the General Assembly may create from time to time. Except as otherwise provided in these Bylaws, the Moderator, in consultation with the Stated Clerk, shall appoint all committees.

11.02 Committees of Commissioners and Youth Advisory Delegates. Prior to each General Assembly, the Moderator, in consultation with the Stated Clerk, shall organize the Commissioners and Youth Advisory Delegates into the following committees: Chaplains/Missions/Pastoral Development, Children's Home/Historical Foundation, Higher Education, Judiciary, Ministry Council/Communications/Discipleship, Stewardship/Elected Officers, and Theology and Social Concerns. Each committee shall consider such matters expected to come before the General Assembly as are referred to it by the Stated Clerk. Any denominational organization, the work of which is affected by a matter before a committee, shall be entitled to address the committee.

11.03 Committee on Nominations.
01. The committee shall consist of ten (10) persons elected by the corporation in such a manner that, immediately following any election, the committee shall have at least one minister and one lay person from each synod. It is preferred but not required that no two members shall be from the same presbytery.
02. Approximately one third of the members of the committee shall be elected each year by the General Assembly and shall serve one term not to exceed three years.
03. The committee shall meet not earlier than February 15 each year and shall nominate to the General Assembly qualified persons to fill all vacancies to be filled by vote of the General Assembly, including vacancies on the Committee on Nominations, unless another method of nomination is provided in these Bylaws. The report of the committee shall list the names of nominees, the presbytery if a minister, and the presbytery and the local congregation if a lay person. The Committee on Nominations shall be intentional in nominating persons who represent the global nature of the Church.
04. Presbyteries and synods and their moderators and stated clerks are requested to assist the Committee on Nominations by recommending persons for any position by providing the name and qualifications of the potential nominees to the Stated Clerk no later than February 1 on a form to be provided by the Stated Clerk. Nominations from the floor shall also be in order.
05. No person shall be nominated for election by the General Assembly unless the nominee has within the past year given his or her consent to the nomination.

11.04 Joint Committee on Amendments. The Judiciary Committee shall appoint as many as five of its members to act in committee with an equal number of members of the Judiciary Committee of the Cumberland Presbyterian Church in America. Upon the request of the General Assembly of the Cumberland Presbyterian Church or the General Assembly of the Cumberland Presbyterian Church in America, this Joint Committee shall prepare for the consideration of both general assemblies proposed amendments to the Confession of Faith, Catechism, Constitution, Rules of Discipline, Directory for Worship, and Rules of Order.

11.05 Judiciary Committee.
01. The committee shall consist of nine (9) persons elected by the corporation in such a manner that, immediately following any election, the committee shall have at least four members (4) who are ordained ministers and at least three (3) members who are licensed attorneys-at-law. The Stated Clerk shall be staff liaison to the committee, attending its meetings and providing resources and counsel.
02. The committee shall meet at least annually upon the call of its chairperson or the Stated Clerk.
03. The committee shall provide advice and counsel to the Stated Clerk. Upon the written request of any judicatory or denominational entity made to the chairperson or Stated Clerk, the committee shall render an advisory opinion on matters of church law or procedure. The chairperson shall secure the views of all members of the committee and write the advisory opinion based on the majority view of the members. The committee shall not render legal opinions on matters of civil law nor otherwise engage in the practice of law.
04. At least one member of the committee shall attend each meeting of the General Assembly to advise with its officers and Commissioners on matters of church law or procedure. At the Moderator's request a member of the committee shall be available to advise the Moderator during the business sessions of the General Assembly.
05. The committee shall be a commission within the meaning of section 2.5 of the Rules of Discipline to hear and determine appeals from synods.

11.06 Our United Outreach Committee.
01. The committee shall consist of five (5) persons elected by the corporation in such a manner that, immediately following any election, the committee shall have one person from each synod. Seven (7) additional members will include a member of the Ministry Council, a member of the Corporate Board, a member of the Board of Stewardship, Foundation and Benefits, a member of the Board of Trustees of the Historical Foundation, and a Cumberland Presbyterian member of the Boards of Trustees of

Bethel University, the Cumberland Presbyterian Children's Home, and Memphis Theological Seminary. The executives of the above named denominational entities shall serve as non-voting, Resource/Advocacy members.

02. The Office of the General Assembly will be responsible for the expenses of the representative of each synod. The represented denominational entities will be responsible for the expenses of their representatives and executives.

11.07 Place of Meeting. The committee shall consist of the Moderator, the Stated Clerk and a representative of the Cumberland Presbyterian Women's Ministries.

11.08 Program Committee. The committee shall consist of the Moderator, Stated Clerk, Director of Ministries, Assistant to the Stated Clerk who serves as secretary, the pastor of the host church, four elected representatives designated by the Ministry Council from among its ministry teams, and one representative designated by each of the following: Bethel University, Board of Stewardship, Foundation, and Benefits, Cumberland Presbyterian Children's Home, Historical Foundation, Memphis Theological Seminary, and the Cumberland Presbyterian Women's Ministry. The committee will begin planning for two years prior to the meeting of a particular General Assembly.

11.09 Unified Committee on Theology and Social Concerns. The committee shall consist of eight (8) members elected by the corporation, the Stated Clerk, and the President of Memphis Theological Seminary. At least one member of the committee other than the Seminary's president shall be a Cumberland Presbyterian member of the faculty of Memphis Theological Seminary.

ARTICLE 12-INDEMNIFICATION

12.01 Indemnification. The corporation shall indemnify any director, officer or employee who is, or is threatened to be, made a party to a completed, pending, or threatened action or proceeding from any liability arising from the director's, officer's or employee's official capacity with the corporation. This indemnification shall extend to the personal representation of a deceased person if the person would be entitled to indemnification under these Bylaws if living.

12.02 Costs and Expenses Covered by Indemnification. Indemnification provided under these Bylaws shall extend to the payment of a judgment, settlement, penalty, or fine, as well as attorney's fees, court costs, and other reasonable and necessary expenses incurred by the director or officer with respect to the action or proceeding.

12.03 Limitation on Indemnification. No indemnification shall be made to or on behalf of any person if a judgment or other final adjudication adverse to that person establishes his or her liability:

01. for any breach of the duty of loyalty to the corporation;
02. for acts or omissions not in good faith or which involve intentional misconduct or a knowing violation of law; or
03. for any distribution of the assets of the corporation which is unlawful under Tennessee law.

ARTICLE 13-TRUSTEE FOR THE CORPORATION

13.01 Trustee. The Board of Stewardship, Foundation and Benefits of the Cumberland Presbyterian Church, a nonprofit corporation existing under the laws of the state of Tennessee, holds certain real property and other assets of the Church as trustee for the use and benefit of the Church. The Board of Stewardship may continue to hold such real property and other assets, but after the adoption of these Bylaws, it shall hold those assets as trustee for the use and benefit of the Cumberland Presbyterian Church General Assembly Corporation.

13.02 Other Assets. Other, additional property may from time to time be conveyed to the Board of Stewardship to be held by it as trustee for the corporation. All assets held by the Board of Stewardship as trustee for the corporation shall be held at the pleasure and direction of the General Assembly.

ARTICLE 14-PARLIAMENTARY AUTHORITY

14.01 Designation. The parliamentary authority of the corporation in all meetings shall be the latest revised edition of the Rules of Order as set out in the Confession of Faith and Government of the Cumberland Presbyterian Church. In matters not provided for in the Rules of Order, the parliamentary authority shall be Robert's Rules of Order, latest revised edition.

14.02 Standing Rules. The following shall be Standing Rules for meetings of the General Assembly and may be suspended as provided in the parlimentary authority. (see Rules of Order 8.34c)

Standing Rules

1. Unless otherwise determined by the General Assembly or by the Stated Clerk in the event of an emergency, the annual General Assembly shall meet on the third or fourth Monday of June at two o'clock in the afternoon to organize, elect a moderator and transact business, and shall close on Thursday or Friday of the same week.

2. Reports of all standing and special committees shall be considered in the order established by the Moderator in consultation with the Stated Clerk. Committee reports may be presented orally or in writing provided to all Commissioners and youth advisory delegates. Those presenting committee reports shall have the opportunity to make remarks and give explanation, such presentations not to exceed ten minutes unless time is extended by two-thirds vote taken without debate. All committee recommendations shall be submitted in writing.

3. All materials from denominational entities for consideration or action by a General Assembly shall be submitted to the Stated Clerk at least thirty (30) days before the meeting of General Assembly.

4. Resolutions and memorials proposed for adoption by individual commissioners rather than denominational entities or judicatories of the Cumberland Presbyterian Church shall be introduced no later than the close of business on the second day of a meeting of General Assembly, and, when introduced, shall be referred by the Moderator, in counsel with the Stated Clerk, to the appropriate committee or committees for report and recommendations to the Assembly.

ARTICLE 15-REPORTS AND AUDITS

15.01 Congregational Reports. Annually by December 1, the Stated Clerk shall send to session clerks statistical forms for reporting congregational data. Session clerks shall mail the completed forms to presbytery clerks by February 1. The presbytery clerk shall mail the composite statistical report for all congregations of a presbytery to the Stated Clerk by February 10.

15.02 Institutional Reports. In order to be considered for inclusion in the General Assembly budget, all denominational entities shall deliver to the Stated Clerk an annual report including a concise description of the organization's work during the previous year and a line item budget for the forthcoming year. Financial reports should be condensed as much as possible while conveying all essential information on the organization's operations. All denominational entities except academic institutions on a fiscal year are requested to maintain their books on a calendar year.

15.03 Reporting Schedule. An electronic copy and two written copies of the annual report signed by two officers of the organization shall be delivered to the Stated Clerk by March 15 each year. Organizations requesting funds from Our United Outreach shall submit multi-year program budgets to the Our United Outreach Committee.

15.04 Audits. Organizations and operations included in the General Assembly budget shall be audited annually by a certified public accountant. Copies of the auditor's report, including any recommendations for changes in the procedures relating to internal financial controls, shall be delivered to the Stated Clerk. Organizations with total receipts of $100,000 or less are not required to have an audit but shall submit their books and financial statements to the Stated Clerk annually.

15.05 Bonds. Each organization or person whose financial records are required to be audited shall have a fidelity bond in an amount adequate to protect all funds held by the organization or person.

ARTICLE 16-AMENDMENTS

16.01 Manner of Amendment. Except as provided below, these Bylaws may be amended or repealed only by the affirmative vote of two-thirds of the votes cast in a duly constituted meeting of the General Assembly. No portion of the Bylaws may be amended or repealed by the Board of Directors. Fair and reasonable notice of any proposed amendment shall be provided as required by state law.

16.02 Extraordinary Actions. In order to be effective the following actions must be approved by (1) the affirmative vote of two consecutive General Assemblies, or (2) a ninety percent (90%) vote of a single General Assembly.

      01. Terminating the existence of a denominational entity named in Bylaw 10.01
      02. Creating a new denominational entity other than a temporary committee or task force.
      03. Decreasing the Our United Outreach budget allocation to a denominational entity by more than 40% of the amount distributed to it during the previous calendar year; or
      04. Taking any other actions which would cause a drastic change in the mission or structure of the Cumberland Presbyterian Church.

MEMORIAL ROLL OF MINISTERS

IN MEMORY OF
MINISTERS LOST BY DEATH

NAME	PRESBYTERY	AGE	DATE
Andrews, Leonard	Nashville	93	05/16/13
Berry, Ephraim A	Cumberland	91	05/07/13
Brown, Richard C	Grace	86	11/16/13
Broyles, Lon B	East Tennessee	68	09/30/13
Butler, George A	West Tennessee	73	08/10/13
Dixon, Robert W	Covenant	78	10/10/13
Hensley, Howard L	Missouri	69	07/23/13
McGregor, David	Columbia	86	01/23/14
Rodriguez, Paul	Cauca Valley		03/10/14
Tant, Robert H	Grace	76	02/19/13
Warren, George H	Hope	92	12/09/13
Watson, David E	Murfreesboro	81	11/04/13
Wilkins, Marvin E	Columbia	65	04/01/14

LIVING GENERAL ASSEMBLY MODERATORS

2014—REV. LISA ANDERSON, 1790 Faxon Avenue, Memphis, TN 38112
2013—REV. FOREST PROSSER, 1157 Mountain Creek Road, Chattanooga, TN 37405
2012—REV. ROBERT D. RUSH, 17822 Deep Brook Drive, Spring, TX 77379
2011—REV. DON M. TABOR, 9611 Mitchell Place, Brentwood, TN 37027
2010—REV. BOYCE WALLACE, Cra 101 No 15-93, Cali, Colombia, South America
2009—ELDER SAM SUDDARTH, 206 Ha Le Koa Court, Smyrna, TN 37167
2008—REV. JONATHAN CLARK, 88 Woodcrest Drive, Winchester, TN 37398
2007—REV. FRANK WARD, 8207 Traditional Place, Cordova, TN 38016
2006—REV. DONALD HUBBARD, 2128 Campbell Station Road, Knoxville, TN 37932
2005—REV. LINDA H. GLENN, 49 Mason Road, Threeway, TN 38343
2004—REV. EDWARD G. SIMS, 2161 N. Meadows Drive, Clarksville, TN 37043
2003—REV. CHARLES MCCASKEY, 679 Canter Lane, Cookeville, TN 38501
2001—REV. RANDOLPH JACOB, 610 W. Adams Street, Broken Bow, OK 74728
1999—ELDER GWENDOLYN G. RODDYE, 3728 Wittenham Drive, Knoxville, TN 37921
1998—REV. MASAHARU ASAYAMA, 3-15-9 Higashi, Kunitachi-shi, Tokyo, JAPAN
1996—REV. MERLYN A. ALEXANDER, 80 N. Hampton Lane, Jackson, TN 38305
1995—REV. CLINTON O. BUCK, 4986 Warwick, Memphis, TN 38117
1993—REV. ROBERT M. SHELTON, 7128 Lakehurst Avenue, Dallas, TX 75230
1992—REV. JOHN DAVID HALL, 109 Oddo Lane SE, Huntsville, AL 35802
1990—REV. THOMAS D. CAMPBELL, PO Box 315, Calico Rock, AR 72519
1989—REV. WILLIAM RUSTENHAVEN, Jr., 703 W. Burleson, Marshall, TX 75670
1988—ELDER BEVERLY ST. JOHN, 806 Evansdale Drive, Nashville, TN 37220
1987—ELDER WILBUR S. WOOD, Box 122, Palestine, AR 72372
1985—REV. VIRGIL H. TODD, 3095 Glengarry Road, Memphis, TN 38128
1982—REV. WILLIAM A. RAWLINS, 3100 Cook Lane, Longview, TX 75604
1981—REV. W. JEAN RICHARDSON, 7533 Lancashire, Powell, TN 37849
1978—REV. JOSE FAJARDO, 101 Vanderbilt, Waxahachie, TX 75165
1975—REV. ROY E. BLAKEBURN, 111 Park Place, Greeneville, TN 37743
1969—REV. J. DAVID HESTER, 1212 Woodbury Court, Knoxville, TN 37922

GENERAL ASSEMBLY OFFICERS

MODERATOR
THE REVEREND LISA HALL ANDERSON
1790 FAXON AVENUE
MEMPHIS, TN 38112
(901)725-0924
anderli@aol.com

VICE MODERATOR
THE REVEREND PAULA LOUDER
98 GALLANT COURT
CLARKSVILLE, TN 37043
(615)804-4809
paula.louder@cmcss.net

STATED CLERK AND TREASURER
THE REVEREND MICHAEL SHARPE
8207 Traditional Place
Cordova, TN 38016
(901)276-4572
FAX (901)272-3913
msharpe@cumberland.org

ENGROSSING CLERK
THE REVEREND VERNON SANSOM
7810 Shiloh Road
Midlothian, TX 76065
(972)825-6887
vernon@sansom.us

THE BOARD OF DIRECTORS OF THE GENERAL ASSEMBLY CORPORATION

(Members whose terms expire in 2015)
(3)REV. MELISSA MALINOSKI, 9087 Fenmore Cove, Cordova, TN 38016
   bobby.coleman@gmail.com
(3)MR. JERRY WEATHERSBY, 119 County Road 743, Cullman, AL 35055
   jerryw@cullmanelectric.com

(Members whose terms expire in 2016)
(1)MR. TIM GARRETT, 150 Third Avenue South, Suite 2800, Nashville, TN 37201
   tgarrett@bassberry.com
(1)REV. BOBBY COLEMAN, 704 E Webb Street, Mountain View, AR 72560
   bobby.coleman@gmail.com

*Ecumenical Partners   +Cumberland Presbyterian Church in America

(Members whose terms expire in 2017)
(1)REV. JOHN BUTLER, PO Box 257, Sacramento, KY 42372
  butler8134@bellsouth.net
(1)MS. BETTY JACOB, PO Box 158, Broken Bow, OK 74728
  chocpres@pine-net.com

MINISTRY COUNCIL

(Members whose terms expire in 2015)
(2)MS. SALLY ALLEN, 3190 Gray Hawk Court, Clarksville, TN 37043
(1)MR. KENNETH BEAN, 1035 Stonewall Street N, McKenzie, TN 38201
(1)MS. MARY ANN COLE, 620 Plum Springs Road, Bowling Green, KY 42101
(3)REV. CARLTON HARPER, 255 Glenview Circle, Lenoir City, TN 37771
(1)REV. RON MCMILLAN, 675 Kimberly Drive, Atoka, TN 38004
(Members whose terms expire in 2016)
(3)MS. JILL CARR, PO Box 1547, Lebanon, MO 65536
(2)REV. TROY GREEN, 105 Cobb Hollow Lane, Petersburg, TN 37144
(3)MS. ELIZABETH HORSLEY, 1200 Imperial Drive, Denton, TX 76201
(3)MS. GWEN RODDYE, 3728 Wittenham Drive, Knoxville, TN 37921
(3)REV. SAM ROMINES, PO Box 127, Lewisburg, KY 42256
(Members whose terms expire in 2017)
(2)REV. DONNY ACTON, 1413 Oakridge Drive, Birmingham, AL 35242
(3)REV. MICHELE GENTRY DE CORREAL, Calle 3 Norte #12-87, Armenia, Quinido,
  COLOMBIA, SOUTH AMERICA
(2)REV. LANNY JOHNSON, 120 S Mill Street, Morrison, TN 37357
(1)MR. ADAM MCREYNOLDS, PO Box 162, Bethany, IL 61914
(2)REV. TOM SANDERS, 4201 W Kent Street, Broken Arrow, OK 74012

(Members whose terms expire in 2015)
YOUTH ADVISORY MEMBERS
(2)MR. EDDIE MONTOYA, JR, 270 Windsor Drive, Roselle, IL 60172
(2)MS. CAROLINA GILLIS, 6243 Sioux Lane, Birmingham, AL 35242
(1)MS. EMILY MAHONEY, 31 Barbara Circle, McMinnville, TN 37110

ADVISORY MEMBERS
REV. LISA ANDERSON, 1790 Faxon Avenue, Memphis, TN 38112
REV. FOREST PROSSER, 1157 Mountain Creek Road, Chattanooga, TN 37405
REV. MICHAEL SHARPE, 8207 Traditional Place, Cordova, TN 38016

COMMUNICATIONS MINISTRY TEAM

(Members whose terms expire in 2015)
(2)REV. MICHAEL CLARK, 338 Royal Oak Drive, Winchester, TN 37398
(2)REV. JAMES D. MCGUIRE, 220-2 Southwind Circle, Greeneville, TN 37743
(Members whose terms expire in 2016)
(1)REV. NICHOLAS CHAMBERS, 11300 Road 101, Union, MS 39365
(1)REV. STEVEN SHELTON, 7886 Farmhill Cove, Bartlett, TN 38135
(Members whose terms expire in 2017)
(3)MS. B. DENISE ADAMS, 126 Ray, Monticello, AR 71655
(2)MRS. DUSTY SHULL, 110 Windmere Cove, Paducah, KY 42001

*Ecumenical Partners   +Cumberland Presbyterian Church in America

DISCIPLESHIP MINISTRY TEAM

(Members whose terms expire in 2015)
(2)MS. JOANNA D. BELLIS, 334 Village Green Drive, Nashville, TN 37217
(1)MS. RACHEL COOK, 210 Bynum Street, Scottsboro, AL 35768
(1)REV. CHRISTIAN SMITH, 475 State Street, Cookeville, TN 38501
(Members whose terms expire in 2016)
(3)REV. MINDY ACTON, 1413 Oak Ridge Drive, Birmingham, AL 35242
(1)REV. NANCY MCSPADDEN, 2011 Woodridge Drive, St Peters, MO 63376
(1)REV. JOSEFINA SANCHEZ, 7 Hancock Street, Melrose, MA 02176
(Members whose terms expire in 2017)
(2)MS. LE ILA DIXON, 4406 John Reagan Street, Marshall, TX 75672
(2)REV. AARON FERRY, 122 Crimson Drive, Winchester, TN 37398
(3)MS. SAMANTHA HASSELL, 510 N Main Street, Sturgis, KY 42459

MISSIONS MINISTRY TEAM

(Members whose terms expire in 2015)
(2)REV. JIM BARRY, 1405 Anna Street, Hixson, TN 37343
(1)MR. TIM CRAIG, 8958 Carriage Creek Road, Arlington, TN 38002
(1)REV. CARDELIA HOWELL-DIAMOND, 1580 Jeff Road NW, Huntsville, AL 35806
(2)MS. SHERRY POTEET, P.O. Box 313, Gilmer, TX 75644
(1)MS. MELINDA REAMS, 10 W Azalea Lane, Russellville, AR 72802
(Members whose terms expire in 2016)
(2)REV. MAKIHIKO ARASE, 3-355-4 Kamikitadai Higashiyamato-Shi, Tokyo, 207-0023 JAPAN
(2)REV. VICTOR HASSELL, 510 N Main Street, Sturgis, KY 42459
(1)MR. DOMINIC LAU, 3820 Anza Street, San Francisco, CA
(1)MS. BRITTANY MEEKS, 2664 Morning Sun Road, Cordova, TN 38016
(1)REV. CHRIS WARREN, 906 Prince Lane, Murfreesboro, TN 37129
(Members whose terms expire in 2017)
(2)REV. JAMES BUTTRAM, 103 Golfcrest Lane, Oak Ridge, TN 37830
(3)REV. JIMMY BYRD, 176 E Valley Road, Whitwell, TN 37397
(1)MS. DONNA CHRISTIE, 3221 Whitehall Road, Birmingham, AL 35209
(3)REV. RICARDO FRANCO, 7 Hancock Street, Melrose, MA 02176
(1)MRS. MS. KAREN TOLEN, 6859 A East County Road 000N, Trilla, IL 62469

PASTORAL DEVELOPMENT MINISTRY TEAM

(Members whose terms expire in 2015)
(1)REV. DUAWN MEARNS, 107 Westoak Place, Hot Springs, AR 71913
(2)REV. LINDA SNELLING, 15791 State Highway W, Ada, OK 74820
(Members whose terms expire in 2016)
(2)MS. MICAIAH THOMAS, PO Box 5204 SBN 499, Princeton, NJ 08543
(1)REV. PATRICK WILKERSON, 3419 Jaydens Nest Way Apt 202, Powell, TN 37849
(Members whose terms expire in 2017)
(2)REV. AMBER CLARK, 338 Royal Oak Drive, Winchester, TN 37398
(2)REV. DREW HAYES, 629 High Street, Union City, TN 38261

*Ecumenical Partners   +Cumberland Presbyterian Church in America

GENERAL ASSEMBLY BOARD OF:

I. TRUSTEES OF BETHEL UNIVERSITY

(Members whose terms expire at the end of 2014)
(1)*MS. LISA COLE, PO Box 198615, Nashville, TN 37219
(3)*DR. PAUL COWELL, c/o Whitestone Country Inn, 1200 Paint Rock Road, Kingston, TN 37763
(1)MR. CHESTER (CHET) DICKSON, 24 W Rivercrest Drive, Houston, TX 77042
(3)REV. LINDA H. GLENN, 49 Mason Road, Three Way, TN 38343
(1)*MR. ARTHUR (ART) LAFFER, JR., 410 Wilsonia Avenue, Nashville, TN 37205
(2)MR. BOBBY OWEN, 1625 Cabot Drive, Franklin, TN 37064
(1)DR. ED PERKINS, 721 Paris Street, McKenzie, TN 38201
(2)REV. ROBERT (ROB) TRUITT, 1238 Old East Side Road, Burns, TN 37029

(Members whose terms expire at the end of 2015)
(3)*MR. MICHAEL (MIKE) CARY, 181 Angel Cove, Huntingdon, TN 38344
(2)MR. CHARLIE GARRETT, 107 Willow Green Drive, Jackson, TN 38305
(1)+REV. ELTON C. HALL, SR., 305 Tiffton Circle, Hewitt, TX 76643
(1)REV. MARK S. HESTER, 763 Finn Long Road, Friendsville, TN 37737
(3)*MS. CHARLENE P. JONES, 137 Moore Avenue W, McKenzie, TN 38201
(1)MS. DEWANNA LATIMER, 1077 Jr. Jones Road, Humboldt, TN 38343
(2)REV. EUGENE LESLIE, 13155 Center Hill Road, Olive Branch, MS 38654
(1)*MS. VIOLA MILLER, 1614 5th Avenue N., Nashville, TN 37208

(Members whose terms expire at the end of 2016)
(1)MR. JEFF AMREIN, 11711 Paramont Way, Prospect, KY 40059
(3)DR. LARRY A. BLAKEBURN, 230 Heathridge Drive, Dyersburg, TN 38024
(2)*JUDGE BEN CANTRELL, 415 Church Street #2513, Nashville, TN 37219
(2)+DR. AMY DANIEL, 3125 Searcy Drive, Huntsville, AL 35810
(3)MR. LAWRENCE (LADD) DANIEL, 13023 Taylorcrest, Houston, TX 77079
(1)MR. BILL DOBBINS 5716 Quest Ridge Road, Franklin, TN 37064
(2)DR. ROBERT LOW, c/o New Prime, Inc., 2740 W Mayfair Avenue, Springfield, MO 65803
(3)MR. BEN T. SURBER, 1145 Hico Road, McKenzie, TN 38201

Trustee Emeritus – Dr. Vera Low, 3653 Prestwick Court, Springfield, MO 65809 (deceased)

II. TRUSTEES OF CUMBERLAND PRESBYTERIAN CHILDREN'S HOME

(Members whose terms expire in 2015)
(2)*MS. KAY GOODMAN, 1042 Bobcat Road, Sanger, TX 76266
(3)MS. PAT HUFF, 249 Rancho Drive, Saginaw, TX 76179
(2)REV. MELISSA KNIGHT, 5730 Haley Road, Meridian, MS 39305
(3)MS. RUBY LETSON, 2921 Alexander, Florence, AL 35633
(2)*MR. BARON H. SMITH, 3401 Hasland Drive, Flower Mound, TX 75022

(Members whose terms expire in 2016)
(1)MR. RICHARD DEAN, 2140 Cove Circle North, Gadsden, AL 35903
(2)MS. PATRICIA LONG, 525 E Oak Street, Aledo, TX 76008
(3)REV. ALFONSO MARQUEZ, 389 Bethel Drive, Lenoir City, TN 37772
(3)MR. MICKEY SHELL, 2143 Griderfield-Ladd Road, Pine Bluff, AR 71601

(Members whose terms expire in 2017)
(3)+MS. MAMIE HALL, 305 Tiffton Circle, Hewitt, TX 76643
(1)MR. CHARLES HARRIS, 3293 Birch Avenue, Grapevine, TX 76051
(3)REV. YOONG KIM, 8601 Dogwood Road, Germantown, TN 38139
(2)MS. TIFFANY SMITH, 2901 Corporate Circle, Flower Mound, TX 75028
(3)REV. DON TABOR, 9611 Mitchell Place, Brentwood, TN 37027

*Ecumenical Partners   +Cumberland Presbyterian Church in America

III. TRUSTEES OF HISTORICAL FOUNDATION

(Members whose terms expire in 2015)
(3)REV. TOMMY JOBE, 807 Rockwood Drive, Nolensville, TN 37135
(2)DR. SIDNEY L. SWINDLE, 4407 Swann Avenue, Tampa, FL 33609

(Members whose terms expire in 2016)
(3)+MS. VANESSA BARNHILL, 819 King Street, Sturgis, KY 42459
(3)MS. PAMELA DAVIS, 5111 County Road 7545, Lubbock, TX 79424
(3)+MS. NAOMI KING, 3850 Millsfield Highway, Dyersburg, TN 38024 (resigned)
(2)REV. MARY KATHRYN KIRKPATRICK, 401 1/2 Henley-Perry Drive, Marshall, TX 75670
(3)MS. SIDNEY MILTON, 27 Kalee Lane, Calvert City, KY 42029

(Members whose terms expire in 2017)
(3)+MS. EDNA BARNETT, 7 Breezewood Cove, Jackson, TN 38305
(2)MR. MICHAEL FARE, 401 E Deanna Lane, Nixa, MO 65714
(2)+ MS. DOROTHY HAYDEN, 3103 Carolina Avenue, Bessemer, AL 35020
(3)+REV. RICK WHITE, 124 Towne West, Lorena, TX 76655

IV. TRUSTEES OF MEMPHIS THEOLOGICAL SEMINARY OF THE CUMBERLAND PRESBYTERIAN CHURCH

(Members whose terms expire in 2015)
(2)REV. KEVIN BRANTLEY, 729 Old Hodgenville Road, Greensburg, KY 42743
(3)REV. JODY HILL, 4030 St Andrew Circle, Corinth, MS 38834
(3)MS. JAN HOLMES, 5209 87th Street, Lubbock, TX 79424
(2)MR. MARK MADDOX, 225 Oak Drive, Dresden, TN 38225
(1)MS. SONDRA RODDY, 2583 Hedgerow Lane, Clarksville, TN 37043
(2)MR. TAKAYOSHI SHIRAI, 25 Minami Kibogaoka Asahi-ku, Yokohama, Kanagawa-ken 241-0824 JAPAN
(1)*REV. MELVIN CHARLES SMITH, 1263 Haynes Street, Memphis, TN 38114
(1)*MS. LATISHA TOWNS, The Med, 877 Jefferson Avenue, Memphis, TN 38103

(Members whose terms expire in 2016)
(2)MR. MICHAEL R. ALLEN, 149 Windwood Circle, Alabaster, AL 35007
(1)*MR. JOHNNIE COOMBS, PO Box 127, Blue Mountain, MS 38610
(2)MS. DIANE DICKSON, 24 West Rivercrest, Houston, TX 77042
(3)*MR. DAN HATZENBUEHLER, 1544 Carr Avenue, Memphis, TN 38104
(1)*DR. RICK KIRCHOFF, 2044 Thorncroft Drive, Germantown, TN 38138
(3)MR. TIM ORR, 1715 Templeton Loop, Newbern, TN 38059
(2)*DR. INETTA RODGERS, 1824 S Parkway E, Memphis, TN 38114
(3)*MRS. K.C. WARREN, 215 Buena Vista Place, Memphis, TN 38112

(Members whose terms expire in 2017)
(2)*REV. ROBERT MARBLE, 515 Shamrock Drive, Little Rock, AR 72205
(3)MS. PAT MEEKS, 8540 Edney Ridge Drive, Cordova, TN 38016
(2)REV. JENNIFER NEWELL, 2322 Marco Circle, Chattanooga, TN 37421
(1)REV. SUSAN PARKER, 655 York Drive, Rogersville, AL 35652
(1)MR. DAVID REED, 281 Reed Farm Road, Martin, TN 38237
(3)REV. ROBERT M. SHELTON, 7128 Lakehurst Avenue, Dallas, TX 75230
(3)+DR. JOE WARD, 2620 Rabbit Lane, Madison, AL 35758
(3)*MS. RUBY WHARTON, 1183 E Parkway South, Memphis, TN 38114

V. STEWARDSHIP, FOUNDATION AND BENEFITS

(Members whose terms expire in 2015)
(2)MR. ANDREW B. FRAZIER, JR., 107 Doris Street, Camden, TN 38320
(3)MR. ROBERT LATIMER, RR 1 Box 123, Miami, MO 65344
(1)MR. MICHAEL ST. JOHN, 324 Carriage Place, Lebanon, MO 65536

*Ecumenical Partners   +Cumberland Presbyterian Church in America

(Members whose terms expire in 2016)
(3)MR. CHARLES G. FLOYD, 1617 Championship Drive, Franklin, TN 37064
(1)REV. CHARLES (BUDDY) POPE, 2391 Fairfield Pike, Shelbyville, TN 37160
(2)MS. SUE RICE, 1301 Brooker Road, Brandon, FL 33511
(2)MS. DEBBIE SHELTON, 1255 MG England Road, Manchester, TN 37355
(Members whose terms expire in 2017)
(1)REV. RANDY DAVIDSON, PO Box 880, Ada, OK 74821
(3)MR. CHARLES DAY, 9312 Owensboro Road, Falls of Rough, KY 40119
(3)MS. SYLVIA HALL, 930 Sherry Circle, Hixson, TN 37343
(3)MR. JACKIE SATTERFIELD, 2303 County Road 730, Cullman, AL 35055

GENERAL ASSEMBLY COMMISSIONS:

I. MILITARY CHAPLAINS AND PERSONNEL

(2) Term Expires in 2015–REV. LOWELL RODDY, 2583 Hedgerow Lane, Clarksville, TN 37043
(1) Term Expires in 2016–REV. CASSANDRA THOMAS, 1920 Dancy Street, Fayetteville, NC 28301
(2) Term Expires in 2017–REV. MARY MCCASKEY BENEDICT, 69 Lennox Court, Richmond Hill, GA 31324

These three persons and the Stated Clerk represent the denomination as members of the Presbyterian Council for Chaplains and Military Personnel, 4125 Nebraska Avenue NW, Washington, DC 20016

GENERAL ASSEMBLY COMMITTEES

I. JUDICIARY

(Members whose terms expire in 2015)
(1)REV. ANNETTA CAMP, 2263 Mill Creek Road, Halls, TN 38040
    anetta@cumberlandchurch.com
(3)MR. CHARLES DAWSON, PO Box 904, Scottsboro, AL 35768
    rdpfcd@scottsboro.org
(2)MS. KIMBERLY SILVUS, 1128 Madison Street, Clarksville, TN 37040
    kgsilvus@gmail.com
(Members whose terms expire in 2016)
(3)REV. SHERRY LADD, 4521 Turkey Creek Road, Williamsport, TN 38487
    revsherryladd@gmail.com
(2)REV. ANDY MCCLUNG, 919 Dickinson Street, Memphis, TN 38107
    scubarev@att.net
(3)MS. FELICIA WALKUP, 179 Mary Anne Lane, Manchester, TN 37355
    fbwalkup@gmail.com
(Members whose terms expire in 2017)
(1)REV. HARRY CHAPMAN, 4908 El Picador Court SE, Rio Rancho, NM 87124
    wrightrev@gmail.com
(2)REV. ROBERT D. RUSH, 17822 Deep Brook Drive, Spring, TX 77379
    rushrd74@comcast.net
(3)MR. WENDELL THOMAS, JR., 1200 Paradise Drive, Powell, TN 37849
    volbaby@comcast.net

*Ecumenical Partners   +Cumberland Presbyterian Church in America

II. JOINT COMMITTEE ON AMENDMENTS

The committee consists of five members of the Judiciary Committee of the Cumberland Presbyterian Church in America and the Cumberland Presbyterian Church.

III. NOMINATING

(Members whose terms expire in 2015)
(1)MR. RICK GAMBLE, 2430 Mount View Road, Manchester, TN 37355
gamble-ra@charter.net
(1)REV. ALAN MEINZER, 25 Rosewood Road, Batesville, AR 72501
brotheralan@suddenlink.net
(Members whose terms expire in 2016)
(1)MS. NANCY BEAN, 3510 Clubhouse Road, Somerset, KY 42503
beann@bethelu.edu
(1)REV. CHARLES MCCASKEY, 679 Canter Lane, Cookeville, TN 38501
charles@cookevillecpchurch.org
(1)REV. JIMMY PEYTON, 1455 County Road 643, Cullman, AL 35055
jakjpeyton@att.net
(1)MS. MARJORIE SHANNON, 2307 Littlemore Drive, Cordova, TN 38016
margieshannon@att.net
(Members whose terms expire in 2017)
(1)REV. TOBY DAVIS, 502 S Alley Street, Jefferson, TX 75657
pastortobydavis@gmail.com
(1)MS. CAROLYN HARMON, 4435 Newport Highway, Greeneville, TN 37743
richardharmon09@comcast.net
(1)MS. ELLIE SCRUDDER, 29688 S 534 Road, Park Hill, OK 74451
escrudder@gmail.com
(1)REV. KEVIN SMALL, 6492 E 400th Road, Martinsville, IL 62442
revkev61@gmail.com

IV. OUR UNITED OUTREACH COMMITTEE

(Members whose terms expire in 2015)
(1)MR. RANDY WEATHERSBY, 1502 Pinecrest Street NW, Cullman, AL 35055
(1)MS. ROBIN WILLS, 4607 E Richmond Shop Road, Lebanon, TN 37090
(Members whose terms expire in 2016)
(3)MR. RON D. GARDNER, 8668 Wood Mills Drive W, Cordova, TN 38016
(Members whose terms expire in 2017)
(3)MS. SHARON RESCH, PO Box 383, Dongola, IL 62926
(3)REV. WILLIAM RUSTENHAVEN III, PO Box 1303, Marshall, TX 75671

V. PLACE OF MEETING

THE STATED CLERK OF THE GENERAL ASSEMBLY
THE MODERATOR OF THE GENERAL ASSEMBLY
A REPRESENTATIVE OF WOMEN'S MINISTRIES OF THE MISSIONS MINISTRY TEAM

*Ecumenical Partners   +Cumberland Presbyterian Church in America

VI. UNIFIED COMMITTEE ON THEOLOGY AND SOCIAL CONCERNS

(Members whose terms expire in 2015)

(1)MR. DAVID PHILLIPS-BURK, 1065 Legacy Lake Circle 104, Collierville, TN 38017
  dlphillipsburk@aol.com
(1)REV. GEORGE ESTES, 7910 Cloverbrook Lane, Germantown, TN 38138
  geoestes@gmail.com
(1)REV. SHELIA O'MARA, 533 Loughton Lane, Arnold, MD 21012
  chaplainshelia@aol.com

(Members whose terms expire in 2016)

(3)MS. LEZLIE P. DANIEL, 13023 Taylorcrest Road, Houston, TX 77079
  lululoop@me.com
(2)+MRS. JIMMIE DODD, c/o Hopewell CPCA, 4100 Millsfield Highway, Dyersburg, TN 38024
  dodd125@gmail.com
(2)REV. BYRON FORESTER, 2376 Eastwood Place, Memphis, TN 38112
  bforester@bellsouth.net
(1)REV. JOHN A. SMITH, 916 Allen Road, Nashville, TN 37214
  john.a.smith.81@gmail.com
(2)+ELDER JOY WALLACE, 6940 Marvin D Love Freeway, Dallas, TX 75237
  jwallace@wlgllc.net

(Members whose terms expire in 2017)

(2)+DR. NANCY FUQUA, 1963 County Road 406, Towncreek, AL 35672
  fug23@bellsouth.net
(2)REV. RANDY JACOB, PO Box 158, Broken Bow, OK 74728
  chocpres@pine-net.com
(3)+REV. NOVALENE SITGRAVES, 3345 Grand Avenue, Louisville, KY 40211

President of Memphis Theological Seminary - Ex-officio Member

OTHER DENOMINATIONAL PERSONNEL

REPRESENTATIVES TO:

American Bible Society: REV. MICHAEL SHARPE, 8207 Traditional Place, Cordova, TN 38016

Caribbean and North American Area Council, World Communion of Reformed Churches:
STATED CLERK MICHAEL SHARPE, 8207 Traditional Place, Cordova, TN 38016

(Member whose terms expire in 2017)
(3)MS. LAURIE SHARPE, 3423 Summerdale Drive, Bartlett, TN 38133

THE REPORT OF THE MODERATOR

I want to express my gratitude to the 183rd General Assembly for the honor of moderating that session in Murfreesboro, Tennessee and for having that distinct honor throughout the rest of 2013 and into this meeting in 2014. I have taken seriously the obligation of representing the Cumberland Presbyterian Church during this year and I hope I have lived up to your expectations. I also express gratitude to Jamie Lively who, as Vice Moderator, has helped me along the way.

In looking back over this year I have experienced a number of surprises.

- I have been surprised by the extent of the work of the Cumberland Presbyterian Church. Of course, I was aware of many of our programs and activities, but by visiting other Presbyteries and sitting in on Board and Committee meetings, I was surprised by what all we are doing! I am amazed at the number of hours of "denotated" labor and support by both our staff and the rest of us. It makes me very proud to be a Cumberland Presbyterian.
- I was surprised by the growth of our mission work. I was aware of our Korean work here in the states and of some of what we are doing in Southeast Asia, but had no real insight into just how big our work in Southeast Asia has grown within the last few years. I was ever more surprised by the growth within South America and Mexico. Now that we have placed Central America "on the front burner" I expect similar growth there. Is the Cumberland Presbyterian Church declining? Not in our global missions!
- I was surprised by the number of women in leadership positions in all our Presbyteries that I had the privilege to visit and I am sure it is true all over our church. We have always had great women leaders but they were few in number. Now they are everywhere! We are gradually working our way out of being a male dominated church. From my observation this is now *okay* with the men. There still remains the problem of churches who either refuse or have hesitancy about accepting women as church pastors, but I predict this will resolve itself over the next few years. Reverend Louisa Woosley started something that could not be overlooked by her generation and which has increased dramatically over the years.
- I was surprised by the dedication and commitment of our Denominational leaders. I have had the privilege of working closely with the Missions Ministry Team in our Korean work, so I knew how helpful they were to us in that ministry. But as Moderator I have had the privilege of working closely with my day to day mentor, Mike Sharpe, and with Mark Davis as I prepared articles for "The Cumberland Presbyterian" magazine. I owe a great debt of gratitude to both for the guidance throughout this year. In addition to these two, I have been graced by the friendship and helpfulness of a lot more of our staff. Over the years, I have heard "gripes" about the "Center Staff," but I definitely did not experience any of that this year. None of the people I had the privilege of being around were doing their job "for the money." They are dedicated to the Cumberland Presbyterian Church now and are tirelessly working for its future.
- I was surprised by the strong support I encountered for unification, not only within the Cumberland Presbyterian Church but also within the Cumberland Presbyterian Church in America. Everywhere I went this was a topic of discussion and the discussions were almost always positive.

One year does not make me an expert, so I do not want to make recommendations, but I would like to make three suggestions:

SUGGESTION 1: Be proud, not negative, about the Cumberland Presbyterian Church. Sure we have problems! But our problems are greatly overshadowed by the dedication and commitment of most of our pastors and laity, our theology (which is the greatest in the world), and our commitment to the commission given to us by Jesus Christ to make disciples all over the world.

SUGGESTION 2: "Renew your mind" as the Apostle Paul asked us to do. I mean by this that we need to "think outside the box." I know that is an overused expression, but the temptation by every committee member is to focus on your committee and not much else. But every committee report is a part of the whole, a part of what will help or hurt us as a church. As an example, please think "globally"…how will this report effect churches in Colombia or Asia. We can no longer afford to think only of our home congregation. We are bigger than that!

SUGGESTION 3: Take advantage of this unique General Assembly as we meet concurrently with our brothers and sisters in the Cumberland Presbyterian Church in America. Please use this setting to make new friends and strengthen existing relationships as we celebrate being a part of God's family. "Being in one place" can help us to "be of one mind." (Acts 2:1) Maybe even pray that the Holy Spirit will shake us up and set us on fire.

My gratitude to the 183rd Assembly and my prayers for the 184th.

Respectively submitted,
Forest Prosser, Moderator

THE REPORT OF THE STATED CLERK

I. THE OFFICE OF THE STATED CLERK

The Constitution, the Rules of Discipline, the Rules of Order, and the General Assembly Bylaws (found in the front of the General Assembly Minutes) list the many responsibilities for the person who holds the position of Stated Clerk, the primary task is to maintain and strengthen a united witness for the Church. The Stated Clerk shall also generally supervise and control the business affairs of the Corporation, and see that all directives of the General Assembly are implemented.

The Office of the General Assembly also provides budgeting, accounting, and support services for commissions, committees, agencies and task forces without executive assistance. This past year, this included assistance to the General Assembly Evaluation Committee and the Unification Task Force (CPC/CPCA).

Additional services and activities provided through the office of the Staed Clerk this past year include:

• Developing and maintaining a web presence for the following General Assembly Committees/Commissions without staff: Nominating Committee, Unified Committee on Theology and Social Concerns, Commission on Military Chaplains and Personnel, Our United Outreach Committee and the Unification Task Force.

• Creation of spring and fall Denominational Updates, a compilation of talking points obtained from each board and agency that may be shared by visiting denominational staff and the moderator when making visits to presbyteries and in other settings. The updates are also shared with presbytery clerks.

• Development of a Travel Chart, to assist with the coordination of travel plans by denominational staff to meetings of presbyteries. The travel chart is also shared with presbytery clerks.

• Provided orientation/training to several of the General Assembly boards, agencies and presbyteries on the use of video conferencing technology for their meetings.

• Hosting the annual conference for Presbytery and Synod Clerks.

• Convened the first meeting of the Web Advisory Committee, comprised of representatives from each board and agency of the denomination. The Committee agreed to meet annually to review and suggest ways to enhance the denominational home page. Any major changes will be delayed until after the unification process with the Cumberlan Presbyterian Church in America is complete.

A significant portion of the Stated Clerk's time has been spent responding to various judicial and legal questions affecting local churches and presbyteries. The Clerk is appreciative for advice provided to this office from both the Judiciary Committee and from Mr. Jamie Jordan who serves as legal counsel for the Office of the General Assembly.

The Stated Clerk is grateful to the Church for calling him to serve in this position and appreciates the support of the Church for the Office and for the person who holds this position.

II. STAFF

Ms. Elizabeth Vaughn continues to serve as the Assistant to the Stated Clerk, a position that requires her to maintain accurate records of ministers, probationers, congregations, record income and expenses and to authorize payment of all items in the Office of the General Assembly budget. The Church is fortunate to have a person with such knowledge, efficiency and dedication to work. The Stated Clerk and the Assistant to the Stated Clerk are currently the only employees of the Office of the General Assembly.

Reverend Vernon Sansom was elected by the 182nd General Assembly to fill the position of Engrossing Clerk, and began his term of service January 1, 2013. Reverend Sansom is to be commended for the accuracy in recording the minutes of the General Assembly. Vernon also leads the orientation session for those who serve as the chair person and co-chair person for each General Assembly appointed Committees and provides valuable assistance in the preparation of committee reports at each meeting of the General Assembly.

III. ECUMENICAL RELATIONSHIPS

The Cumberland Presbyterian Church in America and the Cumberland Presbyterian Church have one heritage, one Confession of Faith and share in several co-operative relationships such as the Historical

Foundation, the United Board of Christian Discipleship, youth ministry, and the Unified Committee on Theology and Social Concerns. The Cumberland Presbyterian Church in America and the Cumberland Presbyterian Church also participate with other Reformed bodies in ministry. Although working through partnerships, the witness of the Cumberland Presbyterian Church in America and the Cumberland Presbyterian Church would be greatly enhanced through a union of the two denominations.

The Stated Clerk attended the Forum of Cumberland Presbyterian Church in America and was invited to present a workshop on the "Rules of Discipline." The Forum was held in Huntsville, Alabama, November 3-7, 2013. The Stated Clerk also attended two meetings of the General Assembly Executive Board (CPCA) during the past year.

The Cumberland Presbyterian Church has always been involved in ecumenical relationships, the oldest of which is the American Bible Society. The American Bible Society seeks to make scriptures available to every person in his/her language. Support for the American Bible Society helps to fulfill this purpose. In order to be able to reach more persons, the American Bible Society works with other Bible societies, some local and some international. The Bible can and does change human lives.

Both The Cumberland Presbyterian Church and the Cumberland Presbyterian Church in a America are members of World Communion of Reformed Churches (WCRC). The WCRC was formed in 2010 by a merger of the World Alliance of Reformed Churches and the Reformed Ecumenical Council. The WCRC represents approximately eighty million members of two hundred thirty denominations from one hundred seven countries, including Reformed, Congregationalists, Presbyterian and United Churches. Resources and updates from the World Communion of Reformed Churches are available on their website: (www.wcrc.ch).

In January of this year, the offices for the WCRC moved from Geneva, Switzerland to Hanover, Germany and shares a building space with the German Reformed Alliance and other ecclesial agencies within the "Calvin Center" in the vicinity of central offices of the Lutheran Church and the national headquarter of the Evangelical Church in Germany.

The election of a new general secretary topped the agenda for the May meeting of the Executive Committee of the World Communion of Reformed Churches (WCRC). Setri Nyomi, current general secretary, will be concluding his second and final term this summer. This past August, Office of the General Assembly had the privelege of hosting a visit by the General Secretary at the Denominational Center in Memphis. The occasion provided an opportunity of dialogue between the Center Staff and guests from Memphis Theological Seminary with Reverend Setri Nyomi.

Through co-operative ministries, chaplains for the military and veteran's hospitals are endorsed, migrant workers and persons in Appalachia are served, and missionaries are sent into a variety of countries. Through ecumenical partnerships disaster relief funds are distributed. Through working co-operatively church school and camping materials are developed. Habitat for Humanity enables many persons throughout the world to secure better housing. The Cumberland Presbyterian witness is more effective through participation with other Christians in these and various other ministries.

IV. THE CORPORATE BOARD

In the called meeting in December 2007, the General Assembly elected a new board of directors for the General Assembly Incorporation. With the merging of program boards into the Ministry Council, trust funds would become more vulnerable in the event the corporation was sued. The General Assembly Bylaws, Article 5 outlines the responsibilities for the Corporate Board.

The board met once this past year. Actions include: reviewed and approved the proposed budgets for 2014 and 2015 for the Office of the General; approved the 2015 housing allowance for the stated clerk; a review of the current status of denominational loans; and a performance review of the Stated Clerk.

As of May 2, 2014 the indebtedness for the denomination:
    Maintenance debt on Union Avenue $69,346.17
    Computer Software Loan $87,194.54

In October of 2013, the Capital Campaign Loan for the Center Property was paid in full. Monthly payments in the amount of $13,054.17 are now being applied to the retirement of the Building and Maintenance Loan (a carryover from the old Center Property on Union Avenue). The annual Shared Services budget for the operation of the Center, also includes $54,000 to pay on the maintenance debt for the Union Avenue Property and $38,049 to pay on the Computer Software Loan. All monies are borrowed from the Board of Stewardship, Foundation and Benefits instead of commercial lenders. At the current rate of payments, it is anticipated that all loans may be paid in full by March 2015.

The Center Interagency Team (CIT) comprised of the Center's Principle Executive Officers, is responsible for oversight of the day-to-day maintenance and property needs at the Denominational Center. Current CIT members include: Mike Sharpe (Office of the General Assembly), Robert Heflin (Board of Stewardship, Foundation and Benefits), Susan Gore (Historical Foundation), and Edith Old (Ministry Council). The Shared Services budget covers the cost for maintaining the Center offices and property (see page 150).

V. MINUTES OF THE GENERAL ASSEMBLY

The 179th General Assembly voted to make the minutes available on a CD, which resulted in a cost saving of over $6,000 for printing minutes and mailing them to persons requesting them. The Stated Clerk is aware that not all persons desiring minutes may have access to a computer and that it will take longer to find information on a disc than in a printed copy. It is permissible to download and print a copy of the minutes from the website (www.cumberland.org/gao). The resource center also prints and sells a few copies of the General Assembly Minutes each year. For information contact Matthew Gore, mhg@cumberland.org.

VI. ENDORSEMENT FOR MODERATOR

The Reverend Paula Louder, Nashville Presbytery, has been endorsed by her presbytery as Moderator of the 184th General Assembly.

VII. STATISTICAL INFORMATION

The annual congregational report forms are sent to the session clerk on December 1, and due in the office of the Stated Clerk of the Presbytery on February 1, and all reports are to be in the Office of the General Assembly by February 10.

In 2013, over a hundred congregations failed to report, thus statistics are not accurate. The statistics for a non-reporting congregation may be several years old, but it is the latest information available. The General Assembly Office continues to shorten and simplify the reporting process. Efforts also continue to further simplify online reporting for those able to utilize the technology. Hard copies of the report forms will still be made available for those congregations who do not have access to the internet.

The 178th and 179th General Assembly directed *"that each presbytery request that its Board of Missions or similar agency, as they minister to the needs of the churches within their presbyteries, remind the churches that it is important that they submit annual reports which are part of our history and offer assistance when needed in preparation of these reports."* If a congregation fails to receive a report, a duplicate form can be requested from the Office of the General Assembly or one may be printed from the web site (www.cumberland.org/gao), and going to the section on congregational reports.

Compiled statistical information is available in the annual Yearbook available online (www.cumberland.org/gao) or in print format, available through Cumberland Resource Distribution – resources@cumberland.org (901-276-4581). Future issues of the Yearbook will reflect a new designation for ministers who have granted the status of Honorably Retired (HR).

VIII. CHURCH CALENDAR 2014-2015

The 182nd General Assembly, directed the Office of the General Assembly to be responsible for reporting the "Church Calendar" to the General Assembly for adoption in 2013 and all future years. Listed below are the dates received from the Boards and Agencies of the denomination.

RECOMMENDATION 1: That the 184th General Assembly approve the following dates for the 2014-2015 Church Calendar:

CHURCH CALENDAR 2014-2015

July-2014
6-11	Cumberland Presbyterian Youth Conference, Bethel, McKenzie, TN
12	Program of Alternate Studies Graduation
12-26	PAS Summer Extension School, Bethel, McKenzie, TN

19	Children's Fest, Bethel, McKenzie, TN
22-26	Ministers Retreat, Bethel, McKenzie, TN

August-2014

23	MTS Fall Semester Begins
31-Sept 28	Christian Education Season

September-2014

10	MTS Opening convocation
14	Senior Adult Sunday
21	Christian Service Recognition Sunday
28	International Day of Prayer and Action for Human Habitat

October-2014

	Clergy Appreciation Month
5	Worldwide Communion Sunday
12	Pastor Appreciation Sunday
26	Native American Sunday

November-2014

	Any Sunday Loaves and Fishes Program
1	All Saints Day
2	Stewardship Sunday
9	World Community Day (Church Women United)
9	Day of Prayer for People with Aids and Other Life-Threatening Illnesses
16	Bible Sunday
23	Christ the King Sunday
30-Dec 25	Advent in Church and Home

December-2014

	Any Sunday Gift to the King Offering
24	Christmas Eve
25	Christmas Day

January-2015

6	Epiphany
11	Human Trafficking Awareness Day
12-13	Stated Clerks' Conference
15	Deadline for receipt of 2014 Our United Outreach Contributions

February-2015

1-28	Black History Month
1	Annual congregational reports due in GA office
1	Denomination Day
1	Historical Foundation Offering
1	Souper Bowl Sunday
8	Our United Outreach Sunday
15	Youth Sunday
18	Ash Wednesday, the beginning of Lent
18–Apr 5	Lent to Easter

March-2015

	Women's History Month (USA)
22-28	National Farm Workers Awareness Week
29	Palm/Passion Sunday
29	One Great Hour of Sharing

April-2015
2   Maundy Thursday
3   Good Friday
5   Easter
12   CPCH Sunday
12-18   Family Week
25-26   30-Hour Famine

May-2015
1   Friendship Day (Church Women United)
10   MTS Closing Convocation & Graduation
24   Memorial Day Offering for Military Chaplains & Personnel for USA churches
24   Pentecost
24   World Mission Sunday

June-2015
19-26   General Assembly, Colombia, South America
19-26   CPWM Convention, Colombia, South America

July-2015
6-11   Cumberland Presbyterian Youth Conference, Bethel, McKenzie, TN
11   Program of Alternate Studies Graduation
11-25   PAS Summer Extension School, Bethel, McKenzie, TN
22-26   Ministers Retreat, Bethel, McKenzie, TN

August-2015
22   MTS Fall Semester Begins
30-Sept 27 Christian Education Season

September-2015
2   MTS Opening convocation
13   Senior Adult Sunday
20   Christian Service Recognition Sunday
20   International Day of Prayer and Action for Human Habitat

October-2015
            Clergy Appreciation Month
4   Worldwide Communion Sunday
11   Pastor Appreciation Sunday
25   Native American Sunday

November-2015
            Any Sunday Loaves and Fishes Program
1   All Saints Day
1   Stewardship Sunday
6   World Community Day (Church Women United)
8   Day of Prayer for People with Aids and Other Life-Threatening Illnesses
15   Bible Sunday
22   Christ the King Sunday
29-Dec 25   Advent in Church and Home

December-2015
            Any Sunday Gift to the King Offering
24   Christmas Eve
25   Christmas Day

IX. CONTINGENCY FUND

The Stated Clerk is to hold, distribute and report annually the General Assembly Contingency Fund (see Bylaws 8.04, #24). Below is a summary of 2013 Contingency Fund Activity.

Summary of 2013 Activity

Balance Forward 1/1/2013 $ 25,715.42

Income in 2013:
- Our United Outreach $1,902.30
- Interest   305.64
- **Total Income:**   **$2,207.94**

Expenditures in 2013:
- General Assembly Evaluation Committee Expense $ 5,101.87
- General Assembly Unification Expense   7,770.35
- Pastoral Development Team   1,104.73
- **Total Expenditures:**   **$13,976.95**

Total Fund Balance as of 12/31/12 *$13,946.41

*Restricted Funds:

$ 4,100.00   The current balance designated by the 178th General Assembly to print the Catechism in the various languages represented in the church.

1,011.51   Pastoral Development Ministry Team/General Assembly Ordination Task Force

Total Amount of *Restricted Funds: $ 5,111.51 (12/31/13)

Total Amount of Unrestricted Amount: $ 8,834.90 (12/31/13)

Total Fund Balance: $13,946.41 (12/31/13)

Respectfully submitted,
Michael Sharpe, Stated Clerk

THE REPORT ONE OF THE MINISTRY COUNCIL

To the 184th General Assembly of the Cumberland Presbyterian Church in session in Chattanooga, Tennessee, June 16-20, 2014.

I. MINISTRY COUNCIL

A. INTRODUCTION

The Ministry Council serves as the primary long- and short-range program planning agency of the Church, striving to ensure that all segments work on a unified mission and that human and material resources are distributed and utilized to carry out ministries of the Church in an effective manner. The Ministry Council is accountable to the General Assembly.

1. Ministry Council (MC) Elected Membership and Terms

Ministry Council elected members are subject to General Assembly requirements of endorsement by presbytery (clergy) or church (laity), synodic geography, and gender representation. *The Ministry Council urges all Commissioners to proactively encourage leaders in their respective presbyteries to seek opportunities to serve as elected board members at the denominational level.*

The term of Mr. Roy Shanks expires in 2014. He has completed three terms and is not eligible to serve another term. Reverend Lisa Scott has moved to a different synod and is not eligible to serve on the Ministry Council. The terms of Reverend Donny Acton, Reverend Michele Gentry de Correal, Reverend Tom Sanders, and Reverend Lanny Johnson expire in 2014, all are eligible for re-election. The Youth Advisory Member term of Mr. Ethan Morgan expires in 2014, and he is not eligible for re-election. The Council expresses appreciation to Reverend Shanks, Reverend Scott, and Mr. Morgan for their contributions to the work of the Ministry Council. The Council also wishes to express appreciation to Reverend Robert Rush for his leadership and participation as a Ministry Council Advisory Member during his two years as Moderator and Immediate Past-Moderator of the General Assembly.

2. The Ministry Council's Ministry Teams plan and implement the program ministries of the Church and are made up of both Staff and Elected Team Members. The Ministry Teams report to the Ministry Council. **Staff Team Members** are employees of the Ministry Council; **Elected Team Members** are elected by the Ministry Council and reflect the General Assembly model to ensure representation among gender, laity and clergy.

Missions Ministry Team elected members having completed their terms of service this year are Mrs. Beverly Stott and Mrs. Nancy Gordon. The Ministry Council and Missions Ministry Team are grateful for their diligent and faithful service.

Ministry Team members recently reelected by the Council include: Mrs. B. Denise Adams, Mrs. Dusty Luthy Shull, Mrs. Le Ila Dixon, Reverend Aaron Ferry, Mrs. Samantha Hassell, Reverend James Buttram, Jr., Reverend Ricardo Franco, Reverend Jimmy Byrd, Reverend Amber Clark, and Reverend Drew Hayes.

New Ministry Team members recently elected by the Council include: Mrs. Karen Tolen, Mr. Tim Craig, and Mrs. Donna Christie.

3. Ministry Team Staff:

• Communications Ministry Team (CMT): Senior Art Director Ms. Sowgand Sheikholeslami and CMT Leader Mr. Mark J. Davis. Prior to her retirement, Ms. Joyce Reeves provided some clerical assistance for CMT.

• Discipleship Ministry Team (DMT): Coordinator of Resource Development and Distribution, Mr. Matthew Gore; Coordinator of Youth and Young Adult Ministry, Mrs. Susan Groce; Coordinator of Adult and Third-Age Ministry, Mrs. Cindy Martin; Coordinator of Children and Family Ministry, Mrs. Jodi Hearn Rush; and DMT Leader Reverend Elinor S. Brown.

• Missions Ministry Team (MMT): Coordinator for Women's Ministry and Congregational Ministry, Reverend Pam Phillips-Burk; Director Global Missions, Reverend Lynn Thomas (Birmingham, Alabama, office); Administration and Finance, Mrs. Jinger Ellis; Evangelism and New Church Development, Reverend T. J. Malinoski; Cross-Culture USA Ministry, Reverend Johan Daza; and new MMT Leader, Reverend Milton Ortiz who began serving on March 1, 2014. On December 31, 2013 MMT Leader

Reverend George R. Estes and part-time Secretary/Receptionist Ms. Joyce Reeves retired. Together they gifted the denomination with nearly 50 years of loyal service. The Ministry Council and Missions Ministry Team express their appreciation to Reverend Estes and Ms. Reeves for their numerous contributions to the former Board of Missions and Missions Ministry Team. The Church is blessed by God to have had such dedicated and competent persons in these positions for nearly five decades.

• Pastoral Development Ministry Team (PDMT): Leader Reverend Milton Ortiz served until March 1, 2014, at which time he accepted the call to serve as MMT Leader. Prior to her retirement, Ms. Joyce Reeves provided some clerical assistance for PDMT.

4. The Global Ministries Leadership Team (GMLT) is made up of the four Ministry Team Leaders and the Director of Ministries. This body works together to apply the vision/mission of the Ministry Council to the many varied programs and resource materials planned and produced by the Ministry Teams, coordinating ministries in a unified, collaborative manner. The GMLT meets monthly and minutes are disseminated to all members of the Ministry Council and four Ministry Teams.

5. Administration: Director of Ministries, Mrs. Edith B. Old, and Executive Assistant to Director of Ministries, Mrs. Megan Warren, provide administrative, financial and human resources to the Ministry Teams. The Director of Ministries is under direct employment of and is responsible to the Ministry Council. The Director gives executive leadership to the Ministry Council in accomplishing duties defined in its Bylaws and supervises the Global Ministries Leadership Team.

B. GENERAL INFORMATION

1. Meetings - The Council has met three times in regular session since the 183rd General Assembly. Meetings included: a) a concurrent/joint meeting with Ministry Teams at the Fogelman Executive Conference Center at the University of Memphis in August 2013, with orientation for newly elected Council and Ministry Team Members prior to the meeting; (b) a joint meeting with Ministry Teams at Faith Cumberland Presbyterian Church in Bartlett, Tennessee, in January 2014; and (c) a regular session at the Denominational Center in April 2014. Ministry Council members are conduits of communication bringing ideas and concerns from their congregations, presbyteries, synods and other spheres of influence to the Council, and in turn taking back information and resources to these same groups. The Ministry Council elected membership includes both clergy and laypersons. In an effort to extend a measure of equity in terms of time taken from work in order to actively attend meetings the Council has one meeting a year that includes a Sunday. In October, President Troy Green sent personal letters to the home churches of elected members thanking them for the support and encouragement they provide to their respective Minstry Council member.

2. Elected member accountability and training - Elected Ministry Council members and elected Ministry Team members attend a day of orientation prior to their first MC/MT meeting to help them become acquainted with the many and varied programs and responsibilities of the Council and four Ministry Teams. Each year, all elected members sign a Covenant reinforcing their commitment to answering the call to serve God through service to the Church. Elected members set individual annual goals and complete annual self-evaluations reflecting on their service. These tools serve as metrics to help guide the Council and Ministry Teams. The Ministry Council Covenant may be seen at *http://ministrycouncil.cumberland.org/ministrycouncilcovenant*.

3. Human Resources - The Council invests time in thorough revision of each MC/MT job description when the position becomes vacant. Input is gathered from elected Team and Council members, GMLT and relevant staff. This year, such review was completed for the MMT Leader, the PDMT Leader and the Secretary/Receptionist. Every MC staff member has an annual performance review completed by his or her supervisor; the Ministry Council appoints a committee to complete the annual review of the Director of Ministries. MC has budgeted funds to be used for "on the spot" performance incentives (gift cards) to be distributed at the discretion of the Team Leaders/Director of Ministries to staff exceeding performance expectations. These performance incentives are in addition to the 2.4% cost of living raise recommended by the 183rd General Assembly that was implemented in 2014.

4. Denominational Pool – The Ministry Council wishes to express our deep appreciation to the Nominating Committee of the General Assembly. That committee has the monumental task of matching individuals to boards in keeping with General Assembly required quotas (gender, synodic representation and clergy/laity) as well as the equally vital challenge of trying to match spiritual gifts of persons to those areas of need identified by the boards. This year, two elected members of the Ministry Council rotate off and the pool of eligible candidates was quite limited in number. It is our belief that God calls people all across the denomination to serve in leadership roles; the limited number of Personal Data Forms and related endorsements on file do not reflect the abundance of qualified leaders within the church. *The Ministry Council challenges all Commissioners to be proactive and intentional in efforts to encourage leaders in their respective spheres of influence to complete the necessary documents to be placed in the pool for future placement on a denominational board.*

C. REFERRALS FROM GENERAL ASSEMBLY

1. Creating 1st Edition Curriculum

The 183rd General Assembly adopted a resolution that "encouraged the Discipleship Ministry Team to pursue creating 1st edition curriculum in native languages that represent all Cumberland Presbyterians." DMT has formed two planning teams to work on curriculum in other languages, one that deals with cross-culture curriculum within the United States and one that deals with curriculum to be used in countries outside the United States. DMT is especially focusing on studies for Guatemala.

2. Mission Work/Mission Fields Relationship with Presbytery

The 183rd General Assembly adopted a recommendation establishing "the Missions Ministry Team as the agency responsible for oversight, guidance and authority for mission work and mission fields that cannot have a meaningful relationship with a presbytery due to distance and/or language." The MMT will fulfill this role as needed when called upon. MMT is the oversight agency of all mission work, as previously determined on various occasions by GA. Complimentary to this role, MMT is now the official host of our mission work until such time as a presbytery can be formed. MMT was tasked by GA to act as a judicatory of GA with respect to mission work outside the United States, and mission work not affiliated with a presbytery.

3. Bylaw Changes

The Ministry Council recommendation to the 183rd General Assembly to change the eligible ages of Youth Advisory members was approved. The Ministry Council is the only denominational entity with youth members. In August, editorial changes to the bylaws were made to reflect the new requirements.

4. Connectionalism

As resources allow, "face to face meetings" and frequent travel take MC/MT staff out into the field because "connectionalism" is important within our denomination. For a list of the locations visited this year by staff, please see *http://ministrycouncil.cumberland.org/2013wherewevebeen* and *http://ministrycouncil.cumberland.org/2014wherewevebeen*. MC/MT staff, including the Director of Ministries, continue to build rapport with individuals and groups throughout the denomination. In order to be good stewards, staff plan multiple events during trips, optimizing the opportunities for connectionalism. The reality of a denomination that includes many cultures and varied approaches to congregational life dictates that Ministry Council staff embrace a high level of cultural intelligence in order to enhance relationship-building with Cumberland Presbyterians around the world.

5. Creating a Curriculum for Elders Serving Communion

Discipleship Ministry Team and Pastoral Development Ministry Team developed and published a curriculum to train elders approved to serve communion called *The Celebration of the Lord's Supper in the Cumberland Presbyterian Church.*

II. MINISTRIES

A. COMMUNICATIONS

1. THE CUMBERLAND PRESBYTERIAN:
The denominational magazine is published 11 times annually, with the November and December issues being combined. In September 2013, the magazine transitioned to all enamel stock and has received entirely positive feedback from the change. For subscription information, navigate to *http://tiny.cc/thecpmagazine*.

2. Missionary Messenger: is a quarterly publication of Missions Ministry Team which is delivered to more than 19,000 households at no charge. The magazine offers up-to-date news of what the denomination is doing in missions, along with inspiring and thought-provoking stories of Cumberland Presbyterians engaged in missions in the United States, in our non-US mission fields, and around the world. To subscribe to the magazine visit the website - *http://ministrycouncil.cumberland.org/themissionarymessenger*, or email Jinger Ellis (jellis@cumberland.org).

3. News of the Church: Developed on a mass-marketing email platform, "News of the Church" (also known as "CP Updates") is an opt-in service designed to deliver news of denominational concern/interest as quickly as we become aware of it, in the most cost-effective manner possible. News of deaths (Elders, Ministers, Presbyterial or Denominational leaders) and prayer requests, event announcements, and public service notices comprise the majority of these "eblasts." To begin receiving News of the Church, navigate to *http://tiny.cc/cpupdates*.

4. New Cumberland Presbyterian materials/books: Ideas for new materials are always being explored and developed as they are needed. The latest resource developed was *Christianity Versus Other Faiths* by Ms. Whitney Brown, a *Faith Out Loud* individual module. CP Resources added *Sixty-Six Devotions from Sixty-Six Great Books* by Reverend Perryn Rice and *God's Mighty Acts Around the Globe* by Reverend Bob Watkins to inventory. CP Resources is also carrying the new Presbyterian hymnal, *Glory to God*.

5. Weekly eblasts: Eblasts go out from the Discipleship Ministry Team staff to all Cumberland Presbyterians in the General Assembly database. The monthly schedule for eblasts: General/Support Ministries (Week 1), Children/Family (Week 2), Adult/Third Age (Week 3), and Youth/Young Adult (Week 4).

B. CROSS-CULTURE USA

1. *Faith Out Loud* translations: A Spanish volume will be available in 2014.

2. Cross-Culture Ministries USA program: Out of 19 presbyteries in the United States, 13 have at least one cross-culture ministry. The United States has a total of 46 cross-culture ministries. Some countries represented include China, Colombia, Cuba, Dominican Republic, El Salvador, Guatemala, Honduras, Japan, Korea, Liberia, Mexico, and Sudan.

3. Naples New Church Development (NCD): Grace Presbytery started a probe in 2011 in Naples, Florida. The probe was approved as a NCD in the fall presbytery meeting in 2013 and is called Nación Santa Internacional Cumberland Presbyterian Church. The goal is to establish a Cumberland Presbyterian Spanish-speaking church in Naples, Florida in the near future.

4. Cumberland East Coast Korean Presbytery: The newest presbytery within the denomination and the first cross-culture presbytery in the United States is a Korean presbytery located on the east coast of the United States. Missions Ministry Team supports this presbytery in various ways.

5. Korean Ministers Conference 2014: This year's theme was New Church Development and Missions. The event was held April 28-May 1 at Ramah Naioth Retreat Center in Vernon, New Jersey. Featured speakers were Reverend Sung W. Cho and Reverend Yoong Kim.

6. Cross-Culture website CP Resources: There are new CP resources available in various languages. Visit: *http://ministrycouncil.cumberland.org/crosscultureusaresources*.

C. EVENTS

1. Prep 1:8 in Nashville: Prep 1:8 is a Missions Ministry Team missionary recruitment and training program. In August 2013, Prep 1:8 met in Nashville, Tennessee to discuss the Cumberland Presbyterian mission program with those exploring the missionary call. Prep 1:8 meets once or twice a year with those interested in future missionary service.

2. 2013 Forum: November 3-6, 2013, at the Brenthaven Cumberland Presbyterian Church in Brentwood, Tennessee. The theme, "Connecting the Dots: Faith, Family and Life," was well represented in the keynotes by Ms. Carol Wehrheim and by the worship leaders Ms. Rosemary Herron and Reverend Tiffany McClung. Almost 50 participants attended the event. The workshops were inspiring and informative and a special recreation time was well received despite the fact some participants weren't sure about "playing."

3. Young Adult Immersion Trip: December 26, 2013-January 5, 2014, 24 young adults from Hong Kong and the United States traveled to Medellin, Colombia. Work included a conference for young adults focusing on connection and evangelism. Events were held in each Cumberland Presbyterian congregation in the Medellin area.

4. Connect: *Connect* is a series of activities for children to be offered at General Assembly in Chattanooga, Tennessee in June, 2014. These events will bring together children from both Cumberland Presbyterian and Cumberland Presbyterian Church in America denominations for the purpose of building relationships and demonstrating unity through a time of fun and fellowship.

5. Children's Fest: June 7, 2014 at Cumberland Presbyterian Children's Home in Denton, Texas, and July 19, 2014 at Bethel University in McKenzie, Tennessee. These events will bring together Cumberland Presbyterian children—kindergarten through 6th grade—for a day of fellowship, Bible study, games, and worship, based on Psalm 139:14, "I will give thanks to you because I have been so amazingly and miraculously made." (God's Word Translation). The events will be from 9:00 am-3:30 pm. The cost is $25 per child. Housing will be available Friday night for groups that need to travel to the event on Friday. The cost for Friday night housing is $25 per person. Scholarships are available. Online registration information is at *http://ministrycouncil.cumberland.org/childrensfest2014*.

6. Women's Ministry Convention: June 18-20, 2013, held concurrently with General Assembly in Murfreesboro, Tennessee. More than 230 attendees participated in worship, workshops, small groups, and a field trip to Thistle Farms, Nashville, Tennessee The combined Convention and General Assembly offering was $22,390.17 and was given to Thistle Farms. The 2013-2014 projects are a passenger van for the Cumberland Presbyterian Children's Home and a theater production by Bethel University's Renaissance, "Project Freedom Curtain."

7. Women's Conference: 52 women participated in *Renew*, a spirituality conference held July 25-27, 2013 in Russellville, Arkansas. The workshops and worship opportunities focused on several spiritual practices. Another conference is scheduled for July 2015, in Bowling Green, Kentucky. Women's Ministry website has more information *http://ministrycouncil.cumberland.org/womensministry*.

8. Pastors Gatherings: MC/MT staff attend meetings of presbytery on a rotating basis to share information; however, the presbytery meetings do not lend themselves to opportunities for extended dialogue between pastors and staff. As a result, two years ago, the Ministry Council initiated regional Pastors Gatherings as a venue to give pastors and other leaders an opportunity to share concerns and ideas. Ministry Council and Team staff will come to your area at no cost to you. Please contact the Director of Ministries to set up a meeting in your region.

9. In a model similar to the Pastors Gatherings, the Ministry Council and Team staff host lunch gatherings for students at Memphis Theological Seminary. Three such lunches are scheduled for calendar year 2014.

D. FUTURE EVENTS

1. Cumberland Presbyterian Youth Conference (CPYC): June 22-27, 2014 at Bethel University. This year's theme is "Rebuild Community." The scripture focus is Isaiah 58:11-12.

2. Children's Fest: July 19, 2014 at Bethel University in McKenzie, Tennessee. Online registration information is at *http://ministrycouncil.cumberland.org/childrensfest2014*.

3. Ministers Retreat: July 22-26, 2014 at Bethel University. This opportunity to retreat is for ministers and probationers at the Summer Extension School (third block of PAS). Take a class or not; follow the schedule or make your own; eat with the students or go out. Scholarships available. *(www.ministrycouncil.cumberland.org/ministersevents)*

4. Sabbath Retreat: October 17-19, 2014 at Ferncliff Camp/Conference Center, Little Rock, Arkansas. When we observe Sabbath, we make space to notice and reflect on instances of God's grace in our lives and in our world. In response to this need, the Discipleship Ministry Team is planning a Sabbath Retreat. The theme is: "Be Free to Enjoy God" (from Isaiah 58:13, The Message). Scholarships available.

5. 2014 Forum: November 2-5, 2014 at Camp Copass in Denton, Texas. Keynote speaker will be Rodger Nishioka (PCUSA) from Columbia Theological Seminary. The theme is "Sparking Imagination and Resilience in God's Changing World" focusing on personal and congregational imagination and resilience. Ten workshops will be offered and a prayer center will be a new feature. Save the Date cards were mailed to all Cumberland Presbyterian congregations, presbyterial Boards of Christian Education and Cumberland Presbyterian Church in America Stated Clerks. Brochures available; register online *http://ministrycouncil.cumberland.org/theforumregistration*.

6. Youth Evangelism Conference (YEC): December 27-20, 2015 in Louisville, Kentucky. A planning team is now being formed.

7. 2015 Ministers Conference: January 13-15, 2015 at Hamilton Lake, Hot Springs, Arkansas. The theme is "Who is in your Pew: Preaching to a Diverse and Global Church!" Keynote speaker is Reverend Dr. Cleophus J. LaRue, and Princeton Theological Seminary's Francis Landey Patton, Professor of Homiletics.

E. GLOBAL INITIATIVES

1. Asia Exchange Committee (AEC): Previously referred to as the Asia Consortium, the AEC has been in discussion for several years. After consultation in Japan and Hong Kong the name was changed to reflect past working arrangements between Hong Kong and Japan Presbyteries. AEC is designed to provide a platform for Cumberland Presbyterian leaders in Asia to meet, learn about all the Cumberland Presbyterian mission work in Asia, share information, plan shared events and activities for Cumberland Presbyterians in Asia and provide a place to develop relational networks. The first AEC meeting was March 21 - 22, 2014 in Japan, with six Asian countries represented. During the initial three-year trial period, AEC will meet annually.

2. New Clinic in Guatemala opened 2014: Early in 2014 a new medical clinic was organized in the Comunidad de Fe CP Church in Guatemala City. The first clinic was established several years ago about 45 minutes outside of Guatemala City on the Casa Shalom orphanage property. The second clinic is housed in a rented facility, which also serves as the Comunidad de Fe Church worship center. The clinic received start-up funds from the *Loaves and Fishes* program. The clinic is under the direct administration of the Comunidad de Fe Church session, as established by action of the Guatemala Council of Cumberland Presbyterian Churches.

3. Organization of the new council of churches in Guatemala: Missions Ministry Team organized a council of three Cumberland Presbyterian churches in Guatemala in the fall of 2013. The intent is to give these churches an opportunity to learn and practice connectionalism and shared decision-making. While not a presbytery, this council has many dynamics similar to and functions in many ways as a presbytery.

4. Organization of Iloilo CP Church in the Philippines: Missions Ministry Team, as the host of the mission work in the Philippines, approved organization of the Iloilo Cumberland Presbyterian Church and installation of missionary Daniel Jang as their pastor. Reverend George Estes and Reverend Lynn Thomas, acting on behalf of MMT, traveled to Iloilo to organize the church and install the pastor.

5. Organization of a Council of CP churches and missions in the Philippines: The Missions Ministry Team organized the Iloilo Cumberland Presbyterian Church and two missions into a Council of Cumberland Presbyterian churches. The council model is used to teach concepts of shared decision-making and shared accountability. It is a step in the direction of future presbytery formation.

6. New Church Development (NCD) Partnership with Andes, Cauca Valley and Missions Ministry Team in Villavicencio, Colombia: Missions Ministry Team entered a partnership with these presbyteries to develop a NCD in the western portion of Colombia on the edge of the Amazon Jungle. Because this is a new area of ministry for the Cumberland Presbyterian Church and at a considerable distance from other Cumberland Presbyterian churches there, MMT helped facilitate and support this NCD, which is currently doing very well with 40 to 50 participants.

7. New Church Development (NCD) Partnership with Mexico Council of Churches and Missions Ministry Team in Ajusco, Mexico: A New Church Development mission plan presented by Missions Ministry Team to the Cumberland Presbyterian Council of Churches in Mexico was approved. MMT is the primary sponsor of the NCD, but the churches in Mexico also support the new church plant. In only a year the NCD has reached about 80 people, using three different home cell groups during the week and a Sunday worship service.

8. Deputation and Deployment of New Missionaries Fhanor and Socorro Pejendino to Guatemala: In March 2014, Missions Ministry Team deployed Fhanor and Socorro Pejendino to Guatemala as new missionaries. They are from the Cauca Valley Presbytery and were recruited because of their experience as church planters. They will be church planters in Guatemala.

9. Development of a new Missionary Liaison program: Missions Ministry Team began a new program that presents those with a call and heart for mission, but who are unable to live on the mission field as a missionary, an opportunity to express their call. The program allows people to apply to MMT to serve as a mission liaison. As a mission liaison they can work with a particular mission field or missionary, or they can provide a particular skill set to the mission field. They may adopt a particular Cumberland Presbyterian institution and advocate for that institution. Mission liaisons are volunteers and in most cases pay their own expenses.

10. Stott-Wallace Missionary Offering: This special offering was approved by both General Assembly and Women's Convention and will support endorsed Cumberland Presbyterian missionaries. The hope is that Missions Ministry Team will be able to sustain salary and benefits packages to Cumberland Presbyterian missionaries via the offering. The focal point of the offering is Pentecost Sunday or Missions Sunday. Churches, youth groups, women's groups, and Sunday school classes are invited to conduct mission education and mission activities to raise money for the offering. It is realistic to expect that the Cumberland Presbyterian Church can raise a million dollars a year for missionaries. The Cumberland Presbyterian Church can provide peace of mind to our missionaries regarding their support, as well as recruit new missionaries for our mission fields.

11. Missions Ministry Team is judicatory host for our mission work where there are no presbyteries: General Assembly gave Missions Ministry Team judicatory responsibility for all mission work outside the United States where there is no presbytery. MMT has a special judicatory committee that meets and reviews what actions need to be taken on the mission field, such as ordinations, installing pastors, organizing churches, etc. Once a presbytery is formed in these countries MMT's judicatory role is terminated. Currently, this responsibility includes 3 churches and 1 pastor in Guatemala; 1 church, two missions, 1 pastor and 8 probationers in the Philippines; and 4 churches, 4 pastors, and 2 probationers in South Korea.

12. Mission Internship in Guatemala in the Summer of 2013 to help with visiting mission groups and work with Cumberland Presbyterian churches in Guatemala: Miss Micaiah Thomas has served as a mission intern for Missions Ministry Team during the summers in Guatemala. She is a student at Princeton Theological Seminary studying spirituality and missions and is a probationer of Grace Presbytery. She helped short-term mission teams that visited Guatemala, as well as worked with Cumberland Presbyterian churches in Guatemala.

13. The first Cumberland Presbyterian women ordained in Mexico and Japan: Luz Dary Guerrero de Rivera was ordained in Mexico City in February 2014. She was the first woman and also the first Cumberland Presbyterian to be ordained in Mexico. She is from Andes Presbytery. Nobuko Seki was ordained in March 2014 by Japan Presbytery. She was the first woman in Japan to be ordained as a Cumberland Presbyterian minister.

14. Formation of Youth Mission Team to Hong Kong: The youth team will begin orientation on June 27, leaving for Hong Kong on July 1. Work will include English as a Second Language and Vacation Bible School (VBS) at the Yao Dao School in Hong Kong, youth worship, and visiting Cumberland Presbyterian churches in Hong Kong Presbytery. The team will work with Glenn Watts, Cumberland Presbyterian missionary to Hong Kong.

15. Certificate in Advanced Cumberland Presbyterian Church Studies: We are excited to announce a new program that we believe will have a positive impact on all aspects of our Church's life, both inside and outside the United States. Memphis Theological Seminary, Missions Ministry Team and Pastoral Development Ministry Team are joining forces to provide Cumberland Presbyterians access to Advanced Cumberland Presbyterian Studies. As a result of rapid growth on the mission field, we realized we needed a way to train experts about all things Cumberland Presbyterian, both inside and outside the United States. The first module was June 4-14, 2014, in Chattanooga, Tennessee and second module will be January 6-16, 2015, in Memphis, Tennessee. The tuition is $1,000. For more information go to *http://www.memphisseminary.edu/become-a-student/certificate-programs/certificate-in-advanced-cp-studies/*.

F. MISSIONARIES (Some names below are represented by initials only, for the protection of our missionaries in politically sensitive areas.)

- Glenn Watts is a layperson serving in Hong Kong. He helps the Xi Lin Cumberland Presbyterian Church with the development of an English worship service.
- Lawrence and Loretta Fung work with Global Operation International. Lawrence is one of the mission's leaders and provides supervision and guidance to missionaries in their program. He is based in Hong Kong.
- D and S are missionaries who live in Laos, a closed country. They have a Cumberland Presbyterian church in Laos. They also travel frequently to Cambodia and have started the Samaki Cumberland Presbyterian Church in Phnom Penh.
- Daniel and Kay Jang are church planters in the Philippines. Daniel is the pastor of the Iloilo Cumberland Presbyterian Church and also works with the Pavia and Oton Cumberland Presbyterian missions.
- P T works with a national church in Nepal. She is from Hong Kong Presbytery and is supported by Cumberland Presbyterian churches in Hong Kong. She is a layperson and works with discipleship.
- N B is a layperson and works with an interdenominational organization in the area of leadership development in China.
- S and L T work for an interdenominational organization in China, directing an orphanage with about 80 children.
- T and T G work with an interdenominational mission in a country in Central Asia. They use a business model as a means to improve the lives of Christians and to develop networks to share Christ.
- M and H W work with an interdenominational mission in Myanmar, using a business school as a means to improve the lives of Christians.
- Boyce and Beth Wallace are semi-retired Cumberland Presbyterian missionaries in Cali, Colombia, who continue to provide leadership in Cauca Valley Presbytery. They remain very involved in the life of the Cumberland Presbyterian Church in Colombia. They have been Cumberland Presbyterian missionaries for more than 50 years.
- Anay Ortega is a layperson from Andes Presbytery. She has been in Guatemala for almost 5 years and helps administer the Casa Shalom medical clinic. She is also working with the Council of Cumberland Presbyterian Churches in Guatemala. Anay has a passion for evangelism and has been called on to lead workshops.
- Fhanor and Socorro Pejendino arrived in Guatemala as new church planters in March 2014. They live in Guatemala City and work with the Council of Cumberland Presbyterian Churches, in addition to their church planting responsibilities.

- Carlos and Luz Dary Rivera are both pastors and from the Andes Presbytery, working in Mexico City with the Mexico Council of Churches. Carlos provides leadership to the churches and pastors and Luz Dary has been developing women's ministry.
- Kenneth and Delight Hopson work with an interdenominational mission in Uganda, Africa. Kenneth is a layperson who uses his talents in printing to help mission organizations and Ugandan churches produce Christian materials. Delight works for the mission with which they are affiliated and also works in an international school.
- S and M S work with an interdenominational mission in language study. Their focus is evangelism to Muslims.
- There are currently 26 Cumberland Presbyterian missionaries, 14 work with interdenominational mission organizations, 12 work in countries closed to the gospel, and 12 are helping plant CP churches.
- Mission Retreat: A retreat was held in Nashville, Tennessee, in March 2014 for people who serve as missions advocates in their churches and presbyteries. More than 60 people attended the retreat and participated in a variety of workshops and worship opportunities.

G. NEW RESOURCES

1. Advent Devotional: *Waiting and Wondering* will be published in the fall of 2014 and is the third Advent devotion book published for Cumberland Presbyterian congregations for use during Advent. *Waiting and Wondering* contains 25 daily devotions written by children, youth and adults from across the Cumberland Presbyterian and Cumberland Presbyterian Church in America. Previous editions were *The Jesse Tree* in 2012 and *Gather 'Round the Circle* in 2013.

2. Intersections - Where Faith and Life Meet: This new adult curriculum for Cumberland Presbyterians is being written by Reverend Cardelia Howell-Diamond. It is thematic and includes a daily devotional component that will reinforce the lesson throughout the week.

3. Missions Gift Catalog: Missions Ministry Team developed a full-color gift catalog featuring many projects/programs, as well as an educational component. The catalog will be distributed to churches/households in the fall of 2014 and will be online on the Ministry Council website.

4. VBS Curriculum: Discipleship Ministry Team is working with Chris Warren to edit, publish, and sell a VBS curriculum that he wrote entitled *Welcome to the Neighborhood*. The curriculum includes lessons, activities, and a music CD with original songs.

5. VBS Missions Resource: Will be created by Discipleship Ministry Team and Missions Ministry Team and will provide information and activities for a VBS mission project for Cumberland Presbyterian congregations that focuses on our churches in Guatemala.

6. CP Resources in different languages: The following CP resources are available at this time in languages other than English: *About Being Cumberland Presbyterian* (Korean, Spanish), *Buenas Nuevas En La Frontera: Historia De La Iglesia Presbiteriana Cumberland* by Reverend Thomas H. Campbell, *El Pacto De Gracia: Un Hilo a Través De Las Escrituras* by Reverend Hubert Morrow, *La Confesion de Fe: Para Los Presbiterianos Cumberland, La Historia Y Las Doctrinas De La Iglelsia Presbiteriana Cumberland* compiled by Reverend Lynn Thomas, *Pacto de Confianza: Ética Ministerial para Presbiterianos Cumberland* by Reverend Milton L. Ortiz. The *Confession of Faith* in Korean is in development at this time. The *Confession of Faith* in Japanese is just being printed and is a joint effort of Japan Presbytery and Discipleship Ministry Team.

7. 50 Days of Prayer: This new resource developed by Missions Ministry Team to support the Stott-Wallace Missionary Offering can be found on the Missions section of the Ministry Council website.

H. PARTNERSHIPS

1. Association of Presbyterian and Reformed Church Educators (APCE): Some years ago, the then Board of Christian Education served as a partner in APCE and helped sponsor their annual event.

There are now a handful of Cumberland Presbyterian Christian educators who are members of APCE and attend the annual event. For this reason, Discipleship Ministry Team staff are looking into renewing this partnership with APCE to help influence this work.

2. Beth-El Farm Worker Ministry: This ministry to migrant farm workers near Tampa, Florida began in 1976 by a small group of Cumberland Presbyterians. Today, the ministry has grown to encompass 27 acres and multi-faceted ministries. Cumberland Presbyterians who serve on the board include Reverend Eddie Jenkins, Reverend Don Schulz, Mrs. Joyce Kalemeris, Mrs. Penny Knight, and Mrs. Sue Rice. Reverend Pam Phillips-Burk represents Missions Ministry Team on the board. To learn more about Beth-El visit their website - *http://www.beth-el.info/index.html*.

3. Coalition of Appalachian Ministries (CAM): Strives to make a positive impact wherever Reformed tradition and Appalachian culture come together by networking with church and community to provide educational and service opportunities. There is Cumberland Presbyterian representation on the board.

4. Ecumenical Stewardship Center (ESC): The Discipleship Ministry Team Leader serves on the Advisory Council of ESC and has done so since 1993 (as staff of the Board of Stewardship). This group of some 25 communions enriches the stewardship ministry of the Cumberland Presbyterian Church and sparks the imagination of its staff. Many pastors and stewardship educators over the years have participated in either the Leadership Seminar or the North American Conference on Christian Philanthropy, both sponsored by ESC.

5. Curriculum Partnerships: Partnerships have been established with publishers of the following curriculum: *Faith Alive* Resources, *Feasting on the Word*, and *Shine* (formally *Gather 'Round*.) All of the partners provide samples, brochures, and support to assist Discipleship Ministry Team in making appropriate curriculum suggestions to Cumberland Presbyterian congregations.

6. National Farm Worker Ministry: This faith-based organization supports farm workers as they organize for justice and empowerment. There are 33 member organizations. Reverend Pam Phillips-Burk represents Missions Ministry Team on the board.

7. Presbyterian and Reformed Educational Partnership (PREP): Comprised of representatives from the Presbyterian Church USA, Moravian Church, Presbyterian Church in Canada, Reformed Church in America, and the Cumberland Presbyterian Church, this group is responsible for the development of *Opening Doors to Discipleship*, an online resource for leaders and seekers. This material is currently being translated into Korean and Spanish. It has been updated to include integrated suggestions for people who have special needs. *Opening Doors to Discipleship* is also available on mobile devices and free to Cumberland Presbyterians. Contact Discipleship Ministry Team for a special access code, then go to *openingdoorstodiscipleship.com* or *odtd.net*.

8. Project Vida: A joint ministry between the Cumberland Presbyterian Church and the Presbyterian Church USA in El Paso, Texas is located in the center of the nation's most impoverished neighborhoods, Project Vida serves more than 1,500 families. The multi-faceted ministry strives to change lives in a holistic and profound way through health, education and economic development. Cumberland Presbyterian who serve on the board are Ms. Diane Sowell and Reverend Lee Bondurant.

I. PLANNING COUNCILS

1. Young Adult Ministry Council (YAMC): Consisting of 12 young adults from the Cumberland Presbyterian Church and Cumberland Presbyterian Church in America, the YAMC seeks to promote, provide, and facilitate opportunities for young adults which create a community of service and fellowship through service projects, missions, spiritual growth, fundraising, and networking in order to foster a sustainable relationship among young adults and the Cumberland Presbyterian Church and Cumberland Presbyterian Church in America as a whole. This Council serves as a voice for young adults and plans opportunities such as the Young Adult Conference.

2. Youth Ministry Planning Council (YMPC): Consisting of 15 youth and 2 adults from the Cumberland Presbyterian Church and Cumberland Presbyterian Church in America, the YMPC has responsibility for planning CPYC and serves as a voice for young people in the Cumberland Presbyterian Church and Cumberland Presbyterian Church in America.

J. PROGRAMS

1. New Candidates and Licentiates: As individuals come under the care of presbyteries and become candidates for the ministry, Pastoral Development Ministry Team gives the following books to them: *Introduction to Christian Ministry*, by Morris Pepper, *The Bible and the Calendar Year*, by Reverend Thomas D. Campbell, *What Cumberland Presbyterians Believe*, by E. K. Reagin, and a copy of the *Confession of Faith*. New licentiates also receive books from PDMT as a way to encourage them on their ministerial journey.

2. Newly Ordained Ministers: Pastoral Development Ministry Team gives a portable communion set, a copy of the *Confession of Faith*, and the books: *Covenant of Grace*, by Hubert Morrow and *Covenant of Trust*, by Reverend Milton L. Ortiz to those who are newly ordained in the Cumberland Presbyterian Church.

3. Work with Presbyterial Committees on Ministry and Clergy Care: Pastoral Development Ministry Team works closely with committees who help to prepare candidates for ministry and those who nurture ordained clergy. PDMT's *Understanding God's Call to Ministry of Word and Sacrament in the Cumberland Presbyterian Church: Guide for Inquirers* helps inquirers understand God's call to the ministry of Word and Sacrament in the Cumberland Presbyterian Church. Also, PDMT's *Understanding the Process for Ordination in the Cumberland Presbyterian Church: Handbook for Presbyterial Committees on the Ministry or Preparation for the Ministry* was developed to help new committee members understand the process of ordination in the Cumberland Presbyterian Church. A manual for Committees on Clergy Care is being developed. (*www.ministrycouncil.cumberland.org/store*)

4. CP Learning Circles: Support for a healthy pastoral journey: The CP Learning Circles are cohorts for pastors who desire support, discernment, and growth in ministry. Participants will join a monthly group coaching call; each participant is assigned a partner from the group for peer support. At least two group members are coached in detail per call; all group members have the opportunity to participate during each call. The CP Learning Circle involves 12, 1½-hour phone calls, with a group size of 8-10 individuals. Sessions consist of structured exercises, input from the coaches, and open sharing. Coaches discern specific tools and approaches depending on group needs and interests. Pastoral Development Ministry Team scholarships one-third of the cost. (*www.ministrycouncil.cumberland.org/learningcircles*)

5. Leadership Referral Services (LRS): This ministry of Missions Ministry Team is designed to provide assistance to churches searching for ministers/leaders and ministers/leaders who want, need, or might be challenged to relocate. Reverend Norlan Scrudder, who has served as the consultant for LRS for the past 12 years retired December 31, 2013. Reverend George Estes is serving as the interim consultant. Work is being done to make LRS a fully automated service by mid-2014. The goal is to make the process more accessible to all interested parties.

6. Birthplace Shrine Summer Chaplaincy: Missions Ministry Team oversees the summer chaplaincy program at the Birthplace Shrine at Montgomery Bell State Park in Dickson, Tennessee. A worship service is held at 9 am each Sunday from Memorial Day to Labor Day. The chaplain for 2013 was Reverend Jesse Freeman.

K. SPECIAL CUMBERLAND PRESBYTERIAN EMPHASIS

1. Christian Service Recognition Sunday: The third Sunday of September is a time to recognize and celebrate the skills and gifts of those who serve within, and outside, the church. Worship resources are available online.

2. Clergy Appreciation Month: October is Clergy Appreciation Month and the second Sunday is Clergy Appreciation Sunday. We encourage and remind all congregations of the opportunity to honor their clergy. *www.ministrycouncil.cumberland.org/clergyappreciation*

3. Family Week: March 1 – 7, 2015. Congregations are encouraged to use this date or select a date that works best with their church calendar to plan *Family Week* activities for their congregations. Each year a planning pack may be requested that includes information to help congregations plan for *Family Week*, which is a week-long observance celebrating and encouraging families to grow in their faith formation.

4. Gift to the King: This focused offering is celebrated on any Sunday in December or Epiphany Sunday. The 2013 offering was $55,861.25 and went toward purchasing the Samaki Cumberland Presbyterian Church in Cambodia a new building so they are not worshipping in a rented facility.

5. Human Trafficking Awareness: January 11 is set aside to raise awareness of sexual slavery and human trafficking worldwide. Resources are available on the Ministry Council website.

6. Loaves and Fishes: This focused offering is celebrated on any Sunday in November. The 2013 offering was $47,670.22 and went toward opening a second medical clinic in Guatemala.

7. National Farm Worker Awareness Week: Celebrated the week closest to March 31, the birthday of Cesar Chavez, founder of National Farm Workers Association. Worship and educational resources are available on the Ministry Council website.

8. One Great Hour of Sharing (OGHS): Annual offering received on Palm Sunday makes the love of Christ real for individuals and communities around the world who suffer the effects of disasters, conflict, or severe economic hardship. There are currently projects underway in more than 100 countries. OGHS is an ecumenical partnership with nine Christian denominations. The 2013 offering was $19,941.31. Seventy-five percent of this offering was sent to Church World Service, official sponsor of OGHS. The remaining 25% was used in support of ministries of compassion on Cumberland Presbyterian fields of service.

9. Safe Sanctuary: General Assembly encourages all congregations and judicatories to have a safe sanctuary policy with those relevant parties trained by December 31, 2014. Resources to assist in creating a plan are available at *http://ministrycouncil.cumberland.org/safesanctuary*. In 2013 and again in 2014 Discipleship Ministry Team provided Safe Sanctuary Pre-Assembly Workshops. This workshop helps churches and judicatories create, train, and implement such a plan for their ministries.

10. Senior Adult Sunday: September 14, 2014. Recognizing the value of our older adult members, in 2003, the then Board of Christian Education established Senior Adult Sunday as a way of celebrating the contributions of this generation. The theme for 2014 will be *There's a Gap for That!* Resources will be available in early August in preparation for the official celebration date.

11. World Missions Day (Pentecost): Beginning in 2014, Missions Ministry Team will no longer observe March of Missions, a program of mission emphasis. Instead, we will focus upon 50 Days of Prayer and Action, from Easter to Pentecost. This time of prayer and action for missions will culminate on Pentecost Sunday and a special offering will be collected for the new Stott-Wallace Missionary Offering Fund. Resources are available on the Stott-Wallace section of the Ministry Council website.

12. Native American Sunday: The Cumberland Presbyterian Church has designated the fourth Sunday of October as the time to recognize and celebrate the first "foreign" mission work of the church. Worship resources are available at *https://ministrycouncil.cumberland.org/liturgyforspecialsundays*.

L. STEP OUT

1. Evangelism
a. Missions Ministry Team hosted a 2013 pre-assembly workshop on "Helping Your Congregation

with the 'E' Word." MMT will host a pre-assembly workshop in 2014 "Step Out: Creating Church Hospitality."

b. 2013 and 2014 summer issues of the *Missionary Messenger* included a Step Out emphasis

c. During the 2013 Forum hosted by Discipleship Ministry Team, the Missions Ministry Team presented a workshop on "How to Share the Gospel without Being a Jerk."

d. During the 2014 Ministers Conference, Missions Ministry Team presented a workshop on "Developing an Evangelistic Sermon."

e. Along with other Ministry Council/Ministry Team staff, Missions Ministry Team staff attended six different Pastors Gatherings to discuss evangelism in the local church.

f. Missions Ministry Team provided evangelism workshops during Arkansas and Grace Presbytery meetings.

2. NCD

a. Missions Ministry Team staff served as consultants for Presbytery of East Tennessee and Tennessee-Georgia Presbytery on New Church Developments within their presbyterial bounds.

b. Missions Ministry Team staff consulted with New Hopewell Presbytery (Cumberland Presbyterian Church in America) on a New Church Development within their presbyterial bounds.

c. Missions Ministry Team is financially assisting 10 New Church Developments/redevelopments within the United States.

d. Missions Ministry Team facilitated multiple church consults in Kentucky, Missouri, Tennessee and Texas.

3. Central America ("Adelante" – "forward")

a. Two All Hands staff meetings provided time to brainstorm and plan collaborative programming for the newest denominational mission field in Guatemala. In March, a group of four staff members representing Communications Ministry Team, Discipleship Ministry Team, and Missions Ministry Team respectively, traveled to Guatemala to provide customized onsite training for in-country church leadership on myriad topics that they had requested including evangelism and church planting, Christian education, Cumberland Presbyterian theology, polity and history, establishing Cumberland Presbyterian Wowmen's Ministry, stewardship, sex education, and human trafficking awareness. Subsequent small groups plan to travel to Guatemala in July and November.

b. Sex Education Curriculum: A curriculum is being developed in response to needs expressed by our congregations and the community in Guatemala. This curriculum should be complete by the fall of 2014.

c. Cumberland Presbyterian theology and polity: Two workshops were developed during the first staff visit to Guatemala. Copies of the *Confession of Faith* in Spanish were given to the participants, and the dialogue was very much appreciated by both the Guatemalans and Ministry Team staff.

d. Youth Ministry: The Ministry Council and Ministry Teams are exploring youth ministry needs including but not limited to training of youth ministers, curriculum needs, and programming for young people such as camping ministry.

e. Leadership Development: Discipleship Ministry Team is working toward developing planning teams that will help in reaching out to those whose first language is not English. One planning team will focus on the educational needs of those outside the United States and the other planning team will focus on the needs of our cross-culture congregations.

4. 2014 Missions Advocate Retreat: The 3Es Global Missions Advocate Retreat was held in Nashville, Tennessee in March 2014 and was well attended. The following topics were addressed: Global Missions Update, Cross-Culture Sensitivity, New Church Development, resources for small congregations, and report on the new mission work in Central America.

5. Living Waters for the World Endeavor for 2015: Living Waters For The World creates a covenantal relationship with a community in need of clean water. Through Living Waters for the World, this relationship provides the community with the training to do the installation and the health and hygiene education to provide a self-sustaining water filtration system.

M. SUSTAINING TRADITIONAL RESOURCES

1. *Live Lent*: Published in 2013, this devotional resource for individuals and congregations encourages readers to "live and learn" about Lent. It is an excellent resource for congregations and families to use to introduce and/or enhance the observance of Lenten disciplines with all ages. *Live Lent* sells for $3.50 each, with a bulletin insert download available for the Lenten season for $12 per congregation.

2. *Faith Out Loud*: A youth curriculum for Cumberland Presbyterian young people written by Cumberland Presbyterians. Currently three volumes are available for hard copy purchase or download. *http://mc.cumberland.org/category/faith*

3. *Encounter*: This curriculum continues to be a staple for more than 6,500 users throughout the denomination. Outlines are developed by the Committee on the Uniform Series, which is a group within the National Council of Churches of Christ. Reverend James McGuire represents the Cumberland Presbyterian Church on that committee and serves as editor. Writers for the next year are Reverend Dwight Liles, Reverend Tom Martin, Reverend Leslie Johnson, and Reverend Victor Hassell.

N. TECHNOLOGY IN MINISTRY

1. **Ministry Council Mobile App:** Developed for use on the iOS and Android operating systems, the app features mobile access to the eVotions daily devotions written by and for Cumberland Presbyterians, contact information for Ministry Council staff and elected membership, the denominational Program Planning Calendar, and links to denominational news and events. Android users should visit Google Play Store and search for "Ministry Council." iOS users should visit App Store and search for "Ministry Council."

2. **cumberlist:** This virtual meeting place/discussion forum for Cumberland Presbyterians was relocated this past February to the Ministry Council website. With the list now on a denominational platform, we anticipate being able to add features and functionalities not formerly available. Future plans include incorporation of the "News of the Church" mailing list functionality (allowing us to reduce costs currently incurred by the necessity of using a commercial platform for that service) and launch of a new denominational social media application. Follow the list at *http://tiny.cc/cumberlist*. To post, log in (or register for an account) on the MC website at *http://tiny.cc/mclogin*.

3. **MC website, Facebook, Twitter:** The Ministry Council maintains a web presence at: *http://www.ministrycouncil.cumberland.org*. Visit the site for resources, news and information, event registration, blogs, announcements, and links of interest and use to Cumberland Presbyterians. Visit us on Facebook at *http://tiny.cc/mconfacebook*. Follow *@MinistryCouncil* on Twitter.

4. **eVotions:** A short online devotion written by youth and adults representing a broad cross-section of Cumberland Presbyterians. Writers are in place through August 2014.

5. **Telling Our Stories:** We are collecting short video clips of Cumberland Presbyterians telling their faith stories. As resources become available, we will visit more and more venues/events with our video booth. To see some of the videos already collected, navigate to *http://tiny.cc/cpfaithstories*. Be sure to visit our booth at the 184th General Assembly, or tell your story when you visit us at the denominational center.

6. **DMT Facebook:** Created to share resources and events with Cumberland Presbyterians who "like" the page.

7. **Liturgies for Special CP Sundays**: Liturgies are available online for Sundays that are particular to Cumberland Presbyterians *http://ministrycouncil.cumberland.org/liturgyforspecialsundays*. Writers were recruited and are already writing and sending in their liturgies for 2014. Liturgies are usually available a month prior to their celebration; 2013 liturgies are also available on the website.

8. **Stewardship Discussion Starters:** Brief articles at *http://ministrycouncil.cumberland.org/stewardshipdiscussionstarters* can help your congregation or small group studying stewardship to begin their talks. Each discussion starter also includes four actions that can be taken to begin practicing stewardship in a concrete way.

9. Stewardship 13-week Study: By the end of 2014, there will be an online 13-week Bible study on stewardship. This study will give broad strokes of the different areas of stewardship, point to particular scriptures that highlight these areas and generally talk about how congregations might work to be more effective stewards in each of the areas.

10. Worship Well: Projected to be online by the end of the year, this webpage for pastors and worship ministry persons will help locate resources when planning and leading worship. It is hoped that Worship Well will be full of resources itself and will also be a place where pastors and others can also recommend resources to one another.

O. UNIFICATION

1. Cumberland Presbyterian Church in America Leaders attend Ministry Council meeting: Building on two previous years of hosting CPCA members during special fellowship events, the Ministry Council invited CPCA leaders to attend the Council's January meeting in its entirety. The Council wishes to thank the following CPCA leaders who enthusiastically responded and actively participated in this meeting: Moderator, Reverend Elton Hall; Vice Moderator, Reverend William Robinson; Stated Clerk, Reverend Theodis Acklin; current chair of the Unification Task Force, Elder Lewis Leon Cole, Jr.; Reverend Anthony Hollis; Elder Craig White; Reverend Al Garrett; and President of the National Missionary Society, Ms. Gladys Canty.

2. United Board of Christian Discipleship (UBCD): The Discipleship Ministry Team Leader suggested that since all activities, ministries and programs are now open to both the Cumberland Presbyterian Church and Cumberland Presbyterian Church in America, that from now on, all meetings will be held as the United Board of Christian Discipleship (UBCD). The DMT concurred. Therefore UBCD met on Friday, January 24, 2014 joining the Ministry Council and other Ministry Teams. DMT will continue to seek ways to promote unification in their area of work.

3. Ministers Conference: During mid-January, more than one hundred Cumberland Presbyterian Church and Cumberland Presbyterian Church in America ministers and licentiates met at Madkin's Chapel CPCA in Huntsville, Alabama to hear gifted and talented preachers. During the three-day conference, each preacher spoke from one of Jesus' parables. What grew out of the conference no one could anticipate. Whether it was from the preaching, the covenant groups, the evangelism workshop, the recognition of 28 clergy women during the Reverend Louisa M. Woosley celebration, the attendance of the two denominations, or a combination of some/all those factors, many participants expressed a deep impression of the presence of the Holy Spirit manifesting itself during worship and conference activities. On the last day, ministers from both denominations experienced a renewal that all who were present could only identify as the power of the Holy Spirit.

III. REALITIES THAT SHAPE MINISTRIES

A. FACTS (Source: Pew Research Religion & Public Life Project)

• Fully 1-in-3 adults under age 30 (30%, and known as "Millennials" because they were born after 1980 and began to come of age around the year 2000) are unaffiliated with any particular faith, describing their religion as "atheist," "agnostic" or "nothing in particular." Compare this with roughly 1-in-10 (9%) of adults 65 and older who are unaffiliated.
• One fifth (20%) of the U.S. public in general report no affiliation.
• Several leading scholars contend that young adults, in particular, have turned away from organized religion because they perceive it as deeply entangled with conservative politics and do not want to have any association with it. Overwhelmingly, they think that religious organizations are too concerned with money and power, too focused on rules and too involved in politics.

B. FUNDING

1. Our United Outreach: The Ministry Council assists with stewardship education efforts that include but are not limited to Our United Outreach. In 2013, Our United Outreach fell short of the goal set by the General Assembly, resulting in a reduction of $130,000 to Ministry Council income. Having consulted with the Stated Clerk to ensure compliance with General Assembly policies, and recognizing that Our United Outreach has not been a consistent/reliable source of dedicated income for many years, the Ministry Council set up a subcommittee to consider long-term financial planning five or more years out. The subcommittee is to identify direction of ministries and initiatives and determine needs that will drive fund development. The subcommittee is charged to explore ways that the Ministry Council can help to promote Our United Outreach while thinking creatively/futuristically about new and additional methods of funding. In a practice begun several years ago, individual members of Ministry Council and Ministry Team staff demonstrate support of Our United Outreach by directing that portions of their paychecks go directly to Our United Outreach. Additionally, Ministry Council and Ministry Team elected members have generously donated back their reimbursed travel expense. As of March 2014, this resulted in donations totaling more than $3,000 from elected members Michele Gentry de Correal, Mary Ann Cole, Troy Green, Samantha Hassell, Victor Hassell, Elizabeth Horsley, Lanny Johnson, Dominic Lau, Ron McMillan, Gwen Roddye, Sam Romines, Tom Sanders, Lisa Scott, and Beverly Stott. It is important to note that while the four Ministry Teams have endowments established over the decades that help address budget deficits when Our United Outreach goals are not met, the Ministry Council, established in 2007, has no such endowments. Ministry Council Administration relies entirely on Our United Outreach funding; when shortfalls occur, there is no endowment income to cover the deficit. We recognize that people are not often inspired to give to administrative budgets, but the structure established by the General Assembly gives the Ministry Council significant administrative function, freeing Ministry Teams to focus on the work of the church. *If you are interested in establishing a MC Administrative Endowment please contact any elected member of the Ministry Council or the Director of Ministries.*

2. All Endowments are listed within the Board of Stewardship section of the General Assembly preliminary minutes. The Ministry Council hopes that highlighting some of the Ministry Team endowments that are not yet viable might prompt potential donors to help move these endowments to the point where interest income can be used to support programs. These include:

Need: $603.66	Christian Education Programs	Endowment No. 806330	Jeff and Angie Sledge	Level to reach: $3,000
Need: $987.55	Christian Education Programs	Endowment No. 806140	Jean Garrett	Level to reach: $5,000
Need: $2,695.85	Children's Ministry	Endowment No. 806370	Jake Tyler Children's Ministry	Level to reach: $5,000
Need: $3,149.86	New Church Development	Endowment No. 803260	Clifford W. & Sarah C. McCall NCD	Level to reach: $10,000
Need: $3,247.52	Counseling, Conference	Endowment No. 810070	James Ratliff	Level to reach: $10,000
Need: $5,450.08	Awards/ Encouragement – CPC/CPCA Students at MTS	Endowment No. 810010	R & R Baugh	Level to reach: $10,000
Need: $8,548.78	Scholarships for Conference (Oklahoma, Red River Presbyteries. & far away)	Endowment No. 810020	L Brown (Beth Brown)	Level to reach: $10,000

3. In recognition of the 125th Anniversary of her ordination, the **Louisa Woosley Endowment for Sustaining Women in Ministry** was established in January 2014. During this inaugural year, those wishing to honor a woman in ministry may have that woman's name entered in the Louisa Woosley Society by contributing $125 to the endowment.

4. Investment Loan Program (ILP): ILPs serve as "savings accounts" for denominational entities. Funds can be set aside in an ILP for future programming. Currently, the Ministry Council has 76 ILPs spread among the four Ministry Teams and Ministry Council Administration. One example of an ILP established this year: rising travel costs and aging vehicles prompted GMLT to explore alternative vehicle travel methods. Subsequently, the Ministry Council sold our two aged vehicles and used the $10,000 proceeds to set up the first ILP for Ministry Council Administration. In February, the Council and Teams initiated a one-year agreement with Enterprise Carshare that is expected to result in measurable cost savings.

5. Clergy Crisis Fund: The purpose is to provide financial support to clergy who are in crisis and in need of support and care. These funds are for emergency use only. The circumstances approved for benefits are: death in the immediate family (i.e. minister, spouse, dependent child); out-of-pocket medical bills; counseling; termination (one-time expenditure); other considerations will be taken under advisement. Presbyterial Clergy Care Committees will explore the need for counseling or additional support. No payment will exceed $500 per year. Counseling fees will be paid at one half (50%) of the annual cost up to $500 per year. Pastoral Development Ministry Team will ask the presbytery to match the amount if possible or contribute a lesser amount if necessary.

6. CP Resources and Sales Figures: In 2013, 2,710 orders were shipped with $191,025.24 total billing for the year. CP Resources serviced approximately 1,975 active accounts in 2013 with 40,296 items. 2013 saw the largest sales total since 2010 (which was boosted by bicentennial activity) and the largest number of shipped orders since the closing of the CP Resource Center.

IV. MINISTRY COUNCIL CONCLUSION

Ministry Council and Ministry Team elected members and staff often say that "it's an exciting time to be a Cumberland!" The Ministry Council and four Ministry Teams are heartened by the work of the Unification Task Force as well as the sacrificial work of staff and volunteers in the many expanding mission fields where Cumberlands have a presence, both official and unofficial. As staff and elected members work alongside Cumberlands who are "eighth generation" and Cumberlands who represent the first generation and/or for whom American English is not their primary language, it IS exciting to see where God is moving among us!

Your Ministry Council and Ministry Teams, both elected members and staff, strive to live out the Great Commission in each event, each resource, each service that we provide serving God through the Cumberland Presbyterian Church. We remain thankful for the guidance of the Holy Spirit as we work to enhance and implement ministries that draw people to Christ and ask that the Church remain in prayer for our work.

Respectfully Submitted,
The Ministry Council of the Cumberland Presbyterian Church
Reverend Troy Green, President
Mary Ann Cole, First Vice President
Reverend Lisa Scott, Second Vice President
Gwen Roddye, Secretary
Edith B. Old, Director of Ministries/Treasurer

THE REPORT NUMBER TWO OF THE MINISTRY COUNCIL

To the 183rd General Assembly of the Cumberland Presbyterian Church in session in Murfreesboro, Tennessee, June 17-21, 2013.

I. MINISTRY COUNCIL
Edith Busbee Old, Director of Ministries

A. INTRODUCTION

The Ministry Council meets three times each year with one of the meetings taking place after the March 15 deadline for board/agency reports to General Assembly. The Ministry Council Corporation Annual Meeting of the Board of Directors was held April 25 and 26, 2014.

Following each Ministry Council meeting, a Summary of Actions is posted on the Council's section of the denominational website. The Council invites all Commissioners to the 184th General Assembly to read the Summary of Actions for the April 2014 meeting (http://ministrycouncil.cumberland.org/april-25-26-2014) as well as the summaries for all the meetings past and future and to encourage others to do so.

B. MINISTRY COUNCIL FUTURE MEETING DATES

The Ministry Council established a formula for setting dates of meetings. The Ministry Council and Ministry Teams meet in concurrent/joint session in August and January at the Center, a location close to Cordova, or possibly a retreat setting. Teams are encouraged to schedule other necessary meetings at the same time as the other Council meetings to facilitate carpooling and sharing expenses. The Ministry Council meetings held between meetings of General Assembly are as follows:

4th weekend of August (Saturday/Sunday) — Ministry Council and Teams in concurrent sessions
Last weekend of January (Friday/Saturday) — Ministry Council and Teams in joint sessions
3rd weekend of April (Friday/Saturday) — Ministry Council

2014 Meeting Dates:
August 22 (Fri) Orientation for new Ministry Council/Ministry Team elected members.
August 23-24 (Sat/Sun); Ministry Council/Teams meet in concurrent sessions. This meeting will take place at the Fogelman Executive Center on the campus of The University of Memphis.

2015 Meeting Dates:
January 30 – 31 (Fri/Sat)
April 17 – 18 (Fri/Sat)

In an effort to extend equity to lay persons who serve, and for whom taking time from work can be costly, challenging or a prohibition to serve the Ministry Council has scheduled one meeting a year to include a Sunday. On that Sunday, a worship service is part of the meeting.

B. MINISTRY COUNCIL CONCLUSION

We encourage all Commissioners to the 184th General Assembly and guests to ask questions and learn more from the Ministry Council/Ministry Teams elected members and staff present at General Assembly and to visit the Ministry Council booth in the display area. As the entity charged with overseeing the ministries of the denomination, Ministry Council/Ministry Team elected members and staff are passionately engaged in providing viable resources to local congregations. Programs, events and materials produced by the Ministry Council/Ministry Teams reflect a deep and wide array of ministries that are part of Cumberland Presbyterian congregational life not just in the United States, but around the world, for individuals in very different cultures speaking more than a dozen languages. We invite all readers, both before, during and after the 184th General Assembly to invest time in reviewing the Ministry Council webpages (http://ministrycouncil.cumberland.org/) as well as reading the MC Reports to General Assembly. The Council hopes that each Commissioner will make it a regular habit throughout the year to share questions and suggestions with Ministry Council/Ministry Team elected members as well as staff. The 57 Ministry Council/Ministry Team elected members are committed to their primary board responsibility to be conduits of information to and from the Council. The Ministry Council/ Ministry Team elected members and staff remain committed to serving God through the Cumberland Presbyterian Church and ask that the Church remain in prayer for our collaborative work. We remain thankful for the guidance of the Holy Spirit as we work to enhance and implement ministries across borders and across generations that draw people to Christ.

Respectfully Submitted,
Reverend Troy Green, President
Mary Ann Cole, First Vice President
Reverend Lisa Scott, Second Vice President
Gwen Roddye, Secretary
Edith B. Old, Director of Ministries/Treasurer

THE REPORT OF THE
BOARD OF STEWARDSHIP,
FOUNDATION, AND BENEFITS

I. GENERAL INFORMATION

A. BOARD MEETINGS AND ORGANIZATION

The Board of Stewardship, Foundation and Benefits under the direction of its officers, President Charlie Floyd, Vice-president Rob Latimer, Secretary Debbie Shanks, and Treasurer Robert Heflin, met two times in regular session.

B. BOARD MEMBERS WHOSE TERMS EXPIRE

Members whose terms expire at the 2013 General Assembly, with their years of service, are as follows: Debbie Shanks, nine years; Charles 'Boyd' Day, six years; Sylvia Hall, six years and Jackie Satterfield, six years. Debbie Shanks is not eligible for another term. We want to thank her for her service and dedication to the Board of Stewardship, Foundation and Benefits. Charles 'Boyd' Day, Sylvia Hall and Jackie Satterfield are eligible to serve another three year term and all three have agreed.

C. BOARD REPRESENTATIVE TO THE 184TH GENERAL ASSEMBLY

The board's representative to the 184th General Assembly is Debbie Shanks.

D. STAFF

Kathryn Gilbert Craig serves as Administrative Assistant, Mark Duck serves as Coordinator of Benefits and Robert Heflin serves as Executive Secretary. Carolyn Harmon serves as the Planned Giving Coordinator for the Presbytery of East Tennessee. The Board appreciates the work Carolyn Harmon does in educating congregations of the legacy ministry that can be accomplished as individuals make planned gifts to their local congregations.

E. 2015 BUDGET

The 2015 line-item budget has been filed with the Office of the General Assembly.

F. 2013 AUDIT

Certified copies of the 2013 audit reports from Fouts and Morgan will be filed with the Office of the General Assembly in compliance with General Regulations E.5. and E.6. The 2013 audit will be printed in the audit section of the 2014 minutes.

II. FINANCIAL FOUNDATION DEVELOPMENT AND MANAGEMENT

A. PURPOSE

One area of the work of the board is in financial foundation development and management. The purpose of this program is as follows:
To secure a firm financial undergirding for the ongoing ministry of congregations and the agencies of presbyteries, synods, and the General Assembly as they bear witness to the saving love of God, the grace of our Lord Jesus Christ, and the fellowship and communion of the Holy Spirit.
The Financial Foundation Program is reported in this section in general terms and more specifically under the headings III. Endowment Program, IV. Investment Loan Program, and V. Property and Casualty Insurance.

B. 2013 IN REVIEW

The year 2013 showed improvement in many sectors of the market and the economy. While we can enjoy increased earnings, we are also cautious moving forward. It is clear that we are part of a global economy. As a result we are always watching what is happening in Europe, Asia and other regions of the world. There is a growing concensus that the world economic condition is improving, global growth is accelerating and the European markets have bottomed out and are slowly improving. Global austerity is much less a concern. The U. S. economy is leading the way out. We have recently experienced an increase production of domestic energy. The housing market and employment numbers are slowly improving.

We need to continue to be cautious about looking too far down the road. Sentiment and emotion rule the short term. We are confident that our investment manager, Gerber/Taylor, can continue to help us navigate the sometimes turbulent ups and downs of the market. Since October 1981, Gerber/Taylor has done a wonderful job for the Cumberland Presbyterian Church.

C. BOARD OF STEWARDSHIP

The Board of Stewardship ended 2013 with an unrestricted surplus of $19,296. We are ever mindful of expenses incurred and try to be good stewards of what has been entrusted to the Board. We are grateful for the faithful support from congregations and individuals through their contributions to Our United Outreach.

D. MANAGEMENT OF FUNDS

In January 2013, we combined the Growth/Income Endowment Fund and the Total Return Endowment Fund with a focus on not only interest and dividends but also growth in realized and unrealized gains/losses.

At the end of 2013 the Endowment Fund portfolio was under the co-management of Gerber/Taylor Management, Metropolitan West Asset Management, RREEF America II and Clarion, 1607 Capital and Eagle MLP. The funds of the Retirement Program were co-managed by Gerber/Taylor Management, Metropolitan West Asset Management, and 1607 Capital.

The church loan portion of the endowment portion of the endowment portfolio and the investments of the Cumberland Presbyterian Church Investment Loan Program, Inc. were under the management of board staff.

III. ENDOWMENT PROGRAM

Since 1836, the board and its corporate predecessors have sought to be faithful trustees of the funds given into their hands to provide a permanent financial foundation for the work of congregations, presbyteries, synods, and General Assembly agencies. The work of the Endowment Program is the oldest responsibility of the board and fulfills a portion of that task to which all Cumberland Presbyterians are called: "Christian stewardship acknowledges that all of life and creation is a trust from God, to be used for God's glory and service."—*Confession of Faith for Cumberland Presbyterians 6:10.*

A. COMMUNICATION

The Endowment Program report will be distributed to all endowment program participants, general assembly board members, churches, and individual contributors.

Agencies, other participants, and interested parties received quarterly detailed reports on the postings to all their endowments. With the addition of names supplied by the agencies during the year, the number of persons receiving these reports continues to expand. In addition, special reports were made as requested.

B. ASSETS, INVESTMENT MIX, AND PERFORMANCE

1. Assets and Investment Mix

The assets of the Endowment Fund totaled $49,941,182 for 2013 at *market value*. The following table provides a breakdown of the investment mix:

INVESTMENT MIX		
Securities & Investments		
15.9%	US Equity	$ 7,949,604
10.3%	Real Assets Investment Trusts	$ 5,168,667
17.3%	Fixed Income	$ 8,616,093
18.8%	Hedged Equity	$ 9,389,903
14.5%	Multi-Strategy	$ 7,262,888
4.4%	Opportunistic	$ 2,185,401
14.0%	International Stocks	$ 6,967,444
4.8%	Emerging Markets	$ 2,401,182
100.0%	Total	$49,941,182

2. Performance of the Endowment Fund

The Endowment Fund generated $6,785,712 in investment earnings. Net contributions and withdrawals were ($5,692,270), including a transfer of funds from the Total Return Fund in the amount of $6,337,550. The change in market value was $1,093,442. Earnings paid and payable to congregations, presbyteries and agencies totaled $1,834,839 for 2013.

With the combining of the Growth/Income Fund and the Total Return Fund in January 2013, we also began paying out 5% (annualized) to the congregations, presbyteries and agencies. Previously agencies had difficulty in preparing budgets because of the unknown amount they would receive from endowment income. Now, they realize they will receive 5% in endowment income over a twelve month period. With this information, they have a better idea how much endowment income they can expect.

3. Rate of Income Paid Out by the Endowment Fund

The rate at which income was paid out to participants in the Endowment Fund for 2013 was 5%

Percentage of Income Paid Out	
2013	5.00%
2012	2.32%
2011	2.01%
2010	3.90%
2009	3.79%
2008	4.03%
2007	4.19%
2006	4.05%
2005	4.20%
2004	4.01%

4. Total Rate of Return for the Endowment Fund

The following table gives the annualized rates of return as contained in the report from Gerber/Taylor Associates for year end 2013:

	One Year Period 01/01/13 12/31/13	Five Year Period 01/01/09 12/31/13	Since Inception 09/30/81 12/31/13
Endowment Fund	14.6%	10.0%	10.4%

C. ESTABLISHING AN ENDOWMENT AS A LEGACY

The Board of Stewardship, Foundation and Benefits manages over 800 endowments established for the benefit of congregations, presbyteries, synods, agencies and other special ministries of the Cumberland

Presbyterian denomination. Many of these endowments were established by individuals as a legacy to continue to benefit long after they are no longer with us. Some of the endowments were established by congregations, presbyteries and synods to help further their specific ministries. Some of the endowments were started with very little. Through the years these endowments have grown and the beneficiaries are reaping the gifts of the endowment income and using it in ministry in their local area or worldwide. Please consider establishing an endowment.

RECOMMENDATION 1: That the General Assembly encourage congregations, presbyteries, synods and individual Cumberland Presbyterians to consider establishing an endowment as their legacy to further the local or worldwide ministry of the Cumberland Presbyterian Church.

D. ENDOWMENT PROGRAM LOANS

Historical Review

Through investing up to 40% of the assets of the Endowment Program in the witness of the Church, the message of good news concerning Christ is strengthened both in the United States and overseas. A recent survey of old files in the Historical Foundation and in the vault of the Board of Stewardship reveals the important role played by this aspect of the investment policy. Over the past sixty-five years from 1944 to 2009, 841 loans were made to congregations, presbyteries, and synods. From 2010 through 2013 an additional 16 loans have been made. Through these loans, $42,474,405 has been provided in financing for expansion of facilities and extension of witness.

A look at the different periods during which loans have been made provides a picture of growing endowments (and of post World War II inflation!).

Period	Loans	Total Loaned	Average
1944-49	35	$ 145,755	$ 4,164
1950-59	171	$ 1,360,441	$ 7,955
1960-69	208	$ 3,056,891	$ 14,697
1970-79	166	$ 3,609,084	$ 21,741
1980-89	101	$ 4,349,120	$ 43,061
1990-99	102	$14,440,837	$141,577
2000-09	58	$10,571,723	$182,271
2010-13	16	$ 4,940,554	$308,785

While looking at the table above, it should be noted that the Cumberland Presbyterian Church Investment Loan Program began January 1, 2001. Since its creation most of the larger loans are made through the Investment Loan Program.

Down through the years, donors to endowments have found satisfaction in the knowledge that the prudent investment of their gifts strengthened not only the work of the particular churches, institutions, and causes which they designated to receive the income but also the broader witness of the Church.

E. OTHER CHURCH LOANS

Although not a part of the Endowment Program, there are two other sources available to the board for investment in loans to churches.

1. Small Church Loan Fund

This fund, formerly none as the Revolving Church Loan Fund, was created through an endowment established by Lavenia Cole and gifts to the "Into the Nineties" Capital Gifts Campaign and all interest earned by the loans is added to the fund to increase the amount available for loans. There were seven loans from the Revolving Church Loan Program at the end of 2013 totaling $173,379.

The rate of interest for the Small Church Loans made during 2013 was based on the loan rate established by the Cumberland Presbyterian Church Investment Loan Program at the beginning of each quarter. These loans are generally small loans of $35,000 or less, amortized over five years.

F. REGIONAL PLANNED GIVING COORDINATORS

1. History

In 1993, the 163rd General Assembly commended the Board of Stewardship for "its vision in developing a program of planned giving in local congregations" and urged congregations "to be open to this new program and to take advantage of the assistance being offered" by the Board.

Further, it adopted recommendations to:

Approve a church-wide annual emphasis on planned gifts as a complementary part of the observation of the Family Week focus provided by the Board of Christian Education during May of each year; and

Urge each congregation to recognize the importance of promoting planned gifts as a part of its overall nurture of Christian stewardship among its members.

In response to the 1993 action, staff of the Board of Stewardship have made presentations to more than 150 congregations on the need to develop congregational endowments and encourage planned giving by church members.

At one time there were four Regional Planned Giving Coordinators. At the moment Carolyn Harmon is the only Regional Planned Giving Coordinators. She is an elder in the Cedar Hill Church, Greeneville, Tennessee, serving the Presbytery of East Tennessee. The other coordinators can no longer serve due to health conditions or other reasons. Though Carolyn is employed by the Presbytery of East Tennessee she has made presentations beyond her presbytery.

Through these regional coordinators education concerning the stewardship opportunities in planned giving has been made readily accessible to many churches. Often times the results of their work is not easily measured. It may be several years before their work bears fruit. The regional coordinators use their presentations to plant the seeds which may bear fruit immediately or years down the road. What is of utmost importance is that the seeds are being planted.

Regional coordinators are employed and their salaries paid by their respective presbyteries or by the Board of Stewardship. They are the living links of a partnership between the General Assembly and their presbyteries and they join in the semi-annual meetings of the Board of Stewardship and the biennial meetings of the North American Conference on Christian Philanthropy. In this partnership, the cost of their materials, travel, and continuing education opportunities are paid by the Board from *Our United Outreach* funds.

The Board of Stewardship would like to begin renewing efforts of educating local congregations about the opportunities available through planned giving. It is through planned giving that current Cumberland Presbyterians can provide for effective ministry long after they are gone.

It is our prayer that God will bless the work of encouraging Cumberland Presbyterians to give generously to enhance the future ministry of all our churches.

VII. CUMBERLAND PRESBYTERIAN CHURCH INVESTMENT LOAN PROGRAM, INC.

In 1976, the board began a program to provide an opportunity for flexible investment of current temporary cash assets of congregations and agencies of the church. The primary purpose of the program is to provide income to participants as a foundation for ministry. As of January 1, 2001, the assets of the original program, Cash Funds Management, were transferred to the new Cumberland Presbyterian Church Investment Loan Program, Inc.

For the year ending 2013, the assets for the Investment Loan Program were $16,307,605. There were 298 individual, congregation and agency accounts. At year end, deposits on account totaled $14,699,957. The total loans were $9,068,809 at year end.

For 2013, the corporation complied with the regulatory requirements in the states of Tennessee and Kentucky and was able to offer investment opportunities to individual Cumberland Presbyterians in the states of Tennessee, Kentucky, Texas, Missouri and New Mexico.

The board of directors is composed of the following: Rob Latimer, president; Charlie Floyd, vice-president and Debbie Shanks, secretary. Robert Heflin serves as Treasurer and Executive Secretary. During the past year, the board met twice in regular session.

In order to simplify administration and focus on the strengths of the Investment Loan Program, the board took action to limit the offering of notes and depository accounts to "ready access accounts." All note holders (individuals) and depository account holders (churches and church agencies) with funds invested in these "on demand" accounts participated in the $425,155 which the program paid in interest. For 2013 the interest rate paid to account holders was 3.0%. The interest rate paid to account holders can fluctuate from one quarter to the next. In recent years there has been renewed interest for congregations to open new accounts because the interest paid is higher than current CD rates.

The table below provides a breakdown of the investment mix.

	INVESTMENT LOAN PROGRAM Securities & Investments	
3.91%	Mutual Funds	$ 332,309
21.24%	Cash Equivalents	$1,803,961
74.85%	Taxable Fixed Income	$6,357,879
100.00%		$8,494,149

At the end of 2013 there were 23 loans to congregations made through the Investment Loan Program. The total loans were $9,068,809. Every accountholder is investing in the future ministry of the Cumberland Presbyterian Church as well as receiving interest on that investment.

RECOMMENDATION 2: That the General Assembly encourage congregations, presbyteries and synods to consider the Cumberland Presbyterian Investment Loan Program when they desire to save money for a special project or other need.

RECOMMENDATION 3: That the General Assembly encourage individual Cumberland Presbyterians who live in the states of Kentucky, Missouri, New Mexico, Tennessee and Texas to consider opening Investment Loan Program accounts to help Cumberland Presbyterian churches to build or expand their facilities.

VIII. EMPLOYEE BENEFITS ADMINISTRATION AND RESEARCH

A. PURPOSE

The second of two broad areas of the work of the board is in employee benefits administration and research. The purpose of this program is as follows:

To support the lay and ordained employees of the church as they venture to be faithful under the call of Christ and the Church to the daily demands of providing leadership to congregations and Church agencies whom are the incarnation of the Body of Christ, the family of God at work in the world.

Employee benefits are reported in detail under headings IX. Retirement Program, X. Ministerial Aid Program, and XI. Insurance Program.

B. VISION

The board has a vision of uniform benefits for all Cumberland Presbyterian clergy, including group health insurance, group long-term disability coverage, and participation in the General Assembly's retirement plan. Ministers would then know what to expect when they are called to another church. No longer would some ministers have to do without what is considered in the secular world to be basic employee benefits. No longer would ministers and their families have to settle for being relegated to second class status. The reality is, as several General Assemblies have recognized, that this is possible if we work together in much the same manner that we send out missionaries and do a lot of other ministry. Good employee benefit plans are in place and they would be healthier and stronger if used and supported by all employees of the Cumberland Presbyterian Church.

IX. RETIREMENT PROGRAM

Since 1952, the board has provided a retirement program open to all church employees. The program gives opportunity for churches and their employees to provide a source of retirement income based on voluntary contributions. In 1987, a new Cumberland Presbyterian Retirement Plan No. 2 was established as a qualified 403(b) defined contribution plan.

A. PLAN AMENDMENTS

As new needs arise or deficiencies in the original plan document for Cumberland Presbyterian Retirement Plan No. 2 become apparent, the General Assembly has the authority under Article IX Section 9.01 of the Plan to amend the same. In 2012 a revised plan document was approved by the General Assembly.

B. YEAR END REPORT

On December 31, 2013, there were 319 active participants in the Retirement Plan. There were also 7 receiving direct monthly payments as a result of their elections under Plan 1. In addition to these participants, there were 12 persons who were receiving annuity payments purchased through the Plan and for whom the Plan issues 1099-R's.

During 2013, $834,080 was dispersed to or for participants, a decrease of 56% over 2012's $1,894,181. Contributions totaled $610,467 and were down .009% over 2012's $616,043. Realized and unrealized gains on investments totaled $2,651,355 compared to a gain in 2012 of $1,124,452. The rate of return credited to the accounts for the year was 14% compared to 11.7% for 2012. (Comparative annual rates of return for: previous three years—+8.3%, previous five years—+12.0%, and from the beginning of professional management in March, 1982—+9.9%.)

Effective January 1, 2011, Gerber/Taylor Management was retained to manage our stock portfolio. We have continued our relationship with MetWest, a bond manager, and RREEF and Clarion, private real estate investment trust managers. Matt Robbins and Stacy Miller of Gerber/Taylor continue to be very helpful with keeping the board updated on market conditions and investment strategies.

RECOMMENDATION 4: That the General Assembly encourage churches to work with their pastor or other church staff to see that they have a retirement account and are saving on a regular basis for their retirement. It is important for a congregation to see that their pastor or other church staff are taken care of during their retirement years.

X. MINISTERIAL AID PROGRAM

A. MINISTERIAL AID

1. Full Benefit Recipients

As of March 2014 there are an equivalent of 3 Cumberland Presbyterian Church recipients of the full benefit of $500 per month (increased from $300 on July 1, 2010). The monthly total of these payments is $1,500.00; annually, $18,000.00 is paid. The equivalent of benefits for four participants at $260, or $1040 per month, $12,480 annually, is sent to Cauca Valley Presbytery in Columbia. These payments are not designated for specific individuals but are distributed by the presbytery as it sees fit.

In October 2005, the board decided to distribute 75% of the previous year's surplus to the remaining recipients. This distribution was made in December 2013 with 2 state side recipients receiving $4,000.00 each for a total distribution of $8,000.00. The Board of Stewardship has approved a cap of a maximum of $4,000 in lieu of large distributions that can have a negative effect on other benefits received, such as SSI, or state assistance.

2. Basic Requirements

The new basic requirements and amount for stateside recipients for the Ministerial Aid program were approved at the General Assembly of the Cumberland Presbyterian Church in June 2010. The poverty levels have been updated to the latest available figures. They are as follows:

Full Benefit of $500 a month for State Side Recipients

1. Minimum age is full retirement age set forth by the Social Security Administration.
2. Minimum years of service to the church - 15.

3. Can qualify for aid if a participant in the Cumberland Presbyterian Retirement Plan if income is below poverty level as established by the US Census Bureau.
4. Physical and/or mental disability (doctor's statement required) at any age, however, a minimum of ten years service is required if less than 60 years of age.
5. Individuals' income cannot exceed federal poverty guidelines set forth for the year by the US Census Bureau. Poverty level is $11,670 a year or $972.50 a month for 2014.
6. Couples income cannot exceed federal poverty guidelines set forth for the year by the US Census Bureau. Poverty level is $15,730 a year or $1,310.83 a month for 2014.
(The GA Board of Stewardship is authorized to look at each case in light of unusual financial hardship; thus, application may be made even if income levels exceed the ceiling.)
7. Presbytery obtains information and approves (approval can be given by the committee or board charged by presbytery with this responsibility); certification of approval is sent to the General Assembly Board of Stewardship.
8. Surviving spouse is eligible if above items 2, 3 and 4 have been met.

**Note: Recipient is responsible to verify if receiving Ministerial Aid would affect his or her SSI, Social Security or other benefits.

Cumberland Presbyterian Church applicants must submit to the board a listing of assets and liabilities so the net worth can be determined. The board urges presbyteries to maintain contact with persons under the Ministerial Aid Program who live within their bounds. Should there be serious unmet needs, the presbytery is urged to contact the board so that it may determine how the Ministerial Aid program can be of assistance in meeting those needs.

3. Cumberland Presbyterian Church in America

The CPCA now has 3 participants who receive monthly payments at the originally agreed upon amount of $109 per month. Benefits for these recipients total $327.00 per month or $3,924.00 annually. The CPCA normally pays its share in June or July following their General Assembly.

4. Ministers in Overseas Presbyteries

Payments for ministers serving in overseas presbyteries (presently, a total of $12,480 annually) are being made to Cauca Valley Presbytery and administered through its budget.

RECOMMENDATION 5: That the General Assembly encourage presbyteries to identify retired pastors who may need some financial assistance and provide the Board of Stewardship, Foundation and Benefits with the name and contact information of those pastors.

B. RETIREMENT RESERVE

Under Retirement Plan No. 1, retirees whose benefits fell below $150 per month could receive a supplement from the Special Reserve Retirement Fund Endowment to bring their benefits up to this level. Spouses of retirees are eligible to continue receiving this benefit after the retiree's death. These payments will eventually cease because no new persons are being added. One individual now receives $150 a month from this fund. Annually, $1,800.00 is paid to the recipient. This endowment has a balance of $1,223,535.52 as of December 31, 2013. The 1996 General Assembly approved the Board's recommendation to use the excess income from this endowment for Ministerial Aid payments. This has freed the Lowrie endowment to be used to meet other ministerial needs.

XI. INSURANCE PROGRAMS

The insurance programs of the board have been assigned by the General Assembly beginning in the middle of the previous century. Dental and Vision Insurance is the newest, begun in December 2008. Property and casualty insurance is the oldest, begun in 1951. While all of the insurance programs are important, group life and health insurance, begun in 1961, touches many lives in a personal way and often at times of deep anxiety. In all, about 310 men, women, and children depend on this program to meet their health care needs.

A. PROPERTY & CASUALTY INSURANCE

The Board of Stewardship, Foundation and Benefits secures property and casualty insurance coverage against accidental loss for the General Assembly Corporation, Board of Stewardship, Discipleship Ministry Team, Missions Ministry Team, Ministry Council, Communications Ministry Team, Pastoral Development Ministry Team, Memphis Theological Seminary, and Historical Foundation.

Our broker is Lipscomb & Pitts of Memphis, Tennessee. For 2014, Travelers Insurance carries our Property & Casualty policy and $2,500,000 in earth quake coverage, Mt. Hawley Insurance Company provides an additional $5,026,211 in earthquake coverage and Lloyds of London provides $10,000,000 in earthquake coverage. Philadelphia carries our Directors & Officers, Crime, Automobile, and Umbrella policies. Workers Compensation coverage has been through FFVA Mutual since October of 2008.

B. GROUP LONG TERM DISABILITY INSURANCE

The presbyteries of Arkansas, Columbia, Covenant, Cumberland, del Cristo, East Tennessee, Missouri, Murfreesboro, Nashville, North Central, Red River, Robert Donnell, Trinity, West Tennessee and The Center have now established non-contributory long term disability programs insured currently through Cigna. This leaves only four stateside presbyteries (Choctaw, Hope, Grace and Tennessee-Georgia) without a program. The quarterly rate applied to participant's salaries is .345 per $100 of salary.

There are three primary reasons for ministers to want the coverage and for presbyteries to want to provide the protection. The group rate is significantly lower than individual policy rates and does not require a large cash outlay to cover all full-time ministers in a presbytery; housing allowance and/or the fair rental value of a manse is included in the definition of salary for ministers; and, there is no medical qualification requirement in order to enroll. These advantages over individual policies make this coverage very attractive, especially to those who have previously purchased their own policies. In addition, a provision was negotiated with Cigna by the Board's consultant, whereby ministers, upon leaving a participating presbytery to serve in a non-participating presbytery, may continue the coverage if he or she so desires. The new employing church is then billed for the quarterly premium. There are now seven ministers and one employee who are receiving or have received benefits from this insurance program. There are approximately 201 participants.

C. GROUP TRAVEL ACCIDENT INSURANCE

This policy provides twenty-four hour coverage on "named employees" for accidental death, dismemberment, or loss of sight while on business travel. The maximum benefit is $50,000 and there is also a $1,000 medical benefit. The annual premium is $900. We renew this policy every 3 years, which will be done in July 2014. Thirty one named positions are covered under this policy.

D. GROUP HEALTH & LIFE INSURANCE

The board has used a fully-insured, managed care approach to provide group health insurance for Cumberland Presbyterian clergy and lay employees since March 1, 1999. Blue Cross / Blue Shield of Tennessee has been our insurance carrier since January 1, 2010. Blue Cross / Blue Shield of Tennessee (BCBST) is an independent, not-for-profit, locally governed health plan company that insures more than 5 million people nationwide. With an extensive network, BCBST is able to effectively service the employees of the Cumberland Presbyterian Church. In 2011 the deductible was increased for the two plans to $1,500 deductible and a $3,500 in-network deductible for the employee and has stayed the same for 2014. Spouse and Family deductibles are twice the amount of the employee only product. Lipscomb & Pitts, a Memphis based insurance company, is our insurance broker, and Craig Wright, our agent.

1. Loss Ratio

A comparison of paid medical premiums and claims is made in order to calculate a loss ratio. The following table contains monthly and cumulative figures for the calendar year of 2013. For 2013, 94% of the medical premiums paid to Blue Cross were used to pay claims and stop-loss premiums. This compares to a loss ratio of 83% for 2012, 91% in 2011, 75% in 2010 (not a full year of claims due to moving to new carrier) 105% for the same period in 2009, 98% in 2008 and 112% in 2007 with our previous carrier, Unicare.

MEDICAL EXPERIENCE REPORT						
	MONTHLY			CUMULATIVE		
MONTH	MEDICAL PREMIUM	PAID CLAIMS	LOSS RATIO	MEDICAL PREMIUM	PAID CLAIMS	LOSS RATIO
Jan. 13	159,850	137,033	86%	159,850	137,033	86%
Feb. 13	160,093	288,867	180%	319,943	425,900	133%
Mar. 13	164,210	186,751	114%	484,153	612,651	127%
Apr. 13	158,942	91,758	58%	643,095	704,409	110%
May 13	152,624	173,071	113%	795,719	877,480	110%
Jun. 13	156,503	125,673	80%	952,222	1,003,153	105%
Jul. 13	155,618	140,151	90%	1,107,840	1,143,304	103%
Aug. 13	153,045	121,888	80%	1,260,885	1,265,192	100%
Sept. 13	158,025	137,637	87%	1,418,910	1,402,829	99%
Oct. 13	157,194	157,167	100%	1,576,104	1,559,996	99%
Nov. 13	154,455	118,156	76%	1,730,559	1,678,152	97%
Dec. 13	156,588	104,173	67%	1,887,147	1,782,325	94%

2. Premiums

Efforts to maintain affordable premiums and comprehensive coverage are the biggest challenges we face. Option 1 has a $1,500 employee only deductible and a $3,000 family deductible. Option 2 has a $3,500 employee only deductible and a $7,000 family deductible. Premiums for 2014 are shown in the table below.

Blue Cross / Blue Shield Health Insurance for 2014		
	Option 1	Option 2
Deductible	$1,500 / $3,000	$3,500 / $7,000
Employee Only	$ 638	$ 545
Employee & Spouse	$1,357	$1,160
Employee & Child(ren)	$1,175	$1004
Family	$1,984	$1,700

The Blue Cross Health Plan is now on a calendar year as far as deductible and pricing is concerned. It is our objective to have the renewal pricing by no later than September 1 so presbyteries and agencies can have the figures for their fall meetings and better plan their budgets for the coming year. Periodically we seek bids from other carriers in an effort to keep premiums competitive. When this is done, we may not have the new premium information by September 1.

Open enrollment period is the month of December. It is during this time that an employee can enroll or change their health insurance coverage unless there are special circumstances.

3. Participation

As of February 1, 2014, 165 employees and 145 dependents for a total of 310 people depend on the Cumberland Presbyterian Church Health Insurance Program. A breakdown of family units by size at February 1, 2014 is listed below.

FAMILY UNITS BY SIZE		
	Number of Units	Total
Emp. Only	94	94
Spouse only		0
E & 1	3	6
E & 2	6	18
E & 3	1	4
E & S	28	56
Families of 3	10	30
Families of 4	15	60
Families of 5	6	30
Families of 6	2	12
Families of 7		0
Total	165	310

The following table shows the enrollment figures from January 2013 to December 2013. As one can see the numbers fluctuate from month to month.

MONTHLY GROUP INSURANCE ENROLLMENT			
	EMPLOYEE COVERAGE	DEPENDENT COVERAGE	TOTAL
13-Jan	93	73	166
13-Feb	93	74	167
13-Mar	93	74	167
13-Apr	91	75	166
13-May	93	72	165
13-Jun	91	72	163
13-Jul	94	72	166
13-Aug	98	70	168
13-Sep	95	71	163
13-Oct	95	72	167
13-Nov	96	71	167
13-Dec	96	71	167

4. Premium Stabilization Reserve (Formerly Emergency Reserve)

The reserve is invested in the Endowment Program Total Return Fund account which had a balance of $985,726 on December 31, 2013. The Emergency Health Insurance Reserve was established in compliance with the 1992 General Assembly directive to be used in "emergency" situations to match presbyterial emergency fund disbursements. The 1998 General Assembly approved the Board's recommendation to allow the Board to use the Emergency Reserve to maintain the stability of the group health and life insurance plan. This allows these funds to be used for purposes outside of the original scope of the reserve. For 2014 the Board of Stewardship reduces the premiums charged by Blue Cross by $40 for Employee coverage and $60 for Dependent coverage. In 2013, the Board of Stewardship used $97,120 to help offset some of the cost of the health insurance premiums.

5. Dental and Vision Insurance

On December 1, 2008, we began offering Dental and Vision insurance, on a voluntary basis, for anyone working at least 30 hours or more for any Cumberland Presbyterian Church, its agencies, boards, and institutions. Peter Whitely is the agent of record. At present there are 72 participating employees.

6. Jessie W. Hipsher Health Insurance Endowment

The Jesse W. Hipsher Health Insurance Endowment was created as the first step in the board's goal to raise $10,000,000 in endowments for the support of the Cumberland Presbyterian Health and Life Insurance Program. The endowment was established on March 6, 2004. At its establishment $11,450 had been raised. The balance of the endowment as of December 31, 2013 was $38,918.

7. Health Education / E-Mail Newsletter

To further educate participants in matters concerning healthcare, participants receive a monthly e-newsletter entitled, TopHealth, published by Oakstone Publishing. The monthly e-newsletter is full of health related tips that can be easily implemented by readers. The two page newsletter can be read within a matter of minutes. Also initiated in 2008 is the E-Mail newsletter that is designed as an information tool to help the participants of the Health and Retirement programs stay on top of happenings within the Board of Stewardship.

8. Wellness Program

With their Well+Wise program, Blue Cross offers health coaching to help make positive lifestyle changes to improve health and wellness, provide support and answer any questions about medical conditions or surgical procedures and treatment decisions. A preventive health guide is also available and has been sent to all participants in the CP health program.

Respectfully submitted,
Debbie Shanks, Board Member
Robert Heflin, Executive Secretary.

THE REPORT OF THE HISTORICAL FOUNDATION

I. GENERAL INFORMATION

A. OFFICERS OF THE BOARD

The officers of the board are as follows: Reverend Rick White, president; Pam Davis, vice-president; Sidney Milton, secretary. Susan Knight Gore is the director and treasurer of the Historical Library and Archives.

B. BOARD REPRESENTATIVE TO THE 184TH CPC GENERAL ASSEMBLY

The board's representative to the 184th General Assembly of the Cumberland Presbyterian Church (CPC) is Tommy Jobe. The alternate is Sidney Milton.

C. MEMBERSHIP AND MEETINGS OF THE BOARD

The board is currently composed of the following members: from the Cumberland Presbyterian Church in America—Edna Barnett, Vanessa Barnhill, Dorothy Hayden, Naomi King, and Rick White, from the Cumberland Presbyterian Church—Pam Davis, Michael Fare, Tommy Jobe, Mary Kathryn Kirkpatrick, Sidney Milton, and Sidney Swindle.
The Board of Trustees met, September 20, 2013.

D. MEMBERS WHOSE TERMS EXPIRE

The first term of Michael Fare expires with the 2014 meeting of the Cumberland Presbyterian General Assembly, and he is eligible for reelection. The second terms of Edna Barnett, Dorothy Hayden, and Rick White expire with the 2014 meeting of the Cumberland Presbyterian General Assembly, and they are eligible for reelection.

E. STAFF

Susan Knight Gore serves as the Archivist of the Historical Foundation. Lauren Gam Gilliland is the archival assistant for the Foundation.

II. ASSEMBLY REPORTING

As a matter of official structure, relative to the CPC, there is a Board of Trustees composed of members from both the CPC and CPCA, and relative to the CPCA, there is a committee composed of members from the CPCA.

III. PROGRAMS AND ACTIVITIES

A. HISTORY INTERPRETATION AND PROMOTIONAL ACTIVITIES

1. The 1810 Circle
In order to enlist the financial support of interested members of our churches in the work of the Foundation, the 1810 Circle was created. Membership is based on a financial contribution of $25 or more per year. Income through such gifts enables the Foundation to meet expenditures and is vital to the continued work of the Foundation.

We appreciate the support given to the Foundation by all members of the 1810 Circle and encourage other members of the Cumberland Presbyterian Church and the Cumberland Presbyterian Church in America to join this donor group.

RECOMMENDATION 1: That the General Assembly make congregations and presbyteries aware of the 1810 Circle and encourage new members to support this endeavor annually.

2. Patrons

Persons who contribute $100 or more to one of the endowments of the Historical Foundation become patron members and receive a certificate. Patron memberships may also be given in honor or in memory of an individual.

3. Heritage Churches

Congregations contributing a minimum of $1,000 to an endowment of the Historical Foundation become Heritage Churches and receive a framed certificate. There are six categories of recognition and churches can move from one level to another.

Heritage Church $1,000 - $4,999
Silver Heritage Church $5,000 to $9,999
Golden Heritage Church $10,000 to $24,999
Platinum Heritage Church $25,000 to $49,999
Diamond Heritage Church $50,000 to $99,000
Jubilee Heritage Church $100,000 and up

4. Presbyterial Heritage Committees/Presbyterial Historians

To promote interest in the work of the Foundation and to nurture the work of history on the presbyterial level, the Historical Foundation seeks to work cooperatively with the Presbyterial Heritage Committees/Presbyterial Historians of both general assemblies. The brochure, *Suggestions for Heritage Committees and Presbyterial Historians*, is available from the Foundation. The board expresses its appreciation to the presbyteries that have Heritage Committees/Presbyterial Historians.

5. Denomination Day Offering

The 2014 Denomination Day Offering was designated for state of the art equipment for use at the Birthplace Shrine to show a video about our denomination.

The Foundation expresses appreciation to congregations and others groups who received special offerings for the work of the Historical Foundation on Denomination Day. This special offering provides an opportunity for congregations to directly contribute to the support of the Historical Foundation as well as the Foundation supplying educational materials to each congregation.

RECOMMENDATION 2: That congregations be encouraged to have a special offering on the Sunday designated as Denomination Day to help support the special project designated for that year.

B. PUBLICATIONS

1. Promotional Materials

The Historical Foundation provides promotional materials describing its purpose and work, the various means of financially supporting this work, and listings of available publications and prints for sale through the Foundation. These materials are available on the Foundation's website.

2. Publication Series

1883 Confession of Faith.
1895 Cumberland Cook Book.
Cumberland Presbyterianism and Arminianism Compared/Contrasted on Selected Doctrines by Joe Ben Irby.
Faith Once Delivered; Some Indispensable Doctrines of the Christian Faith by Joe Ben Irby.
Family of Faith: Cumberland Presbyterians in Harrison County [Texas], 1848-1998 by Rose Mary Magrill.
History of East Side Cumberland Presbyterian Church, Memphis, Tennessee, Memphis Tennessee: 1926-1986, by the Historical Committee.
History of the Cumberland Presbyterian Church by B. W. McDonnold.
Jerusalem Cumberland Presbyterian Church: A Documentary and Pictorial History by Anne Elizabeth Swain Odom.

Legacy of Grace: Louisiana and Texas Cumberland Presbyterian People & Places of Trinity Presbytery by Rose Mary Magrill.
Life and Thought of Finis Ewing by Joe Ben Irby.
Life and Thought of Milton Bird by Joe Ben Irby.
Life and Thought of Reuben Burrow by Joe Ben Irby.
Life and Thought of Robert Verrell Foster by Joe Ben Irby.
Life and Thought of Stanford Guthrie Burney by Joe Ben Irby.
Life and Times of Finis Ewing by F. R. Cossitt.
Soundings by Morris Pepper.
Theological Snippets by Joe Ben Irby.
This They Believed by Joe Ben Irby.
What Cumberland Presbyterians Believe by E. K. Reagin.
Prints of the *Samuel McAdow Home* and the *First Meeting of Cumberland Presbytery*.
These items are available for sale from Cumberland Presbyterian Resources.

RECOMMENDATION 3: That the General Assembly make presbyteries, congregations, and individuals aware that the Historical Foundation is interested and has funds to publish books on topics concerning the Cumberland Presbyterian Church and Cumberland Presbyterian Church in America.

3. Denomination Day Resources

All the Past is but the Beginning of Beginning (Denomination Day resource) is available on the Foundation's web site under the Resources section: http://www.cumberland.org/hfcpc/resource/. It includes eight dramas intended to present the birth of the Cumberland Presbyterian Church and the Cumberland Presbyterian Church in America. A hard copy may be requested from the Foundation office.

4. Online Promotion

Recognizing the increasing value of emerging social media, the Historical Foundation employs a Facebook group, "Historical Foundation of the CPC & CPCA," to engage an expanding audience of Cumberland Presbyterians in denominational history and heritage. By showcasing collection acquisitions, the Foundation expands the knowledge of those materials sought for preservation as well as the nature of archival development.

RECOMMENDATION 4: That the General Assembly encourage presbyteries, congregations, and individuals active on the internet to join the Historical Foundation of the CPC & CPCA Facebook group.

C. HISTORICAL FOUNDATION AWARDS

1. Award in Cumberland Presbyterian History

The Foundation encourages the writing and publication of papers on all aspects of the history of the Cumberland Presbyterian Church in America and the Cumberland Presbyterian Church. One means of promoting such writing is the Historical Foundation Award in Cumberland Presbyterian History. A $300 prize is awarded to the author entering the best paper on any CP or CPCA history subject which meets in form and content the requirements set by the Board of Trustees and judged by the board appointed awards committee. All manuscripts submitted to the competition become property of the Foundation and are added to the Historical Library and Archives.

The contest follows the calendar year, and entries for the 2014 competition are encouraged. All entries will be accepted through December 2014 for this year's contest. Any entries received following the deadline of December 31st will be automatically entered in the 2015 competition.

Guidelines and entry forms for submitting manuscripts to the competition are available from the Foundation office as well as on the internet, http://www.cumberland.org/hfcpc/Awards.htm. The Historical Foundation appreciates the participation of past and future CPCA and CP historians in this program.

The winner of the 2013 competition is Reverend Brittany Meeks for the paper "The Conservative Controversy: How the Upper Cumberland Presbyterian Church was Born."

2. Awards of Recognition

Awards of recognition are certificates given to organizations or individuals in recognition of historic events or contributions to the preservation of our heritage as Cumberland Presbyterians. Appropriate applications for the award are: particular churches celebrating anniversaries of their organization; any judicatory or agency celebrating publication of a written history; celebrations of history or historic event in a creative or unusual manner; individuals who have provided continued service for 50 years or more as members of a local congregation or presbytery; individuals who have served for 40 years or more in a continuing leadership role (including pastors) within a local church. Individuals, churches, or presbyterial heritage committees may make application for the issuing of an award by contacting the Foundation office. Application forms are supplied by the Foundation office as well as the internet, http://www.cumberland.org/hfcpc/Awards.htm.

D. RELATIONSHIPS

Presbyterian Historical Society of the Southwest

The Presbyterian Historical Society of the Southwest is an agency of The Synod of the Sun, Presbyterian Church (USA) and Cumberland Presbyterian Churches in Arkansas, Louisiana, Oklahoma and Texas. Members of the Cumberland Presbyterian Church who serve on the board of this organization are Reverend Norlan Scrudder and Dr. Rose Mary Magrill.

IV. HISTORICAL LIBRARY AND ARCHIVES

A. RESEARCH SERVICE

The Foundation's main research commitment is to the agencies, local congregations, and members of the Cumberland Presbyterian Churches. Since the Historical Library and Archives of the Historical Foundation serves as the official repository for the Cumberland Presbyterian General Assemblies, this is our focus. Although the separation of research into two types designated by their mode of access has been rapid and dramatic, both the traditional and "cyber" mode contribute to and enhance the other.

1. Traditional/Physical Access

Hands on access to primary source material remains the vital heart of historic and theological research. Rather than being diminished by increased electronic resources, traditional research has broadened due to heightened awareness of primary sources in an expanding information age. The Foundation receives research requests by personal visitors, mail, e-mail, and telephone. As time permits, requests are researched. Responses are sent to the requestor, as well as pertinent information on ministers, congregations, presbyteries and synods being placed on our website for future researchers.

2. Electronic Access

The Foundation's website continues to expand in order to provide greater access to the materials in the Historical Library and Archives. As well as being a research tool, the internet provides an invaluable and inexpensive means of promotion for the physical collections of the Historical Library and Archives, the activities of the Historical Foundation, and for the greater community of faith called Cumberland Presbyterians. Information at the site includes: general information about the Foundation, entire texts of important historical documents, historical information on particular congregations, ministers, presbyteries, and synods. The gateway URL to the Foundation's website is http://www.cumberland.org/hfcpc/.

B. ACQUISITIONS

The Historical Library and Archives regularly receives items published by the two denominations, *Minutes of the General Assembly of the Cumberland Presbyterian Church*, *Preliminary Minutes of the General Assembly of the Cumberland Presbyterian Church*, *Yearbook of the General Assembly of the Cumberland Presbyterian Church*, *The Cumberland Presbyterian*, *Missionary Messenger*, *Minutes of the General Assembly of the Cumberland Presbyterian Church in America*, *Preliminary Minutes of the General Assembly of the Cumberland Presbyterian Church in America*, and *The Cumberland Flag*. Synods and presbyteries deposit four copies of their printed minutes in the Historical Library and Archives. In addition, books, pamphlets, theses, dissertations, records and publications of general assembly, boards, agencies, institutions, and task forces; records and publications of synods and presbyteries, session records and other materials of particular churches, biographical material of Cumberland Presbyterian and Cumberland Presbyterian Church in America ministers, photographs, audiovisual materials, and museum items were among the accessions received. The 2012 Accession List closed with 211 accession groups.

Some of the highlights added to the collection in 2013 include:

Books

Campbell, Thomas H. *Buenas Nuevas en la Frontera: Historia de la Iglesia Presbiteriana Cumberland*. Cordova, Tennessee: Iglesia Presbiteriana Cumberland, 2013.

Confession of Faith of the Cumberland Presbyterian Church in the United States of America. Revised and adopted by the General Assembly, at Princeton, Ky., May, 1829. Stereotyped by J. A. James. Published by Cumberland Presbyterian Board of Publication, 1848.

Rice, Edwin W. *The Cumberland Presbyterian Scholar's Hand-book on the International Lessons 1885: Studies in the Acts and Epistles and In the Old Testament*. Nashville, Tennessee: Cumberland Presbyterian Publishing House, 1885.

Stevens, Thomas G. *Tennessee Preacher, Tennessee Soldier: The Civil War Career of Captain John D. Kirkpatrick, CSA One of Morgan's Raiders*. Denver, Colorado: Outskirts Press, 2013.

St. John, Beverly P. and Gary A. Webb. *The Life and Work of Ernest A. Pickup*. [Nashville, Tenn.]: B. P. St. John & G. A. Webb, 2009.

Tao Hsien Cumberland Presbyterian Church. Sham Shui Po, Kowloon, Hong Kong. *25th Anniversary of the Tao Hsien Cumberland Presbyterian Church.: 1985-2010*. Hong Kong, 2011.

General Assembly

Colored Cumberland Presbyterian Church. *Minutes of the Seventy-Eighth General Assembly of the Colored Cumberland Presbyterian Church in the United States of America and Liberia, Africa*. Detroit, Michigan. June 12-15, 1952.

Cumberland Flag. June 1983.

Cumberland Presbyterian Church in America. Planning Calendar. 1996.

Cumberland Presbyterian Pulpit: A Series of Original Sermons, by Clergymen of the Cumberland Presbyterian Church. Vol. 1 No. 6, June 1833.

Cumberland Presbyterian Pulpit: A Series of Original Sermons, by Clergymen of the Cumberland Presbyterian Church. Vol. 1 No. 7, July 1833.

Cumberland Presbyterian Pulpit: A Series of Original Sermons, by Clergymen of the Cumberland Presbyterian Church. Vol. 1 No. 9, September 1833.

Fieldview. Vol. II, No. I (January 1904).

Ladies' Pearl. Vol. VI, No. 1, April 1858. Edited by William S. Langdon and Mrs. Sue D. Langdon. Nashville, Tennessee: published by William S. Langdon.

Ortiz, Milton L. *Covenant of Trust: Ministerial Ethics for Cumberland Presbyterians: A Study Guide for Ministers & Congregations of the Cumberland Presbyterian Church*. Cordova, Tennessee: Pastoral Development Ministry Team of the Ministry Council of the Cumberland Presbyterian Church, 2013.

Second Cumberland Presbyterian Church. Planning Calendar. 1990.

Institutions

Bethel College. McKenzie, Tennessee. "My Graduation Journal." Annie Warren Looney, 1924-1927, scrapbook.

Union College. Virginia, Cass County, Illinois. *Union College Certificate of Scholarship*. B. F. W. Stribling, February 20, 1868.

Waynesburg College. Waynesburg, Pennsylvania. Invitation. "You are cordially invited to be present at the Forty-second Annual Contest between the Union & Philo Literary Societies of Waynesburg College, Wednesday evening, March 25th, 1896."

Yao Dao Cumberland Presbyterian Church. Tin Shui Wai, N. T., Hong Kong. Yao Dao Primary School. DVD. Musicals. 2007-2011.

Minister's Records

Baker, Reverend Nathan Martin (1837-1922). Papers. Contains letters, sermons, photographs.

Museum Items

Austin, First Cumberland Presbyterian Church. Austin, Texas. Commemorative plate. 7th and Lavaca.

Bethel College. McKenzie, Tennessee. Fraternity Patch. Omega Phi. Belonged to Reverend James C. Gilbert.

Bethel College. McKenzie, Tennessee. Fraternity Pin. Omega Phi. Belonged to Reverend James C. Gilbert.

Columbus, First Cumberland Presbyterian Church. Columbus, Mississippi. Mug.

East Gadsden Cumberland Presbyterian Church. Gadsden, Alabama. Commemorative Tile. Probably 1969. Shows old church building.

Fifth Cumberland Presbyterian Church. Memphis, Tennessee. Quilt. 1937. Made by the Missionary Auxiliary Society.

Gilbert, Reverend James C. Gavels and plaques. One box.

Liberty Cumberland Presbyterian Church. Calhoun, Georgia. Plaque. Was on outside of church building.

Liberty Cumberland Presbyterian Church. Calhoun, Georgia. Pulpit. Plaque on it reads "Pulpit Stand, built 1868, identical to and replacement of the original burned by Union soldiers.

Moderator's Cross. Moderator of the General Assembly in 1979. Belonged to Reverend James C. Gilbert.

Ozark Presbytery. Cumberland Presbyterian Church. Banner. "The Holy Spirit Comes Through the Worshiping Community."

West Nashville Cumberland Presbyterian Church. Nashville, Tennessee. Pin Tray. Aluminum. Picture of building and Reverend W. Tom Logan, pastor. 1903.

Other Congregational Records

Advent Cumberland Presbyterian Church. Pinson, Alabama. Files. One box. (Beneath the Cross Cumberland Presbyterian Church-Pinson, Alabama).

Advent Cumberland Presbyterian Church. Pinson, Alabama. Sunday School Records. Class Record Books. 1991-1992 (11), 1999-2000 (4), 2000-2001 (1). (Beneath the Cross Cumberland Presbyterian Church-Pinson, Alabama).

Advent Cumberland Presbyterian Church. Pinson, Alabama. Sunday School Records. Sunday School Secretaries' Record Book. 1991-1991. (Beneath the Cross Cumberland Presbyterian Church-Pinson, Alabama).

Antioch Cumberland Presbyterian Church. Quitman, Louisiana. "100 Year Celebration Antioch Cumberland Presbyterian Church, Quitman, Louisiana: August 1888-August 1988."

Athens, Cumberland Presbyterian Church. Athens, Alabama. Government Document. House of Representatives, 50th Congress, 1st Session. Report No. 142. Cumberland Presbyterian Church of Athens, Ala. January 27, 1888. Committee on War Claims.

Cleveland Cumberland Presbyterian Church. Cleveland, Tennessee. Scrapbook. Friendly Sunday School Class. 1944-1947.

East Lake Cumberland Presbyterian Church. Birmingham, Alabama. Blueprints. 4 prints. (Beneath the Cross Cumberland Presbyterian Church-Pinson, Alabama).

Elm River Cumberland Presbyterian Church. Mt. Erie, Illinois. Cookbook. A Book of Favorite Recipes. Compiled by the ladies of the C.P. Church, 1981.

Falling Water Cumberland Presbyterian Church. Hixson, Tennessee. Church Directory. No date.

Liberty Cumberland Presbyterian Church. Muskogee, Oklahoma. Guest book. October 17, 1987.

Manchester Cumberland Presbyterian Church. Manchester, Tennessee. Minutes. Missionary Auxiliary. January 5, 1961-December 9, 1965.

Mt. Sterling Cumberland Presbyterian Church in America. Sturgis, Kentucky. Photographs, newspaper articles and programs.

Mount Zion Cumberland Presbyterian Church. Mount Zion, Illinois. This congregation went into the union in 1906. *History of the Mt. Zion Presbyterian Church in the U.S.A. From April 1830 to April 1964.*

By Martin J. Myers.

New Hope Cumberland Presbyterian Church. Hardeman County, Tennessee. Cemetery Records. Typescript.

New Hope Cumberland Presbyterian Church. Madisonville, Tennessee. Newsletters. 2006-2009.

Simpson Chapel Cumberland Presbyterian Church in America. Providence, Kentucky. Program. Fall Banquet, November 1, 2008.

Sunshine Cumberland Presbyterian Church in America. Fort Worth, Texas. "Historic Sunshine Cumberland Presbyterian Church in America." Paper 12 pages.

Waverly Cumberland Presbyterian Church. Waverly, Tennessee. Bulletins. Bound. 1953-2004. 49 volumes.

Photographs

Garnett, Reverend Shelby. Photograph. Served at Mt. Sterling, Marion and Fredonia, Kentucky (CPCA).

Ohio Valley Presbytery. Cumberland Presbyterian Church in America. Photograph. Color, 8x10.

Indianola Synod. Synodic Camp. Tecumseh, Oklahoma. 1940. Photographs. Three photographs. Two of groups and one of Joe Ben Irby.

North Point Cumberland Presbyterian Church. North Point, Hong Kong. Photograph. Color, 4x6. Congregation at the 50th anniversary of the church.

West Nashville Cumberland Presbyterian Church. Nashville, Tennessee. Photograph. 8 ½x11, B&W. Building at 51st and Kentucky Avenue with congregation standing in front.

Postcards

Bethel College. McKenzie, Tennessee. Postcard. Divided back, real photo, c1924.

Cleveland Cumberland Presbyterian Church. Cleveland, Tennessee. Postcard. Real Photo. Divided back, c1945.

Cuba Cumberland Presbyterian Church. Cuba, Missouri. Postcard. Divided back, lithograph, c1905.

Presbyterial Records

East Tennessee Presbytery. Missionary Society. Cumberland Presbyterian Church. Minutes. 1902-1928 and 1929-1932.

Ohio Valley Presbytery. Second Cumberland Presbyterian Church. Booklet. "First Decade of the Ohio Valley Presbyterial Musical Clinic 1965-1975.

Ohio Valley Presbytery. Second Cumberland Presbyterian Church. Program. April 3-5, 1975.

Tennessee-Georgia Presbytery. Cumberland Presbyterian Church. "Camp Glancy Cookbook." c2012.

West Tennessee Presbytery. Cumberland Presbyterian Church. Financial Records. 1990-2003.

Sermons

Gilbert, Reverend James Cayce (1925-2012). Sermons. One box.

Session Records

Beech Cumberland Presbyterian Church. Hendersonville, Sumner County, Tennessee. Session Records. 1889-1961. Four original volumes previously on deposit at the Tennessee State Library and Archives.

Blues Hill Cumberland Presbyterian Church. McMinnville, Warren County, Tennessee. Session Records. 1952-1986.

Brooksville Cumberland Presbyterian Church. Brooksville, Noxubee County, Mississippi. Session Records. 1884-1907 and 1926-1954.

Center Hill Cumberland Presbyterian Church. Center Hill, Cannon County, Tennessee. Session Records. 1870-1878. Book continues with Blues Hill Cumberland Presbyterian Church. McMinnville, Warren County, Tennessee. 1886-1951.

Clark's Grove Cumberland Presbyterian Church. Maryville, Tennessee. Session Records. 1996-2008.

Colonial Cumberland Presbyterian Church. Memphis, Shelby County, Tennessee. Session Records. 2012.

Cromwell Cumberland Presbyterian Church. Memphis, Shelby County, Tennessee. Session Records. 1970-1978 and 1979-1984.

Dade City Cumberland Presbyterian Fellowship. Dade City, Florida. Now Immanuel Cumberland Presbyterian Church. Session Records. 2006-2001.

Dilworth Cumberland Presbyterian Church. Horatio, Sevier County, Arkansas. Session Records. 1978-2005.

Dukes Cumberland Presbyterian Church. Hawesville, Hancock County, Kentucky. Mount Vernon Cumberland Presbyterian Church. (1869-1899). Name changed in 1899 to Dukes Cumberland Presbyterian Church. (1899-1904). Session Records. 1869-1904; 1915-1930; 1933 and 1937-1962.

East Gadsden Cumberland Presbyterian Church. Gadsden, Etowah County, Alabama. Session Records. 1964-1980 and 1980-2000.

East Lake Cumberland Presbyterian Church. Birmingham, Jefferson County, Alabama. Session Records. 1934-1942; 1942-1945; 1946-1956 and 1974-1983.

East Lake Cumberland Presbyterian Church. Birmingham, Jefferson County, Alabama. Session Records. 1983-1988. Advent Cumberland Presbyterian Church. 1988-1989. (Beneath the Cross Cumberland Presbyterian Church-Pinson, Alabama)

Eastlake Cumberland Presbyterian Church. Oklahoma City, Oklahoma. Oklahoma City, First Cumberland Presbyterian Church. (1952-1961) St. Mark's Cumberland Presbyterian Church. (1961-1998) Eastlake Cumberland Presbyterian Church. (1998-present) Session Records. 1952-1957; 1957-1968; 1968-1977; 1982-1986; 1987-1995; 2002-2003 and 2005.

Fredonia Cumberland Presbyterian Church. Fredonia, Caldwell County, Kentucky. Session Records. 1980-1994 and 1995-2009.

Harpeth Lick Cumberland Presbyterian Church. College Grove, Williamson County, Tennessee. Session Records. 1951-1971 and 1991-2007.

Lakes of Springfield Cumberland Presbyterian Church. Rowlett, Dallas County, Texas. Session Records. 1992, 1993, 1994, 1996, 1997, 1999, 2001, 2002, 2003, 2004, 2005.

Liberty Cumberland Presbyterian Church. Calhoun, Gordon County, Georgia. Session Records. 1995-2010.

McMinnville Cumberland Presbyterian Church. McMinnville, Warren County, Tennessee. Session Records. 1957-1999 and 2000-2012.

Memphis, First Cumberland Presbyterian Church. Memphis, Shelby County, Tennessee. Session Records. 1985-1986; 1987-1988; 1989-1990; 1991-1992; 1993-1994; 1994-1995; 1995-1996; 1996-1997; 1997-1998; 2000-2001 and 2001-2001.

Moberly Cumberland Presbyterian Church. Moberly, Randolph County, Missouri. Session Records. 1947-1968.

Olive Branch, First Cumberland Presbyterian Church. Olive Branch, DeSoto County, Mississippi. Session Records. 2002-2004.

Park Avenue Cumberland Presbyterian Church. Memphis, Shelby County, Tennessee. Session Records. 1930-1936; 1936-1947; 1947-1953; 1953-1961; 1961-1969; 1970-1973; 1973-1975; 1976-1977; 1977-1979; 1979-1980; 1980-1981; 1982-1983.

Park Avenue Cumberland Presbyterian Church. Memphis, Shelby County, Tennessee. Session Records. 1984-1984. Also contains: Cromwell-Park Avenue Cumberland Presbyterian Church. Memphis, Shelby County, Tennessee. Session Records. 1984-1985.

Rutherford Cumberland Presbyterian Church. Rutherford, Gibson County, Tennessee. Session Records. 1955-1958 and 1958-1977.

Sedalia Cumberland Presbyterian Church. Sedalia, Pettis County, Missouri. Session Records. 1977-1979.

Shawnee Mound Cumberland Presbyterian Church. Chilhowee, Henry County, Missouri. Session Records. 1870-1884; 1884-1897; 1898-1937 and 1957-1979.

Shiloh Cumberland Presbyterian Church. McKenzie, Carroll County, Tennessee. Session Records. 2000-2010.

Silverdale Cumberland Presbyterian Church. Chattanooga, Hamilton County, Tennessee. Session Records. 1974-1983.

Yorkville Cumberland Presbyterian Church. Yorkville, Gibson County, Tennessee. Session Records. 1900-1914; 1947-1965; 1965-1979; 1979-1985 and 1986-1999.

Synodical Records

Cumberland Presbyterian Church in America. Kentucky States Synod. Synodical Sunday School. August 5-7, 2010, Mayfield, Kentucky. Program.

RECOMMENDATION 5: That the General Assembly encourage all congregations to preserve their session records by depositing them in the Historical Foundation.

RECOMMENDATION 6: That the General Assembly instruct each synod and presbytery to deposit their minutes in a timely fashion with the Historical Foundation.

The Historical Foundation can provide on-site assistance to both presbyteries and individual congregations. On the presbyterial level, we can assist the appropriate agency to evaluate materials left when a church has ceased to be viable and has been closed. This can eliminate speculation on the presbytery's part as to what is, or is not, material to be preserved. For congregations we can provide a similar service helping them to determine what can and should be archived.

RECOMMENDATION 7: That the General Assembly instruct presbyteries to locate the session records when closing a church and then deposit them in the Historical Foundation.

V. BIRTHPLACE SHRINE

The Birthplace Shrine located at Montgomery Bell State Park near Dickson, Tennessee was dedicated June 18, 1960. This site consists of the Memorial Chapel and a replica of the Reverend Samuel McAdow's log house. Since 1994, the Foundation has been responsible for the preservation of the Birthplace Shrine. Four endowments provide funds for maintenance and repairs: the Grace Johnson Beasley Birthplace Shrine Fund, the Birthplace Shrine Fund, the Henry Evan Harper Endowment for Cumberland Presbyterian History, and the P.F. Johnson Memorial Endowment. Gifts to these endowments provide for the continued preservation of the Birthplace Shrine. Interested donors are encouraged to contact the Foundation office. Another means of support are the fees collected from couples who use the chapel for their wedding ceremony. These funds are added to the Birthplace Shrine Fund and earnings are used for maintenance and special projects. The Board encourages individuals and groups to visit the Birthplace Shrine as an act of remembering our heritage and envisioning our future as Cumberland Presbyterians.

Groups and individuals are encouraged to contact the Foundation to set up work days and special projects. The Foundation thanks the Heritage Committee of Nashville Presbytery and the Charlotte Cumberland Presbyterian Church for their continuing volunteer upkeep of the property.

VII. FINANCIAL CONCERNS AND 2015 BUDGET

A. BUDGETS

The 2015 line-item budget of the Historical Foundation has been filed with the CPC General Assembly Office.

B. ENDOWMENTS

Anne Elizabeth Knight Adams Heritage Fund
Rosie Magrill Alexander Trust
Paul H. and Ann M. Allen Heritage Fund
Grace Johnson Beasley Birthplace Shrine Fund
Birthplace Shrine Fund
James L. and Louise M. Bridges Heritage Fund
Mark and Elinor Swindle Brown Heritage Fund

Sydney and Elinor Brown Heritage Fund
Centennial Heritage Endowment
Walter Chesnut Heritage Fund
Lavenia Campbell Cole Heritage Fund
Cumberland Presbyterian Church in America Heritage Fund
Cumberland Presbyterian Women Archival Supplies Endowment
Bettye Jean Loggins McCaffrey Ellis Heritage Fund
Samuel Russell & Mary Grace (Barefoot) Estes Endowment
Family of Faith Endowment
Gettis and Delia Snyder Gilbert Heritage Fund
James C. and Freda M. Gilbert Heritage Fund
James C. and Freda M. Gilbert Trust
Mamie A. Gilbert Trust
Henry Evan Harper Endowment for Cumberland Presbyterian History
Ronald Wilson and Virginia Tosh Harper Endowment
Historical Foundation Trust
Donald and Jane Hubbard Heritage Fund
Cliff and Jill Hudson Heritage Fund
Robert and Kathy Hull Endowment
Into the Nineties Endowment
Joe Ben Irby Heritage Fund
P.F. Johnson Memorial Endowment
Irene A. Kiefer Endowment
Chow King Leong Endowment
Dennis Lawrence & Elmira Castleberry Magrill Trust
J. Richard Magrill Heritage Fund
Joe Richard and Mary Belle Magrill Trust
Gwendolyn McCaffrey McReynolds Heritage Fund
Jimmie Joe McKinley Heritage Fund
Edith Louise Mitchell Heritage Fund
Lloyd Freeman Mitchell Heritage Fund
Snowdy Clifton and Lillian Walkup Mitchell Heritage Fund
Rev. Charles and Paulette Morrow Endowment
Virginia Sue Williamson Morrow Heritage Fund
Anne Elizabeth Swain Odom Heritage Fund
Martha Sue Parr Heritage Fund
Florence Pennewill Heritage Fund
Morris and Ruth Pepper Endowment
Publishing House Endowment
Mable Magrill Rundell Trust
Samuel Callaway Rundell Heritage Fund
Paul and Mary Jo Schnorbus Heritage Fund
Roy and Mary Seawright Shelton Heritage Fund
Shiloh CPC Ellis County Texas Endowment
Hinkley and Vista Smartt Heritage Fund
John William Sparks Heritage Fund
Irvin Scott and Annie Mary Draper Swain Heritage Fund
F. P. Waits Historical Trust

Respectfully submitted,
Rick White, President
Susan Knight Gore, Archivist

THE REPORT OF THE BOARD OF TRUSTEES OF MEMPHIS THEOLOGICAL SEMINARY

Introduction

Memphis Theological Seminary of the Cumberland Presbyterian Church is the only seminary of the Cumberland Presbyterian Church. Our history is traced back through the Cumberland Presbyterian Theological Seminary in McKenzie to the organization of the graduate School of Theology at Cumberland University and the Theological Department at Bethel College, both of which began in 1852. Those two schools of theology continued the legacy begun in the work of founder Finis Ewing, who educated candidates for the ministry in his home, and many other ministers, who trained young candidates in homes, churches, and on the trail. For one hundred fifty seven years, Cumberland Presbyterians have been providing formal theological education for the church's ministers. For almost two hundred years, the Cumberland Presbyterian Church has valued the importance of an educated ministry.

With the denomination's decision to move its seminary to Memphis in 1964, Memphis Theological Seminary of the Cumberland Presbyterian Church began to serve a larger and more diverse student body. Though students from other denominations were admitted during the McKenzie years, the move to a major metropolitan area opened the opportunity to attract more students from more denominations. Today, Memphis Theological Seminary has one of the most diverse student populations, in terms of denomination and race, of any seminary in the United States. This theological and denominational diversity provides a rich environment for educating pastors, chaplains, Christian educators, and other leaders for the church of Jesus Christ. The sign on our campus that faces Union Avenue reads: "Memphis Theological Seminary: an Ecumenical Mission of the Cumberland Presbyterian Church." Every Cumberland Presbyterian can be proud of the mission our seminary fulfills of educating our own church leaders, and leaders from more than 25 other denominations.

This year marks the 50th anniversary of our move to Memphis. We are planning appropriate celebrations to mark this important anniversary in our witness and work. We are grateful for the step of faith taken by the MTS Board, the Cumberland Presbyterian General Assembly, and the church as a whole that has enabled our seminary to grow and thrive for the past 50 years.

We, the trustees and administration of Memphis Theological Seminary are privileged to be a part of this legacy, born out of and guided by the ecumenical and evangelical spirit of the Cumberland Presbyterian Church. We look forward to what God has in store for our ministry in the future. With gratitude for God's grace, guidance and provision in the past year, we make the following report to the 184th General Assembly of the Cumberland Presbyterian Church, meeting June 16-20 in Chattanooga, Tennessee.

I. BOARD OF TRUSTEES

A. OFFICERS

The following officers were elected by the Board of Trustees to serve during the past academic year: Moderator – Reverend Dr. Tom Bell (United Methodist minister, North Alabama Conference); Vice-moderator – Mrs. K. C. Warren (Presbyterian Church laywoman, Memphis); Secretary – Ms. Pat Meeks (Cumberland Presbyterian elder, Bartlett, Tennessee); Treasurer – Mrs. Cassandra Price-Perry (Vice President of Operations and CFO, MTS). In February, Dr. Bell had to resign his position on the Board in order to care for his wife, who is recovering from a stroke. Mr. Tim Orr (Cumberland Presbyterian elder, Newbern, Tennessee) was elected Moderator to fill Dr. Bells term.

B. BOARD REPRESENTATIVE

Mr. Mark Maddox, MTS Trustee, was elected to serve as the Board's representative to this meeting of the General Assembly.

C. MEETINGS

The Board has met twice since the last meeting of General Assembly: October 3-4, 2013 and February 13-14, 2014. It is scheduled to meet one more time before the meeting of General Assembly, on May 16, 2014. In addition to full Board meetings, standing committees meet on a regular schedule between Board meetings, usually by conference call.

Members of our Board of Trustees devote significant time and resources to their work on behalf of the seminary. By rule of the General Assembly, thirteen of the twenty-four members are Cumberland Presbyterians. The other eleven members of the Board represent six different denominations.

D. EXPIRATION OF TERMS

The terms of eight of twenty-four members of the Board of Trustees expire each year. Seven of the eight whose terms expire this year are eligible to succeed themselves and have agreed to serve another three year term: Reverend Dr. Doy Daniels (Cumberland Presbyterian, Milan, Tennessee); Ms. Pat Meeks (Cumberland Presbyterian, Bartlett, Tennessee); Reverend Jennifer Newell (Cumberland Presbyterian, Chattanooga, Tennessee); Reverend Dr. Robert M. Shelton (Cumberland Presbyterian, Dallas, Texas), Reverend Bob Marble (United Methodist, Little Rock, Arkansas); Dr. Joe Ward (Cumberland Presbyterian Church in America, Madison, Alabama); and Mrs. Ruby Wharton (Roman Catholic, Memphis, Tennessee). All have served faithfully and contributed greatly to the life of the seminary. We are grateful for their willingness to continue serving if re-elected.

One trustee submitted his resignation in February, having completed all but five months of third term: Reverend Dr. Tom Bell (United Methodist, United Methodist, Birmingham, Alabama). Tom has served faithfully for eight and one half years, and served as Moderator for seven months during his tenure. We thank God for his faithful service.

RECOMMENDATION 1: That the General Assembly express its gratitude to Reverend Dr. Tom Bell for his faithful service to Memphis Theological Seminary and the Cumberland Presbyterian Church.

E. WORK OF THE BOARD

The trustees continue to develop their administrative procedures and practices to provide the best possible governance to the life of the seminary. For the past seven years we have had 100% participation by trustees in giving to the Annual Fund, and in participating actively in the work of MTS.

In the past year, the Board repurposed its Administration Committee as a Trusteeship Committee with responsibility to recruit, engage, and support each trustee in our common work. This committee will also be responsible for strategic long range planning and ensuring the Board remains focused on the Mission, Vision and Values of the seminary.

F. "MINISTRY FOR THE REAL WORLD"

The 183rd General Assembly approved a recommendation from our Board granting us permission to engage in a major capital campaign for Memphis Theological Seminary. The quiet phase of the campaign is now underway and we are raising funds for the purposes of building a new chapel, building our endowments, and securing the financial future of MTS. The case statement for the program is included here:

MINISTRY FOR THE REAL WORLD
Scholarship, Piety and Justice
MEMPHIS THEOLOGICAL SEMINARY

March 24, 2014

MINISTRY FOR THE REAL WORLD
TWO CENTURIES OF MAKING A DIFFERENCE.

"Academic scholarship is a major hallmark of Memphis Theological Seminary. The school feeds both the minds and spirits of its students. Rigorous scholastic study and intellectual discussion of the Bible from different points of view are encouraged." "The goal is to foster informed critical thinkers. It is not to promote the agenda of Memphis Theological Seminary. When students graduate, they have the knowledge and practical tools to be effective ministers. They live their lives according to the teachings and values of the Bible. Graduates are well prepared to positively impact individuals, congregations and society." – Mrs. Ruby Wharton, Esq., Trustee

In 1821, a pastor's dedication to theological education and inclusiveness gave rise to the first theological school west of the Mississippi. Thirty years later, out of the same Spirit, a theological department was established at Bethel College (now Bethel University) in McKenzie, Tennessee, an institution of the Cumberland Presbyterian Church.

Over one hundred years later, in 1964, in order to reach more ministers for the Gospel, the seminary was moved to Memphis and renamed Memphis Theological Seminary. It was intentionally opened as an ecumenical seminary that welcomes men and women of all faiths, cultures and ages. The philosophy and values of the seminary are as meaningful today as they were two centuries ago. The school focuses on scholarship, piety and justice. Inherent in these three words are powerful concepts that differentiate MTS from other seminaries.

- Scholarship implies disciplined, traditional study, but it also involves becoming a discerning critical thinker. Graduates are compelling spiritual servant leaders and thoughtful ministers. They are able to explain Biblical passages within both their historical context and their relevancy in today's world—and in such a way that lives are transformed.
- Piety involves our heart-felt devotion to God. True piety leads to compassion, selflessness, universal love and respect for all of God's creation. As Dr. Martin Luther King Jr. described so eloquently when he wrote, "Our goal is to create a beloved community, and this will require a qualitative change in our souls as well as a quantitative change in our lives."
- Justice does not refer to civil law. It is much more. Without the practice of justice as described in the Bible, love, liberty and even life cannot flourish. Love alone does not ensure equality. Biblical justice involves care for the poor and powerless and leads to inclusiveness, understanding and compassion. It is respecting all people, even those who are very different from you. It is actively participating in righting wrongs whenever and however they present themselves.

Our student population is very diverse and reflects the real world. There are no age, gender, economic, cultural, theological or racial barriers here. Our graduates will be ministering to many different populations and denominations. Their experience at MTS helps them understand how to work toward a beloved community.

Some of the most respected and influential ministers in the Mid-South are graduates of Memphis Theological Seminary. They are acknowledged for their depth of Biblical and religious knowledge and their ecumenism. They are respected for their ability to influence both religious and secular communities.

Wherever our graduates serve, they impact the lives of those they touch. They are formed to be ministers in the real world.

Our graduates touch thousands of lives in their chosen ministry. They become pastors, youth ministers, educators and chaplains in hospitals, prisons and the military.

For over fifty years, the seminary has occupied the magnificent turn-of-the-century Newburger Mansion in midtown Memphis. We have worked hard to maintain the original beauty of this grand home. Warmth and intimacy are created by cascading stairways, arched doorways, and handcrafted woodwork. It is the beautiful face we show to the public. In more recent years, we have added two adjoining mansions in response to a growing student body and the faculty and staff hired to serve them.

The three homes have served us well, but with enrollment reaching 325 students, we have outgrown them. Because of the reputation and impact of our graduates, our enrollment continues to grow. We believe we can reach an enrollment of 450 students in the not-too-distant future. Together students will represent over 30 denominations, several states and a few countries.

The Newburger Mansion's prized Ballroom is our makeshift chapel. Unfortunately it can only seat one-fifth of our student body. We are grateful to have resided in the homes on beautiful East Parkway during our time of growth. We will always maintain them. They will continue to serve us well as library space, offices and intimate gathering spaces for small discussion groups. But it is urgent that we expand our campus and construct a chapel and an academic building. We have acquired property adjacent to our campus for both structures. Now we must build. Our future depends on it.

PREPARING FOR ANOTHER TWO HUNDRED YEARS OF MINISTRY FOR THE REAL WORLD

The Board and administration of Memphis Theological Seminary have thought long and hard about the future of the seminary. We have prayed for God to guide us in our decision making. In order to ensure our future, we must undertake three important and much-needed projects without delay.

1. A new chapel is a top priority. We have made do with a small converted ballroom for too long.

2. We need a building to house our new, groundbreaking Methodist House of Studies. Methodists represent the single largest contingent of students at MTS. With faculty offices and meeting space, the Methodist House of Studies will relieve pressure on MTS's limited academic facilities.

3. Significantly increasing our endowment and underwriting an important faculty chair will enable MTS to prosper and grow. It will help us become financially stable and ready to withstand any potential financial crises for the next two hundred years. Like most seminaries, we are tuition dependent. At last report our endowment was $9.2 million. This does not generate sufficient interest income to meet the growing demands of our expanding student body. It is crucial that we double the endowment immediately. It will allow us to meet the increasing need for scholarships and financial aid. And it will be a cushion to protect MTS from unforeseen emergencies.

While MTS serves a variety of denominations, its' roots extend back to the Cumberland Presbyterian tradition. By fully endowing the Baird-Buck Chair in Cumberland Presbyterian Studies, we will ensure that our Cumberland Presbyterian students are fully prepared to serve the congregation to which they are sent.

Successfully completing these projects will enable MTS to aggressively pursue its mission well into the twenty-first century: To educate men and women for ordained and lay Christian ministry in the church and the world by shaping and inspiring lives devoted to scholarship, piety and justice.

<u>Project One: Construct a new free-standing chapel</u>

We are blessed to have already received two wonderfully generous gifts designated for our new chapel. The first is an extraordinary cash donation of $1 million. This significant gift is a vote of confidence in Memphis Theological Seminary. It recognizes the difference our graduates make in the world.

The second is one of the oldest and finest pipe organs in the South. It was donated to us by the Union Avenue United Methodist Church. It is an acknowledgement of the role we play in preparing strong spiritual leaders. The pipe organ was manufactured in 1924 by the M.P. Moller Organ Company. In today's dollars, it is estimated to be worth $550,000—a valuable and prestigious gift. Moller pipe organs are also installed in the chapels at Camp David and Lincoln Center.

Both gifts are true blessings and will enable MTS to construct a chapel that

- Reflects our identity, purpose and excellence.
- Is large and adaptable enough for different denominations within the seminary to conduct worship services reflective of their cultures and expressions of faith.
- Provides a place of worship that will accommodate our entire student body.
- Replicates in a small way the churches in which graduates will preach. This will give students the experience of speaking from a real pulpit rather than a small podium.
- Has the proper acoustics to showcase the beautiful Moller pipe organ.
- Will allow us to offer certificates or degrees in church music and organ music.

<u>Project Two: Construct a home for the Methodist House of Studies</u>

There has long been a perceived gap between "the academy" and "the church." We at MTS have become convinced that such a binary way of thinking is deeply flawed. The relationship between seminary and church ought to be marked by an organic, mutually beneficial partnership. Within that partnership, it is the seminary's calling to be in service to the church—preparing women and men for pastoral leadership and resourcing the current ministry needs of pastors and congregations.

We at MTS believe that there is a point of intersection between the mission of the seminary and the mission of the church. Our commitment is to focus our resources and attention at that point of intersection. We are planning a major new initiative in the life of MTS—the Methodist House of Studies. Under the direction of faculty member Dr. Andrew C. Thompson, the Methodist House of Studies will serve as a "community within a community" where our Methodist students can take advantage of the best in Wesleyan theological formation within MTS' richly ecumenical context. The House of Studies will also serve as a vehicle for connecting the resources of MTS with the needs of the wider church. This link will offer pastors and congregations new avenues and contexts for mission and ministry.

The proposed building will house professors' offices and provide meeting space for this groundbreaking program. Given our facilities limitations, the additional space will contribute to the success of this important program.

The ecumenical partnership between Memphis Theological Seminary and the United Methodist Church goes back for decades. And from a strong foundation we believe a vital future can be cultivated and grown. At this crucial juncture in the life of both seminary and church, we are excited to anticipate advancing the relationship between the two with the creation of a home at MTS for the Methodist House of Studies.

Project Three: Significantly increase our endowment and endow the Baird-Buck Chair in Cumberland Presbyterian Studies

Without a larger endowment, we cannot fully execute our mission. Cassandra Price-Perry, Vice President of Operations/CFO, explains this very well.

"I am here to use my financial skills to help students respond to their call by God to ministry. Because of our small endowment, the number and size of our scholarships and financial aid packages are limited. We are not able to enroll as many highly qualified and motivated students as we would like because they can't afford the cost of attendance—books, fees, travel, food and other miscellaneous expenses."

Our tuition is certainly not exorbitant, but nor is it cheap. Many students find it difficult to fund the entire three years required to receive a degree.

Sadly, this compromises our commitment to being an ecumenical school that welcomes everyone who meets our academic requirements. We have cut our operating expenses to the bone during the economic downturn. Still, we can only offer financial assistance to just a portion of the students who apply. Only with philanthropy will it be possible to provide financial assistance to the many motivated and qualified students who are called to serve.

Founded by the Cumberland Presbyterian Church, Memphis Theological Seminary has proclaimed the inclusiveness of the Gospel message for more than 150 years. A fully endowed Baird-Buck Chair in Cumberland Presbyterian Studies will ensure that the vibrant tradition which has guided MTS for eight generations will inspire seminarians for many years to come.

MAKING A REAL DIFFERENCE: MINISTRY FOR THE REAL WORLD

The graduates of Memphis Theological Seminary proclaim and embody God's message of redemption, justice and peace in service to others. Our graduates guide people in their faith and help them understand why they believe. This is powerful. They ignite people's hearts in love for Jesus Christ and support them in walking in His way. They model Christ-like behavior, and in doing so they transform the lives of those they touch—in church, in the grocery store, on a bus or in prisons. They shatter prejudice. They stand in the face of desperation and offer hope. They provide for those with nothing, and they teach others to do the same. The world is a better place because of their real world ministry—a ministry that is persuasive, practical and purposeful.

"Today, mainline religions are grappling with retaining membership. Our emphasis is on academics, practical application and an inclusive approach to theology. This prepares our graduates to be relevant and meaningful ordained and lay ministers in the real world today. This is the only way they can serve and embody God's mission of redemption, justice and peace in service to the New Creation of Jesus Christ. My father attended this seminary, so it was only natural that I followed in his footsteps. Now that I am president, I am blessed to be leading the initiative to bring our facilities into the twenty-first century. We cannot wait. Our campus must reflect the extraordinary academic excellence within its walls." – Dr. Daniel J. Earheart-Brown, President

Angel, must I give again, I ask in dismay. And must I keep giving and giving and giving it away? Oh no, said the angel, his glance pierced me through. Just keep giving 'til the Lord stops giving to you.

THIS MINISTRY FOR THE REAL WORLD CAMPAIGN IS
NOT REALLY ABOUT NEW BUILDINGS

It is about the people.

It is about the highly qualified professors who work inside them. It is about the committed and passionate students who are following God's call to ministry. Sometimes they leave successful careers. Their families make significant economic and lifestyle changes. They do this to serve God, humanity and all of creation. Their lives are transformed. And as a result, our lives are changed. And the world is a better place because of them. Adequate classrooms and a student center will support students on their rigorous academic and spiritual journey. They deserve a real chapel in which to pray, preach, meditate and seek God's further counsel. A chapel filled with the music of a real pipe organ. And joyous voices joined in praise. Finally, Memphis Theological Seminary deserves facilities that truly reflect the excellence of its high academic standards. Its commitment to forming extraordinary ministers for the real world must be celebrated with quality facilities.

You have the power make a real and powerful difference. Your support ensures the success of our campaign. It also secures the future of Memphis Theological Seminary. With your support we will be able to continue to graduate outstanding ministers for the real world. Prayerfully consider your role in supporting our important undertaking. And as you do, please consider the wisdom of this poem. It reflects the insights of a very generous philanthropist.

YOUR SUPPORT HAS A POWERFUL RETURN

A donation to Memphis Theological Seminary means that your investment will be leveraged in extraordinary ways.

A message from Tim Orr, Chair of the Board Trustees, Memphis Theological Seminary:

Dear Friends,

As you consider your participation in the Ministry for the Real World Campaign, you can rest assured that your investment will be leveraged in extraordinary ways. The check I write to Memphis Theological Seminary is multiplied many times over. I am not just writing a check for the seminary. My donation impacts global society.

Here is what I mean. People come here because they are called to ministry. MTS forms them into leaders—Christian leaders with Christian values. Their lives are changed forever. But it doesn't stop there. Everyone touched by one of our graduates is changed also. MTS prepares ministers to be relevant and compelling in the real world. In a world that is spiritually bankrupt, they are effective in their congregation and in all of society. Their lives are transformed, and they are given the tools and skills to transform the spirit of our global society— and they do. I ask you, 'what investment has this powerful a return?'

I hope you will join me at this turning point in the life of Memphis Theological Seminary. Your prayers and generosity will ensure that MTS continues to prepare men and women for transformation ministry to the real world.

Faithfully,
Tim Orr

II. ADMINISTRATION

A. PRESIDENT

Daniel J. (Jay) Earheart Brown, Ph.D., became the seventh President of Memphis Theological Seminary August 1, 2005. Jay had served on the faculty of MTS since August, 1997, having previously served as a pastor in Nashville, Tennessee, and Lexington, Kentucky. He is a life-long Cumberland Presbyterian and son of a Cumberland Presbyterian minister. He is a graduate of Bethel College (B.A.), Memphis Theological Seminary (M.Div.), and Union Theological Seminary in Richmond, Virginia (Ph.D.). He will complete his ninth year in this position at the end of the current academic year.

B. VICE PRESIDENT OF ACADEMIC AFFAIRS/DEAN

Reverend R. Stan Wood, D.Min., was appointed to serve as Interim Vice President of Academic Affairs and Dean in May, 2010. Dr. Wood had previously served MTS as Clara Scott Associate Professor of Ministry and Director of the D.Min. Program. He is an ordained minister in the Cumberland Presbyterian Church in America and currently serves as Pastor of the Mt. Tabor CPCA in Jackson, Tennessee.

D. VICE PRESIDENT OF ADVANCEMENT

In January 2007, Mrs. Cathi Johnson began work as Vice President of Advancement, coming to MTS after over six years as Development Director for The Baddour Center, a residential home for adults with mental disabilities.

Cathi has brought to her work at MTS a proven track record of non-profit fundraising, a commitment to the mission of MTS, and the ability to manage and build on the efforts of those who have gone before her. She is a United Methodist laywoman, active in her local church in Collierville, Tennessee, a Memphis suburb. There she sings in the choir and takes an active part in all the programs of the church. Cathi's skills and experience have been a great asset to the seminary over the last six years.

E. VICE PRESIDENT OF OPERATIONS/CFO

Mrs. Cassandra Price-Perry began work with MTS in August 2010 as Vice President of Operations and Chief Financial Officer. She is a Certified Public Accountant with over 20 years of experience in business and accounting. Cassandra is an active laywoman in her Roman Catholic Church in Southaven, Mississippi. She has received high praise from our auditors and our Board for her work over the past almost three years.

III. INSTRUCTION

A. DEGREE PROGRAMS

Memphis Theological Seminary offers four degree programs and three certificate programs, including the certificate offered through the Program of Alternate Studies. The Master of Divinity is the basic degree program for persons preparing for ordained ministry in many denominations. It continues to be our largest degree program, with over 70% of students enrolled. The M.Div. requires 87 semester hours and takes three years of full-time study to complete.

The Master of Arts (Religion) degree is an academic degree for persons seeking to pursue further graduate studies. The M.A.R. requires 48 semester hours and takes two years of full-time study to complete. Because of declining interest in this degree program, we will not be admitting new candidates for this degree in the fall of 2014. The faculty and administration are in conversation about discontinuing this degree and instead launching a two year master's degree in the practice of ministry.

The Doctor of Ministry degree is a professional degree designed for pastors and other ministers who have at least three years of full-time work in ministry after their M.Div. and who want to engage in further theological reflection on the practice of ministry. The D.Min. is designed around five two-week residencies, in January and July, and the implementation of and report on a major project in ministry.

In the spring of 2013, we awarded our first new degree in several years: the Master of Arts in Youth Ministry (MAYM). Through our partnership with the Center for Youth Ministry Training in Brentwood, Tennessee, and the new certificate program in youth ministry through the Cumberland Presbyterian Church, we have 33 students enrolled in this degree program.

At Commencement in May of 2013, Memphis Theological Seminary awarded the Master of Arts in Youth Ministry degree to nine graduates. Thirteen persons were awarded the Master of Arts (Religion) degree. Thirty-one persons were awarded the Master of Divinity degree, and one was awarded the Doctor of Ministry degree. Of these fifty-four graduates, six were Cumberland Presbyterians.

Cumberland Presbyterian Master of Arts in Youth Ministry graduate was:
    Joanna Bellis, Missouri Presbytery

Cumberland Presbyterian Master of Divinity graduates were:
    Thomas G. Clark, Murfreesboro Presbytery
    Jeffrey W. DeWees, Nashville Presbytery
    Stewart Patton Salyer, Nashville Presbytery
    Laura Rose Todd, West Tennessee Presbytery
    Elisabeth Joy Warren, Nashville Presbytery

B. FACULTY

For the current academic year, Memphis Theological Seminary has eleven full-time teaching faculty and four administrative faculty members who teach part-time. In addition, the seminary curriculum is greatly enhanced by the work of twenty-five to thirty adjunct professors, most of whom are active in pastoral or other ministries.

Members of the MTS faculty continue to publish books and articles both for the academy and the church. Many faculty members preach in area churches on a regular basis, deliver lectures for local churches and judicatories, deliver papers at academic conferences, and write articles for a wide range of readers.

Under the leadership of VP/Dean Wood, the faculty is currently engaged in a major curriculum review and re-visioning process.

C. ENROLLMENT

Total enrollment in Memphis Theological Seminary for the fall term was 333. We had a significant decrease in enrollment in the M.Div. program, which was partially offset by the Drug & Alcohol Addiction Counseling program. This dip in our enrollment in the fall led to budget adjustments during the year, and an increased effort to recruit new students. In the spring semester of 2013, we saw an increase in enrollment, and are working hard to get enrollments up in all our programs. Our largest number of students come from the United Methodist Church, with 25% of total enrollment. Cumberland Presbyterians are the second largest denomination represented in the student body with just under 15% of all students.

The following table presents a picture of the growth in the student body at MTS since 1990. The figures are based on fall semester enrollment. Figures included are for total enrollment, enrollment in three of our four degree programs, and enrollment of Cumberland Presbyterian Students.

	Total enroll	M.Div.	Master-other	D.Min.	CPC
1990	140	114	12	-	37
1991	189	126	22	14	40
1992	198	130	23	21	37
1993	227	155	23	24	37
1994	238	175	27	18	37
1995	268	181	29	24	40
1996	287	184	37	29	42
1997	282	191	32	34	47
1998	266	177	34	28	40
1999	286	197	26	26	34
2000	282	201	31	25	37
2001	323	212	45	32	39
2002	326	211	50	34	39
2003	349	230	58	30	38
2004	351	240	51	27	42
2005	346	236	57	24	37
2006	332	236	44	26	42
2007	305	218	38	26	39
2008	313	206	41	34	43
2009	352	234	40	35	46
2010	313	218	31	22	44
2011	320	227	34	22	41
2012	315	190	29	28	44
2013	333	194	55	42	49

We continue to work to recruit Cumberland Presbyterian students, and to lift up the call of God to ordained ministry in the church. We call on all Cumberland Presbyterians to pray that God will continue to call men and women to the office of ministry, and that they will be well prepared through our educational institutions to lead growing and vibrant congregations in the ministry of Jesus Christ to the world.

RECOMMENDATION 2: That the General Assembly urge all probationers to consider Memphis Theological Seminary and the Program of Alternate Studies as their first options for meeting educational requirements for ordained ministry.

D. PROGRAM OF ALTERNATE STUDIES

The Program of Alternate Studies is an alternate route to ordination for Cumberland Presbyterian men and women designed to accommodate those who possess significant gifts for ministry, yet whose circumstances hinder them from completing the regular course of study in a graduate school of theology. It is administered as a certificate program of Memphis Theological Seminary.

1. APPRECIATION EXPRESSED

The vitality of any program depends, long-term, on the continued input and faithfulness from the church at large. Those who serve on the PAS Advisory Council perform an essential service that continues to bless the church through those we prepare for leadership. Please join us in profound appreciation for the faithful commitment of Dr. Clinton Buck and Dr. Jennifer Williams who fulfilled their maximum eligibility and rotated off the council in December, 2013. Dr. Ron McMillan and Dr. Pat Pickett have been elected to replace them.

We would also recognize with deep gratitude the contribution of Dr. J. David Hester, President Emeritus of Memphis Theological Seminary. Dr. Hester has taught many courses for PAS over the span of its existence as a mainstay of the "Bethel Experience." He has decided that the summer of 2014 will reluctantly end this labor of love for him and he will pass the baton.

We are pleased to announce, then, that Dr. J. David Hester will serve as the featured speaker for the 2014 PAS Commencement Service held July 12th, at 11:00 AM, in Bouldin Auditorium, on the campus of Bethel University. We would like to invite all Cumberland Presbyterians with the opportunity to do so to join us to mark this significant milestone for our graduates, for our program, and for Dr. Hester who will soon add another "Emeritus" to his title.

2. PAS-COLOMBIA

We look forward to celebrating, along with all the denomination, the blessings of PAS-Colombia when the General Assembly meets next year in Cali. We hope to be able to showcase for those in attendance the great progress that has been made through the sacrificial efforts of many. The focus of the first phase has been to provide Cumberland Presbyterian studies, not only to candidates but to all probationers and all ministers serving the Cumberland Presbyterian Church in Colombia. Ninety-five percent (95%) of the ministers and probationers in country, over 100, have now taken at least one of the Cumberland Presbyterian courses through PAS-Colombia. The Program of Alternate Studies is proud to be a part of what the Spirit of God is doing on yet another new frontier.

3. PRESBYTERY RELATIONS

The original plan for PAS required "That presbyteries be instructed to take steps, in cooperation with Memphis Theological Seminary, to assume responsibilities in the administration of the Program of Alternate Studies." The collaboration has worked well and our current administration has continued to improve communication with the many Probationer Care Committees. We appreciate the consistent affirmation of the General Assembly for PAS to continue to embody the denomination's historic dual values of insistence on quality education for its ministers accompanied by a willingness to remain flexible in its approach to achieving this goal. We would all also benefit from continuing the path of clarifying roles.

The proliferation of varying kinds of graduate degree and certificate programs, and the increasing availability of purely online versions of Master of Divinity degrees, complicates the issue for those attempting to assess a student's record. The PAS Director highlighted this complexity in an open letter sent to all stateside probationer care committees in 2013.

The review process for PAS, as it has evolved, is that the Director reviews all transcripts and makes recommendations to the presbytery committee regarding which courses should be required. Regardless of the degree or status, if there are gaps in an applicant's record compared to the requirements of the PAS curriculum, it is recommended that the student take specific courses. The PAS Advisory Council this year established an Academic Review Committee to assist in any areas of uncertainty regarding academic credit and course requirements. No system is perfect but this process gives comforting assurance to all that, within the framework of flexibility, the anticipated standard has been met.

What happens, then, if the probationer care committee of the student's presbytery disagrees with the determination of what courses a particular probationer needs? Most instances are easily managed in the spirit of mutual respect for the role of the presbytery (ordaining body) and the Program of Alternate Studies (certifying body). But, in the rare instance that agreement cannot be reached, who has the final say?

It has been the commonly-held understanding that PAS certifies that a student has met the constitutional requirements regarding education for ordained ministers in the Cumberland Presbyterian Church, not that they have completed certain courses as prescribed by their presbytery committee. The form used to notify presbytery, signed by the Director of PAS and the President of MTS, clearly envisions this view in this explanatory note:

When signed, the above form serves notice to presbyteries that the above named person is constitutionally qualified, regarding their educational preparation, to be ordained or to have their previous ordination recognized.

This respects the historic authority of the presbytery over ordination (they may or may not choose to ordain based on this one factor). It also gives the Program of Alternate Studies the final say in whether an individual meets the educational standards of the constitution. If the General Assembly would affirm this understanding it could help clarify our role.

4. ONLINE COURSES

Our first experiment with online education, a six-week Old Testament survey course taught by Dr. Pat Pickett, was a most enriching success. We anticipate the first two Cumberland Presbyterian Studies will be ready late this Spring in an online format. We will publicize a roll-out when prudent for the special circumstances that require distance education. We express appreciation to the IT department of MTS for their critical and creative assistance.

5. C.P. STUDIES

We want to remind everyone that there are now four (4) required courses of C.P. studies through PAS. The accessibility to the second CP Theology course has gone very well in 2013. Everyone who needed it for ordination had the opportunity to take it in a WES reasonably accessible to them. With online classes soon available there should be no impediment to completing all four courses within a year's time.

6. MONEY MATTERS

The Program of Alternate Studies relies on three essential sources of funding. OUO and gift income supplies about 24%. The bulk of our operating expenses must be collected in the form of tuition or fees. We have made concerted effort to get the program in a position to pay its own way so that generosity of MTS in housing the program does not unduly burden its own limited resources. I am pleased to report that we are on the cusp of that goal. I am equally pleased to announce that we will be holding tuition steady in the next year at $315 per course. The next increase is not envisioned until August of 2015. Along with budgetary constraint, the willingness of presbyteries to pay for PAS students has helped keep this educational approach reasonable and move us to break-even status.

The process outlined in our catalog urges presbyteries to pay "all, or at least a significant part" of the expenses for students who attend PAS. Each presbytery is left to determine what to do and a wide variety of approaches exist. It is not uncommon for months to elapse in a convoluted collection process, creating difficulties for the MTS Business Office which now does all billing.

As first steps toward uniformity we propose to revise the catalog for 2014 to assure prospective PAS students have been counseled about program costs, method of payment, and the details of their presbytery's policy for paying educational expenses. We will ask local presbyteries, as part of their commitment, to serve as guarantors for their student's expense. This puts the presbytery, on the frontlines with the students, in a position of mutual accountability.

E. NEW ACADEMIC INITIATIVES

In Fall 2010, we began offering courses toward a certificate in drug and alcohol addiction counseling. This new program, which has been led by Cumberland Presbyterian minister and counselor Dr. Johnie Welch, promises to meet an important need in our society and in our region. Due to health concerns, Dr. Welch was unable to continue in this role after the 2012 academic year. Reverend Bill Warr, an experienced counselor recommended to us by Dr. Welch, began coordinating this program in the fall of 2012.

In the spring of 2012, we began a new certificate program targeted for African American ministers in the Memphis area who do not have the educational background to enroll as degree students at MTS. We believe that there is a need for such certificate level education for many in our area and hope to expand this work in the near future.

F. ACCREDITATION

Memphis Theological Seminary holds dual accreditation by the Association of Theological Schools in the United States and Canada (ATS), and the Southern Association of Colleges and Schools (SACS). Every ten years, member schools go through an extensive process of re-accreditation review.

Our last accreditation visit occurred in 2008, at which time we were fully affirmed for the next ten years by both accrediting bodies.

IV. FACILITIES

A. LEADERSHIP

Since the fall of 2011, our facilities and safety department has been ably led by Mr. Greg Spencer and a dedicated staff of facilities technicians. Mr. Spencer is a member of the West Union Cumberland Presbyterian Church in Millington, Tennessee, and has more than twenty years of experience in construction and facilities management.

B. PURCHASE OF PROPERTY

Thanks to the support of the 177th General Assembly, we have been given approval to purchase additional properties within the bounds of our long range campus plan. Because of the recession we have not purchased any properties in the past four and a half years, and do not intend to borrow any more money for this purpose. Due to the recession we have been in arrears on our loan payments to the Board of Stewardship, but have a plan in place to catch up on those payments. All interest due is current as of the writing of this report, and we hope to pay significant amounts on the principal due on notes in the coming fiscal year.

C. COMMUTER HOUSING

MTS began to convert its student housing from individual rentals to commuter housing in the 1998. Currently, MTS provides commuter housing, with very reasonable nightly rates, for about fifty students each week of the regular term. The need for such commuter housing has continued to grow, as has income from such rentals. Our ability to serve students from about a 250 mile radius around Memphis, through block scheduling of classes and provision of affordable commuter housing, has had a significant impact on the growth of the student body over the past ten years.

D. CAMPUS WORK GROUPS

We have been blessed in recent years by adult and youth work groups who have come to MTS during the summer months to help repair and maintain our campus housing. Groups have come from Trilla, Illinois; Greeneville, Tennessee; Florence, Alabama; Bowling Green, Kentucky; and Collierville, Tennessee; and the youth from West Tennessee Presbytery to volunteer their time in a variety of areas. We encourage work groups who would be willing to help the seminary in this way to contact Mr. Greg Spencer in the Facilities Office, or Mrs. Cathi Johnson in the Advancement Office of the seminary.

E. SAFETY

The Office of Safety of MTS continues to explore ways to enhance the safety of our students in the context of our urban campus. Through the use of lighting, security officers, secure locks, and well articulated safety plans, the seminary seeks to provide a safe environment for students and visitors to our campus.

During past four years, MTS has contracted with a local security company to provide regular patrols around our neighborhood. This additional safety measure has been well received by our students and by our neighbors. We continue to seek ways to provide a safe environment for our campus community.

V. ADVANCEMENT AND FINANCE

A. BUDGET

Our Board of Trustees will approve a budget for the 2013-2014 academic year at its May meeting. Copies of that budget will be provided at the meeting of General Assembly.

After two years of significant budget reductions in the worst of the recession, we have begun to restore some of the cuts as income has improved the past two years. We continue to be very conservative in our budget planning as we work to recover from the effects of the recession. We hope to be able to give modest raises to our employees next year, after four years of flat or reduced compensation. Our employees deserve much credit for hanging in with us through some tough economic times.

B. SCHOLARSHIPS AND GRANTS

We continue to cultivate relationships with foundations whose mission closely aligns with ours. The following grants for scholarships and other projects have been received in recent years:

1. The Henry Luce Foundation (2012-2014)

To support At the River: Theology & Arts Program at MTS, the Henry Luce Foundation granted $150,000 payable over 3 years, double their initial investment in 2009-2011. The Luce Foundation is located in New York City and funds programs like these on a large scale across the country. In 2014, we conclude this round of funding, but with a new Theology & Arts director and program focus, we anticipate a new opportunity for Luce Foundation funding.

2. The Varnell Artist-in-Residence

For five years, Mr. and Mrs. Henry and Jeanne Varnell, long-time friends of MTS, have provided financial and practical support for the Artist-in-Residence of At the River: Theology & Arts program.

3. The Wilson Family Foundation

The Wilson family, founders of the Holiday Inn hotel chain and great philanthropists in Memphis, has renewed their funding of the Wilson Scholarships at $15,000 for 2013-14.

4. The H.W. Durham Foundation

In 2013, the Memphis-based H.W. Durham Foundation renewed its gift of $5,000 to provide 5 $1,000 scholarships for students who are 55+ years of age. These Durham Scholars will represent much of our student body who are second-career students.

5. The First Tennessee Foundation

This Foundation provides a gift of $10,000 to partner with MTS in the course "Money, Markets & Ministry," taught by Dr. Jay Earheart-Brown. We are in our fourth year of this level of support.

6. The Lilly Endowment (2013-2015)

With a three-year grant totaling $249,371, MTS is creating a program to increase financial literacy and decrease debt among our student population, and long term, the congregations they serve.

C. ENDOWMENTS

1. The Baird-Buck Chair of Cumberland Presbyterian Studies

Dr. Clinton Buck, Professor Emeritus of Christian Education at MTS, knowing the need for more focused teaching in CP heritage, has converted an existing endowment that was originally begun with the hopes of endowing a chair in Christian Education. Subsequent to Dr. Buck's decision, the late Mrs. Thalia Baird, widow of former President and Professor Dr. Colvin Baird, converted an endowment they had designated for general operations. Together with The Rev. J.T. Buck Scholarship Endowment Fund established in 1979 to provide scholarship assistance for Cumberland Presbyterian students at Memphis Theological Seminary, the new endowment was established with an initial principal balance of approximately $112,000. To-date, the fund has grown to more than $316,308, thanks to generous contributions from many Cumberland Presbyterians.

The purpose of this endowment is to strengthen the Cumberland Presbyterian Church by establishing an endowed professorship with a primary focus of teaching Cumberland Presbyterian history, theology, church administration and the practice of ministry that is particular to the Cumberland Presbyterian Church. The goal is to raise $1.5 million to fully fund this endowed chair.

2. Rev. Hillman and Lorene Moore Endowed Scholarship Fund

Hillman Moore established this endowment fund on October 10, 2013, to be funded with a future gift of a bequest from his estate. It will be used to provide scholarship funds for training Cumberland Presbyterian students at Memphis Theological Seminary.

3. Wes and Susan Brantley Endowment

On October 15, 2013, the Brantley family of Ada, OK, was deeply saddened by the death of Susan Brantley, wife of former MTS trustee Wes Brantley, and mother of current trustee Kevin Brantley. In her memory, Wes has established the Wes and Susan Brantley Endowment to support general operating expenses of the seminary.

4. Brooksville Cumberland Presbyterian Church Scholarship Endowment

After 129 years of ministry in the Brooksville, Mississippi, area, the Session of the Brooksville CP Church decided to close the church due to lack of growth in the changing rural town. The closing service of praise and thanksgiving was held on January 13, 2013, led by Reverend Jearl Hunley (M.Div. '67), who served the church for 12 years. Many family, friends and former members came back for this occasion. In March, Grace Presbytery held its spring meeting and voted to use one-half of the proceeds of the sale of the church building to establish a memorial scholarship that will provide tuition support for CP students in the years to come. First preference will be given to MTS students from Grace Presbytery.

5. The Davis/Winston Scholarship for National Baptist Students

In the waning days of the spring semester 2013, one CP and one United Methodist student listened as three fellow students talked about the struggles they have in paying their seminary tuition. For these two students, all or most of their tuition is paid by their denomination. For the others, all National Baptists, humble servants with sweet spirits, the story is completely different.

Moved by the Holy Spirit through their student colleagues, they sought a way to establish a scholarship to help future National Baptist students. In recognition of the blessing received when seminary education is paid in full or in part by scholarship and/or denominational assistance, and in honor of exemplary and invigorating teaching by professors Dr. Christopher B. Davis and Dr. Eric Winston, they established a scholarship to support National Baptist students at MTS.

6. Dr. Alfred DeWayne Hill Scholarship Endowment Fund

Mrs. Doris Thomas Hill remembers that her late husband was always grateful for the financial assistance he received to attend seminary. "In his memory and because of our need to continue Dr. Hill's practice of sowing into the lives of students, especially faith leaders, I am pleased to establish the Dr. Alfred DeWayne Hill Scholarship Endowment Fund" to support scholarships for African American students.

7. Rev. David and Leota Watson Scholarship Endowment Fund

A new endowment has been established to honor the ministry of the late Reverend David Watson. His widow, Mrs. Leota Watson, has chosen to direct the endowment earnings to support scholarships for Cumberland Presbyterian students attending MTS. Those who knew and loved Reverend Watson and appreciate his and Leota's ministry are invited to send a gift to fully establish the Reverend David and Leota Watson Scholarship Endowment Fund. Every gift matters. Perhaps in the Fall semester 2014, a David Watson Scholar will be announced.

8. Other Endowment funds

Many Cumberland Presbyterians and others continue to support endowments that have been established through the years to fund our work. The Advancement Office and President are available at any time to discuss endowment gifts with potential donors.

D. FACULTY CHAIRS

1. The Rev. Marlon and Sheila Foster Professor of Pastoral Theology and Homiletics (2008-2013)

An anonymous donor established this six-year named professorship to encourage ministerial candidates to attend Memphis Theological Seminary, in support of the great need for training in pastoral care, and in honor of the designees. Reverend Marlon Foster is a recent graduate of MTS. Tenured Professor of Pastoral Theology and Homiletics, Dr. G. Lee Ramsey Jr., B.A., M.Div., Ph.D., is filling this role.

2. The Dr. James L. Netters Chair in African American Studies (2009-2013)

Memphis Theological Seminary is dedicated to becoming the premier seminary in the country for those who are devoted to racial reconciliation under the banner of the gospel. Working together with a group of pastors and lay leaders, the Elders for Education have established a named professorship that will signal to the local and global community that we at MTS are serious about working toward the fulfillment of peace and justice. It is named in honor of beloved pastor of Mt. Vernon Baptist Church – Westwood in Memphis, Dr. James L. Netters. Dr. Andre Johnson, B.S., M.Div., Ph.D. is filling this role.

3. The Mary Magdelene Professor of New Testament (2012-2014)

Former students and friends of Dr. Mitzi Minor contributed to this named professorship in honor of her 20th year of ordination to the ministry in the Cumberland Presbyterian Chuch, and in appreciation for her excellence in teaching New Testament.

E. ESTATE GIFTS

MTS received no estate gifts during the past year. We do continue to have conversations with friends and donors about the importance of remembering MTS in their estate plans. We publish a list of those who have informed our office that they have included MTS in their will. That group is known as the Heritage Society.

F. SEMINARY SUNDAY

We have many churches in our denomination, and in other denominations we serve who recognize Seminary Sunday in their local churches. This provides time for education of members about the work of MTS and the Program of Alternate Studies and provides an opportunity for members to make a special one-time gift to support the work of the seminary. Please contact the seminary for more information on how you can recognize Seminary Sunday in your local church, and to request a speaker for the occasion.

RECOMMENDATION 3: That the General Assembly encourage all churches to recognize and support Seminary Sunday.

G. ANNUAL FUND

Memphis Theological Seminary could not operate without the faithful contribution of its alumni and friends. Annual Fund contributions help us keep the cost of tuition down, so that students do not leave seminary with a large burden of debt to have to pay during their early years in ministry. Annual Fund contributions have grown steadily over the past fifteen years, as income from Our United Outreach has declined.

In some respects, the income we receive from OUO puts us in a better position than many theological seminaries, whose income from denominational sources has declined significantly over the past twenty years. Our income from OUO has remained relatively steady and over that time period. However, as a percentage of our total income, OUO has fallen from almost 20% to about 3% of our operating budget. We are grateful for the commitment of Cumberland Presbyterians to the ministry of MTS, and all our common ministries, expressed so tangibly through giving to Our United Outreach.

At the same time, we do not expect income from denominational contributions to increase significantly in the future. This means that we are required to put more time and energy into fund raising than ever before. We are grateful for the many alumni who have made a financial contribution to our ministry this year. We are also grateful for all the faithful laypersons who have given to the Annual Fund because they know the importance of an educated ministry to the life and health of our denomination.

H. AUDIT REPORT

The auditing firm of Zoccola Kaplan, P.C. has audited the books of Memphis Theological Seminary for the 2012-2013. The audit was unqualified, and noted several significant improvements in the financial position of MTS. Copies of that report have been filed with the office of the Stated Clerk.

Respectfully submitted,
Tim Orr, Moderator of the Board of Trustees
Daniel J. Earheart-Brown, President
Memphis Theological Seminary

THE REPORT OF THE
OUR UNITED OUTREACH COMMITTEE

The 2009 General Assembly established a denominational Our United Outreach Committee to be made up of 12 voting representatives, one from each Synod and the rest from the church programs and institutions. Executives from the church programs and institutions participate on the Committee as advisory members. This Committee has meets annually unless there is a needed called meeting.

A goal of the Our United Outreach Committee is to encourage ALL churches to contribute to Our United Outreach. Approximately 30 percent of the churches do not give anything with a high percentage of other churches not giving at the 10 percent level. This past year, 2013, the budgeted goal for Our United Outreach was $2,800,000 – 91% giving was achieved. While this was an admirable achievement, the Committee seeks to involve ALL churches with Our United Outreach giving and at a greater level of giving.

I. OUR UNITED OUTREACH FUNDS ALLOCATION

The Our United Outreach Committee met March 28, 2014, to allocate the Our United Outreach funds for the 2015 year. The Our United Outreach allocation basis for 2015 is $2,900,000. The 2012 General Assembly had two funding requests which affected the allocation process beginning in 2014. The 2013 General Assembly had one funding request from the Unification Task Force which was for $20,000 a year starting in 2014.

- That $3,500 a year for three years—2014, 2015, 2016—be budgeted out of Our United Outreach funds for the use of the Evaluation Committee when doing agency evaluations.
- That a fund be established to make money available for any legal expenses of the Office of the General Assembly, that $25,000 from Our United Outreach allocation be designated for that fund in 2014 and 2015 and that a balance of $50,000 remain in that fund each year thereafter.
- That $20,000 be set aside for expenses incurred by the Unification Task Force beginning in 2014.

These requests, along with the Debt Retirement and the Fund Development Coordinator's salary, have been approved as guaranteed amounts and are deducted from the goal amount prior to allocation purposes.

RECOMMENDATION 1: We ask General Assembly that the following allocation for incoming 2015 for Our United Outreach funds be adopted:

The allocation is to be as follows: $2,900,000.00

Development Coordinator	79,000.00	
Debt Retirement	119,993.00	
Legal Expenses—Insurance Deductible	25,000.00	
Evaluation Committee	3,500.00	
Unification Task Force	20,000.00	
Sub-total	$ 247,403.00	
Ministry Council	$1,326,254.00	50%
Bethel University	132,625.00	5%
Children's Home	79,575.00	3%
Stewardship	159,150.00	6%
General Assembly Office	212,201.00	8%
Memphis Theological Seminary/ Program of Alternate Studies	185,676.00	7%
Historical Foundation	79,575.00	3%
Shared Services	450,926.00	17%

(next 5 items total 1%)

Comm. on Chaplains	9,284.00	.350%
Judiciary Committee	8,753.00	.330%
Theology/Social Concerns	3,249.00	.123%
Nominating Committee	2,719.00	.103%
Contingency Fund	2,520.00	.095%
	$2,652,507.00	

        Our United Outreach Goal $2,900,000.00

From the agencies listed above, all should be self-explanatory except maybe Shared Services. Maintenance, utilities, mowing, trash pick-up, pest extermination, and custodial are all examples of Shared Services for agencies sharing the Cumberland Presbyterian Center.

II. DIRECTOR FOR OUR UNITED OUTREACH

The 2012 General Assembly approved the establishment of a full-time position to work with Our United Outreach denomination inclusive and the title of this position was Fund Development Coordinator, which was changed to Development Director for Our United Outreach at the 2013 General Assembly. This full-time position was filled by Reverend George (Cliff) Hudson, who accepted the call to the position May, 2013.

Reverend Hudson has represented Our United Outreach in all venues to individuals, Churches, and Presbyteries. Through discussions in these venues, the need for electronic methods of giving surfaced. The younger generation has migrated towards the paperless society and look to electronic means to participate in their giving.

The Committee authorized the Our United Outreach Committee and Development Director to investigate and institute electronic giving opportunities such as PayPal, PaySimple, Intuit, automatic bank deduction, or electronic funds transfer for receiving contributions to Our United Outreach.

RECOMMENDATION 2: That congregations and individuals consider the use of electronic giving when making contributions to Our United Outreach.

III. OUR UNITED OUTREACH EDUCATION

In an effort to further educate all churches and to continue towards the goal of 100 percent of the churches participating in Our United Outreach giving, the segment of our denomination served by other denomination ministers should be educated about Our United Outreach.

RECOMMENDATION 3: We ask General Assembly to encourage Presbyterian Boards of Missions and other appropriate agencies to cooperate with Our United Outreach Director of Development to educate ministers of other denominations who are serving as Stated Supplies on the significance of Our United Outreach.

The Our United Outreach Committee members are enthusiastic in their approach to the development of total participation in this program of the church

Respectfully submitted,
Ron Gardner, Chairperson
Reverend Lanny Johnson, Vice-Chairperson
Sharon Resch, Secretary
and the Our United Outreach Committee

THE REPORT OF THE COMMISSION ON MILITARY CHAPLAINS AND PERSONNEL

The Commission on Military Chaplains and Personnel represent the Cumberland Presbyterian Church on the Presbyterian Council for Chaplains and Military Personnel (PCCMP). The commission does its work through the Council which has its headquarters in Washington D.C. and represents also the Cumberland Presbyterian Church inAmerica, Presbyterian Church (USA) and the Korean Presbyterian Church Abroad. The Cumberland Presbyterians who are members of the Commission for the Cumberland Presbyterian Church and hence the broader group known as the PCCMP include Reverend Lowell Roddy, Reverend Mary Catherine Benedict, Reverend Cassandra Thomas, and Stated Clerk Reverend Michael Sharpe.

I. REPRESENTATION

The The term of the Reverend Mary Catherine Benedict expires in 2014, but she is eligible for reelection. For 2014, three of the four PCCMP Executive Board positions are filled by CPC members: Reverend Lowell G. Roddy serves as the Chairperson, Reverend Cassandra O. Thomas is Secretary and Reverend Mary Catherine Benedict is the Treasurer of the PCCMP Council.

Retiring PCCMP Director, the Reverend Ed Brogan, and his wife Sandy, were given an official farewell in May 2014. We applaud and commend Ed and Sandy for 13 years of wonderful care, compassion, and service to our chaplains and their families in these crucial years our nation has been in war. Effective June 1, 1014, the new PCCMP Director is Lawrence Greenslit (PCUSA), after 27 years of active duty service, in Navy, Coast Guard, and Marine Corps billets. The Associate Director of the PCCMP is Reverend Don Wilson.

II. RESPONSIBILITY OF THE COMMISSION

1. To provide ecclesiastical endorsement for chaplains of the United States Armed Forces, who are on active duty, in the Reserves/National Guard and also chaplains of Veterans Affairs Medical Centers.
2. To provide pastoral support for their chaplains and their families.
3. To provide a unified and influential voice for the member denominations to the national government in matters relating to the ministry and welfare of Presbyterians serving in the United States Armed Forces and Veterans Affairs Medical Centers.
4. To provide representation to denominational agencies and ecumenical bodies in their concerns with matters relating to United States military personnel, veterans and their families.
5. To consider other duties as may be requested by the member denominations.
6. To promote closer communications between chaplains and their judicatories.

III. ANNUAL COMMISSION MEETING

The annual convening of the PCCMP usually takes place in the fall, with representatives of the member denominations in attendance. This past year the Council met at St. Paul's College in Washington, D.C. on October 21-23, 2013. It is at this time that potential chaplain candidates are interviewed by a committee of the Council who must determine whether the candidate will receive ecclesiastical endorsement. Council members may use other opportunities to schedule interviews such as at the PCCMP Annual Chaplain Training which happens at Montreat Retreat Center, North Carolina in August.

Each candidate is required to submit an application, school transcripts, presbyterial approval, and letters of reference. After the documents are gathered, we interview the candidates to determine if they should be endorsed for active duty or service with the Reserve/National Guard and Veteran's Administration (VA). A recommendation for each candidate is then submitted to the Council. If they are approved by the Council, then they make application to the various branches of service. The PCCMP maintains sound working relations with the Chief of Chaplains for each branch of the ministry and the VA.

IV. SUPPORT OF THE COUNCIL

The Council receives its financial support from the four denominations, individuals, judicatories, and churches. The current economic challenges in our country are creating a need to redesign how to minister to our chaplains and their families. We will be faithful stewards as we care for our military and veterans and their families.

One of the best ways Cumberland Presbyterian churches can support this vital ministry is to participate in the annual Memorial Day Offering or other special offering time convenient to your church such as the Sunday closest to Independence Day or Veteran's Day. In this way, we remember and show our support for all men and women, who serve and have served in the United States Armed Services, and their families. The offerings are sent to the General Assembly Stated Clerk and are then forwarded to the Council for its outreach, mission, and maintenance efforts. The Commission would like to express its deepest appreciation to all churches that collected offerings for the PCCMP during 2013 and 2014 to date. All Cumberland Presbyterian Churches in the United States are urged to consider their involvement in this vital ministry to God, country, and Presbyterians.

V. CUMBERLAND PRESBYTERIAN CHAPLAINS

We are proud to say that our denomination has a total of 10 men or women currently involved in various forms of chaplaincy around the world and 3 chaplain candidates.

	Active Duty	Reserves
Army	3	2
Air Force	1	1

VA	National Guard	Chaplain Candidates
Full time 1	1	3
Part time 1		

Please remember to pray for these servings in this important ministry. Names and addresses are included in the Yearbook of the Cumberland Presbyterian Church. Stand with these heroes of faithful service.

Anyone desiring more information can check our website: www.cumberland.org/ccmp.

Respectively Submitted,
Mary Catherine Benedict
Lowell Roddy
Cassandra Thomas

THE REPORT OF THE
PERMANENT JUDICIARY COMMITTEE

The Judiciary Committee met February 28, 2014 in Huntsville, Alabama. Present were Annetta Camp, Charles Dawson, Andy McClung, Robert Rush, Kimberly Silvus, Wendell Thomas, and Felicia Walkup. Also attending were Jaime Jordan, legal counsel, and Mike Sharpe, Stated Clerk of General Assembly. Sherry Ladd and Perryn Rice were excused.

I. ORGANIZATION OF THE COMMITTEE

Kimberly Silvus was elected chairperson and Andy McClung was elected secretary.

II. MEMORIAL

The committee reviewed a memorial from Murfreesboro Presbytery to General Assembly and found it not to be inproper order. The memorial calls for General Assembly to take actions which violate the incorporated status of the Ministry Council and other agencies of the denomination. The memorial and a statement of opinion from this committee as to its not being in proper order were returned to Murfreesboro Presbytery.

III. ACTION OF THE 183RD GENERAL ASSEMBLY

As an interpretation of Constitution 9.4.d, j, and m, the 183rd General Assembly (2013) adopted Recommendation 8 of The Report Number Two of the Ministry Council, which was under the subheading "III. Missions Ministry Team" (p.128, *2013 Minutes of the General Assembly*). The recommendation read as follows:

RECOMMENDATION 8: The General Assembly, following previously approved guidelines and in interpretation of the Constitution, sections 9.4 d, j, and m, designates the Missions Ministry Team (elected and staff members) or its successor as the agency responsible for oversight, guidance and authority for missionwork and mission fields that cannot have a meaningful relationship with a presbytery due to distance and/or language. The Missions Ministry Team is authorized to conduct all actions typical of a presbytery in oversight of such mission work until such time as a presbytery can be formed to accommodate the mission churches, pastors and probationers. As part of its oversight, the Missions Ministry Team may, if circumstances warrant, attach mission work to an existing presbytery, with its approval, following General Assembly-approved guidelines for host presbyteries.

Adoption of this recommendation by the 183rd General Assemblywas unconstitutional. According to the Constitution of the Cumberland Presbyterian Church, only a duly-formed presbytery may receive and license probationers, and establish congregations. Constitutional rules being violated by this interpretation include but are not limited to:

5.6.a. The presbytery is charged with pastoral oversight and has the responsibility to: Receive, examine, dismiss, and license candidates and ordain them to the ministry.

5.6.c. The presbytery is charged with pastoral oversight and has the responsibility to: Approve ministers to serve as pastors and in other types of ministry.

5.6.o. The presbytery is charged with pastoral oversight and has the responsibility to: Form and receive new churches and concert measures for the enlargement of the church within its bounds.

6.12 To be received as a candidate for the ministry, a person must be a member in good standing of a particular church in the receiving presbytery. Persons desiring to become candidates for the ministry shall confer with the committee on the ministry prior to presenting themselves to presbytery.

6.14 The committee on the ministry shall examine candidates respecting personal religious experience, motives leading to the seeking of the office of the ministry and the internal call to it, and plans for education. Such prior examination by the committee shall not preclude examination by the presbytery at the time of reception.

6.15 The reception of candidates for the ministry shall be at a duly constituted meeting of presbytery.... Proper record of the reception shall be made in the minutes of presbytery.

6.201 Licensure is a judgment by presbytery that a candidate for the ministry has exhibited certain qualities and abilities suitable to the office of ministry and has achieved a certain level of preparation for the ministry.... The report of the committee on the ministry of its examination shall not preclude examination by the presbytery.

6.203 The licensing of candidates shall be done at a duly constituted meeting of the presbytery or by a commission of the presbytery.... Proper record of the licensure shall be made in the minutes of presbytery.

The committee praises the passion and ministry of the Missions Ministry Team and rejoices in what is happening with the non-USA growth of our denomination. The committee also reaffirms the mentioned guidelines, adopted by the 182nd General Assembly (p.103, *2012 General Assembly Minutes*). The committee has considered the various ways to insure that this important work continues, but continues legally. The following recommendations are made not to hamper the international growth of the Cumberland Presbyterian Church nor the work of the Mission Ministry Team, but to insure that this work continues immediately and legally.

RECOMMENDATION 1: That the unconstitutional action of the 183rd General Assembly, which authorized the Missions Ministry Team to conduct all actions typical of a presbytery in oversight of non-USA mission work, be rescinded.

RECOMMENDATION 2: That the 184th General Assembly direct Mission Synod of the Cumberland Presbyterian Church to establish immediately a non-geographic presbytery called New Missions Presbytery of the Cumberland Presbyterian Church to serve as atransitional presbytery which will facilitate new mission work and provisional congregations outside the United States until membership in an existing or new geographic presbytery has been established.

IV. CLERGY TAX LAW

The committee encourages all sessions and ministers to pay attention toa possible upcoming change in tax law regarding clergy housing allowance.

V. REVIEW OF SYNODICAL MINUTES

The committeer reviewed the minutes of Synod of the Southeast and Synod of the Midwest and found both to be in order.

VI. GENERAL ASSEMBLY REPRESENTATIVES

Kimberly Silvus will serve as this committee's representative to the 184th General Assembly and Wendell Thomas will serve as the alternate.

Respectfully submitted,
The Judiciary Committee

THE REPORT OF THE NOMINATING COMMITTEE

The Nominating Committee consists of a minister and a lay person from each synod, preferably from different presbyteries. Members may serve a three year term, but cannot succeed themselves. Cumberland Presbyterian members of any board or committee can be re-elected to the same board after a two year absence. Ecumenical representatives may be re-elected to the same board after a one year absence. With the exception of the Nominating Committee any person elected to serve on a denominational entity may serve three consecutive terms. Filling an unexpired term counts as one term, thus members of any entity do not always serve nine years before completing eligibility on a board/agency.

The members of the various Ministry Teams are no longer elected by the General Assembly, but are to be appointed by the Ministry Council.

*Ecumenical Representative   +Cumberland Presbyterian Church in America

The Committee submits the following list of nominees:

I. BOARD OF DIRECTORS, GENERAL ASSEMBLY CORPORATION

Reverend John Butler, Cumberland Presbytery, Synod of Midwest, for a three-year term.
Ms. Betty Jacob, McGee Chapel Congregation, Choctaw Presbytery, Mission Synod, for a three-year term.

II. MINISTRY COUNCIL

Reverend Donny Acton, Grace Presbytery, Synod of the Southeast, to succeed himself for a three-year term.
Mr. Kenneth Bean, McKenzie Congregation, West Tennessee Presbytery, Synod of Great Rivers, to fill the one-year unexpired term of Reverend Lisa Scott, who has moved outside the bounds of Synod of Great Rivers.
Reverend Michele Gentry de Correal, Andes Presbytery, Mission Synod, to suceed herself for a three-year term.
Reverend Lanny Johnson, Murfreesboro Presbytery, Tennessee Synod, to succeed himself for a three-year term.
Ms. Emily Mahoney, Youth Advisory Member, Liberty Congregation, Murfreesboro Presbytery, Tennessee Synod, for a one-year term.
Mr. Adams McReynolds, Bethany Congregation, North Central Presbytery, Synod of Midwest, for a three-year term.
Reverend Tom Sanders, Red River Presbytery, Mission Synod, to succeed himself for a three-year term.

III. HISTORICAL FOUNDATION

Mr. Michael Fare, Springfield Congregation, Missouri Presbytery, to suceed himself for a three-year term.

IV. MEMPHIS THEOLOGICAL SEMINARY

*Mr. Robert Marble, an ecumenical partner, to succeed himself for a three-year term.
Ms. Pat Meeks, Faith Congregation, West Tennessee Presbytery, Synod of Great Rivers, to succeed herself for a three-year term.
Reverend Jennifer Newell, Tennessee-Georgia Presbytery, Synod of Southeast, to succeed herself for a three-year term.
*Mr. David Reed, an ecumenical partner for a three-year term.
Reverend Robert M. Shelton, Red River Presbytery, Mission Synod, to succeed himself for a three-year term.
+Dr. Joe Ward, CPCA, to succeed himself for a three-year term.
*Ms. Ruby Wharton, an ecumenical partner to succeed herself for a three-year term.
Reverend Susan Parker, Hope Presbytery, Synod of Southeast, for a three-year term.

V. BOARD OF STEWARDSHIP, FOUNDATION AND BENEFITS

Mr. Randy Davidson, Covenant Congregation, Red River Presbytery, Mission Synod, for a three-year term.
Mr. Charles Day, Short Creek Congregation, Cumberland Presbytery, Synod of Midwest, to succeed himself for a three-year term.
Ms. Sylvia Hall, Red Bank Congregation, Tennessee-Georgia Presbytery, Synod of Southeast, to succeed herself for a three-year term.

Mr. Jackie Satterfield, Welti Congregation, Hope Presbytery, Synod of Southeast succeed himself for a three-year term.

VI. COMMISSION ON CHAPLAINS AND MILITARY PERSONNEL

Reverend Mary McCaskey Benedict, Murfreesboro Presbytery, Tennessee Synod, to succeed herself for a three-year term.

VII. JUDICIARY

Reverend Harry Chapman, Presbytery del Cristo, Mission Synod, for a three-year term.
Reverend Robert D. Rush, Trinity Presbytery, Mission Synod, to succeed himself for a three-year term.
Mr. Wendell Thomas, Beaver Creek Congregation, Presbytery of East Tennessee, Synod of the Southeast, to succeed himself for a three-year term.

VIII. NOMINATING

Reverend Toby Davis, Trinity Presbytery, Mission Synod, for a three-year term.
Ms. Carolyn Harmon, Cedar Hill Congregation, Presbytery of East Tennessee, Synod of the Southeast, for a three-year term.
Reverend Alan Meinzer, Arkansas Presbytery, Synod of Great Rivers, to fill the one-year unexpired term of Reverend Isaac Gray.
Ms. Ellie Scrudder, Faith Congregation, Red River Presbytery, Mission Synod, for a three-year term.
Reverend Kevin Small, North Central Presbytery, Synod of the Midwest, for a three-year term.

IX. OUR UNITED OUTREACH COMMITTEE

Ms. Sharon Resch, Zion Congregation, Covenant Presbytery, Synod of the Midwest, to succeed herself for a three-year term.
Reverend William Rustenhaven, III, Trinity Presbytery, Mission Synod, to succeed himself for a three-year term.

X. UNIFIED COMMITTEE ON THEOLOGY AND SOCIAL CONCERNS

Reverend George Estes, Presbytery del Cristo, Mission Synod, to fill the one year unexpired term of Reverend Steve Parrish.
Reverend Randy Jacob, Choctaw Presbytery, Mission Synod, to succeed himself for a three-year term.

XI. ITEMS FOR CONSIDERATION

The Committee notes that the current General Assembly Bylaws 11.09 requires that "At least one member of the Committee other than the Seminary's President shall be a Cumberland Presbyterian member of the faculty of Memphis Theological Seminary."

Due to the decrease in the number of Cumberland Presbyterians serving on the faculty at Memphis Theological Seminary, it has become difficult in an effort to comply with this bylaw. We therefore make the following recommendations:

RECOMMENDATION 1: That Memphis Theological Seminary be encouraged to hire Cumberland Presbyterian faculty.

RECOMMENDATION 2: That "faculty" at Memphis Theological Seminary referred to in the General Assembly Bylaw 11.09, be expanded to include adjunct faculty.

In an effort to bring uniformity and strengthen the overall nominating process, the Committee makes the following recommendation:

RECOMMENDATION 3: That the requirements for endorsement process currently in place for Cumberland Presbyterian nominees filling vacancies on the Ministry Council, be utilized for all General Assembly boards and agencies.

THE REPORT OF THE PLACE OF MEETING COMMITTEE

The Place of Meeting Committee consists of the Moderator, a representative of the Cumberland Presbyterian Women's Ministry, and the Stated Clerk who serves as the chairperson. The representative of the Cumberland Presbyterian Women's Ministry is the Convention Coordinator.

The 165th General Assembly, "authorized the committee to select meeting places up to five years in the future and that preference be given that keeps, insofar as possible, the General Assembly and the Convention of Cumberland Presbyterian Women's Ministry, and guest rooms in one facility. It is recognized that these places are hard to find and may cost some additional monies. The place of meeting committee will use its best judgment." The 173rd General Assembly approved exploring the use of college campuses and very large conference centers in addition to hotels/convention centers. When the Office of the General Assembly receives an invitation from a congregation or a presbytery, the Stated Clerk makes a site visit. If adequate facilities are discovered, a follow up visit is made by the Stated Clerk, the Assistant to the Stated Clerk, and the Convention Coordinator of the Cumberland Presbyterian Women's Ministry.

Unless the General Assembly sets aside Bylaw 14.02 Standing Rules 1 to allow for a different meeting time, the annual meeting is the third or the fourth week of June.

Commissioners, delegates to Conventions, and visitors are encouraged to stay at the General Assembly/Convention hotel, to assure meeting the contracted room block. Hotel contracts also include a commitment on food and beverages, thus it is important for boards/agencies to continue to sponsor special meal functions. The luncheons/dinners provide opportunities for the sponsoring agencies/boards to keep the church informed about their respective programs, thus enhancing support.

I. INFORMATION ABOUT FUTURE GENERAL ASSEMBLIES

The 181st General Assembly accepted the invitation of Cauca Valley and Andes Presbyteries to host the 185th General Assembly in Colombia, South America. The General Assembly will meet on the campus of the Colegio Americano in Cali, Colombia on June 19-26, 2015 with the nineteenth and the twenty-sixth being travel days. The opening worship will be Saturday afternoon, June 20. Participants/visitors at General Assembly and the women attending the Cumberland Presbyterian Women's Ministry Convention will be able to attend worship in the various churches in Cauca Valley Presbytery on Sunday, June 21. The General Assembly will have the primary day of business on Tuesday, June 23. The Convention of the Cumberland Presbyterian Women's Ministry will have their program on Monday and Tuesday. Wednesday, June 17 and Thursday, June 18 be used for sight seeing and visiting some of the ministries in within Cauca Valley and Andes Presbyteries. The Colegio will offer a meal package (3 lunches, 3 dinners and snacks) for Saturday, Monday and Tuesday at a cost of $100 per person. Lunch Sunday will be provided by the host church. Additional costs for sight seeing options will be made available through the General Assembly Office and on the website (www.cumberland.org/gao) when that information becomes available from the host committee.

In February the Stated Clerk and the Director for Women's Ministry, traveled to Colombia to meet with the joint host committee to work on the arrangements for the 2015 meeting and to make site visits to hotels. The hotel rate will be $800 per room for the week spent in Colombia. All lodging arrangements and payments should be made through the Office of the General Assembly.

Although the exact airfare will not be known until late July, current estimates for airfare will range from $1,200 to $1,500 (depending on the departure city). Once airline schedules are available for next June (sometime in late August or September), a group promotion code through American Airlines will be made available. The promotion code would give each passenger a 5% discount on the lowest available fare.

Passports are required to go to Colombia, visas and shots are not required. It will be wise to allow two to three months to secure the passport. Many post offices will have passport applications forms. A birth certificate, picture and fee of $135 per person (for first time applicants) is required to secure a passport.

II. SCHEDULE OF FUTURE GENERAL ASSEMBLIES

185th   Cauca Valley & Andes Presbyteries   June 19-26, 2015

III. FUTURE INVITATIONS

Nashville Presbytery has extended an invitation to host the 186th General Assembly. The Convention Coordinator of the Cumberland Presbyterian Women's Ministry, the Moderator and the Stated Clerk have made site visits and have determined that there is adequate facilities in Nashville, Tennessee.

RECOMMENDATION 1: That the 184th General Assembly accept the invitation of Nashville Presbytery to host the concurrent meetings of the 186th General Assembly (CPC) and the General Assembly of the Cumberland Presbyterian Church in America, June 17-21, 2016.

There are no invitations on file for hosting the General Assembly/Convention after 2016. There has been some initial communications with the Chandler Congregation and Bethel University about the possibility of hosting General Assembly. Continued discussions with the leadership of the Cumberland Presbyterian Church in America regarding joint meetings of the General Assemblies in 2017 and 2018 may impact location. It is essential to continue scheduling a few years in advance of the meeting to assure that adequate hotel/convention space is available. If a congregation or a presbytery is interested in hosting the General Assembly/Convention, the Office of the General Assembly will provide information on hosting responsibilities. Hosting the General Assembly/Convention is a service to the Church, allowing the Church to celebrate the good ministries occurring within a particular presbytery, and provides persons within a presbytery the opportunity to participate more fully in the annual meeting.

In the event that no invitation is received in a particular year or a situation arises requiring a change of venue for a particular year, the Corporate Board will be responsible for selecting a place of meeting.

IV. SCHEDULE OF MEETINGS BY PRESBYTERIES

The following schedule shows the annual meetings and the year that the General Assembly last met in the bounds of a particular presbytery.

Presbytery	Year	Presbytery	Year
Murfreesboro	2013	Covenant	2002
Hope & Robert Donnell	2012	del Cristo	2001
Missouri	2011	Cumberland	2000
Nashville	2010	Tennessee-Georgia	1998
West Tennessee	2009	Robert Donnell	1996
Japan	2008	Nashville	1995
Arkansas	2007	North Central	1980
Grace	2006	Trinity	1969
Columbia	2005	Hope	1961
Red River	2004	Murfreesboro	1956
East Tennessee	2003		

Respectfully submitted,
Michael G. Sharpe
Pam Phillips-Burk
Robert D. Rush

THE REPORT OF THE UNIFIED COMMITTEE ON THEOLOGY AND SOCIAL CONCERNS

I. MEETING AND OFFICERS

The Unified Committee on Theology and Social Concerns met at the Cumberland Presbyterian Center on October 11-12, 2013 and on February 21, 2014. The following officers were elected during the fall meeting: Joy Wallace (CPCA), Chair; Reverend Byron Forester (CPC), Vice Chair; and Reverend Nancy Fuqua (CPCA), Secretary. The treasurer's position is handled by the Office of the Stated Clerk (CPC).

II. EXPIRATION OF TERMS

The Committee notes that the term of the Reverend Randy Jacobs expires in 2014, but is eligible to be reelected. The Committee also notes that Dr. Steve Parrish has asked to be replaced on the Committee due to his heavy teaching schedule at Memphis Theologcial Seminary. The Committee expresses gratitude for his service.

III. GENERAL ASSEMBLY REPRESENTATIVES

The committee elected Ms. Lezlie Daniel to serve as the representative to the meetings of General Assembly. Reverend Nancy Fuqua was elected as the alternate.

IV. WORKS IN PROGRESS

There are currently two papers being studied by the Committee.

Worship in the Third Millennium by Reverend Paul Criss, is still being reviewed. The Committee has sent the paper back to Reverend Criss with a request that study questions accompany the paper and that the paper be made more lay friendly for local congregations. The committee will explore developing companion resources for this paper in an effort to encourage inter generational involvement.

Come, Let Us Reason Together, Being Faithful in the Midst of Conflict by Reverend Mitzi Minor. The development of a PowerPoint demonstration is still in progress along with the development of a study guide, Bible Study resources, simulation of the resource in action, and a case study.

A previous paper, *Theological and Biblical Reflections on Women in Ministry*, has been added to the website with updated information on women in ministry from both denominations.

A new paper, *Illegal, Undocumented, or Unauthorized Immigrant…Commonly Used Terms; Which Is Right?* by Reverend Johan Daza was presented to the committee. The committee discussed ways to raise awareness of the impact of the use of the terminology "illegal" versus "undocumented" or "unauthorized" and to assist persons and congregations with information and resources on obtaining documentation.

The Committee invites the submission of Reflection or Position Papers on current issues that individuals or groups feel called to address. *A Guide to the Process of Writing Papers* by Reverend Paul Criss has been added to the website.

The Committee will explore how to interface with presbyteries that do not have Theological and Social Concerns Committees and will also work on developing some guidelines for use by presbytery committees.

V. UNIFICATION EFFORTS

It is the hope of the Committee that presbyteries and local churches that have not yet read the study paper *Reflections On A Divided Church* will do so and will find opportunities to participate in the following action steps that have been approved by both General Assemblies:

1. That local congregations where the churches have overlapping boundaries to organize joint activities between the CPC and CPCA to provide opportunities to build better relationships between the two churches such as holding joint activities through worship, pulpit exchange, times of fellowship, revivals, VBS, and discussion of the papers produced by this committee.

2. That presbyteries of the CPC and CPCA might also consider ways that committees boards and agencies might begin working together. Committees on ministry and missions, Christian education committees, and camping programs would all benefit from joint interaction. Examples of ways presbyteries can work together include having advisory members participate in the other denomination's meetings, workshops, projects for the Cumberland Presbyterian Women, working together on local, regional, and even denominational mission efforts including Habitat for Humanity, and raising money for disaster areas around the world.

The committee also recommends utilizing the resource from Reverend Andy McClung, *CPC & CPCA, Siblings in Faith*.

Respectfully Submitted,
Unified Committee on Theology and Social Concerns

THE REPORT OF THE UNIFICATION TASK FORCE

I. MEETING AND OFFICERS

The Unification Task Force (UTF) of the Cumberland Presbyterian Church in America (CPCA) and the Cumberland Presbyterian Church (CPC) met on September 6, 2013 and December 12-13, 2013 in Nashville, Tennessee, and on April 3-4, 2014 in Franklin, Tennessee. Officers elected at the September 2013 meeting were the Elder Leon Cole (CPCA) and the Reverend Gloria Villa-Diaz (CPC), co-chairs; the Reverend Joy Warren (CPC) continuing as secretary. Members of the UTF include Reverend Jay Earheart-Brown (CPC), Reverend Elton Hall (CPCA), Elder Arthur Haywood (CPCA), Reverend Lynne Herring (CPCA), Reverend William Robinson (CPCA), Reverend Anthony Hollis (CPCA), Reverend Steve Mosley (CPC), Reverend Perryn Rice (CPCA/CPC), Reverend Robert Rush (CPC), Elder Leon Cole (CPCA), Reverend Gloria Villa-Diaz (CPC), Reverend Mitchell Walker (CPCA), Reverend Joy Warren (CPC), Craig White (CPCA) and Reverend Mike Sharpe (CPC).

II. SUMMARY OF MEETINGS

In early September 2013, the UTF developed and circulated a survey to solicit feedback from both denominations on a wide variety of topics pertaining to unification, and had over 500 responses. In October, the UTF used the websites and social media to dispel commonly heard myths regarding unification. UTF members visited presbytery and synod meetings with the dual purpose of information sharing and gathering. The task force reviewed responses to the survey in its December meeting and named a subcommittee to draft the proposed plan of union. This subcommittee brought a draft of the plan to the April meeting, where the full UTF edited its contents for submission to both Assemblies.

Following a devotional time, each meeting of the UTF begins with celebration of joint activities and reports from task force members' speaking engagements. Some highlights of the past year include the CPCA Forum in Huntsville, Alabama; the Ministers' Conference hosted by Madkins Chapel CPCA; presbytery meetings with time devoted to extensive discussion of unification; and an informal poll taken at CPYC, overwhelmingly in favor of unification. Task force members strive to communicate a consistent message in each setting, allowing for as many questions and comments as possible. The UTF desires the plan of union to be a true "people's plan," with input from the membership of both denominations.

Education and communication through face to face meetings are vital aspects of the work of the UTF. In order to perform these functions, the UTF requires presence at meetings on all judicatorial levels and funding from both denominations.

RECOMMENDATION 1: That the Unification Task Force be given time at Summer and Fall 2014 and Spring 2015 presbytery and synod meetings to present updates on unification and to get feedback on the plan for union.

RECOMMENDATION 2: That joint clusters of churches also schedule a time for a presentation on unification by a member of the task force, unification advocates, and/or other leaders within both denominations.

RECOMMENDATION 3: That the General Assembly continue its funding for the programming and travel of the Unification Task Force.

The UTF, after much prayer and joint work, has developed a proposed plan of union. The members seek input from membership of both denominations in the finalization process. A guiding principle to the work of the UTF has been that members of the UTF represent the membership, the people around the globe who must desire unity for this plan to be successful. The plan leaves much of the real work of unification in the hands of the people. With this proposed plan and a process of reflection in mind, the UTF also constructed a timeline of events for unification.

Proposed Plan for Union of Cumberland Presbyterian Church and
Cumberland Presbyterian Church in America (with Reflection Questions)

"There is one, holy, universal, apostolic church. She is the body of Christ, who is her Head and Lord" (Confession of Faith 5.01). "The church is one because her head and Lord is one, Jesus Christ. Her oneness under her Lord is manifested in the one ministry of word and sacrament, not in any uniformity of covenantal expression, organization, or system of doctrine" (5.02). "The church, as the covenant community of believers who are redeemed, includes all people in all ages, past, present, and future, who respond in faith to God's covenant of grace, all who are unable to respond, for reasons known to God, but who are saved by his grace" (5.06). It is on this belief that the Unification Task Force recommends the union of the Cumberland Presbyterian Church in America (CPCA) and the Cumberland Presbyterian Church (CPC). We are one in Christ by the grace of God and the power of the Holy Spirit! We believe that becoming one will strengthen our witness as Christian believers in the world, and that together we will be able to accomplish more for the glory of God. United together in Christ by faith, we are united to one another in love. In this communion we share the grace of Christ with one another, bear one another's burdens, and reach out to all other persons (5.10).

1.00 The Name of the New Denomination
The name of the denomination shall be the United Cumberland Presbyterian Church.

> *Reflect:* Do you think this is a good name? Why or why not?

2.00 The Logo of the New Church
A new logo will be fashioned by the new church.

> *Reflect:* Do you have an idea for a new logo? Some suggestions of the survey included comments about maintaining the global nature of the new church and incorporating components of both denominations' current logos. What do you think about this idea?

3.00 Mission Statement for the New Church
The United Cumberland Presbyterian Church affirms the great commission of Christ: "Go, therefore, and make disciples of all nations, baptizing them in the name of the Father, and of the Son, and of the Holy Spirit, and teaching them to obey everything that I have commanded you. And remember I am with you until the end of the age"(Matthew 28:19-20). We celebrate our oneness in faith. As disciples, we seek through worship, global witness, and service to be the hands and feet of Christ and to live out the inclusive love of Jesus Christ to the glory of God.

> *Reflect:* What would you add or remove from this statement, if anything? Is there another scripture text that you would suggest for a mission statement?

4.00 The Confession of Faith and Government
The United Cumberland Presbyterian Church will use the Confession of Faith and Government of the Cumberland Presbyterian Church and the Cumberland Presbyterian Church in America, approved by both General Assemblies of the former denominations in 1984 as its system of faith and government.

> *Reflect:* Did you know that the Confession of Faith and the Government of the Cumberland Presbyterian Church and Cumberland Presbyterian Church in America include the following: the Constitution, the Rules of Discipline, the Directory for Worship and the Rules of Order? Find a copy and explore this important document! (Current printing Jan 2014)

It should be noted that in the Constitution (4.6, 5.6p) the CPC allows for the session to request permission from Presbytery for a designated elder to serve communion for a one year period of time. This is an exception, NOT A RULE for general practice, for those presbyteries that have difficulty supplying each church with an ordained minister. The responsibility lies with presbytery for proper training and oversight of the designated elder. Again, is this an EXCEPTION. No presbytery is required to apply this exception.

> *Reflect:* Is this an issue in your presbytery? Are there ordained clergy in your presbytery who are not serving a church or could make arrangements to fill this need? How do you feel about elders being trained to serve communion?

4.01 The United Cumberland Presbyterian Church will use the *Catechism for Cumberland Presbyterians* (2008) for instruction in the faith and will include it in an updated Confession of Faith.

> *Reflect:* Does your church use the catechism for study? Do you know where to locate it? Ask your pastor or session clerk

4.02 The CP Digest (CPC) and Summaries of Actions (for both denominations) will continue to serve as resource tools. A new Digest will begin with the formation of the United Cumberland Presbyterian Church.

> *Reflect:* These resources are interpretations of actions by both churches and there may be value in retaining them in the new church. What do you think? Why or why not?

5.00 The Presbyteries and Synods

5.01 In an effort to make union something more than just an idea on paper, and to engage the grassroots in creating the new church, we recommend a restructure of the synod boundaries in the following way –

Mission	Midwest	Tennessee	Alabama
Angelina (6 – 107)	Cleveland, OH (4 – 315)	Columbia (34 – 3,003)	Birmingham (6 – 203)
Arkansas (60 – 3,343)	Covenant (42 – 5,133)	Elk River (11 – 89)	Florence (5 – 274)
Brazos River (9 – 432)	Cumberland (64 – 4,939)	Hiawassee (9 – 758)	Grace (38 – 3,946)
Choctaw (7 – 140)	Missouri (24 – 1,185)	Murfreesboro (43 – 4,699)	Hope (10 – 1,502)
Del Cristo (11 – 3,917)	New Hopewell (11 – 387)	Nashville (39 – 5,231)	Huntsville (18 – 3178)
East Texas (4 – 101)	North Central (35 – 2,548)	East Tennessee (37 – 5,199)	Robert Donnell (21 – 1,726)
Red River (27 – 3,795)	Ohio Valley (4 – 128)	Tennessee-Georgia (37 – 2,622)	South Alabama (6 – 328)
Trinity (23 – 2,689)	Purchase (3 – 44)	Cumber E Coast Korean (5 – 194)	Tennessee Valley (8 – 523)
Andes (10 – 1,917)	West Tennessee (95 – 9,892)		Tuscaloosa (7 – 251)
Cauca Valley (20 – 2,972)			
Hong Kong (10 – 1,947)			
Japan (14 – 2,314)			

For relationship building during the first six years, all synods will be an annual general meeting (Constitution 8.2) as opposed to a delegated meeting. Synods may petition General Assembly at any point for a change in boundaries.

> Reflect: In which synod is your presbytery? What is your opinion of this structure? Can you suggest a different synod structure? If you could redraw synod boundaries how might that look?

5.02 Presbyteries will remain as they are constituted at the time of union for a period of six years, during which a study of restructure will be made by synods. The constitutional processes for restructuring presbyteries will be applicable (Constitution 8.5c).

> *Reflect:* If you were on a committee to restructure presbytery boundaries, what would be important to you? Look in your Confession of Faith to review the process for restructuring presbyteries. What are your thoughts? What are some of the benefits of restructuring? What are some challenges? What are some benefits/challenges to the current structure?

6.00 Commissioners and Youth Advisory Delegates to the General Assembly

6.01 The current formula for representation will prevail for six years or until the restructuring of presbyteries occurs, whichever comes first.

CPCA		CPC	
1-200 active membership in Presbytery	1 minister/1 elder	1-1000	1 minister/ 1 elder
201-400	2 ministers/2 elders	1001-2000	2 ministers/2 elders
401-1000	3 ministers/3 elders	Above 2000	Continue in the above proportions
1001- above	4 ministers/4 elders		

> *Reflect:* Did you know that CPCA representation at General Assembly is 52 and the CPC General Assembly representation is 120? What are your thoughts about the difference in representation? Once the new church is formed, what would be your suggestion for a new representation ratio?

6.02 Each presbytery is entitled to send up to two Youth Advisory delegates to the General Assembly.

> *Reflect:* Did you know that at the 2013 CPC General Assembly, the YADs voted unanimously in favor of unification when polled by the Moderator? What do the young people in your setting think about unification?

7.00 Moderator and Vice Moderator of General Assembly

7.01 The moderator/vice moderator will be elected each year during the first six years with both offices alternating between the two former denominations.

7.02 The moderator and vice moderator of the United Cumberland Presbyterian Church will reflect its diverse nature, to include international representatives. The church expects the moderator and vice moderator to travel within the denomination, sharing and gathering information among its local churches. Travel expenses for the moderator and vice moderator will be paid.

> *Reflect:* Currently, the CPCA provides an honorarium as well as travel reimbursement for the moderator and vice moderator. In the CPC, the moderators receive only travel reimbursements. What do you think would be fair in the new denomination?

8.00 Stated Clerk and Associate Stated Clerk of the General Assembly

8.01 The new church shall employ a Stated Clerk and an Associate Stated Clerk. Both positions will be full-time jobs. During the first six years of the United Cumberland Presbyterian Church, the Stated Clerk will serve six years and the Associate Stated Clerk will serve four years, after which each would be elected for a four-year period. One position will be filled by a former CPCA and the other position filled by a former CPC during their first terms. The subsequent election of each position will allow for continuity during transitions.

> *Reflect:* After the initial six (6) years, these positions will be elected from the new church. Currently, there are no term limits in the CPC, but in the CPCA it is 12 years. Although they have the same title, the job duties of the Stated Clerk vary greatly between the two denominations. The CPC Stated Clerk includes many duties of the CPCA Administrative Director. The Associate Clerk position is a new position for both denominations. What type of leadership do you think would best serve the new church? How do you see these?

9.00 Boards and Agencies of the General Assembly
9.01 Each church has programs in various stages of planning and implementation that are the result of commitment to ministry through the church. Insofar as possible, these plans and programs will be continued without interruption for a period of three years. The United Cumberland Presbyterian Church will continue ecumenical partnerships, such as the World Communion of Reformed Churches.

> *Reflect:* There are already a number of joint ministries between the two denominations - Coalition of Appalachian Ministries, Federated Board of Christian Education, Unified Committee on Theology and Social Concerns, Historical Foundation, Memphis Theological Seminary, Commission on Military Chaplains & Personnel. Were you aware of how much we work together already? Have you served on any of these joint ministries?

9.02 Institutional Boards
The General Assembly shall have the following institutional boards: Trustees of Memphis Theological Seminary to include the Program of Alternate Studies and School of Continuing Education Committee, and Trustees of the Historical Foundation. Representation on each Board of Trustees will remain as they are constituted at the time of union.

9.03 The General Assembly shall have the following commission: Chaplains and Military Personnel. Representation on the commission will be merged as they are constituted at the time of union until natural rotation occurs.

9.04 GA shall have the following standing committees: Theology and Social Concerns, Judiciary, Our United Outreach, Nominating, and Multi-Cultural Ministry. Committee representation on Theology and Social Concerns will remain as constituted at the time of union until natural rotations occurs. Judiciary and Nominating committees in both denominations will each be merged at the time of union. Committee representation for Our United Outreach will be expanded to include two elected representatives from each new synod (one voting representative from each of the former denominations until natural rotation occurs). Committee on Multi-Cultural Ministry is a new committee that will reflect the diversity of the United Cumberland Presbyterian Church.

> *Reflect:* The Multi-Cultural Committee is a NEW committee. Representation will reflect the diversity of the United Cumberland Presbyterian Church. What voices do you think need to be around this table? What can you do in your local setting to promote education about cultural intelligence within the new denomination?

9.05 The General Assembly shall have the following administrative Boards: The Board of Stewardship, Foundation and Benefits and The Board of Directors of the General Assembly Corporation. During the transition period, each of these boards will have equal number of members from each of the former denominations.

9.06 The United Cumberland Presbyterian Church will have a Mission Programming Agency to provide coordination and oversight for those ministries formally planned and implemented by the two former denominations. After the three-year period, the new programming and denominational structure will consist of the following ministries and entities –

    Christian Education & Nurture (Youth Convention & National Sunday School, Convention, Discipleship Ministry)
    Missions (Evangelism, Missionary Auxiliary, Women's Ministry)

Clergy Care & Development
Communications (Cumberland Flag, Cumberland Presbyterian Magazine,
   Missionary Messenger, website)

> *Reflect:* What would you call this new programming entity? What name would you give to each programming area of the new church? Are there any ministry areas missing? If so, describe other ministries that need to be included in this new entity

Composition of each ministry entity will include equal number of persons from each of the former denominations in the new church at the time of union. Composition of the new Mission Agency will include one staff and one elected member from each ministry entity, along with two elected members (one each from the former denominations) representing each of the synods. The Associate Stated Clerk position would provide executive leadership for the Mission Agency.

10. Denominational Staff Personnel & Offices
Currently, the CPCA employs two full time staff members; the CPC employs twenty-five staff members.

10.01 The new organizational structure will discontinue the positions of Administrative Director (CPCA) and the Director of Ministries (CPC) and will create the position of Associate Stated Clerk. The Stated Clerk and Associate Stated Clerk will be elected during the General Assembly of 2018. The Implementation Task Force will make recommendations to the 2018 Assembly about the transition in staffing to be complete by the 2019 Assembly.

10.02 Staffing for the United Cumberland Presbyterian Church will reflect the diversity of the new church. As new staff positions become available, equal opportunity employment practices will prevail.

10.03 Denominational Centers – During the first six years, steps are to be taken to assure that regional centers be located in a minimum of three and a maximum of five locations. Thus, neither the Center in Huntsville nor the Center in Memphis will be designated as " the denominational center." By placing regional centers in a variety of locations this will assure that all areas of the church will be served equally. (possible regional locations could be Memphis, Huntsville, Louisville, Texas, South America, and Asia)

> *Reflect:* What do you think about the possibility of regional centers? How do you envision these centers working for the benefit of the denomination? Are there certain regions that would be good areas for particular ministries?

10.04 Global Staff
There will be endorsed missionaries and partner missionaries in the new church. The new church will continue to support the current and future missionaries and global work. Current missionaries include – Boyce & Beth Wallace (Colombia, South America), Glenn Watts (Hong Kong), Anay Ortega (Guatemala), Phanor & Socorro Pejendino (Guatemala), Daniel & Kay Jang (Philippines), Kenneth & Deligh Hopson (Uganda), Lawrence and Loretta Fung (Asian ministry USA), Carlos and Luz Dary Rivera (Mexico), Missionaries in undisclosed (6), CP missionaries supported by their presbyteries – Iwao Satoh and Keishi and Kazuko Ishitsuka

11.00 Stewardship and Finance
11.01 Legal control of assets of both churches will be transferred to the United Cumberland Presbyterian Church through appropriate legal transaction. The intent of all designated gifts and endowments will be honored.

11.02 The United Cumberland Presbyterian Church will develop an approach to the financing of the programs of the church that reflects the stewardship understanding of the new constituency. Such a unitary approach will be developed as soon as possible after formation and no later than the end of the first six years.

> *Reflect:* Within the CPC, ministries are funded through "Our United Outreach (OUO)" on a denominational level. Each congregation gives 10% to OUO based on their annual income. Presbyteries are funded by apportionments or the like, and synods are funded indirectly through the presbyteries. Within the CPCA, ministries are funded by a congregational tithe of 10%. 7% goes to the General Assembly, 2% to Presbytery, and 1% to synod. In both denominations, some income is exempt from the tithe calculation. What does this new approach to giving in the United Cumberland Presbyterian Church mean? Does it mean churches no longer give to their presbytery or denomination? NO
> - Each local congregation will continue in their giving practices until a new plan is approved by General Assembly.

12.00 Recognition of Ordination
12.01 All ordinations, both clergy and lay (elders and deacons), of both denominations will be recognized by the United Cumberland Presbyterian Church. All future ordinations will be governed by the conditions specified in the Constitution.

RECOMMENDATION 4: That the proposed plan of union and reflection questions be received by General Assembly and circulated widely among the people, and that feedback be provided to the Office of General Assembly by July 1, 2015.

Proposed Time Line for Unification

Planning Phase
1. Beginning June 2014: Individuals, groups, congregations, presbyteries, synods, and all others, study the proposed Plan of Union prayerfully and send responses to both General Assembly Offices by July 1, 2015.

2. By the 2016 General Assemblies: The UTF will review responses to the proposed Plan of Union and formulate a revised Plan of Union. A draft plan of the bylaws and standing rules will also be presented to the General Assemblies. The Assemblies will be asked to approve the Plan of Union and send it to presbyteries for ratification. The Assemblies will form a Joint Implementation Task Force and dissolve the Unification Task Force.

3. Between June 2016 and June 2017: The Plan of Union will be sent to presbyteries in each denomination for ratification. The draft plan of the bylaws and standing rules will be available for study and response. Implementation Task Force will work with attorneys to finalize new bylaws and standing rules.

4. By the 2017 General Assemblies (concurrent called meeting of CPCA): Ratification Process for the Plan of Union will be complete. Revised bylaws and standing rules will be presented to Assemblies for approval. Both Assemblies will adjourn in 2017 to meet together as the United Cumberland Presbyterian Church in 2018.

5. 2018: Celebration of the United Cumberland Presbyterian Church!

Implementation Phase
The first six years after unification (2017-2023), implementation of the plan for union for the new church (which will include chartering the new church, monitoring changes to synod/presbytery boundaries, development of unified denominational programming and staff, exploration of new regional centers).

> Reflect: What are your thoughts on this time line? Does it need to be longer? Shorter? What are any additional tasks that need to be done during the implementation phase? What specific things will you do to help implement this plan?

RECOMMENDATION 5: That this timeline for unification be approved.

Respectfully submitted,
Unification Task Force

THE REPORT OF BOARD OF TRUSTEES OF BETHEL UNIVERSITY

Bethel University is the only Cumberland Presbyterian University in the world. It has been in existence since 1842. Bethel University has a Covenant Relationship with the Cumberland Presbyterian Church and values this long and trusted relationship and is fully committed to maintaining it.

Bethel University operates with a Board of Trustees of no more than 30 persons, of which the majority must be active members of the Cumberland Presbyterian Church. Currently the Board of Trustees has 27 members. Bethel University is a 501(c)(3) Corporation.

Bethel University's enrollment for the fall of 2013 was 5625, an increase over the 5214 enrollment in the fall of 2012. The students are enrolled in one of the following: School of Arts and Sciences, School of Professional Studies, School of Public Service, or School of Health Sciences.

Bethel currently has more than 11,000 alumni. We have alumni living in all but four of the U.S. states. More than 8,000 live right here in Tennessee. That is 5 alumni for every square mile of the state. That number of alumni stands to grow exponentially with the increasing enrollment.

We also have student athletes who come from all over the U.S. - this past year we served more than 700 student athletes. They too are exposed to Cumberland Presbyterian ideals and they take that with them when they leave Bethel.

Renaissance, Bethel's performing arts group, has become a leader on our campus and spreading the Bethel message. Probably, more than any other group on campus, these students are exposed to the Cumberland Presbyterian ideals. They visit churches; they stay in church members' homes; they see how we do things. We now have more than 1,000 students who have been a part of Renaissance and who have a very strong sense of what the Cumberland Presbyterian faith is all about. It is a part of who they are now, and they are bringing it into their daily lives.

Our alumni have been exposed to the Cumberland Presbyterian faith and value system, and they are living and having an impact based on what our denomination believes.

Our men's basketball team was ranked in the top 15 in the nation (NAIA). Our women's basketball team was ranked in the top 20 in the nation (NAIA). Our bass fishing team was ranked #1 in the nation by BassRanking.com, the largest bass ranking organization in America. Our hockey team is nationally ranked. Track, shooting and bowling are also enjoying successful seasons. Our women's swimming team went to the Nationals in Oklahoma City. Renaissance is on the road weekly and has been in many of your churches or towns. Our Hendrix scholarship competition (academic and overall student excellence) was very successful this year. We had more applicants for this scholarship than ever before. Winner is Matthey Gainey from Seymour, Tennessee. He will major in Theatre and participate in the Renaissance Program. Matthew attends the Seymour Heights Christian Church. Runner-up is Tyler Vernon from Bartlett, Tennessee. He will have a double major in History (Pre-Law interest) and Theatre and participate in the Renaissance program. Tyler attends Ellendale United Methodist Church. Our Nursing Program received a letter in February, 2014 from the Tennessee Board of Nursing noting that the Baccalaureate Nursing Program at Bethel University had a 100% National Council Licensure Examination passing rate in 2013. This is a significant achievement.

We are currently actively fund raising for the Cumberland Chapel. Bethel wants to build a new chapel that will serve our entire student body and help to foster a closer relationship with our Creator. Our fundraising is off to a solid start and we hope to announce plans to start the building soon.

Our last two years of audited financials are enclosed. For the fiscal year that ended July 31, 2013, we had a very solid showing.

We solicit your prayers and your support. We pray you will encourage students to consider us. Bethel looks forward to our common goal in the future.

Bethel Forevermore!

THE REPORT OF THE BOARD OF TRUSTEES OF THE CUMBERLAND PRESBYTERIAN CHILDREN'S HOME

Thank you for reading our Report to the 184th General Assembly of the Cumberland Presbyterian Church. These brief pages offer you a glimpse of the life changing new beginnings children and families experience at The Cumberland Presbyterian Children's Home (Cumberland or Children's Home). Thank you for your prayers, thoughtful and sacrificial giving of time and resources and your sustaining commitment to Christ's command to "suffer the little children to come to me." We look forward to your questions and comments about our ministry.

I. OVERVIEW

Our 110 year ministry at the Children's Home serves children and families in different ways:

- **Children's Residential Care,**
- **Children's Emergency Shelter Care,**
- **Single Parent Family Services, and**
- **Cumberland Family Services Counseling.**

In the 21st Century, we focus our ministry on ending the maltreatment of children. Child abuse and neglect not only injure children, but impact the lives and families of adults who were once abused. We must stop the cycle of harm, a harm that can be measured in many ways. Foremost, I believe we are called to this redemptive ministry by God. God has called us to feed, clothe, teach, and love the little, the last, the lost and the least.

The harm also creates a toll in human tragedy correlated with crime, addiction, unemployment, incarceration, broken relationships, mental and emotional dysfunction, ill health, violence and self destructive actions. The cost to society is numbing.

So Cumberland provides a safe, nurturing and loving residence where children and families can live and grow. It also provides tools for healing and health through counseling and parenting training. And most importantly, the Children's Home enacts Christ's command to serve in His name. Here are some numbers to give you a flavor of the scope of our ministry.

Cumberland directly served over 1,090 children, youth, teens, parents and families in 2013.

Cumberland helps children and families in residential and non-residential programs.
- In its residential programs, Cumberland served 119 children and 16 single parents.
- Over 950 additional children and families were served through intake and referral services, counseling sessions, or classes in our non-residential programs.
- Cumberland held over 1,670 separate counseling sessions and fielded almost 800 calls for service.

In all, 2,147 lives were touched with healing and hope by The Cumberland Presbyterian Children's Home during 2013.

A. MISSION

*In response to Christ's love and example,
we serve children and families
by providing healing and hope.*

B. GUIDING VALUES

We categorize our guiding values under the headings of *faith*, *acceptance*, *care*, and *excellence*.

Faith: In response to the gift of life given to us by Jesus Christ and the ministry entrusted to us by God, we serve God by serving others.
Acceptance: We accept individuals as they are and help them develop the capacity for change

in their own lives.

Care: *Our service to others is framed by a positive, strength-based and solution-focused approach to all our relationships.*

Excellence: *In our service to others, we strive for excellence, efficiency and professionalism in all that we do.*

C. CAMPUS

Cumberland's 17-acre campus in Denton, Texas, includes three residential cottages for children and teens and 8 apartments for single parent families. Other features include the Parr Family Resource Building, which houses the Library and Technology Center, therapy rooms, meeting facilities and staff offices. The campus is also home to the Gilbert-Parr Activities Building, which houses Cumberland's recreational facilities and a chapel, the 250-seat Lela Stricklen Hall.

D. CORPORATE ENTITY AND GOVERNANCE

Cumberland is a non-profit corporation incorporated under the laws of the state of Texas. Cumberland is tax-exempt under IRS Code section 501(c)(3). Cumberland is governed by a board of 15 Trustees. The Cumberland Board of Trustees hired the President, CEO & General Counsel to manage the agency.

Trustees: There are currently 14 trustees: eleven Cumberland Presbyterians and three ecumenical partners *(the Board is in the process of filling a vacated seat)*

Ecumenical Partners: Kay Goodman, Tiffany Smith, and Baron Smith

Cumberland Presbyterians: Mamie Hall, Reverend Melissa Knight, Patricia Huff, Reverend Don Tabor, Richard Dean, Mickey Shell, Reverend Dr. Yoong Kim, Ruby Letson, Reverend Norlan Scrudder, Reverend Alfonso Marquez, and Patricia Long

Officers: President—Kay Goodman; Vice-President—Reverend Norlan Scrudder; Secretary—Patricia Huff.

Leadership:
- *President, CEO & General Counsel*: Rev. Richard A. Brown, Esq., LCCA
- *Vice President, Programs:* Dr. Jennifer Livings, LPC-S
- *Vice President & CFO:* Warren Nagumo
- *Vice President of Development*: Larry Brown
- *Chaplain:* Rev. Stephanie Brown

E. ORGANIZATIONAL STRUCTURE

Because our mission calls us to a ministry of service, we have adopted the following "Pyramid of Care©" as an organizational structure. Rather than organizing from the top down, we wish to follow in Christ's example of servant leadership. We place the people we serve, both in residential care and in non-residential care, at the top of the pyramid.

PYRAMID OF CARE ©

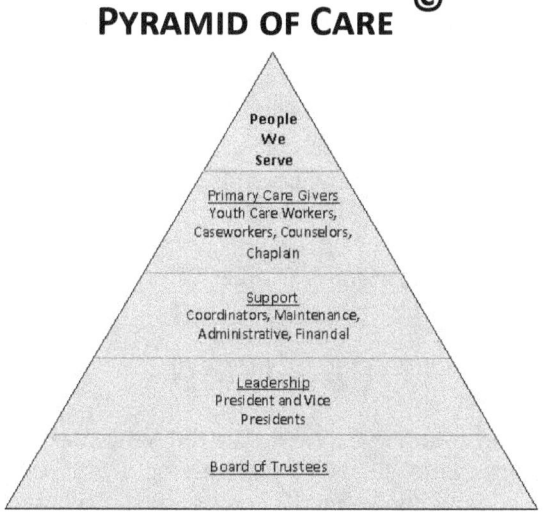

II. OUTCOMES

In our efforts to serve families and children, Cumberland looks for quantitative ways to measure our work. Beginning in 2010, Cumberland contracted with a third party to create an unbiased and verifiable method of measuring outcomes. This process helps us constantly improve our programs and maintain accountability with our donors and service partners. Below are a few of the positive outcomes from our study covering the calendar year 2013:

A. RESIDENTIAL CARE

Residents completed or made progress with over 8 out of 10 of their goals. Children that remain in care six months or longer on average are 33% more effective with their goals and improve behaviorally 35%. Teens involved in extracurricular activities and services activities averaged 5 hours per week in those activities. One-third of eligible residents were employed working an average of 22 hours per week. Behavior scores over the past four years at CPCH on average are 40% better than a clinical population of teens in Texas.

B. SHELTER

Shelter residents stayed an average of 53 days. 80% of all shelter discharges were planned. This is significant considering behavior scores are closely aligned with a clinical population of teens in Texas. During the time in the shelter, residents improved 10% in their sense of wellbeing in areas of safety, relationships, skills, and hope for their future.

C. SINGLE PARENT FAMILY

Over 9 out of 10 SPF residents were employed during their stay with CPCH and they worked an average of 33 hours per week. Half reported they were actively involved in church. Residents in the SPF program grow on average 21% in their goals for each month they are in the program. This statistically significant growth is important as it demonstrates the stability the SPF program provides families allows them to focus and grow in goals they have chosen.

D. CUMBERLAND FAMILY SERVICES

Counseling hours in 2013 doubled from those reported in 2012. 7 out of 10 identified positive progress in their ability to achieve change. 7 out of 10 identified progress in skills to manage challenges. 2 out 3 said they were more aware of their personal strengths as a result of counseling. 2 out of 3 reported that they were more aware of their options because of counseling. 97% said the counseling services they received were good or excellent. 94% counseling participants agreed or strongly agreed with the statement "My counselor works with me to set therapy goals." 97% of counseling participants agreed or strongly agreed with the statement "I feel accepted and respected by my counselor." 92% of counseling participants agreed or strongly agreed with the statement "My counselor encourages me to make my own decisions." Therapist perceptions of client growth and client self-reports of wellbeing/growth are highly correlated and indicative of a high level of rapport between clients and therapists.

Over 8 out of 10 training participants reported positive or very positively that:
- "The material in this training was helpful."
- "The presentation was well delivered."
- "My expectations were met."
- "I would recommend this training to others."
- "Overall evaluation."

III. GIVING

Cumberland Presbyterian Children's Home exists today because of the commitment Cumberland Presbyterian individuals and congregations have made in giving every year and through planned gifts. In her will, Miss Victoria Jackson of Bowling Green, Kentucky, created a home for widows and orphans. Her final act of generosity has allowed thousands of lives to be touched by this ministry. For the past 110 years, many faithful and forward thinking people have blessed the children's home, including the increasingly needed family services, with annually recurring and estate gifts.

We are grateful that more than half of CP churches made direct gifts to the children's home this last year. Through these reliable annual gifts and the endowment built from planned giving, Cumberland Presbyterian Children's Home can keep the church's promise to do more than house, clothe and feed our children. The opportunities for spiritual growth and practical life skills for children and families would not exist without the continued prayers and support from the women and men of Cumberland Presbyterian Churches.

The sad reality is the cost for care increases every year. Those innocents caught in difficult circumstances often experience a higher rate of inflation than the national average, compounding the difficulty to escape. Even though the cost of basic needs and necessary services has steadily climbed over our 110 year history, annual giving from most of our closest CP Churches has remained the same or declined over the past 3 decades. Many can point to declining membership, demographic changes and regional economic issues for the lack of increase but the needs of our children and the promise of the church remains.

IV. FINANCIAL INFORMATION

A. EXPENSES

Based on the unaudited 2013 Financial Statements, Cumberland spent $2.4 million bringing healing and hope to children and families. Only 11 cents of every dollar was spent on administrative and fund raising costs. Expenses break down into the following categories:

Residential Childcare	51.1%
Emergency Shelter Childcare	32.8%
Cumberland Family Services	7.3%
Single Parent Family	8.8%

B. INCOME

Based on the unaudited 2013 Financial Statements, Cumberland derived over $1.7 million in operational income from the following sources:

$ 771,746	Contributions	45.5%
$ 579,775	Service Compensation	34.2%
$ 267,990	Endowment Income	15.8%
$ 46,727	OUO	2.8%
$ 31,408	Other	1.9%
$1,697,646	Total	100.0%

V. STRATEGIC PLAN

With a history of innovation, the Cumberland Board of Trustees has developed a Strategic Vision and a 10-year Strategic Plan. The strategic vision looks to a self-sustaining, fully-staffed ministry in our current location. This vision also sees the replication of our existing programs in other locations, and the vision recognizes the possibility of new programs serving children and families. The 10-year Strategic Plan will work toward fulfilling the vision by improving programs, expanding our outreach and creating sustainability.

A. STRATEGIC VISION

1. Self-Sustaining, fully-staffed agency in Denton, Texas
2. Replication of our programs
3. Work toward complete social service ministry for children and families

B. 2012-2022 STRATEGIC OBJECTIVES

1. Program Development

Cumberland will examine, continue to improve on, and strive for excellence in the existing programs as well as add at least one new, self-sustaining program to the agency's continuum of care.

Cumberland's Denton campus will be a beautiful fully-functioning, synergistic model for other multiple program agencies. Cumberland will replicate one or more of its programs in at least one new geographic location.

2. Outreach Development

Cumberland will develop reciprocal professional relationships with institutions such as hospitals, area churches, social service agencies, Bethel University, Memphis Theological Seminary, Texas Woman's University and University of North Texas combining relevant research and mature faith ensuring the long-term sustainability of social service ministry. Cumberland will develop relationships at the highest level with the Texas Department of Family and Protective Services by serving on committees and boards at the state and local level.

Cumberland will be a significant provider of social services to children and families in Texas and will be the primary social service resource to the Cumberland Presbyterian denomination.

3. Agency Development

Cumberland will have a minimum operating budget of $2.5 million with contributions accounting for no more than 20% of the income, be fully staffed for optimum programming outcomes in all locations, and have a total endowment valued at more than $10.2 million.

Cumberland will become a self-governing agency within a covenant, but not legal relationship, with the General Assembly of the Cumberland Presbyterian Church. The Board of Trustees will meet a minimum of three times per year and become more active in resource development, i.e. recruiting major donors, planned giving, forming relationships with businesses, participating in special events and making gifts of their own that indicate significant support for the agency.

VI. PRESIDENT'S MESSAGE

This year I invite you to join us in celebrating and honoring the life and legacy of Reverend Dr. James C. Gilbert, a man who touched so many lives with a grace that kindled hope. Dr. Gilbert's tireless efforts to faithfully serve God, to support and nurture the Cumberland Presbyterian Church and to follow Christ's love and example in service to children and families made possible so many transformations and new beginnings. Thank you, Dr. Gilbert, for your words and works that brought healing and hope to so many of God's children.

A year ago at General Assembly in Murfreesboro, Tennessee, we remained fresh in the grief of our loss. Dr. Gilbert's death in November 2012 left an enormous void in the hearts of family, friends and the ministries he devoted so much of his life to serving. For us who continue to serve at the Cumberland Presbyterian Children's Home, that "great cloud of witnesses" encourages and inspires us to serve the children and families entrusted to our care today just as they have been served since Miss Victoria Jackson made possible the first campus of the Children's Home in Bowling Green now 110 years ago. So many faithful servants have helped give substance to her vision. Thank you, Miss Jackson, for your words and works that brought healing and hope to so many of God's children.

2013 was a humbling year for those of us at the Cumberland Presbyterian Children's Home. Yet our burdens were small compared to the burdens of those children and teenagers, those single moms and that single dad who lived on our campus. Compared to the burdens that were brought to our counseling rooms, our challenges were light. We sought to be God's face and hands to those who needed to hear the good news that they are loved and valuable beyond imagination. We sought to be the vehicle of God's blessing upon the lives of God's children in need. In the midst of our challenges we felt lifted up. Thanks be to God.

We invite you to join us in the midst of God's stirring at The Cumberland Presbyterian Children's Home. The challenges remain. Yet we rest upon the Lord to lead us and sustain us as we strive to serve as we have seen in the lives of those whose service has given us an example.

Respectfully Submitted,
Reverend Richard A. Brown, Esq., LCCA
President, CEO & General Counsel

GENERAL ASSEMBLY AGENCIES

I. OFFICE OF THE GENERAL ASSEMBLY

A. GENERAL ASSEMBLY OFFICE

	Revised 2014	Proposed 2015
INCOME		
Our United Outreach	$212,201	$212,201
Endowments/Interest	20,000	20,000
Interest on Cash Funds Management	2,500	2,500
Sales of yearbook/digest	2,000	2,000
Our United Outreach Committee	7,000	7,000
TOTAL INCOME	**$243,701**	**$243,701**
EXPENSE		
ECUMENICAL RELATIONS		
World Communion of Reformed Churches	$ 6,000	$ 6,000
CANAAC	2,000	2,000
Ecumenical Travel	1,000	1,000
Sub-Total	$ 9,000	$ 9,000
LIAISON WITH CHURCH		
General Assembly Meeting	$ 10,000	$ 10,000
Preliminary Minutes	5,000	5,000
GA Minutes/Mailing	500	500
Yearbook/Mailing	2,500	2,500
Travel/Moderator	8,500	8,500
Travel/Stated Clerk & Staff	8,500	8,500
Sub-Total	$ 35,000	$ 35,000
OFFICE		
Computer Supplies	$ 2,000	$ 2,000
Equipment/Supplies	2,500	2,500
Postage	2,000	2,000
Sub-Total	$ 6,500	$ 6,500
PERSONNEL		
Salaries/Housing	$139,420	$139,420
FICA (Asst to Stated Clerk)	4,300	4,300
Retirement	6,800	6,800
Health Insurance	30,000	30,000
Disability Insurance/Worker's Compensation	800	800
Sub-Total	$181,320	$181,320
STATED CLERK'S CONFERENCE/BOARD EXPENSE/ COMMITTEE EXPENSE		
Legal Fees / Clerk's Conference	$ 1,963	$ 1,963
Corporate Board Expense	2,000	2,000
Our United Outreach Committee	7,000	7,000
Sub-Total	$ 10,963	$ 10,963
TOTAL EXPENSE	**$236,201**	**$236,201**
From Reserves	$ 0	$ 0

B. GENERAL ASSEMBLY COMMISSIONS AND COMMITTEES

	Revised 2014	Proposed 2015
INCOME		
Contingency	$ 2,425	$ 2,425
Nominating Committee	2,629	2,629
Commission on Chaplains	8,934	8,934
Judiciary Committee	8,423	8,423
Theology and Social Concerns Committee	3,140	3,140
TOTAL INCOME	**$ 25,551**	**$ 25,551**

	Revised 2014	Proposed 2015
EXPENSE		
Contingency	$ 2,425	$ 2,425
Nominating Committee	2,629	2,629
Commission on Chaplains	8,934	8,934
Judiciary Committee	8,423	8,423
Theology and Social Concerns Committee	3,140	3,140
TOTAL EXPENSE	**$25,551**	**$ 25,551**

II. MINISTRY COUNCIL

	Revised 2014	Proposed 2015
INCOME		
Contributions		
Contributions/Gifts	$ 36,000	$ 78,400
ILP Contributions - unrestricted	**-	20,000
ILP Contributions Earnings - unrestricted	-	2,000
ILP Contributions - temporary restricted (MMT)	-	350,000
ILP Contributions Earnings - temporary restricted (MMT)	-	40,000
Endowment Contributions	-	185,000
Endowment Earnings	-	300,000
Fund Development	-	105,000
CarShare Program	25,200	-
Transfers		
Endowment Distributions	550,000	-
ILP Contributions - unrestricted	322,685	-
Our United Outreach		
OUO Income	1,311,270	1,368,000
In lieu of Our United Outreach	6,720	6,720
Events		
CP Youth Conference Fees	45,000	45,000
Pres. Youth Triennium Fees	***0	0
Youth Evangelism Conference	0	0
The Event	1,100	1,100
Forum Fees	3,000	3,000
Young Adult Conference	0	1,000
Children's Fest	1,000	0
Minister's Conference Fees	7,200	7,200
Writers Conference	5,000	10,000
WM Officers Retreat	2,000	2,000
New Program Iniatives: Sabbath Retreat	7,000	-
CPWM Convention Fees	8,000	12,000
Sales and Subscriptions		
Opening Doors	0	0
Encounter	94,500	94,500
Faith Out Loud	3,000	3,000
Ministry Council Cards	0	0
Publications/Stock for Resale	58,300	58,500
CP Resources Shipping	22,500	22,500
CP Magazine subscriptions	30,000	30,000
Sales (Planning Calendar)	8,000	8,000
Curriculum Resources	125,000	-
Grants	10,000	10,000
Congregational Websites	5,000	5,000
TOTAL INCOME	**$2,562,475**	**$2,767,920**

	Revised 2014	Proposed 2015
EXPENSE		
Salaries		
Salaries	$ 806,165	$ 877,923
Housing Allowance	123,315	131,136
Benefits		
Health Insurance	160,992	137,092
Retirement	46,024	46,561
FICA	42,798	43,234
Insurance/Disability	3,214	6,448
Events		
Conference/Event	215	15,215
CPWM Convention	12,000	12,000
WM Work Trip	0	2,500
Pres BOM/CW Officers Retreat	0	6,000
New Church Development/Cross-Culture Pastor's Retreat	2,000	4,000
CPWM Leadership Development	0	2,500
Rural Church Development	0	4,000
New Program Iniative: Support Ministries	2,000	5,000
New Program Iniative: Online Database	10,000	10,000
New Program Iniative: Children's CP Cirriculum	0	10,000
New Program Iniative: Sabbath Retreat	10,000	12,000
New Program Iniatives	18,000	29,400
The Forum	10,000	10,000
General Assembly	2,000	3,000
General Assembly Meals	500	500
Presbytery Meeting Visits material	500	1,100
The Event	5,000	5,000
Children's Fest	10,000	10,000
CP Youth Conference	50,100	50,100
Young Adult Ministry	8,000	9,000
Young Adult Conference	8,000	10,000
Youth Ministry Planning Council	4,000	4,000
Faith in 3D	5,000	10,000
Youth Evangelism Conference	8,000	13,000
Pres. Youth Triennium	5,000	5,000
Ministers' Conference	6,000	6,000
Clergy Crisis Support	6,000	6,000
Minister's Encouragement & Recognition	1,200	2,000
Missionary Recruitment/Prep 1:8	3,000	6,500
Writer's Conference	5,000	10,000
Team Expenses		
Elected Team Travel	48,750	49,900
MC/Elected Team Recognition	1,000	1,000
Publications		
Missionary Messenger - Printing	28,800	28,800
Missionary Messenger - Other/Postage	20,800	20,800
Missionary Messenger - Mailing Service	4,500	4,500
Educational Publications for Distribution	7,200	7,200
Web Dev./Maintenance	6,000	6,000
Electronic Publications	10,670	12,670
Forum Notes	750	750
These Days	0	0

	Revised 2014	Proposed 2015
Planning Calendar	$ 6,000	$ 6,000
Planning Calendar Postage	600	600
Resource Packets	2,300	2,800
Opening Doors	0	0
Encounter	42,750	42,750
Faith Out Loud	6,000	6,000
CP Magazine Publications	42,000	42,000
CP Magazine Postage	9,000	9,000
Photography	1,300	2,000
Resource Purchases		
Publications/Stock for Resale	30,500	30,500
CP Resources: Promotion	0	0
Contracted Services		
Legal	2,000	2,000
General Consultants	50,212	77,000
Temporary Help	28,793	26,100
Birthplace Shrine Chaplaincy	2,500	2,500
Missionary Support	218,447	170,000
Internship	12,000	0
Ecumenical Partnerships		
Church Women United	1,300	1,300
National Farm Worker	2,200	2,200
Project Vida	8,500	8,500
Coalition-Appalachian Ministries	11,500	11,500
Beth-El Farm Worker	40,000	35,000
Ecumenical Stewardship Center	4,500	4,500
Cooperative Uniform Series	1,000	1,000
Protestant Church Owned Publications Association	100	100
Ecumenical Youth Ministry Staff Team	500	500
CPCA Partnerships	1,700	3,700
Building and Maintenance		
Telephone/Internet	6,820	8,600
Rent Expense	-	2,400
Professional Development		
Staff Resources	5,200	10,700
Training Missionary Crisis Support	0	2,500
Subscriptions & Membership	1,900	1,900
Continuing Education	4,000	0
Payment/Subsidies		
Designated Control Disbursement	277,400	296,000
Scholarships	8,400	8,400
Choctaw Scholarships	3,500	3,500
Church Development Subsidies	-	-
Choctaw Field Budget	0	50,000
Church Paper Sunday	-	-
Colombia South America Missionary Council	-	-
Missionaires Office	-	-
ILP Withdrawal - unrestricted	0	0
ILP Withdrawal - temporary restricted (MMT)	0	0

	Revised 2014	Proposed 2015
International Representative Subsidies	$ -	$ -
Growth/Income Disbursements	0	0
Volunteers in Action	-	-
Congregational Websites	10,000	10,000
Presbytery Partnerships	500	1,000
Equipment		
Office Equipment	0	2,500
Office Equipment Maintenance	250	0
Computer Equipment	7,700	11,500
Computer Maintenance	0	0
Computer Software	5,600	7,100
Supplies		
Office Supplies	11,379	9,590
Postage/Shipping		
CP Resources Shipping	19,500	19,500
Postage	9,440	10,240
Employee Recognition		
Employee Recognition	3,840	3,840
Employee Incentives	5,000	-
Employee Events	1,000	1,500
Travel		
Staff Travel	110,608	130,000
CarShare Program	25,200	-
Vehicle - NEW	-	15,000
Vehicle Insurance & Maintenance - NEW	-	1,998
Vehicle Insurance & Maintenance - Dodge	-	1,998
Vehicle Insurance & Maintenance - Ford	-	1,998
WM Executive Com/Pres Expense	9,000	9,000
Convention Coordinator Travel	2,000	2,000
CPCA Travel to MC Meeting	1,500	-
Fund Development Travel & Materials	450	450
Advertising/Promotion		
Advertising & Promotion	2,000	2,000
Miscellaneous		
Annual Credit Card Fees	1,699	1,717
Credit Card Acceptance Fees	2,000	3,500
Government Fees (Annual Reports)	40	40
Relocation Expense	0	0
Transfers		
Endowment Transfers - Growth Income	0	0
Projects - Transfers In	0	0
TOTAL EXPENSES	**$2,562,306**	**$2,765,850**
Surplus/(Deficit)	$169	$2,070

* Symbol (-) depicts line items that have been added/removed to better reflect the budget as we continue to refine budgets.

** Zeros (0) depict a budgeted amount of $0

III. BOARD OF STEWARDSHIP

	Revised 2014	Proposed 2015
INCOME		
Contributions		
Contributions/Gifts	$ 2,000	$ 2,000
ILP Contributions	5,000	2,000
Endowment Contributions	55,000	60,000
Total Contributions	**62,000**	**64,000**
Our United Outreach	146,000	160,000
Investment Earnings		
Endowment Earnings	76,500	90,000
Total Investment Earnings	**76,500**	**90,000**
Service Fees		
Management Fees - Acct Coordinator	2,000	1,600
Management Fees	46,000	46,000
Total Service Fees	**48,000**	**47,600**
TOTAL INCOME	**$332,500**	**$ 361,600**
EXPENSE		
Salaries		
Salaries	$173,050	$ 181,703
Housing Allowance	20,000	21,000
Total Salaries	**193,050**	**202,703**
Benefits		
Health Insurance	70,000	75,000
Retirement	9,653	10,135
FICA	8,595	9,025
Insurance/Disability	5,000	5,000
Total Benefits	**93,248**	**99,160**
Events		
Conference/Events	500	500
Tax Guide for Ministers	3,000	3,100
Total Events	**3,500**	**3,600**
Board Expense		
Board/Agency Travel	13,500	12,500
Board/Agency Training	0	250
Board/Agency Recognition	0	550
Total Board Expense	**13,500**	**13,300**
Resource Purchases		
Subscriptions	100	100
Total Resources Purchases	**100**	**100**
Contracted Services		
Legal	500	500
Temporary Help	1,500	1,500
Total Contracted Services	**2,000**	**2,000**
Professional Development		
Subscriptions & Membership	2,000	2,000
Total Professional Development	**2,000**	**2,000**
Payment/Subsidies		
ESC Stewardship Expense	2,000	2,000
ILP Withdrawal	6,000	7,000
Endowment Distribution	1,000	2,000
Total Payments/Subsidies	**9,000**	**11,000**
Equipment		
Office Equipment	500	500
Computer Equipment	1,000	2,087
Computer Maintenance	0	150
Computer Software	500	500
Total Equipment	**2,000**	**3,237**

	Revised 2014	Proposed 2015
Supplies		
Computer Supplies	$ 1,000	$ 1,000
Office Supplies	3,502	3,500
Total Supplies	**4,502**	**4,500**
Postage/Shipping		
Postage	2,500	2,700
Shipping	500	500
Total Postage/Shipping	**3,000**	**3,200**
Employee Recognition		
Employee Recognition	1,000	1,200
Total Employee Recognition	**1,000**	**1,200**
Travel		
Staff Travel	5,000	15,000
Total Travel	**5,000**	**15,000**
Miscellaneous		
Miscellaneous	500	500
Total Miscellaneous	**500**	**500**
Organization		
Organizational Expense	100	100
Total Organization	**100**	**100**
TOTAL EXPENSE	**$332,500**	**$ 361,600**

IV. HISTORICAL FOUNDATION

	Revised 2014	Proposed 2015
INCOME		
Our United Outreach	$ 79,575	$ 79,575
Endowments	30,000	44,000
Gifts	10,000	9,000
ILP Earnings	6,000	6,000
Denomination Day Offering	5,000	5,000
TOTAL INCOME	**$ 130,575**	**$ 143,575**
EXPENSE		
Salaries	$ 83,264	$ 85,450
FICA / Retirement	12,860	14,542
Health, LTD, Dental & Vision Insurance	8,100	8,100
Board Travel	6,000	7,000
Legal Fees	200	200
Staff Training	300	500
Subscriptions/Memberships	1,000	1,000
Computer Supplies	300	500
Office Supplies	1,000	1,000
Postage	500	500
Acquisitions ILP	4,000	6,000
Photography	300	300
Birthplace Shrine	2,000	2,000
Employee Recognition	450	450
Staff Travel	5,000	7,000
Denomination Day Project	5,000	5,000
TOTAL EXPENSE	**$ 130,274**	**$ 139,542**

	Revised 2014	Proposed 2015

V. MEMPHIS THEOLOGICAL SEMINARY

REVENUE

Student Tuition Fees	$2,517,160	$ 2,926,825
Investment	335,834	379,280
Gifts and Grants	1,277,731	1,326,325
Other Revenues	226,338	93,919
TOTAL REVENUES	**$4,357,063**	**$ 4,726,349**

EXPENSES

Business Office	$ 280,648	$ 337,750
Dean's Office	123,107	145,446
Chapel	52,206	44,487
Formation For Ministry	115,801	117,311
Financial Leadership Ministry	0	76,325
Educational Development Committee	17,250	17,250
Advancement Office	283,458	314,617
Doctor of Ministry	67,970	66,920
Facilities	524,459	556,818
Faculty	826,643	916,026
Summer Classes	37,600	37,600
January Classes	11,000	11,000
Financial Aid	62,211	64,199
Information Technology	188,693	194,015
Library	195,347	220,958
President's Office	257,660	264,250
Admissions & Student Services	174,206	235,646
Registrar & Institutional Research	121,049	130,692
Public Relations	126,081	85,849
Communications	0	38,544
Student Housing	217,664	142,280
Certificate & Continuing Education	41,140	40,390
Student Government	3,255	3,255
Theology & Arts	94,617	23,288
Scholarships	433,478	562,473
Program of Alternate Studies	127,319	130,476
Depreciation	0	233,317
TOTAL EXPENSES	**$4,458,093**	**$4,993,182**
Increase (Decrease) in Net Assets	(101,030)	(266,833)

VI. SHARED SERVICES

	Revised 2014	Proposed 2015
REVENUE		
Our United Outreach	$ 416,504	337,131
TOTAL REVENUES	**$ 416,504**	**$ 337,131**
EXPENSES		
Salaries	$ 47,462	$ 48,601
Health Insurance	21,000	23,940
Retirement	2,373	2,430
FICA	3,623	3,718
Accounting Coordinator	1,600	1,600
Audit	20,000	20,000
Payroll Service	7,800	8,200
Bank Charges	15,000	15,000
Technology System Consultants - EMS	18,000	18,000
Technology System Consultants - Blackbaud	-	-
Software Maintenance Agreement - Blackbaud	13,200	13,200
Building & Maintenance	12,000	12,000
Pest Control	840	840
Lawn & Ground Maintenance	18,000	18,000
Lawn Treatment	-	1,500
Loan Interest	7,500	3,000
Computer Loan	38,049	38,049
Utilities - Building 1	22,866	23,552
Utilities - Building 2	15,244	15,701
Janitorial Service	8,100	8,100
Security System Monitoring	1,100	1,100
Trash Collection	1,850	1,850
Telephone/Internet	14,400	7,500
Heating & AC Maintenance Agreement	5,000	5,000
Building & Maintenance Debt - Union	54,000	-
Insurance/Liability	34,000	34,000
Office Equipment Maintenance	13,000	13,000
Computer Maintenance	3,000	3,000
Office Supplies	2,500	2,500
Postage	750	750
Employee Events	1,000	1,000
TOTAL EXPENSE	$ 403,257	$ 337,131
Surplus/Deficit	$ 13,247	$ 0

AUDITED FINANCIAL STATEMENTS OF

THE AGENCIES OF
THE CUMBERLAND PRESBYTERIAN
CHURCH CENTER

DECEMBER 31, 2013

THE AGENCIES OF
THE CUMBERLAND PRESBYTERIAN CHURCH CENTER

TABLE OF CONTENTS
DECEMBER 31, 2013

	PAGE
Independent Auditor's Report	1
Combined Statement of Financial Position	2
Combined Statement of Activity	3
Combined Statement of Cash Flows	4
Individual Statements of Financial Position	
Our United Outreach	5
General Assembly Corporation	6
Ministry Council	7
Shared Services	8
Historical Foundation	9
Board of Stewardship, Foundation, and Benefits	10
Small Church Loan Program	11
Insurance Program	12
Ministerial Aid	13
Investment Loan Program	14
Retirement Fund	15
Endowment Program	16
Individual Statements of Activity	
Our United Outreach	17
General Assembly Corporation	18
Ministry Council	19
Shared Services	20
Historical Foundation	21
Board of Stewardship, Foundation, and Benefits	22
Small Church Loan Program	23
Insurance Program	24
Ministerial Aid	25
Investment Loan Program	26
Retirement Fund	27
Endowment Program	28
Notes to Financial Statements	29 - 42

To the General Assembly Corporation
The Agencies of The Cumberland Presbyterian Church Center
Memphis, Tennessee

INDEPENDENT AUDITOR'S REPORT

We have audited the accompanying combined financial statements of The Agencies of The Cumberland Presbyterian Church Center, which comprise the combined statement of financial position as of December 31, 2013, and the related combined statements of activities and cash flows for the year then ended, and the related notes to the financial statements.

Management's Responsibility for the Financial Statements

Management is responsible for the preparation and fair presentation of these financial statements in accordance with accounting principles generally accepted in the United States of America; this includes the design, implementation, and maintenance of internal control relevant to the preparation and fair presentation of financial statements that are free from material misstatement, whether due to fraud or error.

Auditor's Responsibility

Our responsibility is to express an opinion on these financial statements based on our audit. We conducted our audit in accordance with auditing standards generally accepted in the United States of America. Those standards require that we plan and perform the audit to obtain reasonable assurance about whether the financial statements are free from material misstatement.

An audit involves performing procedures to obtain audit evidence about the amounts and disclosures in the financial statements. The procedures selected depend on the auditor's judgment, including the assessment of the risks of material misstatement of the financial statements, whether due to fraud or error. In making those risk assessments, the auditor considers internal control relevant to the entity's preparation and fair presentation of the financial statements in order to design audit procedures that are appropriate in the circumstances, but not for the purpose of expressing an opinion on the effectiveness of the entity's internal control. Accordingly, we express no such opinion. An audit also includes evaluating the appropriateness of accounting policies used and the reasonableness of significant accounting estimates made by management, as well as evaluating the overall presentation of the financial statements.

We believe that the audit evidence we have obtained is sufficient and appropriate to provide a basis for our audit opinion.

Opinion

In our opinion, the combined financial statements referred to above present fairly, in all material respects, the individual and combined financial position of The Agencies of The Cumberland Presbyterian Church Center as of December 31, 2013, and the changes in their net assets and their cash flows for the year then ended in accordance with accounting principles generally accepted in the United States of America.

FOUTS & MORGAN
Certified Public Accountants

Memphis, Tennessee
May 27, 2014

THE AGENCIES OF
THE CUMBERLAND PRESBYTERIAN CHURCH CENTER

COMBINED STATEMENT OF FINANCIAL POSITION
DECEMBER 31, 2013

ASSETS

Cash	$ 664,663
Due from other agencies, boards, and divisions	6,048,406
Accounts receivable	12,631
Interest and dividends receivable, net of allowance for uncollectible interest	91,106
Health insurance tax credit receivable	44,516
Securities and investments	
Cash and cash equivalents	4,913,439
Mortgage backed securities	6,690,189
Bond mutual funds	9,385,365
Closed-end bond funds	3,153,887
Equity mutual funds	1,758,892
Real estate investment trusts	4,777,111
Private investment entities	52,250,400
Real estate	90,573
Inventory - at lower of cost or market	1,371
Prepaid expenses	6,422
Loans receivable, net of allowance for loan losses	12,591,380
Buildings and land	2,760,412
Furniture and equipment	156,745
Less: accumulated depreciation	(548,482)
Total Assets	**$ 104,849,026**

LIABILITIES AND NET ASSETS

Liabilities:	
Accounts payable	$ 2,371
Accrued expenses	46
Notes payable to individual investors	790,635
Unearned subscriptions	11,675
Due to other agencies, boards, and divisions	6,376,361
Funds held in trust for others	32,505
Depository accounts held for church organizations	9,338,177
Total liabilities	16,551,770
Net Assets:	
Unrestricted	6,513,212
Temporarily restricted	2,907,634
Permanently restricted	56,015,419
Net assets available for benefits, at fair value	22,860,991
Total net assets	88,297,256
Total Liabilities and Net Assets	**$ 104,849,026**

See accompanying notes.

THE AGENCIES OF
THE CUMBERLAND PRESBYTERIAN CHURCH CENTER

COMBINED STATEMENT OF ACTIVITY
FOR THE YEAR ENDED DECEMBER 31, 2013

	Unrestricted	Temporarily Restricted	Permanently Restricted	Net Assets Available for Benefits	Totals
Revenues, gains, and other support:					
Contributions and gifts	$ 3,159,914	$ 306,612	$ 1,277,448	$ -	$ 4,743,974
Insurance program premium revenue	2,145,692	-	-	-	2,145,692
Endowment earnings	-	-	740,161	-	740,161
Interest and dividend income	242,248	76,988	14,302	189,944	523,482
Management service fees	47,614	-	-	(16,222)	31,392
Registration fees	156,599	-	-	-	156,599
Sales and subscription income	222,987	-	-	-	222,987
Net realized and unrealized gain on investments	(540,227)	-	6,204,208	2,456,153	8,120,134
Other income	77,732	-	-	-	77,732
Participant retirement contributions	-	-	-	610,467	610,467
Net assets released from restriction	1,467,709	(364,194)	(1,103,515)	-	-
Total revenues, gains, and other support	6,980,268	19,406	7,132,604	3,240,342	17,372,620
Provision for loan losses	33,000	-	-	-	33,000
Net revenues, gains, and other support - after provision	7,013,268	19,406	7,132,604	3,240,342	17,405,620
Expenses:					
Our United Outreach	559,509	-	-	-	559,509
General Assembly Corporation	373,848	-	-	-	373,848
Ministry Council	3,062,933	-	-	-	3,062,933
Shared Services	399,225	-	-	-	399,225
Historical Foundation	166,351	-	-	-	166,351
Board of Stewardship, Foundation and Benefits	269,107	-	-	-	269,107
Small Church Loan Program	50,439	-	-	-	50,439
Insurance Program	2,230,291	-	-	-	2,230,291
Ministerial Aid	74,350	-	-	-	74,350
Investment Loan Program	54,886	-	-	-	54,886
Retirement Fund	-	-	-	834,081	834,081
Endowment Program	-	-	2,523,173	-	2,523,173
Total expenses	7,240,939	-	2,523,173	834,081	10,598,193
Change in net assets	(227,671)	19,406	4,609,431	2,406,261	6,807,427
Net assets at beginning of year	6,740,883	2,888,228	51,405,988	20,454,730	81,489,829
Net assets at end of year	$ 6,513,212	$ 2,907,634	$ 56,015,419	$ 22,860,991	$ 88,297,256

See accompanying notes.

THE AGENCIES OF
THE CUMBERLAND PRESBYTERIAN CHURCH CENTER

COMBINED STATEMENT OF CASH FLOWS
FOR THE YEAR ENDED DECEMBER 31, 2013

Cash flows from operating activities	
Combined change in net assets	$ 6,807,427
Adjustments to reconcile combined change in net assets to net cash used in operating activities:	
Depreciation	92,994
Net realized/unrealized (gain) loss on investments - Investment Loan Program	648,228
Net realized/unrealized (gain) loss on investments - Retirement Fund	(2,456,152)
Net realized/unrealized (gain) loss on investments - Endowment Program	(6,203,724)
Provision for loan losses	(33,000)
(Increase) decrease in operating assets:	
Due from other agencies, boards, and divisions	83,706
Accounts receivable	79,180
Interest and dividends receivable	82,416
Health insurance tax credit receivable	(14,824)
Prepaid assets	(542)
Increase (decrease) in operating liabilities:	
Accounts payable	(22,755)
Accrued expenses	34
Unearned subscriptions	(4,629)
Due to other agencies, boards, and divisions	87,941
Unallocated earnings	(33)
Funds held in trust for others	2,173
Notes payable to individual investors	386,055
Depository accounts held for church organizations	422,645
Net cash provided by (used in) operating activities	(42,860)
Cash flows from investing activities	
Proceeds from sale of investments:	
Endowment Program	25,483,830
Retirement Fund	8,439,377
Investment Loan Program	7,319,874
Purchase of investments:	
Endowment Program	(25,462,907)
Retirement Fund	(8,408,625)
Investment Loan Program	(8,611,580)
Loan principal payments received	1,387,637
Loan principal disbursed	(142,000)
Net cash provided by (used in) investing activities	5,606
Net increase (decrease) in cash	(37,254)
Cash at the beginning of the year	701,917
Cash at the end of the year	$ 664,663

See accompanying notes.

THE AGENCIES OF
THE CUMBERLAND PRESBYTERIAN CHURCH CENTER
OUR UNITED OUTREACH
STATEMENT OF FINANCIAL POSITION
DECEMBER 31, 2013

ASSETS

Endowment earnings receivable	$ 41,865
Endowments - held by Endowment Program	2,468,487
Total Assets	$ 2,510,352

LIABILITIES AND NET ASSETS

Liabilities:	
Cash borrowed from other agencies, boards, and divisions	$ 10,547
Due to outside church organizations	55,455
Total liabilities	66,002
Net Assets:	
Unrestricted	(24,137)
Permanently restricted	2,468,487
Total net assets	2,444,350
Total Liabilities and Net Assets	$ 2,510,352

See accompanying notes.

THE AGENCIES OF
THE CUMBERLAND PRESBYTERIAN CHURCH CENTER
GENERAL ASSEMBLY CORPORATION
STATEMENT OF FINANCIAL POSITION
DECEMBER 31, 2013

ASSETS

Endowment earnings receivable	$	5,345
Health insurance tax credit receivable		9,318
Inventory		1,371
Due from other agencies, boards, and divisions		129,931
		145,965
Endowments - held by Endowment Program		466,565
Total Assets	$	612,530

LIABILITIES AND NET ASSETS

Liabilities:		
Accounts payable	$	822
Cash borrowed from other agencies, boards, and divisions		192,499
Due to other agencies, boards, and divisions		13,339
Funds held in trusts for others		32,505
Total liabilities		239,165
Net Assets:		
Unrestricted		(93,200)
Permanently restricted		466,565
Total net assets		373,365
Total Liabilities and Net Assets	$	612,530

See accompanying notes.

THE AGENCIES OF
THE CUMBERLAND PRESBYTERIAN CHURCH CENTER
MINISTRY COUNCIL
STATEMENT OF FINANCIAL POSITION
DECEMBER 31, 2013

ASSETS

Cash	$ 24,057
Accounts receivable	7,855
Endowment earnings receivable	153,289
Health insurance tax credit receivable	21,734
Due from other agencies, boards, and divisions	3,175,144
Securities and investments	
Real estate	51,818
	3,433,897
Endowments - held by Endowment Program	15,088,642
Total Assets	$ 18,522,539

LIABILITIES AND NET ASSETS

Liabilities:	
Accounts payable	$ 806
Accrued expenses	46
Unearned subscriptions	11,675
Total liabilities	12,527
Net Assets:	
Unrestricted	698,139
Temporarily restricted	2,723,230
Permanently restricted	15,088,643
Total net assets	18,510,012
Total Liabilities and Net Assets	$ 18,522,539

See accompanying notes.

THE AGENCIES OF
THE CUMBERLAND PRESBYTERIAN CHURCH CENTER
SHARED SERVICES
STATEMENT OF FINANCIAL POSITION
DECEMBER 31, 2013

ASSETS

Cash	$	34,994
Accounts receivable		1,835
Buildings and land		2,760,412
Less: accumulated depreciation		(391,737)
Furniture and equipment		156,745
Less: accumulated depreciation		(156,745)
Total Assets	$	2,405,504

LIABILITIES AND NET ASSETS

Liabilities:		
Due to other agencies, boards, and divisions	$	236,205
Net Assets:		
Unrestricted		2,169,299
Total Liabilities and Net Assets	$	2,405,504

See accompanying notes.

THE AGENCIES OF
THE CUMBERLAND PRESBYTERIAN CHURCH CENTER
HISTORICAL FOUNDATION
STATEMENT OF FINANCIAL POSITION
DECEMBER 31, 2013

ASSETS

Cash	$	48,940
Endowment earnings receivable		15,605
Health insurance tax credit receivable		1,326
Due from other agencies, boards, and divisions		178,749
Securities and investments		
Real estate		38,755
		283,375
Endowments - held by Endowment Program		1,460,756
Total Assets	$	1,744,131

LIABILITIES AND NET ASSETS

Net Assets:		
Unrestricted	$	59,963
Temporarily restricted		184,404
Permanently restricted		1,499,764
Total net assets		1,744,131
Total Liabilities and Net Assets	$	1,744,131

See accompanying notes.

THE AGENCIES OF
THE CUMBERLAND PRESBYTERIAN CHURCH CENTER
BOARD OF STEWARDSHIP, FOUNDATION, AND BENEFITS
STATEMENT OF FINANCIAL POSITION
DECEMBER 31, 2013

ASSETS

Endowment earnings receivable	$ 20,386
Health insurance tax credit receivable	12,138
Due from other agencies, boards, and divisions	456,486
	489,010
Endowments - held by Endowment Program	1,935,307
Total Assets	$ 2,424,317

LIABILITIES AND NET ASSETS

Liabilities:	
Cash borrowed from other agencies, boards, and divisions	$ 32,209
Net Assets:	
Unrestricted	456,801
Permanently restricted	1,935,307
Total net assets	2,392,108
Total Liabilities and Net Assets	$ 2,424,317

See accompanying notes.

THE AGENCIES OF
THE CUMBERLAND PRESBYTERIAN CHURCH CENTER
SMALL CHURCH LOAN PROGRAM
STATEMENT OF FINANCIAL POSITION
DECEMBER 31, 2013

ASSETS

Interest receivable, net of allowance for uncollectible interest	$ 954
Loans receivable, net of allowance for loan losses	172,425
Due from other agencies, boards, and divisions	229,376
Total Assets	$ 402,755

LIABILITIES AND NET ASSETS

Net Assets:	
Permanently restricted	$ 402,755
Total Liabilities and Net Assets	$ 402,755

See accompanying notes.

THE AGENCIES OF
THE CUMBERLAND PRESBYTERIAN CHURCH CENTER
INSURANCE PROGRAM
STATEMENT OF FINANCIAL POSITION
DECEMBER 31, 2013

ASSETS

Cash	$	171,673
Accounts receivable		2,943
Prepaid expenses		6,422
Due from other agencies, boards, and divisions		1,066,461
Total Assets	$	1,247,499

LIABILITIES AND NET ASSETS

Liabilities:		
Accounts payable	$	743
Net Assets:		
Unrestricted		1,246,756
Total Liabilities and Net Assets	$	1,247,499

See accompanying notes.

THE AGENCIES OF
THE CUMBERLAND PRESBYTERIAN CHURCH CENTER
MINISTERIAL AID
STATEMENT OF FINANCIAL POSITION
DECEMBER 31, 2013

ASSETS

Cash	$ 64,379
Endowment earnings receivable	14,721
Due from other agencies, boards, and divisions	312,843
	391,943
Endowment Funds - held by Endowment Program	3,965,289
Total Assets	$ 4,357,232

LIABILITIES AND NET ASSETS

Net Assets:	
Unrestricted	$ 391,943
Permanently restricted	3,965,289
Total net assets	4,357,232
Total Liabilities and Net Assets	$ 4,357,232

See accompanying notes.

THE AGENCIES OF
THE CUMBERLAND PRESBYTERIAN CHURCH CENTER
INVESTMENT LOAN PROGRAM
STATEMENT OF FINANCIAL POSITION
DECEMBER 31, 2013

ASSETS

Interest and dividends receivable, net of allowance for uncollectible interest	$	30,672
Securities and investments		
Cash equivalents		1,792,350
Bonds and mortgage backed securities		6,690,189
Loans receivable, net of allowance for loan losses		7,794,394
Total Assets	$	16,307,605

LIABILITIES AND NET ASSETS

Liabilities:		
Notes payable to individual investors	$	790,635
Due to other agencies, boards, and divisions		4,571,145
Depository accounts held for church organizations		9,338,177
Total liabilities		14,699,957
Net Assets:		
Unrestricted		1,607,648
Total Liabilities and Net Assets	$	16,307,605

See accompanying notes.

THE AGENCIES OF
THE CUMBERLAND PRESBYTERIAN CHURCH CENTER
RETIREMENT FUND
STATEMENT OF FINANCIAL POSITION
DECEMBER 31, 2013

ASSETS

Interest and dividends receivable, net of allowance for uncollectible interest	$ 16,365
Securities and investments	
Cash and cash equivalents	1,460,571
Bond mutual funds	2,905,775
Closed-end bond funds	1,017,383
Equity mutual funds	549,887
Real estate investment trusts	1,121,148
Private investment entities	15,789,862
Total Assets	$ 22,860,991

LIABILITIES AND NET ASSETS

Net Assets:	
Net assets available for benefits, at fair value	$ 22,860,991
Total net assets	22,860,991
Total Liabilities and Net Assets	$ 22,860,991

See accompanying notes.

THE AGENCIES OF
THE CUMBERLAND PRESBYTERIAN CHURCH CENTER
ENDOWMENT PROGRAM
STATEMENT OF FINANCIAL POSITION
DECEMBER 31, 2013

ASSETS

Cash equivalents	$ 555,875
Due from other agencies, boards, and divisions	248,205
Interest and dividends receivable, net of allowance for uncollectible interest	43,115
Securities and investments	
Cash equivalents	1,660,518
Bond mutual funds	6,479,590
Closed-end bond funds	2,136,504
Equity mutual funds	1,209,005
Real estate investment trusts	3,655,963
Private investment entities	36,460,538
Loans receivable, net of allowance for loan losses	4,624,561
	57,073,874
Less: net endowment assets of The Agencies of The Cumberland Presbyterian Church Center, as reflected on separate statements of financial position	(25,385,048)
Total Assets	$ 31,688,826

LIABILITIES AND NET ASSETS

Liabilities:	
Due to other agencies, boards, and divisions	$ 1,500,217
Net Assets:	
Permanently restricted:	
Cumberland Presbyterian Children's Home	6,806,618
Discipleship Ministry Team	2,083,987
Missions Ministry Team	12,656,072
Memphis Theological Seminary	9,677,003
Board of Stewardship, Foundation, and Benefits	1,935,309
Our United Outreach	2,468,488
General Assembly Corporation	466,565
Communications Ministry Team	108,638
Pastoral Development Ministry Team	239,944
The Historical Foundation	1,460,756
Ministerial Aid	3,965,289
Bethel University	2,997,983
Other designated persons and organizations	10,707,005
Total net assets	55,573,657
Less: net endowment assets of The Agencies of The Cumberland Presbyterian Church Center, as reflected on separate statements of financial position	(25,385,048)
Total Liabilities and Net Assets	$ 31,688,826

See accompanying notes.

THE AGENCIES OF
THE CUMBERLAND PRESBYTERIAN CHURCH CENTER
OUR UNITED OUTREACH
STATEMENT OF ACTIVITY
FOR THE YEAR ENDED DECEMBER 31, 2013

	Unrestricted	Temporarily Restricted	Permanently Restricted	Totals
Revenues, gains, and other support:				
Contributions	$ 2,441,242	$ -	$ 97,459	$ 2,538,701
Endowment earnings	-	-	29,891	29,891
Income from oil royalties	25,392	-	-	25,392
Net realized and unrealized gain on investments	-	-	260,367	260,367
Net assets released from restriction	102,594	-	(102,594)	-
	2,569,228	-	285,123	2,854,351
Expenses:				
Distribution to other agencies, boards, and divisions of The Cumberland Presbyterian Church:				
Bethel University	114,610	-	-	114,610
Board of Stewardship	137,531	-	-	137,531
Commission on Chaplains	8,023	-	-	8,023
Committee on Theology and Social Concern	2,820	-	-	2,820
Committee on Judiciary	7,564	-	-	7,564
Communications Ministry Team	253,690	-	-	253,690
Contingency Fund	2,178	-	-	2,178
Cumberland Presbyterian Children's Home	68,765	-	-	68,765
Discipleship Ministry Team	282,875	-	-	282,875
General Assembly Council	183,376	-	-	183,376
Historical Foundation	68,765	-	-	68,765
Memphis Theological Seminary	131,572	-	-	131,572
Ministry Council	136,278	-	-	136,278
Missions Ministry Team	372,676	-	-	372,676
Nominating Committee	2,361	-	-	2,361
OGA - Contingency Loan	168,492	-	-	168,492
Pastoral Development Ministry Team	100,578	-	-	100,578
Program of Alternate Studies	28,881	-	-	28,881
Shared Service (Accounting)	58,242	-	-	58,242
Shared Service (Computer Tech)	63,982	-	-	63,982
Shared Service (Maintenance/Operations)	198,324	-	-	198,324
Shared Service (Old Building)	69,126	-	-	69,126
Shared Service (OUO Committee)	79,000	-	-	79,000
Property tax	4,389	-	-	4,389
	2,544,098	-	-	2,544,098
Change in net assets	25,130	-	285,123	310,253
Net assets at beginning of year	(49,267)	-	2,183,364	2,134,097
Net assets at end of year	$ (24,137)	$ -	$ 2,468,487	$ 2,444,350

See accompanying notes.

THE AGENCIES OF
THE CUMBERLAND PRESBYTERIAN CHURCH CENTER
GENERAL ASSEMBLY CORPORATION
STATEMENT OF ACTIVITY
FOR THE YEAR ENDED DECEMBER 31, 2013

	Unrestricted	Temporarily Restricted	Permanently Restricted	Totals
Revenues, gains, and other support:				
Our United Outreach	$ 183,376	$ -	$ -	$ 183,376
Contributions and gifts	93,630	-	-	93,630
Endowment earnings	21,141	-	-	21,141
Interest income	2,968	-	-	2,968
Other income	52,340	-	-	52,340
Net realized and unrealized gain on investments	-	-	50,338	50,338
Net assets released from restriction	15,367	-	(15,367)	-
	368,822	-	34,971	403,793
Expenses:				
Conferences and events	39,930	-	-	39,930
Employee benefits	31,117	-	-	31,117
Equipment maintenance	1,729	-	-	1,729
Grants made	80,371	-	-	80,371
Miscellaneous	78	-	-	78
Office expense	1,949	-	-	1,949
Payroll taxes	4,188	-	-	4,188
Postage and shipping	1,814	-	-	1,814
Printing and publications	1,210	-	-	1,210
Retirement	8,213	-	-	8,213
Salaries	181,938	-	-	181,938
Supplies	705	-	-	705
Travel	20,606	-	-	20,606
Total expenses	373,848	-	-	373,848
Change in net assets	(5,026)	-	34,971	29,945
Net assets at beginning of year	(88,174)	-	431,594	343,420
Net assets at end of year	$ (93,200)	$ -	$ 466,565	$ 373,365

See accompanying notes.

THE AGENCIES OF
THE CUMBERLAND PRESBYTERIAN CHURCH CENTER
MINISTRY COUNCIL
STATEMENT OF ACTIVITY
FOR THE YEAR ENDED DECEMBER 31, 2013

	Unrestricted	Temporarily Restricted	Permanently Restricted	Totals
Revenues, gains, and other support:				
Our United Outreach	$ 1,205,243	$ -	$ -	$ 1,205,243
Contributions	-	278,481	152,403	430,884
Endowment earnings	60,253	-	185,004	245,257
Gifts - designated	85,169	-	-	85,169
Gifts - undesignated	347,520	-	-	347,520
Interest income	16,037	71,212	-	87,249
Registration fees	156,599	-	-	156,599
Sales of materials, literature, etc.	183,020	-	-	183,020
Subscription income	39,967	-	-	39,967
Net realized and unrealized gain on investments	-	-	1,614,768	1,614,768
Net assets released from restrictions	932,769	(316,084)	(616,685)	-
	3,026,577	33,609	1,335,490	4,395,676
Expenses:				
Automobile expenses	3,241	-	-	3,241
Computer expenses	12,670	-	-	12,670
Conferences and events	231,314	-	-	231,314
Consulting fees	30,973	-	-	30,973
Contract labor	20,855	-	-	20,855
Dues and subscriptions	468	-	-	468
Employee benefits	173,932	-	-	173,932
Equipment maintenance	480	-	-	480
Grants made	802,689	-	-	802,689
Miscellaneous expense	20,954	-	-	20,954
Missionary support	290,936	-	-	290,936
Occupancy expenses	42	-	-	42
Office expense	1,802	-	-	1,802
Payroll taxes	39,110	-	-	39,110
Postage and shipping	44,178	-	-	44,178
Printing and publications	150,860	-	-	150,860
Purchases for resale	55,628	-	-	55,628
Rent expense	383	-	-	383
Retirement	44,222	-	-	44,222
Salaries	934,726	-	-	934,726
Supplies	14,691	-	-	14,691
Telephone	3,812	-	-	3,812
Training expenses	3,803	-	-	3,803
Travel expenses	181,164	-	-	181,164
Total expenses	3,062,933	-	-	3,062,933
Change in net assets	(36,356)	33,609	1,335,490	1,332,743
Net assets at beginning of year	734,495	2,689,621	13,753,153	17,177,269
Net assets at end of year	$ 698,139	$ 2,723,230	$ 15,088,643	$ 18,510,012

See accompanying notes.

THE AGENCIES OF
THE CUMBERLAND PRESBYTERIAN CHURCH CENTER
SHARED SERVICES
STATEMENT OF ACTIVITY
FOR THE YEAR ENDED DECEMBER 31, 2013

	Unrestricted	Temporarily Restricted	Permanently Restricted	Totals
Revenues, gains, and other support:				
Our United Outreach	$ 389,674	$ -	$ -	$ 389,674
Gifts	169,793	-	-	169,793
	559,467	-	-	559,467
Expenses:				
Accounting fees	18,760	-	-	18,760
Bank fees	15,616	-	-	15,616
Computer expenses	2,118	-	-	2,118
Consulting fees	36,313	-	-	36,313
Depreciation expense	92,994	-	-	92,994
Employee benefits	21,612	-	-	21,612
Equipment maintenance	17,357	-	-	17,357
Insurance expense	33,046	-	-	33,046
Interest expense	17,039	-	-	17,039
Legal fees	510	-	-	510
Occupancy expenses	72,474	-	-	72,474
Office expense	95	-	-	95
Payroll taxes	3,546	-	-	3,546
Postage and shipping	733	-	-	733
Retirement	2,318	-	-	2,318
Salaries	46,350	-	-	46,350
Supplies	2,758	-	-	2,758
Telephone	15,586	-	-	15,586
Total expenses	399,225	-	-	399,225
Change in net assets	160,242	-	-	160,242
Net assets at beginning of year	2,009,057	-	-	2,009,057
Net assets at end of year	$ 2,169,299	$ -	$ -	$ 2,169,299

See accompanying notes.

THE AGENCIES OF
THE CUMBERLAND PRESBYTERIAN CHURCH CENTER
HISTORICAL FOUNDATION
STATEMENT OF ACTIVITY
FOR THE YEAR ENDED DECEMBER 31, 2013

	Unrestricted	Temporarily Restricted	Permanently Restricted	Totals
Revenues, gains, and other support:				
Our United Outreach	$ 68,765	$ -	$ -	$ 68,765
Contributions and gifts	11,908	28,131	16,594	56,633
Endowment earnings	-	-	17,953	17,953
Interest income	-	5,776	-	5,776
Net realized and unrealized gain on investments	-	-	156,431	156,431
Net assets released from restriction	109,207	(48,110)	(61,097)	-
	189,880	(14,203)	129,881	305,558
Expenses:				
Archival acquisitions	29,117	-	-	29,117
Archival equipment	10,479	-	-	10,479
Birthplace shrine	3,854	-	-	3,854
Computer equipment and supplies	1,848	-	-	1,848
Conferences and events	100	-	-	100
Contract labor	350	-	-	350
Dues and subscriptions	1,028	-	-	1,028
Employee benefits	7,349	-	-	7,349
Insurance expense	1,303	-	-	1,303
Legal fees	1,347	-	-	1,347
Payroll taxes	5,728	-	-	5,728
Postage and shipping	641	-	-	641
Printing and publications	482	-	-	482
Purchases for resale	353	-	-	353
Retirement	6,742	-	-	6,742
Salaries	74,873	-	-	74,873
Supplies	595	-	-	595
Training expenses	2,848	-	-	2,848
Travel expenses	17,314	-	-	17,314
Total expenses	166,351	-	-	166,351
Change in net assets	23,529	(14,203)	129,881	139,207
Net assets at beginning of year	36,434	198,607	1,369,883	1,604,924
Net assets at end of year	$ 59,963	$ 184,404	$ 1,499,764	$ 1,744,131

See accompanying notes.

THE AGENCIES OF
THE CUMBERLAND PRESBYTERIAN CHURCH CENTER
BOARD OF STEWARDSHIP, FOUNDATION AND BENEFITS
STATEMENT OF ACTIVITY
FOR THE YEAR ENDED DECEMBER 31, 2013

	Unrestricted	Temporarily Restricted	Permanently Restricted	Totals
Revenues, gains, and other support:				
Our United Outreach	$ 137,531	$ -	$ -	$ 137,531
Contributions and gifts	3,617	-	122,200	125,817
Endowment earnings	5,623	-	22,817	28,440
Interest income	14,101	-	-	14,101
Management service fees	47,614	-	-	47,614
Net realized and unrealized gain on investments	-	-	199,790	199,790
Net assets released from restriction	79,264	-	(79,264)	-
	287,750	-	265,543	553,293
Expenses:				
Accounting	575	-	-	575
Computer expenses	578	-	-	578
Contract labor	1,706	-	-	1,706
Dues and subscriptions	2,000	-	-	2,000
Employee benefits	53,690	-	-	53,690
Grants made	14,239	-	-	14,239
Legal	116	-	-	116
Miscellaneous	501	-	-	501
Payroll taxes	6,363	-	-	6,363
Postage and shipping	2,600	-	-	2,600
Printing and publications	2,809	-	-	2,809
Relocation expenses	83	-	-	83
Retirement	7,930	-	-	7,930
Salaries	157,786	-	-	157,786
Stewardship fees	2,000	-	-	2,000
Stewardship materials and events	302	-	-	302
Supplies	2,796	-	-	2,796
Travel and board meetings	13,033	-	-	13,033
Total expenses	269,107	-	-	269,107
Change in net assets	18,643	-	265,543	284,186
Net assets at beginning of year	438,158	-	1,669,764	2,107,922
Net assets at end of year	$ 456,801	$ -	$ 1,935,307	$ 2,392,108

See accompanying notes.

THE AGENCIES OF
THE CUMBERLAND PRESBYTERIAN CHURCH CENTER
SMALL CHURCH LOAN PROGRAM
STATEMENT OF ACTIVITY
FOR THE YEAR ENDED DECEMBER 31, 2013

	Unrestricted	Temporarily Restricted	Permanently Restricted	Totals
Revenues, gains, and other support:				
Contributions	$ -	$ -	$ 50,739	$ 50,739
Interest income	-	-	14,302	14,302
Net assets released from restriction	50,439	-	(50,439)	-
	50,439	-	14,602	65,041
Expenses:				
Distribution to other agencies, boards, and divisions of The Cumberland Presbyterian Church:				
Investment Loan Program	50,439	-	-	50,439
Change in net assets	-	-	14,602	14,602
Net assets at beginning of year	-	-	388,153	388,153
Net assets at end of year	$ -	$ -	$ 402,755	$ 402,755

See accompanying notes.

23

THE AGENCIES OF
THE CUMBERLAND PRESBYTERIAN CHURCH CENTER
INSURANCE PROGRAM
STATEMENT OF ACTIVITY
FOR THE YEAR ENDED DECEMBER 31, 2013

	Unrestricted	Temporarily Restricted	Permanently Restricted	Totals
Revenues, gains, and other support:				
Premium revenue	$ 2,145,692	$ -	$ -	$ 2,145,692
Contributions	5,810	-	-	5,810
Interest income	14,739	-	-	14,739
Net realized gain on investments	(3,175)	-	-	(3,175)
Net unrealized gain on investments	111,176	-	-	111,176
	2,274,242	-	-	2,274,242
Expenses:				
Insurance premiums	2,204,083	-	-	2,204,083
Payroll taxes	1,670	-	-	1,670
Postage and shipping	812	-	-	812
Retirement	1,091	-	-	1,091
Salaries	22,635	-	-	22,635
Total expenses	2,230,291	-	-	2,230,291
Change in net assets	43,951	-	-	43,951
Net assets at beginning of year	1,202,805	-	-	1,202,805
Net assets at end of year	$ 1,246,756	$ -	$ -	$ 1,246,756

See accompanying notes.

THE AGENCIES OF
THE CUMBERLAND PRESBYTERIAN CHURCH CENTER
MINISTERIAL AID
STATEMENT OF ACTIVITY
FOR THE YEAR ENDED DECEMBER 31, 2013

	Unrestricted	Temporarily Restricted	Permanently Restricted	Totals
Revenues, gains, and other support:				
Contributions	$ 1,225	$ -	$ 30,000	$ 31,225
Endowment earnings	-	-	48,061	48,061
Interest income	9,234	-	-	9,234
Net realized and unrealized gain on investments	-	-	418,936	418,936
Net assets released from restriction	91,052	-	(91,052)	-
	101,511	-	405,945	507,456
Expenses:				
Ministerial aid	72,550	-	-	72,550
Retirement resident distribution	1,800	-	-	1,800
Total expenses	74,350	-	-	74,350
Change in net assets	27,161	-	405,945	433,106
Net assets at beginning of year	364,782	-	3,559,344	3,924,126
Net assets at end of year	$ 391,943	$ -	$ 3,965,289	$ 4,357,232

See accompanying notes.

THE AGENCIES OF
THE CUMBERLAND PRESBYTERIAN CHURCH CENTER
INVESTMENT LOAN PROGRAM
STATEMENT OF ACTIVITY
FOR THE YEAR ENDED DECEMBER 31, 2013

	Unrestricted	Temporarily Restricted	Permanently Restricted	Totals
Revenues, gains, and other support:				
Interest income	$ 610,324	$ -	$ -	$ 610,324
Interest expense	(425,155)	-	-	(425,155)
Net interest income - before provision	185,169	-	-	185,169
Provision for loan losses	33,000	-	-	33,000
Net interest income - after provision	218,169	-	-	218,169
Net gain (loss) on investments	(648,228)	-	-	(648,228)
	(430,059)	-	-	(430,059)
Expenses:				
Accounting fees	4,725	-	-	4,725
Legal fees	4,003	-	-	4,003
Management fee	46,000	-	-	46,000
Office expenses	112	-	-	112
Postage and shipping	46	-	-	46
Total expenses	54,886	-	-	54,886
Change in net assets	(484,945)	-	-	(484,945)
Net assets at beginning of year	2,092,593	-	-	2,092,593
Net assets at end of year	$ 1,607,648	$ -	$ -	$ 1,607,648

See accompanying notes.

THE AGENCIES OF
THE CUMBERLAND PRESBYTERIAN CHURCH CENTER
RETIREMENT FUND
STATEMENT OF ACTIVITY
FOR THE YEAR ENDED DECEMBER 31, 2013

	Net Assets Available for Benefits
Additions to Net Assets attributed to:	
Investment income:	
Interest and dividend income	$ 189,944
Management service fees	(16,222)
Net realized gain on investments	30,910
Net unrealized gain on investments	2,425,243
Net investment income	2,629,875
Contributions:	
Contributions by participants	610,467
	3,240,342
Deductions from Net Assets attributed to:	
Disbursements to participants	834,081
Change in plan assets available for benefits	2,406,261
Net assets available for benefits at beginning of year	20,454,730
Net assets available for benefits at end of year	$ 22,860,991

See accompanying notes.

THE AGENCIES OF
THE CUMBERLAND PRESBYTERIAN CHURCH CENTER
ENDOWMENT PROGRAM
STATEMENT OF ACTIVITY
FOR THE YEAR ENDED DECEMBER 31, 2013

	Unrestricted	Temporarily Restricted	Permanently Restricted	Totals
Changes in Permanently Restricted Net Assets:				
Revenues, gains, and other support:				
Contributions	$ -	$ -	$ 1,277,448	$ 1,277,448
Interest and dividend income	-	-	740,161	740,161
Net realized gain on investments	-	-	(174,672)	(174,672)
Net unrealized gain on investments	-	-	6,378,880	6,378,880
	-	-	8,221,817	8,221,817
Expenses:				
Distribution for designated purposes	-	-	2,101,894	2,101,894
Distribution of earnings	-	-	1,417,674	1,417,674
Other expenses	-	-	107,418	107,418
	-	-	3,626,986	3,626,986
Change in net assets	-	-	4,594,831	4,594,831
Net assets at beginning of year	-	-	50,978,826	50,978,826
Net assets at end of year	$ -	$ -	$ 55,573,657	$ 55,573,657
Represented by funds held in trust for others:				
Bethel University	$ -	$ -	$ 2,997,983	$ 2,997,983
Cumberland Presbyterian Children's Home	-	-	6,806,618	6,806,618
Memphis Theological Seminary	-	-	9,677,003	9,677,003
Other designated persons and organizations	-	-	10,707,005	10,707,005
	-	-	30,188,609	30,188,609
Represented by funds held for The Agencies of The Cumberland Presbyterian Church Center:				
Discipleship Ministry Team	-	-	2,083,987	2,083,987
Missions Ministry Team	-	-	12,656,072	12,656,072
Board of Stewardship, Foundation, and Benefits	-	-	1,935,309	1,935,309
Our United Outreach	-	-	2,468,488	2,468,488
General Assembly Corporation	-	-	466,565	466,565
Communications Ministry Team	-	-	108,638	108,638
Pastoral Development Ministry Team	-	-	239,944	239,944
The Historical Foundation	-	-	1,460,756	1,460,756
Ministerial Aid	-	-	3,965,289	3,965,289
	-	-	25,385,048	25,385,048
Net assets at end of year	$ -	$ -	$ 55,573,657	$ 55,573,657

See accompanying notes.

THE AGENCIES OF
THE CUMBERLAND PRESBYTERIAN CHURCH CENTER

NOTES TO FINANCIAL STATEMENTS
DECEMBER 31, 2013

Note A - Nature of Activities and Significant Accounting Policies

Nature of Activities - By the covenant of Abraham and his descendants according to faith, God has established the church in the world through His Son Jesus Christ. This household of faith, the universal church, consists of all those persons in every nation and every age who confess Jesus Christ as Lord and Savior and who respond to His call for discipleship. The church in the world never exists for herself alone, but to glorify God and work for reconciliation through Christ. Christ claims the church and gives her the word and sacraments in order to bring God's grace and judgment to persons.

The General Assembly is the highest judicatory of this church and represents in one body all the particular churches thereof. It bears the title of the General Assembly of the Cumberland Presbyterian Church and constitutes the bond of union, peace, correspondence, and mutual confidence among all its churches and judicatories. The Agencies of The Cumberland Presbyterian Church Center have been established by the General Assembly and in 2000 it caused the Cumberland Presbyterian Church General Assembly Corporation to be formed. The Agencies consist of the following entities:

Cumberland Presbyterian Church General Assembly Corporation
Ministry Council of the Cumberland Presbyterian Church, Inc.
Board of Stewardship, Foundation, and Benefits of the Cumberland Presbyterian Church, Inc.
Historical Foundation of the Cumberland Presbyterian Church and the Cumberland Presbyterian Church
  in America

Contributions - Contributions received are recorded as unrestricted, temporarily restricted, or permanently restricted, depending on the existence and/or nature of any donor restrictions.

Support that is restricted by the donor is reported as an increase in unrestricted net assets if the restriction expires in the reporting period in which the support is recognized. All other donor restricted support is reported as an increase in temporarily or permanently restricted net assets depending on the nature of the restriction. When a restriction expires, temporarily restricted net assets are reclassified to unrestricted net assets.

Donated Equipment and Services - Donated equipment is reflected as contributions in the accompanying financial statements at their estimated values at the date of receipt. No equipment was donated to the Center during the year ended December 31, 2013. No amounts have been reflected in the statements for donated services because they did not meet the criteria for recognition under FASB ASC 958-605-25.

Use of Estimates - The preparation of financial statements in conformity with generally accepted accounting principles requires management to make estimates and assumptions that affect the reported amounts of assets and liabilities and disclosure of contingent assets and liabilities at the date of the financial statements and the reported amounts of revenues and expenses during the reporting period. Actual results could differ from these estimates.

NOTES CONTINUED

Note A - Nature of Activities and Significant Accounting Policies - Continued

The Cumberland Presbyterian Church Investment Loan Program, Inc.'s notes receivable will consist of loans made to congregations, governing bodies, church organizations, and other qualifying related entities. The ability of each borrower to repay its loan generally depends upon the contributions received from its members. The number of members of each congregation and its revenue is likely to fluctuate.

The Program must rely on the borrower's or guarantor's continued financial viability for repayment of loans. If a borrower or guarantor experiences a decrease in contributions or revenues, payments on that loan may be adversely affected. Even though the loans are collateralized by real estate, realization of the appraised value upon default is not assured and is dependent upon the local economic conditions of the borrower. Therefore, the determination of the adequacy of the allowance for notes receivable losses is based on estimates that are particularly susceptible to significant changes in the economic environment and market conditions for the geographic areas where the borrowers are located.

While management uses available information to recognize losses on notes receivable, further reductions in the carrying amounts of notes receivable may be necessary based on changes in the economic conditions for the geographic area of the borrowers. It is therefore reasonably possible that the estimated losses on notes receivable may change materially in the near term. However, the amount of the change that is reasonably possible cannot be estimated.

Promises to Give - Unconditional promises to give are recognized as revenue or gains in the period received and as assets or decreases of liabilities depending on the form of the benefits received. Conditional promises to give are recognized when the conditions on which they depend are substantially met. The Center has no promises to give at December 31, 2013.

Inventory - Inventories are stated at the lower of cost or market. Cost is determined using the average cost method.

Depreciation - In years past, Shared Services has recorded property and equipment as assets and depreciated them. Depreciation of property and equipment was computed using the straight-line method over the estimated useful lives of the assets. Purchases of equipment after 1996 are not capitalized, but expensed when purchased; therefore, no depreciation expense has been recorded for items acquired in 1997 and thereafter. The difference between the cost of fixed assets expensed and depreciation expense that would be recorded is immaterial. In 2008, the Center purchased land and two incomplete office buildings. The cost of these plus the construction costs necessary to complete the new Center were capitalized and are being depreciated over an estimated useful life of 39 years. In 2009, the Shared Services agency purchased a large amount of computer equipment and capitalized these costs. The computer equipment purchased is being depreciated over an estimated useful life of four years.

Property and Equipment - Property and equipment is recorded at historical cost. Donated property and equipment is recorded at fair market value at the date of donation. Such donations are reported as unrestricted support unless the donor has restricted the donated asset to a specific purpose. Assets donated with explicit restrictions regarding their use and contributions of cash that must be used to acquire property and equipment are reported as restricted support. Absent donor stipulations regarding how long those donated assets must be maintained, the Center reports expirations of donor restrictions when the donated or acquired assets are placed in service as instructed by the donor. The Center re-classes temporarily restricted net assets to unrestricted net assets at that time.

NOTES CONTINUED

Note A - Nature of Activities and Significant Accounting Policies - Continued

Investments - Investments are stated at fair value. Investments in private investment entities are valued based on the Center's proportional share of the net asset valuations reported by the general partners of the underlying entities. The reported values of all other investments (with the exception of notes receivable) are measured by quoted prices in active markets. Realized and unrealized gains and losses are reflected in the statement of activities. (See Note L)

The Center's investments include various types of securities in various companies within various markets. Investment securities are exposed to several risks, such as interest rate, market and credit risks. Due to the risks associated with certain investment securities, it is at least reasonably possible that changes in the values of investment securities will occur in the near term and those changes could materially affect the amounts reported in the Center's combined financial statements.

Fair Value Measurements - Fair value under accounting principles generally accepted in the United States of America is defined as the price that would be received to sell an asset or paid to transfer a liability in an orderly transaction between market participants at the measurement date. Generally accepted accounting principles establishes a three-tier fair value hierarchy that prioritizes the inputs used to measure fair value. These tiers include: Level 1, defined as observable inputs such as quoted prices available in active markets for identical assets or liabilities; Level 2, defined as pricing inputs other than quoted prices in active markets that are either directly or indirectly observable; and Level 3, defined as unobservable inputs about which little or no market data exists, therefore requiring an entity to develop its own assessment about the assumptions the market participants would use in pricing an asset or liability.

Income Tax Status - The Center is a not-for-profit organization exempt from federal income taxes under Internal Revenue Code (IRC) Section 501 (c)(3). Thus, no provision for federal income taxes has been made. The Center has a defined contribution retirement plan which is qualified under Internal Revenue Code Section 403 (b); no provision for income taxes has been included in the Plan's financial statements.

Cash and Cash Equivalents - For purposes of the statement of cash flows, all highly liquid investments with a maturity of three months or less are considered to be cash equivalents. However, cash and cash equivalents reported as securities and investments by the Endowment Program, Investment Loan Program and Retirement Fund are considered investments for purposes of the statement of cash flows.

Loans Receivable and Allowance for Losses - Loans receivable are stated at unpaid principal balances, less the allowance for notes receivable losses. Inter-agency loans are shown as due to/from other agencies, boards, and divisions.

The allowance for loans receivable is maintained at a level which, in management's judgment, is adequate to absorb credit losses inherent in the loans receivable portfolio. The amount of the allowance is based on management's evaluation of the collectability of the portfolio, including the nature of the portfolio, credit concentrations, trends in historical loss experience, economic conditions, and other risks inherent in the portfolio. Although management uses available information to recognize losses on notes receivable, because of uncertainties associated with the various local economic conditions of the borrowers and collateral values, it is reasonably possible that a material change could occur in the allowance for notes receivable in the near term. However, the amount of the change that is reasonably possible cannot be estimated. When considered necessary, the allowance is increased by a charge to expense and reduced by actual charge-offs, net of recoveries.

NOTES CONTINUED

Note B - Retirement Plan

General - The Cumberland Presbyterian Church Retirement Plan Number Two is available to certain employees of the Church and its agencies. All agencies, boards, and divisions match each employee's contribution up to five percent of the employee's salary. The total retirement contribution expense for The Agencies of The Cumberland Presbyterian Church Center for 2013 was $69,425.

The Plan obtained its latest determination letter on January 31, 1972, in which the Internal Revenue Service stated that the Plan, as then designed, was in compliance with the applicable requirements of the Internal Revenue Code. The Plan has been amended since receiving the determination letter. However, the Plan administrator and the Plan's tax counsel believe that the plan is currently designed and being operated in compliance with the applicable requirements of the Internal Revenue Code. The Plan is a "church plan" and is, therefore, not subject to ERISA.

Eligibility - Employees who are 18 years of age are immediately eligible to participate in the plan.

Vesting - Participants are immediately 100% vested in their accounts.

Investments - The Plan's investments are held by a bank-administered trust fund. The trust is the funding vehicle for the Plan, and all contributions are made to the trust. The cost and market value of the Plan's investments at December 31, 2013, are as follows:

	Cost	Market Value
Total	$ 19,332,707	$ 22,860,991

Note C - Endowment Program

The Endowment Program includes assets of The Agencies of The Cumberland Presbyterian Church Center and the assets of other agencies, boards, and divisions.

Effective January 1, 2013, the Board of Stewardship, Foundation, and Benefits merged the two previously-separated Endowment Programs, the Growth/Income Fund and the Total Return Fund, into one single Endowment Program in order to more efficiently and effectively administer the investment of endowment funds and help beneficiaries of said funds carry out their purpose. As of December 31, 2012, the total net assets for the Growth/Income Fund and the Total Return Fund were $46,091,258 and $4,887,568, respectively. The merger results in total beginning net assets of the single Endowment Program of $50,978,826 for 2013.

The Program's investments, other than notes receivable, real estate, and certificates of deposit, are held by a bank-administered trust fund. The costs and market value of the Program's investments held in trust at December 31, 2013, are as follows:

	Cost	Market Value
Total	$ 44,419,339	$ 51,645,226

NOTES CONTINUED

Note C - Endowment Program - Continued

The Center has interpreted the Uniform Prudent Management of Institutional Funds Act ("UPMIFA") requiring a portion of a donor restricted endowment of perpetual duration be classified as permanently restricted assets. The amount of the endowment that must be retained permanently is in accordance with explicit donor stipulations as outlined in their respective trust agreements.

The primary objective of these endowments is to provide a balance between capital appreciation, preservation of capital, and current income. This is a long-term goal designed to maximize returns without undue risk. The Board of Stewardship has set distribution rates with certain beneficiaries of the Endowment Program.

Unless otherwise stated in the donor agreement, the Board of Stewardship shall select the investment portfolio where the endowments will be invested as described in the Investment Policy of the Center. The Investment Policy of the Center outlines the asset allocations, permissible investments, and objectives of the portfolios.

Endowment Net Asset Composition by Type of Fund as of December 31, 2013:

	Permanently Restricted	Total
Donor-restricted endowment funds	$ 55,573,657	$ 55,573,657
Total funds	$ 55,573,657	$ 55,573,657

Changes in Endowment Net Assets for the year ended December 31, 2013:

	Permanently Restricted	Total
Endowment net assets, beginning of year	$ 50,978,826	$ 50,978,826
Investment return	6,836,951	6,836,951
Contributions	1,277,448	1,277,448
Withdrawal of principal balances	-	-
Appropriation of endowment assets for expenditures	(3,519,568)	(3,519,568)
Endowment net assets, end of year	$ 55,573,657	$ 55,573,657

Description of Amount Classified as Permanently Restricted Net Assets (Endowment Only):

Permanently Restricted Net Assets -

The portion of perpetual endowment funds that is required to be retained permanently either by explicit donor stipulation or by UPMIFA	$ 55,573,657
Total endowment funds classified as permanently restricted net assets	$ 55,573,657

NOTES CONTINUED

Note D - Investment Loan Program

Nature of Activities - On March 19, 1999, the State of Tennessee approved the charter for the Cumberland Presbyterian Church Investment Loan Program, Inc., a subsidiary corporation of the Board of Stewardship, Foundation and Benefits of the Cumberland Presbyterian Church, Inc. The Program is designed to allow participants to help provide the loans needed to finance the growth of Cumberland Presbyterian congregations in the 21st century.

1. It provides building loans secured by first mortgages to congregations, presbyteries, and church agencies.

2. It allows congregations, presbyteries, church agencies, and individual members of the Cumberland Presbyterian Church to invest their funds in interest bearing accounts from which withdrawals can be made "on demand" replacing the function of the Cash Funds Management Program.

3. All participants have the opportunity to invest funds for specific terms (such as three years or five years) in order to receive a higher rate of interest. A prospectus outlines the added investment options offered.

Securities and Investments - The cost and market values of Investment Loan Program investments at December 31, 2013, are as follows:

	Cost	Market Value
Total	$ 9,196,653	$ 8,482,539

Notes Payable to Individual Investors - Notes payable to individual investors are made through a general offering in the states of Kentucky, New Mexico, Tennessee, and Texas to eligible individual investors and must be purchased in minimum face amounts of $500. All notes payable to individual investors shown in these financial statements are Adjustable Rate Ready Access Notes. Adjustable Rate Ready Access Notes are payable on demand and pay an adjustable interest rate that may be adjusted each month. Additions of principal may be made to Adjustable Rate Ready Access Notes at any time. Withdrawals from Adjustable Rate Ready Access Notes may be made at any time and are payable upon written request of the investor; however, the Program reserves the right to require the investor to provide up to thirty (30) days written notice of any intended withdrawal before such withdrawal is made. Both additions to and withdrawals from Adjustable Rate Ready Access Notes must be made in minimum amounts of $250. The Program may review certain factors, such as investment gap analysis, loan demand, cash flow needs, and the current policy of the Federal Reserve, before establishing each month's rate of interest.

The notes are non-negotiable and may be assigned only upon the Program's written consent. The notes are unsecured and of equal priority with all other current indebtedness of the Program.

NOTES CONTINUED

Note D - Investment Loan Program - Continued

Depository Accounts Held for Church Organizations - The Cumberland Presbyterian Church Investment Loan Program, Inc. accepts depository accounts in which church organizations may place funds with the Program, in minimum amounts of $500. All depository accounts shown in these financial statements are Adjustable Rate Ready Access accounts. Like the Program's notes, depository accounts are general obligations of the Program, are unsecured and not insured, and are of equal priority with all other current indebtedness of the Program including notes. The interest rate on the depository accounts is adjusted pursuant to the policies of the Cumberland Presbyterian Church Investment Loan Program, Inc. as they may be adopted from time to time by its Board of Directors. The Cumberland Presbyterian Church Investment Loan Program, Inc. may terminate any depository account upon sixty (60) days written notice to the church organization.

Loans Receivable - Amounts that have been loaned are included on the Statement of Financial Position as loans receivable. There are 24 loans outstanding at December 31, 2013.

Loans receivable are collectible primarily through monthly payments based on up to a twenty-five year amortization period. Interest rates, as determined by the board, are based on the Prime Interest Rate as reported in the Wall Street Journal plus 2.5% per annum. On loans originated for $500,000 or less, the interest rate will be adjusted triennially. On loans originated for more than $500,000, the interest rate will be adjusted annually for the term of the loan.

The composition of loans is as follows:

Loans receivable (secured by real estate)	$ 8,830,394
Less: allowance for loan losses	(1,036,000)
	$ 7,794,394

A summary of changes in the allowance for loan losses is as follows:

Balance at beginning of year	$ 1,069,000
Provision charged to operations	(33,000)
Loans charged off	-
Recoveries	-
Balance at end of year	$ 1,036,000

Estimated receipts of principal payments for the five years subsequent to 2013 are:

Year ending December 31,	Amount
2014	$ 424,552
2015	381,275
2016	399,711
2017	419,229
2018	785,740
Thereafter	5,383,887
	$ 7,794,394

NOTES CONTINUED

Note E - Funds Held in Trust

The Discipleship Ministry Team leader of the Ministry Council is responsible for certain funds held in trust for outside groups. Funds invested by the executive director in Investment Loan Program amounted to the following as of December 31, 2013:

P.R.E.M. $ 240,427

The General Assembly Corporation is responsible for funds held in trust for certain committees and commissions. These funds are shown as liabilities in the Statement of Financial Position of the General Assembly Corporation. Activity in these funds for the year ended December 31, 2013, is as follows:

	Nominating Committee	Committee on Judiciary	Non-USA Moderator Travel Fund
Balance January 1, 2013	$ 7,132	$ 4,080	$ 5,847
Our United Outreach	2,361	6,327	-
Contributions	-	352	-
Disbursements	(3,312)	(7,154)	-
Balance December 31, 2013	$ 6,181	$ 3,605	$ 5,847

	Committee on Theology and Social Concerns	Commission on Chaplains
Balance January 1, 2013	$ 14,805	$ 4,315
Our United Outreach	6,900	8,395
Contributions	-	-
Disbursements	(6,703)	(7,230)
Balance December 31, 2013	$ 15,002	$ 5,480

Note F - Insurance Program

The Cumberland Presbyterian Group Health and Life Insurance Program is a fully insured, experience-rated plan with a policy year ending on the last day of February. Any excess of premium over medical claims and other plan expenses is retained by the insurer; excess losses are no longer carried forward as a charge against the experience for subsequent policy years, as in the past, but must be absorbed by the insurer. The plan is the responsibility of the Board of Stewardship, Foundation, and Benefits.

The plan has one Investment Loan Program account and one account in the Endowment Program. Both are used as a stabilization reserve to provide some protection against unexpected medical claims volatility. The balance at December 31, 2013 of the Investment Loan Program account is $80,735. The balance at December 31, 2013 of the Endowment Program account is $985,726.

NOTES CONTINUED

Note G - Concentrations of Credit Risk Arising from Cash Deposits in Excess of Insured Limits

The Center maintains its cash balances in a financial institution located in Memphis, Tennessee. The balances are insured by the Federal Deposit Insurance Corporation up to $250,000 as of December 31, 2013. At various times there were balances that exceeded these FDIC limits. Cash and cash equivalents classified as securities and investments are items held in equities backed by the Federal Government. These equities, while backed by the Federal Government, are not insured by the Federal Deposit Insurance Corporation.

Note H - Real Estate

Real estate assets of both the Ministry Council and the Historical Foundation are held for investment and are therefore not depreciated. These assets amounted to the following at December 31, 2013:

Property Location	Ministry Council	Historical Foundation	Total
San Francisco, California	$ 51,818	$ -	$ 51,818
Birthplace Shrine Chapel, Dickson County, Tennessee	-	21,500	21,500
McAdow Home, Dickson County, Tennessee	-	17,255	17,255
Total	$ 51,818	$ 38,755	$ 90,573

Note I - Leases

The Ministry Council leases three copiers and two postage machines for use in its offices. Lease payments for the year ended December 31, 2013, totaled $14,514. The minimum lease payments for the next five years ended December 31 are as follows:

2014	$ 8,922
2015	4,255
2016	-
2017	-
2018	-
Thereafter	-
	$ 13,177

NOTES CONTINUED

Note J - Combined Statement of Activities Expenses

The total expenses of various Agencies are included in the Combined Statement of Activities as follows:

Expense Description	Agencies
Our United Outreach	Our United Outreach
General Assembly Corporation	General Assembly Corporation
Ministry Council	Ministry Council
Shared Services	Shared Services
Historical Foundation	Historical Foundation
Board of Stewardship, Foundation and Benefits	Board of Stewardship, Foundation, and Benefits
Small Church Loan Program	Small Church Loan Program
Insurance Program	Insurance Program
Ministerial Aid	Ministerial Aid
Investment Loan Program	Investment Loan Program
Retirement Fund	Retirement Fund
Endowment Program	Endowment Program

Costs originating from Shared Services (formerly Central Services - made up of Building and Maintenance, Computer Services Division, and Central Accounting Division) are now funded by Our United Outreach appropriations instead of being charged to the various applicable agencies based on usage.

Inter-agency revenue and expense items for Our United Outreach and endowment earnings have been eliminated on the combined statement of activity.

Note K - Fair Value Measurements

Prices for closed-end bond funds and equity mutual funds are readily available in the active markets in which those securities are traded, and the resulting fair values are categorized as level 1.

Prices for mortgage backed securities, bond mutual funds, and real estate investment trusts are determined on a recurring basis based upon inputs that are readily available in public markets or can be derived from information available in publicly quoted markets and are categorized as level 2.

NOTES CONTINUED

Note K - Fair Value Measurements - Continued

There is limited or no observable data for the prices of private investment entities that are held by the Center and the resulting fair values of these securities are categorized as level 3.

Fair values of assets measured on a recurring basis at December 31, 2013 are as follows:

		Fair Value Measurements at Reporting Date Using		
	Fair Value	Quoted Prices In Active Market for Identical Assets (Level 1)	Significant Other Observable Inputs (Level 2)	Significant Unobservable Inputs (Level 3)
December 31, 2013				
Mortgage backed securities	$ 6,690,189	$ -	$ 6,690,189	$ -
Bond mutual funds	9,385,365	-	9,385,365	-
Closed-end bond funds	3,153,887	3,153,887	-	-
Equity mutual funds	1,758,892	1,758,892	-	-
Real estate investment trusts	4,777,111	-	4,777,111	-
Private investment entities	52,250,400	-	-	52,250,400
Total	$ 78,015,844	$ 4,912,779	$ 20,852,665	$ 52,250,400

Because of the multiple number and complexity of the calculations necessary, management does not believe it is practicable to estimate fair value of loans receivable, net of allowance for loan losses. Therefore, no adjustment has been made to the net carrying value of $12,591,380 listed on the Combined Statement of Financial Position.

NOTES CONTINUED

Note K - Fair Value Measurements - Continued

The following table provides information related to the previously mentioned investments that are valued based primarily on net asset value at December 31, 2013:

	Fair Value	Unfunded Commitments	Redemption Frequency (If Currently Eligible)	Redemption Notice Period
Private Investment Entities				
GT Emerging Markets (QP), L.P.	$ 3,453,253	None	Annual	90 Days
GT Offshore Fund, Ltd. (Class A)	7,262,902	None	Annual	90 Days
GT Offshore Fund, Ltd. (Class B)	9,389,898	None	Annual	90 Days
GT ERISA Fund, Ltd. (Class A)	3,036,102	None	Annual	90 Days
GT ERISA Fund, Ltd. (Class B)	4,300,894	None	Annual	90 Days
GT Real Assets, L.P.	441,528	None	Annual	90 Days
GT Special Opportunities III, L.P.	3,087,360	None	see note	see note
Midland Intl Equity QP Fund, L.P.	10,119,259	None	Quarterly	60 Days
Midland U.S. QP Fund, L.P.	11,159,204	None	Quarterly	60 Days
	$ 52,250,400			

The GT Special Opportunities III, L.P. provides for an annual redemption upon 90 days notice after an initial lock-up period of eighteen months.

The following table summarizes fair value by fund for investments in private investment entities that are valued based primarily on net asset value at December 31, 2013:

	Retirement Fund	Endowment Program	Total Fair Value
Private Investment Entities			
GT Emerging Markets (QP), L.P.	$ 1,050,528	$ 2,402,725	$ 3,453,253
GT Offshore Fund, Ltd. (Class A)	-	7,262,902	7,262,902
GT Offshore Fund, Ltd. (Class B)	-	9,389,898	9,389,898
GT ERISA Fund, Ltd. (Class A)	3,036,102	-	3,036,102
GT ERISA Fund, Ltd. (Class B)	4,300,894	-	4,300,894
GT Real Assets, L.P.	137,026	304,502	441,528
GT Special Opportunities III, L.P.	901,959	2,185,401	3,087,360
Midland Intl Equity QP Fund, L.P.	3,152,053	6,967,206	10,119,259
Midland U.S. QP Fund, L.P.	3,211,300	7,947,904	11,159,204
	$ 15,789,862	$ 36,460,538	$ 52,250,400

NOTES CONTINUED

Note K - Fair Value Measurements - Continued

Assets measured at fair value on a recurring basis using significant unobservable inputs (Level 3):

Fair value at beginning of year	$ 35,022,627
Investments and distributions, net	3,487,161
Realized/unrealized gains (losses)	13,740,612
Fair value at end of year	$ 52,250,400

Gains and losses (realized and unrealized) for Level 3 assets included in net assets for the year are reported as follows:

On the Combined Statement of Activity, under Revenues, gains, and other support:

Permanently restricted net assets:	
Endowment program	$ 9,339,275
Net assets available for benefits:	
Retirement fund	4,401,337
Total net assets	$ 13,740,612

These investments without readily determinable values comprise approximately 50% of total assets at December 31, 2013.

All assets have been valued using a market approach.

A description of the Private Investment Entities and the investment objectives is as follows:

<u>GT Emerging Markets (QP), L.P.</u> - This fund is organized as a "fund of funds" which seek to achieve long-term capital appreciation through investments in limited partnerships, off-shore corporations, open-end mutual funds, closed-end mutual funds, commingled trust funds, and separately managed accounts that invest primarily in "emerging markets." Investments may also be made in industrialized nations such as the United States and Japan.

<u>GT Offshore Fund, Ltd. / GT ERISA Fund, Ltd.</u> - These are open-ended "umbrella" funds, incorporated as exempted companies in the Cayman Islands with multiple classes of Shares. Each class of share is separately valued and pursues its own clearly defined investment objective(s) and strategy(ies). These funds overall investment objectives are as follows:

Class A is broadly diversified among multiple investment managers and multiple investment strategies. The strategies employed may include multi-strategy arbitrage, capital structure arbitrage, distressed debt, long/short equity or niche financing.

Class B seeks to achieve a superior rate of return exceeding that of the MSCI World Index with less volatility while minimizing market risk through a hedged approach. The primary investment strategy will be a long/short equity strategy. This class is broadly diversified among multiple investment managers and multiple long/short equity strategies.

NOTES CONTINUED

Note K - Fair Value Measurements - Continued

GT Real Assets, L.P. - This fund is organized as a "fund of funds" investment vehicle that will pool and invest funds, generally through "Managed Investment Vehicles," for the purpose of generating attractive risk-adjusted returns by opportunistically investing in a broad spectrum of resources, real assets, and other investment strategies.

GT Special Opportunities, III, L.P. - This fund is organized as a "fund of funds" investment vehicle that will pool and invest funds, generally through "Managed Investment Vehicles," for the purpose of achieving a superior rate of return. The fund focuses on a very limited number of investment strategies that are considered to be opportunistic based upon prevailing market conditions. At times, the fund may only invest in one strategy and do so in a non-diversified manner, perhaps with only a single manager. The strategies sought by the fund will often be niche-focused. Accordingly, the risk level for the fund is anticipated to be extremely high.

Midland International Equity QP Fund, L.P. - This is an international equity fund which seeks to identify listed companies selling at a discount to intrinsic net worth on liquid stock exchanges of non-U.S. countries. The focus of this fund is long-term capital appreciation. This fund seeks to outperform the MSCI EAFE Index, net of fees and taxes, over a full market cycle.

Midland U.S. QP Fund, L.P. - This fund's objective is to outperform the broad U.S. equity market, defined as the Russell 3000 Index, net of fees and taxes over a full market cycle. The fund seeks to compound capital at attractive rates through direct and indirect long-term ownership of publicly traded businesses domiciled in the United States.

Note L - Securities and Investments

Securities and investments at December 31, 2013 are as follows:

	Ministry Council	Historical Foundation	Investment Loan Program	Retirement Fund	Endowment Program	Total
Cash and cash equivalents	$ -	$ -	$ 1,792,350	$ 1,460,571	$ 1,660,518	$ 4,913,439
Mortgage backed securities	-	-	6,690,189	-	-	6,690,189
Bond mutual funds	-	-	-	2,905,775	6,479,590	9,385,365
Closed-end bond funds	-	-	-	1,017,383	2,136,504	3,153,887
Equity mutual funds	-	-	-	549,887	1,209,005	1,758,892
Real estate investment trusts	-	-	-	1,121,148	3,655,963	4,777,111
Private investment entities	-	-	-	15,789,862	36,460,538	52,250,400
Real estate	51,818	38,755	-	-	-	90,573
	$ 51,818	$ 38,755	$ 8,482,539	$ 22,844,626	$ 51,602,118	$ 83,019,856

Note M - Subsequent Events

Subsequent events were evaluated through May 27, 2014, which is the date the financial statements were available to be issued.

BETHEL UNIVERSITY

FINANCIAL STATEMENTS
AND OTHER INFORMATION

JULY 31, 2013 AND 2012

BETHEL UNIVERSITY

Table of Contents

	Page
INDEPENDENT AUDITOR'S REPORT	1 - 2
FINANCIAL STATEMENTS	
Statements of Financial Position	3
Statements of Activities	4 - 5
Statements of Cash Flows	6 - 7
Notes to Financial Statements	8 - 31
OTHER INFORMATION	
Schedule of Expenditures of Federal Awards	32
Notes to Schedule of Expenditures of Federal Awards	33
INDEPENDENT AUDITOR'S REPORT ON INTERNAL CONTROL OVER FINANCIAL REPORTING AND ON COMPLIANCE AND OTHER MATTERS BASED ON AN AUDIT OF FINANCIAL STATEMENTS PERFORMED IN ACCORDANCE WITH *GOVERNMENT AUDITING STANDARDS*	34 - 35
INDEPENDENT AUDITOR'S REPORT ON COMPLIANCE FOR THE MAJOR PROGRAM AND ON INTERNAL CONTROL OVER COMPLIANCE REQUIRED BY OMB CIRCULAR A-133	36 - 37
SCHEDULE OF FINDINGS AND QUESTIONED COSTS	38 - 39
SUMMARY SCHEDULE OF PRIOR AUDIT FINDINGS	40 - 41

Independent Auditor's Report

The Board of Trustees
Bethel University
McKenzie, Tennessee

Report on the Financial Statements

We have audited the accompanying financial statements of Bethel University (the "University"), which comprise the statements of financial position as of July 31, 2013 and 2012, and the related statements of activities and cash flows for the years then ended, and the related notes to the financial statements.

Management's Responsibility for the Financial Statements

Management is responsible for the preparation and fair presentation of these financial statements in accordance with accounting principles generally accepted in the United States of America; this includes the design, implementation, and maintenance of internal control relevant to the preparation and fair presentation of financial statements that are free from material misstatement, whether due to fraud or error.

Auditor's Responsibility

Our responsibility is to express an opinion on these financial statements based on our audits. We conducted our audits in accordance with auditing standards generally accepted in the United States of America and the standards applicable to financial audits contained in *Government Auditing Standards*, issued by the Comptroller General of the United States. Those standards require that we plan and perform the audit to obtain reasonable assurance about whether the financial statements are free from material misstatement.

An audit involves performing procedures to obtain audit evidence about the amounts and disclosures in the financial statements. The procedures selected depend on the auditor's judgment, including the assessment of the risks of material misstatement of the financial statements, whether due to fraud or error. In making those risk assessments, the auditor considers internal control relevant to the entity's preparation and fair presentation of the financial statements in order to design audit procedures that are appropriate in the circumstances, but not for the purpose of expressing an opinion on the effectiveness of the entity's internal control. Accordingly, we express no such opinion. An audit also includes evaluating the appropriateness of accounting policies used and the reasonableness of significant accounting estimates made by management, as well as evaluating the overall presentation of the financial statements.

The Board of Trustees
Bethel University

We believe that the audit evidence we have obtained is sufficient and appropriate to provide a basis for our audit opinion.

Opinion

In our opinion, the financial statements referred to above present fairly, in all material respects, the financial position of Bethel University as of July 31, 2013 and 2012, and the changes in its net assets and its cash flows for the years then ended in accordance with accounting principles generally accepted in the United States of America.

Other Matters

Other Information

Our audit was conducted for the purpose of forming an opinion on the financial statements as a whole. The accompanying schedule of expenditures of federal awards, as required by Office of Management and Budget Circular A-133, *Audits of States, Local Governments, and Non-Profit Organizations,* is presented for purposes of additional analysis and is not a required part of the financial statements. Such information is the responsibility of management and was derived from and relates directly to the underlying accounting and other records used to prepare the financial statements. The information has been subjected to the auditing procedures applied in the audit of the financial statements and certain additional procedures, including comparing and reconciling such information directly to the underlying accounting and other records used to prepare the financial statements or to the financial statements themselves, and other additional procedures in accordance with auditing standards generally accepted in the United States of America. In our opinion, the information is fairly stated, in all material respects, in relation to the financial statements as a whole.

Other Reporting Required by Government Auditing Standards

In accordance with *Government Auditing Standards*, we have also issued our report dated December 8, 2013, on our consideration of the University's internal control over financial reporting and on our tests of its compliance with certain provisions of laws, regulations, contracts, and grant agreements and other matters. The purpose of that report is to describe the scope of our testing of internal control over financial reporting and compliance and the results of that testing, and not to provide an opinion on internal control over financial reporting or on compliance. That report is an integral part of an audit performed in accordance with *Government Auditing Standards* in considering the University's internal control over financial reporting and compliance.

Crosslin + Associates, P.C.
Nashville, Tennessee
December 8, 2013

BETHEL UNIVERSITY
STATEMENTS OF FINANCIAL POSITION

ASSETS

	July 31, 2013	July 31, 2012
Cash	$ 879,267	$ 1,674,470
Perkins loan cash	112,743	131,225
Receivables:		
Contributions, net (Note B)	4,768,311	3,109,676
Students, net of allowances of $1,851,395 and $1,401,395 respectively	2,968,649	5,086,410
Perkins loans, net of allowances of $223,290 and $211,084, respectively	266,751	258,600
Other	106,500	-
Note receivable	8,200,000	-
Inventories	280,849	184,585
Prepaid expenses and deposits	127,786	212,873
Investments (Note C)	3,395,719	5,047,967
Beneficial interest in assets held by others (Note D)	3,489,347	3,208,813
Property, buildings, and equipment:		
Land	711,511	711,511
Buildings and improvements	62,460,515	53,333,023
Equipment, furniture and automobiles	7,906,789	7,371,323
Library books	1,284,514	1,267,209
Property held under capital leases (Note F)	5,508,296	3,595,455
Construction in progress	1,092,977	14,921,570
	78,964,602	81,200,091
Less: Accumulated depreciation	(20,387,270)	(14,560,405)
Total property and equipment, net	58,577,332	66,639,686
Total assets	$ 83,173,254	$ 85,554,305

LIABILITIES AND NET ASSETS

	2013	2012
Liabilities:		
Accounts payable	$ 7,104,700	$ 11,999,719
Accrued payroll and benefits	886,993	645,409
Deferred tuition revenue	9,211,604	6,965,761
Annuities payable	707	707
Debt (Note E)	44,125,905	49,265,366
Obligations under capital leases (Note F)	535,935	2,331,206
Advances from the federal government	411,781	1,673,773
Total liabilities	62,277,625	72,881,941
Net Assets:		
Unrestricted	6,166,553	927,573
Temporarily restricted (Notes G and H)	4,853,004	2,184,331
Permanently restricted (Notes G and H)	9,876,072	9,560,460
Total net assets	20,895,629	12,672,364
Total liabilities and net assets	$ 83,173,254	$ 85,554,305

See accompanying notes to financial statements.

BETHEL UNIVERSITY
STATEMENTS OF ACTIVITIES

	Year Ended July 31, 2013			
	Unrestricted	Temporarily Restricted	Permanently Restricted	Total
Revenue, gains and other support:				
Regular tuition and fees	$ 54,394,364	$ -	$ -	$ 54,394,364
Degree completion tuition	12,693,723	-	-	12,693,723
Institutional scholarships and grants	(14,330,903)	-	-	(14,330,903)
Net tuition and fees	52,757,184	-	-	52,757,184
Bookstore income	2,200,323	-	-	2,200,323
Private gifts and contracts	11,225,480	3,705,081	35,077	14,965,638
Investment income	150,116	137,643	-	287,759
Unrealized (loss) gain on beneficial interests in assets held by others	-	-	280,535	280,535
Auxiliary fund revenues	7,623,967	-	-	7,623,967
Government grants	421,791	-	-	421,791
Other income	1,388,519	-	-	1,388,519
Net assets released from restrictions	1,174,051	(1,174,051)	-	-
Total revenue, gains (losses) and other support	76,941,431	2,668,673	315,612	79,925,716
Expenses:				
Education and general:				
Instruction	41,178,333	-	-	41,178,333
Academic support	1,069,385	-	-	1,069,385
Student services	7,429,354	-	-	7,429,354
Institutional support	13,438,273	-	-	13,438,273
Auxiliary enterprises	8,587,106	-	-	8,587,106
Total expenses	71,702,451	-	-	71,702,451
Net increase (decrease) in net assets	5,238,980	2,668,673	315,612	8,223,265
Net assets, beginning of year	927,573	2,184,331	9,560,460	12,672,364
Net assets, end of year	$ 6,166,553	$ 4,853,004	$ 9,876,072	$ 20,895,629

See accompanying notes to financial statements.

	Year Ended July 31, 2012			
	Unrestricted	Temporarily Restricted	Permanently Restricted	Total
	$ 42,568,565	$ -	$ -	$ 42,568,565
	14,276,913	-	-	14,276,913
	(11,923,689)	-	-	(11,923,689)
	44,921,789	-	-	44,921,789
	2,136,631	-	-	2,136,631
	1,131,401	2,285,128	144,641	3,561,170
	(303)	25,394	-	25,091
	-	-	(148,002)	(148,002)
	6,937,146	-	-	6,937,146
	650,988	-	-	650,988
	259,238	-	-	259,238
	1,709,983	(1,709,983)	-	-
	57,746,873	600,539	(3,361)	58,344,051
	36,079,270	-	-	36,079,270
	1,529,400	-	-	1,529,400
	6,947,912	-	-	6,947,912
	13,725,445	-	-	13,725,445
	6,835,307	-	-	6,835,307
	65,117,334	-	-	65,117,334
	(7,370,461)	600,539	(3,361)	(6,773,283)
	8,298,034	1,583,792	9,563,821	19,445,647
	$ 927,573	$ 2,184,331	$ 9,560,460	$ 12,672,364

See accompanying notes to financial statements.

BETHEL UNIVERSITY
STATEMENTS OF CASH FLOWS

	Year ended July 31,	
	2013	2012
CASH FLOWS FROM OPERATING ACTIVITIES:		
Increase in net assets	$ 8,223,265	$ (6,773,283)
Adjustments to reconcile change in net assets to net cash provided by operating activities		
Non-cash:		
Allowance for doubtful student accounts, contributions and Perkins loans receivable	543,859	1,555,548
Disposal of property and equipment	-	156,149
Unrealized (gain) loss on investments and beneficial interests in assets held by others	(568,296)	93,060
(Gain) on the change in fair value of interest rate swap	(166,961)	100,460
Depreciation	6,010,614	4,636,749
(Increase) decrease in:		
Perkins loan cash	18,482	14,979
Contributions receivable	(1,740,706)	(1,748,992)
Student accounts receivable	1,667,761	(1,553,676)
Perkins loans receivable	(19,939)	5,548
Other receivables	(106,500)	70,177
Inventories	(96,264)	(36,468)
Prepaid expenses and deposits	85,087	(107,550)
Increase (decrease) in:		
Accounts payable	(868,416)	1,423,258
Accrued payroll and benefits	241,584	365,370
Deferred tuition revenue	2,245,843	4,458,477
Contributions restricted for long-term investments	(35,077)	(144,641)
Total adjustments	7,211,071	9,251,980
Net cash provided by operating activities	15,434,336	2,478,697
CASH FLOWS FROM INVESTING ACTIVITIES:		
Withdrawal of investments, net	1,940,010	314,608
Payment of accounts payable for property, buildings and equipment	(4,026,603)	(6,473,629)
Purchases of property, buildings and equipment	(4,235,419)	(10,374,948)
Net cash used in investing activities	(6,322,012)	(16,533,969)
CASH FLOWS FROM FINANCING ACTIVITIES:		
Payments on annuity obligations	-	(720)
Proceeds from notes payable and line-of-credit	26,183,740	20,702,153
Payments on notes payable and line-of-credit	(31,156,240)	(7,062,961)
Repayments of capital lease obligations	(3,708,112)	(1,963,376)
Contributions restricted for long-term investments	35,077	144,641
Changes in advances from the federal government	(1,261,992)	1,261,992
Net cash (used in) provided by investing activities	(9,907,527)	13,081,729

See accompanying notes to financial statements.

BETHEL UNIVERSITY
STATEMENTS OF CASH FLOWS - Continued

	Year ended July 31,	
	2013	2012
Net decrease in cash and cash equivalents	(795,203)	(973,543)
Cash and cash equivalents at beginning of year	1,638,002	2,611,545
Cash and cash equivalents at end of year	$ 842,799	$ 1,638,002
Supplemental disclosures of cash flow information:		
Interest paid	$ 2,405,667	$ 1,948,270
Non-cash financing and investing activities:		
Purchases of property and equipment	6,148,260	23,630,976
Amount financed through capital leases, accounts payable, or debt	(1,912,841)	(13,256,028)
Total paid for property and equipment	$ 4,235,419	$ 10,374,948

See accompanying notes to financial statements.

BETHEL UNIVERSITY
NOTES TO FINANCIAL STATEMENTS
JULY 31, 2013 AND 2012

A. SUMMARY OF SIGNIFICANT ACCOUNTING POLICES

Organization and Business Purpose

Bethel University (the "University") is a private, residential, coeducational University affiliated with the Cumberland Presbyterian Church, dedicated primarily to educating students in the liberal arts and science while also offering select pre-professional programs, a graduate teacher education program, a masters of business administration program, and an online criminal justice program. In addition to its traditional academic programs, the University also offers a degree-completion program. The University is accredited by the Commission on Universities of the Southern Association of Universities and Schools and its education emphasizes academic excellence, high achievement, intellectual and personal integrity, and participation in community life. Its Christian heritage finds expression in commitment to the values of personal growth, justice, community, and service.

Accrual Basis and Financial Statement Presentation

The financial statements of the University have been prepared on the accrual basis of accounting.

The University classifies its revenue, expenses, gains, and losses into three classes of net assets based on the existence or absence of donor-imposed restrictions. Net assets of the University and changes therein are classified as follows:

Unrestricted net assets - Net assets that are not subject to donor-imposed stipulations.

Temporarily restricted net assets - Net assets subject to donor-imposed stipulations that may or will be met either by actions of the University and/or the passage of time.

Permanently restricted net assets - Net assets subject to donor-imposed stipulations that are required to be maintained permanently by the University. Generally, the donors of these assets permit the University to use all or part of the income earned on related investments for general or specific purposes.

The amount for each of these classes of net assets is displayed in the statements of financial position and the amount of change in each class of net assets is displayed in the statements of activities.

BETHEL UNIVERSITY
NOTES TO FINANCIAL STATEMENTS
JULY 31, 2013 AND 2012

A. SUMMARY OF SIGNIFICANT ACCOUNTING POLICES - Continued

Use of Estimates in the Preparation of Financial Statements

The preparation of financial statements in conformity with accounting principles generally accepted in the United States of America requires management to make assumptions that affect the reported amounts of assets and liabilities, disclosure of contingent assets and liabilities at the date of the financial statements and the reported amounts of revenues and expenses during the reporting period. The more significant areas include the recovery period for property and equipment, the allocation of certain operating expenses to functional categories, the collection of contributions receivable and the adequacy of the allowance for doubtful student receivables. Management believes that such estimates have been based on reasonable assumptions and that such estimates are adequate. Actual results could differ from those estimates.

Contributions

The University reports gifts of cash and other assets as restricted support if they are received with donor stipulations that limit the use of the donated assets. When a donor restriction expires, that is, when a stipulated time restriction ends or the purpose of the restriction is accomplished, temporarily restricted net assets are reclassified to unrestricted net assets and reported in the statement of activities as net assets released from restrictions. The University has elected to report contributions received with donor-imposed restrictions as an increase to unrestricted net assets if the restrictions are met in the same fiscal year that the contributions are received.

The University reports gifts of land, equipment and other assets as unrestricted support unless explicit donor stipulations specify how the donated assets must be used. Gifts of long-lived assets with explicit restrictions that specify how the assets are to be used and gifts of cash or other assets that must be used to acquire long-lived assets are reported as restricted support. Absent explicit donor stipulations regarding how long the long-lived assets must be maintained, the University reports expirations of donor restrictions when the donated or acquired long-lived assets are placed in service.

Contribution of services are recognized if the services received (a) create or enhance non-financial assets or (b) require specialized skills, provided by individuals possessing those skills and would typically need to be purchased if not provided by donation.

In the event a donor makes changes to the nature of a restricted gift which affects its classification among the net asset categories, such amounts are reflected as reclassifications in the statement of activities.

BETHEL UNIVERSITY
NOTES TO FINANCIAL STATEMENTS
JULY 31, 2013 AND 2012

A. SUMMARY OF SIGNIFICANT ACCOUNTING POLICES - Continued

Perkins Loan - Cash

As required by federal regulations, cash related to the Federal Perkins Loan Program is maintained in a separate bank account.

Student Accounts Receivable

The University records accounts receivable at their estimated net realizable value. An allowance for doubtful accounts is recorded based upon management's estimate of uncollectible accounts determined by analysis of specific student balances and a general reserve based upon agings of outstanding balances. Past due balances and delinquent receivables are charged against the allowance when they are determined to be uncollectible by management.

Notes Receivable - Students

Notes receivable from students at July 31, 2013 and 2012, totaled $266,751 and $258,600, respectively, net of allowances of $223,290 and $211,084, respectively. Student loans are granted by the University under the federally funded Perkins loan program. These funds are disbursed based upon the demonstration of financial need on the Perkins loan, at which time the loan will also begin accruing interest. Perkins loan amounts are then repaid through a third party billing service. Student loans are considered past due when payment has not been received within 30 days. At July 31, 2013 and 2012, student loans represented 0.32% and 0.30% of total assets, respectively.

The allowance for doubtful accounts is established based on prior collection experience and current economic factors which, in management's judgment, could influence the ability of loan recipients to repay the amounts per the loan terms. Loan balances are written off only when they are deemed to be permanently uncollectible.

Contributions Receivable

Contributions receivable are recorded at their estimated fair value using a discount rate commensurate with the rate on U.S. Government Securities whose maturities correspond to the maturities of the contributions. Contributions receivable are considered to be either conditional or unconditional promises to give. A conditional contribution is one which depends on the occurrence of a specified uncertain future event to become binding on the donor. Conditional contributions are not recorded as revenue until the condition is met, at which time they become unconditional. Unconditional contributions are recorded as revenue at the time verifiable evidence of the promise to give is received.

BETHEL UNIVERSITY
NOTES TO FINANCIAL STATEMENTS
JULY 31, 2013 AND 2012

A. SUMMARY OF SIGNIFICANT ACCOUNTING POLICES - Continued

Inventories

Inventories consist primarily of books and supplies and are stated at the lower of cost or market. Cost is determined using the average cost method.

Investments

Investments in marketable equity securities with readily determinable fair values and investments in debt securities are stated at their fair values in the statements of financial position. Fair value of investments is determined based on quoted market prices or using Level 2 or 3 inputs as described in Note I. All gains and losses (both realized and unrealized) and other investment income are reported in the statements of activities.

Property and Equipment

Property and equipment are recorded at cost at the date of acquisition or fair value at the date of donation in the case of gifts. Depreciation on property and equipment is calculated on the straight-line method over estimated useful lives of 20-70 years for buildings and improvements, 18 months - 10 years for equipment, furniture, and library books, 5 years for automobiles, and 20 years for other property. Property held under capital leases is being depreciated on the straight-line method based on the shorter of the estimated useful life of the property to the University or the life of the capital lease. Repairs and renovations that do not add value or extend the life of the assets are expensed as incurred. Depreciation and operation and maintenance charges are allocated to appropriate functional expense categories.

The estimate to complete construction in progress is $656,244 as of July 31, 2013.

Deferred Revenue

Deferred revenue consists primarily of charges and cash receipts collected prior to year-end for services rendered after year-end. These receipts pertain to upcoming tuition and fees.

Advances from the Federal Government for Student Loans

The Perkins Loan Program is a campus-based program providing revolving loan funds for financial assistance to eligible postsecondary school students based on financial need. The Department of Education provides funds along with the University which are used to make loans to eligible students at low interest rates. Refundable government advances for Perkins at July 31, 2013 and 2012 totaled $411,781 and $1,673,773, respectively.

BETHEL UNIVERSITY
NOTES TO FINANCIAL STATEMENTS
JULY 31, 2013 AND 2012

A. SUMMARY OF SIGNIFICANT ACCOUNTING POLICES - Continued

Derivative Instruments

The University accounts for its derivative instruments under Financial Accounting Standards Board Accounting Standards Codification (ASC) 815, *Derivatives and Hedging*, which establishes accounting and reporting standards requiring that derivative instruments be recorded in the statement of financial position at estimated fair value. Changes in a derivative's fair value are included in the statement of activities as a component of the change in net assets in the period of change. As described in Note E, the University has interest rate swap agreements which are considered to be derivative instruments. The University's interest rate risk management strategy is to stabilize cash flow requirements by maintaining interest rate swap contracts to convert certain variable-rate debt to a fixed rate.

Advertising Costs

Advertising costs are expensed as incurred and totaled approximately $1,296,474 and $1,506,537 for the years ended July 31, 2013 and 2012, respectively.

Tax Status

The University is exempt from Federal income taxes under 501(a) of the Internal Revenue Code ("IRC") as an organization described in IRC Section 501(c)(3). Accordingly, no provision for income taxes has been made in the accompanying financial statements. The University is not classified as a private foundation.

The University accounts for the effect of any uncertain tax positions based on a more likely than not threshold to the recognition of the tax positions being sustained based on the technical merits of the position under examination by the applicable taxing authority. If a tax position or positions are deemed to result in uncertainties of those position, the unrecognized tax benefit is estimated based on a cumulative probability assessment that aggregates the estimated tax liability for all uncertain tax positions. Tax positions for the University include, but are not limited to, the tax-exempt status and determination of whether certain income is subject to unrelated business income tax; however, the University has determined that such tax positions do not result in an uncertainty requiring recognition.

BETHEL UNIVERSITY
NOTES TO FINANCIAL STATEMENTS
JULY 31, 2013 AND 2012

A. SUMMARY OF SIGNIFICANT ACCOUNTING POLICES - Continued

Fair Value Measurements

Assets and liabilities recorded at fair value in the statements of financial position are categorized based on the level of judgment associated with the inputs used to measure their fair value. Related disclosures are included in Note I. Level inputs, as defined by Financial Accounting Standards Board Accounting Standards Codification ("ASC") 820, *Fair Value Measurements and Disclosures*, are as follows:

Level 1 - Values are unadjusted quoted prices for identical assets and liabilities in active markets accessible at the measurement date.

Level 2 - Inputs include quoted prices for similar assets or liabilities in active markets, quoted prices from those willing to trade in markets that are not active, or other inputs that are observable or can be corroborated by market data for the term of the instrument. Such inputs include market interest rates and volatilities, spreads and yield curves.

Level 3 - Certain inputs are unobservable (supported by little or no market activity) and significant to the fair value measurement. Unobservable inputs reflect the University's best estimate of what hypothetical market participants would use to determine a transaction price for the asset or liability at the reporting date.

Classification of Expenses

Expenses are classified functionally as a measure of service efforts and accomplishments. Direct expenses incurred for a single function are allocated entirely to that function. Joint expenses applicable to more than one function are allocated on the basis of objectively summarized information or management estimates.

B. CONTRIBUTIONS RECEIVABLE

Contributions receivable at July 31, 2013 and 2012 consist of the following:

	2013	2012
Contributions receivable (present value)	$ 6,071,724	$ 4,413,089
Less: allowance for doubtful contributions	(1,303,413)	(1,303,413)
	$ 4,768,311	$ 3,109,676

BETHEL UNIVERSITY
NOTES TO FINANCIAL STATEMENTS
JULY 31, 2013 AND 2012

B. CONTRIBUTIONS RECEIVABLE - Continued

Expected maturities of contributions receivable at July 31, 2013 are as follows:

Fiscal Year Ending July 31,	Amount
2014	$ 3,428,151
2015	668,587
2016	438,270
2017	353,337
2018	331,577
Thereafter	1,012,200
Total expected contributions	6,232,122
Less: allowance for net present value using a weighted average discount rate of 1.00%	(160,398)
Present value of contributions receivable	$ 6,071,724

C. INVESTMENTS

The investments of the University are principally administered by the University or by the Board of Stewardship of the Cumberland Presbyterian Church, Inc. (the "Board"). The funds administered by the Board are co-mingled with funds of other agencies of the Church. The University's portion represents approximately 5% of the funds administered by the Board at July 31, 2013 and 2012. The investments of the University are invested as follows:

	2013	2012
Administered by the Board:		
Marketable equity and debt securities	$2,865,236	$2,678,531
Administered by the University:		
Marketable equity and debt securities	76,967	10,533
Certificates of deposits (partially pledged, see Note E)	428,567	2,333,954
Other	24,949	24,949
	$3,395,719	$5,047,967

- 14 -

BETHEL UNIVERSITY
NOTES TO FINANCIAL STATEMENTS
JULY 31, 2013 AND 2012

D. BENEFICIAL INTEREST IN ASSETS HELD BY OTHERS

Beneficial interest in assets held by others represents arrangements in which a donor establishes and funds a perpetual trust administered by an individual or organization other than the University. The fair value of perpetually held trusts in which the University had a beneficial interest as of July 31, 2013 and 2012, was $3,489,347 and $3,208,813, respectively. The University records these trusts at estimated fair value. Income distributed to the University from the beneficial interest assets is temporarily restricted for scholarships.

E. DEBT

The University has the following debt obligations at July 31, 2013 and 2012:

	2013	2012
Note payable to Regions Bank, payable in monthly installments of $25,737 including interest of 4.79% through July 17, 2015, with a final payment of $1,396,516 due August 17, 2015; collateralized by certain real property.	$ 1,852,033	$ 2,066,553
Note payable to Regions Bank, payable in monthly installments of $25,936 including interest of 4.79% through July 17, 2015, with a final payment of $2,636,959 due August 17, 2015; collateralized by certain real property.	2,979,452	3,143,681
Note payable to Regions Bank, payable in monthly installments of $10,108 including interest of 4.18% through February 28, 2016; collateralized by certain real property.	787,135	873,559
Step down revolver credit agreement with Regions Bank, bearing interest of 6.35%. Monthly principal payments of $26,000 plus accrued interest are due through September 12, 2013 at which time all unpaid principal and interest are due; collateralized by substantially all real property.	4,679,146	4,987,891

- 15 -

BETHEL UNIVERSITY
NOTES TO FINANCIAL STATEMENTS
JULY 31, 2013 AND 2012

E. DEBT - Continued

	2013	2012
Notes payable to various financial institutions, with interest incurred at rates ranging from 3.29% to 5.5%. Certain notes are unsecured with the remaining notes collateralized by certificates of deposit, specified real estate, or specified equipment.	7,590	9,814
Line-of-credit totaling $2,000,000 with First Tennessee Bank, bearing interest at the prime rate plus 2% with a maturity date of August 31, 2013; collateralized by all bank accounts held at the bank. During fiscal 2013, the balance was paid in full.	-	2,000,000
Note payable to First Cumberland Presbyterian Church of McKenzie, payable in monthly principal installments of $2,000 through January 2013; collateralized by certain real property. During fiscal 2013, the balance was paid in full.	-	14,000
Bond bearing interest at the greater of 3.25% a variable per annum rate based on LIBOR plus certain basis points (6.12% at July 31, 2013), payable in monthly principal payments of $26,389 plus interest through April 4, 2015, with a final payment of $3,203,965 due May 4, 2015; collateralized by certain real property.	3,747,222	4,063,889
Credit loan totaling $2,000,000 with Regions Bank, bearing interest at 6.25%, payable in equal monthly principal and interest payments with a maturity date of August 16, 2016; collateralized by certain real property.	1,309,006	1,680,012

BETHEL UNIVERSITY
NOTES TO FINANCIAL STATEMENTS
JULY 31, 2013 AND 2012

E. DEBT - Continued

	2013	2012
Note payable to a related party private company totaling $9,000,000, bearing interest at 3.50%, payable in varying month installments; principal payments due in quarterly installments of $667,000, with the remaining balance due at final maturity on June 1, 2015. This note was renegotiated in fiscal 2013. (See Note R).	-	9,000,000
Bond bearing interest at a variable per annum rate based on LIBOR plus certain basis points (5.32% at July 31, 2013), payable in monthly principal and interest payments through July 28, 2016, with a final payment of $1,558,366 due August 30, 2016; collateralized by certain real property.	1,945,910	2,054,082
Bond bearing interest at a variable per annum rate based on LIBOR plus certain basis points (4.99% at July 31, 2013), payable in monthly principal and interest payments through July 28, 2016, with a final payment of $1,551,166 due September 16, 2016; collateralized by certain real property.	1,945,910	2,054,082
Bond bearing interest at a variable per annum rate based on LIBOR plus certain basis points (3.33% at July 31, 2013), payable in monthly principal and interest payments through July 28, 2016, with a final payment of $1,561,066 due September 1, 2016; collateralized by certain real property.	1,945,910	2,054,082
Bond bearing interest at a variable per annum rate based on LIBOR plus certain basis points (5.00% at July 31, 2013), payable in monthly principal and interest payments through July 28, 2016, with a final payment of $1,562,902 due September 15, 2016; collateralized by certain real property.	1,945,910	2,054,082

BETHEL UNIVERSITY
NOTES TO FINANCIAL STATEMENTS
JULY 31, 2013 AND 2012

E. DEBT - Continued

	2013	2012
Demand line-of-credit totaling $220,000 with McKenzie Banking Company, bearing interest at 2.80% payable on demand with a stated maturity date of February 23, 2014; collateralized by certificates of deposit.	202,635	219,900
Line-of-credit totaling $2,000,000 with Farmers and Merchants Bank, bearing interest at 6% with the full principal payment due on January 29, 2015; collateralized by accounts receivable.	975,810	2,000,000
Note payable to First Bank, bearing interest at 4%, with monthly payments of interest plus $5,000 of principal due beginning on February 15, 2013 through final maturity on August 2, 2013 upon which the remaining principal balance was paid; collateralized by certificate of deposit.	-	2,000,000
Line-of-credit totaling $500,000 with First Bank, bearing interest at 4.0%, maturing on July 30, 2013; collateralized by real property.	476,755	476,675
Note payable at First Bank, bearing interest at 5%, with the full principal balance maturing and paid in full on August 28, 2012.	-	300,000
Note payable to related party private Company, bearing interest at 3.5% with the full principal balance maturing in August 2013. This note was renegotiated in fiscal 2013. (See Note R).	-	1,174,985
Debt agreement through the City of Paris, Tennessee, bearing interest at SIFMA rate, plus 180 basis points (5% at July 31, 2013) and a trustee fee of $125. Interest payments are due monthly through June 1, 2026. Principal amounts totaling $6,500,000 are due in varying amounts ranging from $330,000 to $625,000 annually beginning June 1, 2013 through 2026. This amount was paid in full in August 2013.	288,363	6,500,000

BETHEL UNIVERSITY
NOTES TO FINANCIAL STATEMENTS
JULY 31, 2013 AND 2012

E. DEBT - Continued

	2013	2012
Note payable to a related party private company totaling $16,666,000, bearing interest at one year LIBOR plus 7%, payable in monthly installments of interest only. Starting on August 31, 2013, and continuing until January 31, 2015; principal payments due in monthly installments of $308,629.63, with the remaining balance due at final maturity on July 1, 2019. (See Note R).	16,666,000	-
Line-of-credit with a related party private company totaling $5,000,000, bearing interest at one year LIBOR plus 9%, payable in monthly installments of interest only starting on August 31, 2013, and continuing until August 31, 2015; first advance on this Note was on June 28, 2013 in the amount of $2,000,000. (See Note R).	2,000,000	-
	43,754,787	48,727,287
Interest rate swap	371,118	538,079
	$44,125,905	$49,265,366

The anticipated maturities of the University's notes payable are as follows:

Fiscal Year Ending July 31,	Amount
2014	$12,531,767
2015	9,598,582
2016	9,573,637
2017	12,050,801
	$43,754,787

BETHEL UNIVERSITY
NOTES TO FINANCIAL STATEMENTS
JULY 31, 2013 AND 2012

E. DEBT - Continued

Interest Rate Swap

During fiscal year 2011, the University entered into interest rate swap agreements with Regions Bank having an original notional amount of $6,337,500 to reduce the risk associated with debt interest rate fluctuations on portions of the Special Project bonds payable. During fiscal year 2012, the notional amount was increased to $8,450,000 in line with the related bonds payable. The University does not engage in trading these derivatives. The financial instruments are used to manage interest rate risk. The notional amounts are being amortized over the life of the agreements and at July 31, 2013 and 2012, the remaining amounts totaled $7,783,640 and $8,216,327, respectively. The interest rate swap agreements provide for the University to receive interest at a variable rate of 63.456% of LIBOR plus 321 basis points and to pay a fixed monthly interest rate of 5.32% expiring in August 2016.

Gains or losses on the derivatives are included as a component of the change in unrestricted net assets in the statement of activities. The University's interest rate risk management strategy is to stabilize cash flow requirements by maintaining the interest rate swap contracts to convert certain variable-rate debt to fixed rate. The fair value of the derivative was a liability at July 31, 2013 and 2012, totaling $371,118 and $538,079, respectively.

Interest Expense

For the years ending July 31, 2013 and 2012, Bethel University incurred interest expense of $2,405,667 and $1,948,270, respectively.

Compliance with Covenants

Certain loan agreements contain various covenants and establish certain financial ratios. The University was not in compliance with certain covenants and ratios at July 31, 2013. However, the University has obtained waivers from the relevant financial institution.

BETHEL UNIVERSITY
NOTES TO FINANCIAL STATEMENTS
JULY 31, 2013 AND 2012

F. OBLIGATIONS UNDER CAPITAL LEASES

The University has entered into capital lease agreements for certain computer equipment relating to the University's notebook computer program. The agreements expire at various dates through June 2014. Equipment under capital lease at July 31, 2013 and 2012, totaled $1,669,460 and $2,166,132, net of accumulated depreciation of $3,838,836 and $1,429,323, respectively.

Minimum future lease payments under capital leases as of July 31, 2013, are as follows:

Fiscal Year Ending July 31,	Amount
2014	$ 300,075
2015	253,910
	553,985
Less: Amount representing interest	(18,050)
Present value of net minimum lease payments	$ 535,935

Interest rates on capitalized leases are 3.20% and are imputed based on the lessor's implicit rate of return.

G. TEMPORARILY AND PERMANENTLY RESTRICTED NET ASSETS

At July 31, 2013 and 2012, temporarily restricted net assets are available for the following purposes:

	2013	2012
Scholarships	$ 84,693	$ 387,837
Contributions and other	4,768,311	1,796,494
	$4,853,004	$2,184,331

- 21 -

BETHEL UNIVERSITY
NOTES TO FINANCIAL STATEMENTS
JULY 31, 2013 AND 2012

G. TEMPORARILY AND PERMANENTLY RESTRICTED NET ASSETS - Continued

At July 31, 2013 and 2012, permanently restricted net assets are as follows:

	2013	2012
Beneficial interest in assets held by others	$3,489,348	$3,208,813
Student loan fund	3,965	3,965
Endowments	6,382,759	6,347,682
	$9,876,072	$9,560,460

The endowments represent nonexpendable funds that are subject to restrictions requiring the principal to be invested and only the income used as specified by the donors. The student loan fund consists of funds subject to donor restrictions related to loan requirements.

Net assets were released from donor restrictions by incurring expenses satisfying the restricted purposes. The following is a summary of the assets released from restrictions for the years ended July 31, 2013 and 2012:

	2013	2012
Institutional support expenditures	$ 654,580	$1,070,373
Scholarship and grant expenditures	55,466	262,286
Endowment expenditures	464,005	377,324
Auxiliary expenditures	-	-
	$1,174,051	$1,709,983

- 22 -

BETHEL UNIVERSITY
NOTES TO FINANCIAL STATEMENTS
JULY 31, 2013 AND 2012

H. ENDOWMENT

The University's endowment consists of individual donor-restricted funds established for a variety of purposes. As required by U.S. generally accepted accounting principles, net assets associated with endowment funds are classified and reported based on the existence or absence of donor-imposed restrictions.

Interpretation of Relevant Law

The Board of Trustees of the University has interpreted the applicable state laws as requiring the preservation of the original gift as of the gift date of the donor-restricted endowment funds absent explicit donor stipulations to the contrary. As a result of this interpretation, the University classified as permanently restricted net assets (a) the original value of gifts donated to the permanent endowment, (b) the original value of subsequent gifts to the permanent endowment, and (c) accumulations to the permanent endowment made in accordance with the direction of the applicable donor gift instrument at the time the accumulation is added to the fund. The remaining portion of the donor-restricted endowment fund that is not classified in permanently restricted net assets is classified as temporarily restricted net assets until those amounts are appropriated for expenditure by the University in a manner consistent with the standard of prudence prescribed by applicable state laws. In accordance with applicable state laws, the University, considers the following factors in making a determination to appropriate or accumulate donor-restricted endowment funds:

- The duration and preservation of the fund
- The purposes of the University and the donor-restricted endowment fund
- General economic conditions
- The possible effect of inflation and deflation
- The expected total return from income and the appreciation of investments
- Other resources of the University
- The investment policies of the University

BETHEL UNIVERSITY
NOTES TO FINANCIAL STATEMENTS
JULY 31, 2013 AND 2012

H. ENDOWMENT - Continued

Changes in Endowment Net Assets

	Temporarily Restricted	Permanently Restricted	Total
Endowment net assets, August 1, 2011	$ 674,784	$ 9,563,821	$ 10,238,605
Investment return:			
Investment income	25,394	-	25,394
Net depreciation (realized and unrealized)	-	(148,002)	(148,002)
Total investment return	25,394	(148,002)	(122,608)
Contributions	64,983	144,641	209,624
Appropriation of endowment assets for expenditure (scholarships)	(377,324)	-	(377,324)
Endowment net assets, July 31, 2012	387,837	9,560,460	9,948,297
Investment return:			
Investment income	137,643	-	137,643
Net appreciation depreciation (realized and unrealized)	-	280,535	280,535
Total investment return	137,643	280,535	418,178
Contributions	23,218	35,077	58,295
Appropriation of endowment assets for expenditure (scholarships)	(464,005)	-	(464,005)
Endowment net assets, July 31, 2013	$ 84,693	$ 9,876,072	$ 9,960,765

Return Objectives and Risk Parameters

The University has adopted investment and spending policies for endowment assets that attempt to provide a predictable stream of funding to programs supported by its endowment while seeking to maintain the purchasing power of the endowment assets. Endowment assets include those assets of donor-restricted funds that the University must hold in perpetuity or for a donor-specified period(s). Under this policy, as approved by the Board of Trustees, the endowment assets are invested with an overall total return objective as established for each time horizon: 1) Short Term, 2) Intermediate, and 3) Long Term according to the funding needs of the University. The returns will be compared with the generally accepted indices, i.e., the S&P 500, certain Bond Indices,

BETHEL UNIVERSITY
NOTES TO FINANCIAL STATEMENTS
JULY 31, 2013 AND 2012

H. ENDOWMENT - Continued

and MSCI EAFE stock indices, and an index of U.S. Treasury Bills depending on the time horizon in place. At July 31, 2013 and 2012, the endowment assets consist of investments in certificates of deposit, marketable debt and equity securities, beneficial interests in assets held by others.

Strategies Employed for Achieving Objectives

To satisfy its rate-of-return objectives, the University relies on a total return strategy in which investment returns are achieved through both capital appreciation (realized and unrealized) and current yield (interest and dividends). The University targets an investment allocation based on the three time horizons described above and that places emphasis on diversification of assets within prudent risk constraints.

Spending Policy and How the Investment Objectives Relate to Spending Policy

During fiscal year 2009, the University's Board of Trustees adopted a spending policy, which is based on the "Total Return" concept of determining the amount available for distribution. Total Return takes into consideration all of the elements of long-term investment return. The appropriate spending amount is based on the projected long-term Total Return of the funds, less an estimate of future inflation. The goal of the Total Return approach is to provide for a level of current income that protects the future purchasing power of the fund, thereby providing for increasing amounts of future income. The University anticipates that this percentage will be in the range of 3 to 5% of market value based on historical measurements of Total Return and Inflation. The market value of the fund will be noted each year on a specific date and a three-year rolling average market value will be established. The rolling three-year market value will be multiplied by the approved spending percentage which will be set annually.

BETHEL UNIVERSITY
NOTES TO FINANCIAL STATEMENTS
JULY 31, 2013 AND 2012

I. FAIR VALUES OF FINANCIAL INSTRUMENTS

Required disclosures concerning the estimated fair values of financial instruments are presented below. The estimated fair value amounts have been determined based on the University's assessment of available market information and appropriate valuation methodologies. The following table summarizes required fair value disclosures under ASC 825, *Financial Instruments*, and measurements at July 31, 2013 and 2012 for the assets and liabilities measured at fair value on a recurring basis under ASC 820, *Fair Value Measurements and Disclosures*:

	Carrying Amount	Estimated Fair Value	Measured at Fair Value	Fair Value Measurements Using		
				Level 1	Level 2	Level 3
July 31, 2013						
Assets:						
Investments	$3,395,719	$3,395,719	$3,395,719	$863,904	$516,808	$2,015,007
Beneficial interests in trusts	3,489,347	3,489,347	3,489,347	-	3,489,347	-
Liabilities:						
Notes payable and long-term obligation	44,661,840	49,665,811	-	-	-	-
July 31, 2012						
Assets:						
Investments	$5,047,967	$5,047,967	$5,047,967	$2,531,449	$1,277,376	$1,239,142
Beneficial interests in trusts	3,208,813	3,208,813	3,208,813	-	3,208,813	-
Liabilities:						
Notes payable and long-term obligation	51,596,572	57,377,520	-	-	-	-

BETHEL UNIVERSITY
NOTES TO FINANCIAL STATEMENTS
JULY 31, 2013 AND 2012

I. FAIR VALUES OF FINANCIAL INSTRUMENTS - Continued

Changes in Level 3 assets are as follows:

	Fair Value Measurements Using Significant Unobservable Inputs (Level 3)	
	2013	2012
Beginning Balance	$1,239,142	$ 1,443,976
Purchases and sales, net	696,570	24,331
Unrealized gain (loss)	79,295	(229,165)
Ending Balance	$2,015,007	$ 1,239,142

The following methods and assumptions were used to estimate the fair value of each class of financial instruments:

Cash equivalents, receivables, accounts payable and accrued payroll and benefits, deferred revenue and advances from the Federal government for student loans

The carrying values of these items approximate their fair values due to the short maturities of these instruments.

Investments

Fair values are based on quoted market prices, where available, and Level 2 and 3 inputs. The carrying amounts and the fair values of the University's investments are presented in Note C.

Notes payable and obligations under capital leases

For fixed rate debt, fair value was estimated using discounted cash flow analyses based on the University's current incremental borrowing rates for similar types of borrowing arrangements.

J. DEGREE-COMPLETION PROGRAM

Revenue from the degree-completion program in fiscal years 2013 and 2012 was $12,693,723 and $14,276,913, which represents approximately 19% and 25% of the University's unrestricted revenue, respectively.

BETHEL UNIVERSITY
NOTES TO FINANCIAL STATEMENTS
JULY 31, 2013 AND 2012

K. FUND RAISING ACTIVITIES

The University conducts fund raising activities each year. The total cost of these activities for fiscal years 2013 and 2012, was $712,179 and $789,314, respectively.

L. RETIREMENT PLAN

The University's full-time employees may participate in either a retirement plan which is administered by the Cumberland Presbyterian Board of Finance or the TIAA/CREF Plan, which is a national pension plan. Payments are made to the plans by withholding five percent of the employee's salary with the University paying a matching amount. Total matching contributions were made by the University for fiscal years 2013 and 2012, of $242,434 and $500,022, respectively.

M. HEALTH BENEFITS

The University provides group health benefits coverage for participating employees through its membership in the TICUA Benefit Consortium ("Consortium"). The Consortium is a partially self-insured health benefit plan consisting of eight private colleges and universities in Tennessee, and is exempt under Section 501(c)(9) of the Internal Revenue Code. Funding for the plan has been based upon actuarial calculations using historical experience of claims paid and estimates of claims outstanding.

N. CONCENTRATION OF RISKS

Concentration of Risk

The University generates revenue predominantly from tuition and fees, investment income, gifts, auxiliary enterprises and contributions. In planning and budgeting during a fiscal year, significant reliance is placed on meeting tuition, gift, auxiliary, investment earnings and contribution goals in order for the University to sustain successful operations. In the event that enrollment or gifts and contributions significantly decrease in any one year, operations could be adversely affected.

Financial instruments that potentially subject the University to concentrations of credit risk and market risk consist principally of cash equivalents, investments, and student receivables.

The University, in connection with its activities, grants credit to students that involves, to varying degrees, elements of credit risk. The maximum accounting loss from credit risk is limited to the amounts that are recognized in the accompanying statements of financial position as student accounts receivable at July 31, 2013 and 2012.

BETHEL UNIVERSITY
NOTES TO FINANCIAL STATEMENTS
JULY 31, 2013 AND 2012

N. CONCENTRATION OF RISKS - Continued

The University also has several bank deposits in excess of those insured under regulatory insurance limits.

O. OPERATING LEASES

The University leases office space for satellite campuses relating to its degree-completion program. These leases expire at various dates through fiscal year 2016. Minimum future rental payments under non-cancelable operating leases as of July 31, 2013 are as follows:

Fiscal Year Ending July 31,	Amount
2014	$ 2,340,293
2015	1,866,843
2016	1,792,359
2017	1,443,300
2018	1,443,300
Thereafter	1,443,300
	$10,329,395

Rent expense under the non-cancelable operating leases totaled $953,964 and $972,560 for the years ended July 31, 2013 and 2012, respectively.

On July 31, 2013, the University entered into a sale-leaseback agreement with a related party for a building in Paris, Tennessee. The purchasor entered into a note receivable with the University for $8,200,000, which approximated the carrying value of the building, and therefore, no gain or loss was recognized. The purchasor will be paying the note receivable over 30 years at an interest rate of 2%. The University will lease the building for six years with monthly payments of $120,275.

BETHEL UNIVERSITY
NOTES TO FINANCIAL STATEMENTS
JULY 31, 2013 AND 2012

P. FUNCTIONAL ALLOCATION OF EXPENSES

During the years ended July 31, 2013 and 2012, the University allocated the cost of certain professional fees and the operation and maintenance of physical plant, including depreciation expense of $6,010,614 and $4,636,749, respectively, over the cost of providing instruction, research, academic support, institutional support and auxiliary enterprises as follows:

	2013	2012
Instruction	$3,979,934	$3,275,409
Academic support	103,809	139,641
Student services	721,192	634,373
Institutional support	1,304,498	1,249,231
Auxiliary enterprises	833,579	624,092
Total operation and maintenance of physical plant	$6,943,012	$5,922,746

Q. LITIGATION AND CONTINGENCIES

The University is a defendant in legal actions from time to time in the normal course of operations. It is not currently possible to state the ultimate liability, if any, in these matters. In the opinion of management, any resulting liability from these actions will not have a material adverse effect on the financial position of the activities of the University.

R. RELATED PARTY TRANSACTIONS

During fiscal years 2013 and 2012, the University had an agreement with a company owned by a member of the University's faculty. Under the agreement, the company developed and is maintaining the University's online masters of business administration program. Specifically, the company is responsible for developing course work, producing lectures and graphic presentations, and maintaining student records. Fees under the agreement are $300 per student, per course and the agreement has no contractual expiration. Total fees incurred during fiscal years 2013 and 2012 were $7,635,564 and $5,967,850, respectively.

During fiscal years 2013 and 2012, the University contracted with companies owned by members of the Board of Trustees. Under the contract, the companies were responsible for the construction of certain University buildings. Total charges incurred and capitalized during the fiscal years 2013 and 2012 were $1,106,656 and $7,881,587, respectively.

- 30 -

BETHEL UNIVERSITY
NOTES TO FINANCIAL STATEMENTS
JULY 31, 2013 AND 2012

R. RELATED PARTY TRANSACTIONS - Continued

During fiscal years 2013 and 2012, the University entered into note payable with a private company owned by a member of the Board of Trustees. Total outstanding balances during fiscal years 2013 and 2012 were $18,666,000 and $10,174,985 respectively (See Note E).

The University entered into a leasing arrangement with a related party as described in Note O.

S. SUBSEQUENT EVENTS

The University has evaluated subsequent events through December 8, 2013, the issuance date of the University's financial statements, and has determined that there are no subsequent event requires disclosure.

OTHER INFORMATION

BETHEL UNIVERSITY
SCHEDULE OF EXPENDITURES OF FEDERAL AWARDS
YEAR ENDED JULY 31, 2013

Federal Grantor/Pass-through Grantor/ Program or Cluster Title	Federal CFDA Number	Federal Expenditures
U.S. Department of Education - Direct Awards		
Student Financial Assistance - Cluster: (1)		
Federal Direct Student Loans Program (Note C)	84.268	$62,870,520
Federal Perkins Loan Program (Note B)	84.038	103,065
Federal Work-Study Program	84.033	153,688
Federal Supplemental Educational Opportunity Grants Program	84.007	235,850
Federal Pell Grant Program	84.063	15,391,275
Teacher Education Assistance for University and Higher Education Grant	84.379	43,000
Total Student Financial Assistance - Cluster		78,797,398
U.S. Department of Education - Pass-through Program from:		
Special Education: Grants to States Tennessee Teachers Assistants Grant	84.027A	116,002
Total Expenditures of Federal Awards		$78,913,400

(1) Tested as a major program

See independent auditor's report.

BETHEL UNIVERSITY
NOTES TO SCHEDULE OF EXPENDITURES OF FEDERAL AWARDS
YEAR ENDED JULY 31, 2013

A. BASIS OF PRESENTATION

The accompanying schedule of expenditures of federal awards is presented in accordance with the requirements of OMB Circular A-133, *Audits of States, Local Governments, and Non-Profit Organizations*, on the accrual basis of accounting consistent with the basis of accounting used by the University in the preparation of its financial statements.

B. FEDERAL PERKINS LOAN PROGRAM - CFDA #84.038

The outstanding loan balance for the Federal Perkins Loan Program at July 31, 2013 was $266,751, net of the allowance for uncollectible loans of $223,290. Total loan disbursements for the program for the year ended July 31, 2013, were $103,065. These disbursements include expenditures such as loans to students, repayments of fund capital, and administrative expenditures.

C. FEDERAL DIRECT LOANS PROGRAM - CFDA #84.268

During the fiscal year ending July 31, 2013, the University processed $62,870,520 of new loans under the Federal Direct Loans program (which includes subsidized and unsubsidized Stafford Loans, Parents' for Undergraduate Students, and Supplemental Loans for Students)

D. MATCHING FUNDS

The University provided matching funds of $78,614 for the Federal Supplemental Educational Opportunity Grants program and $51,229 for the Federal Work Study program during the fiscal year ended July 31, 2013.

Independent Auditor's Report on Internal Control Over
Financial Reporting and on Compliance and Other Matters
Based on an Audit of Financial Statements Performed in
Accordance with *Government Auditing Standards*

The Board of Trustees
Bethel University
McKenzie, Tennessee

We have audited, in accordance with the auditing standards generally accepted in the United States of America and the standards applicable to financial audits contained in *Government Auditing Standards* issued by the Comptroller General of the United States, the financial statements of Bethel University (the "University"), which comprise the statement of financial position as of July 31, 2013, and the related statements of activities and cash flows for the year then ended, and the related notes to the financial statements, and have issued our report thereon dated December 8, 2013.

Internal Control Over Financial Reporting

In planning and performing our audit of the financial statements, we considered the University's internal control over financial reporting (internal control) to determine the audit procedures that are appropriate in the circumstances for the purpose of expressing our opinion on the financial statements, but not for the purpose of expressing an opinion on the effectiveness of the University's internal control. Accordingly, we do not express an opinion on the effectiveness of the University's internal control.

A *deficiency in internal control* exists when the design or operation of a control does not allow management or employees, in the normal course of performing their assigned functions, to prevent, or detect and correct misstatements on a timely basis. A *material weakness* is a deficiency, or a combination of deficiencies, in internal control such that there is a reasonable possibility that a material misstatement of the entity's financial statements will not be prevented, or detected and corrected on a timely basis. A *significant deficiency* is a deficiency, or a combination of deficiencies, in internal control that is less severe than a material weakness, yet important enough to merit attention by those charged with governance.

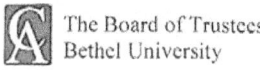
The Board of Trustees
Bethel University

Our consideration of the internal control was for the limited purpose described in the first paragraph of this section and was not designed to identify all deficiencies in internal control that might be material weaknesses or significant deficiencies. Given these limitations, during our audit we did not identify any deficiencies in internal control that we consider to be material weaknesses. However, material weaknesses may exist that have not been identified.

Compliance and Other Matters

As part of obtaining reasonable assurance about whether the University's financial statements are free from material misstatement, we performed tests of its compliance with certain provisions of laws, regulations, contracts, and grant agreements, noncompliance with which could have a direct and material effect on the determination of financial statement amounts. However, providing an opinion on compliance with those provisions was not an objective of our audit, and accordingly, we do not express such an opinion. The results of our tests disclosed no instances of noncompliance or other matters that are required to be reported under *Government Auditing Standards*.

Purpose of this Report

The purpose of this report is solely to describe the scope of our testing of internal control and compliance and the results of that testing, and not to provide an opinion on the effectiveness of the University's internal control or on compliance. This report is an integral part of an audit performed in accordance with *Government Auditing Standards* in considering the University's internal control and compliance. Accordingly, this communication is not suitable for any other purpose.

Crosslin & Associates, P.C.
Nashville, Tennessee
December 8, 2013

Independent Auditor's Report on Compliance For The Major
Program and on Internal Control Over Compliance
Required by OMB Circular A-133

The Board of Trustees
Bethel University
McKenzie, Tennessee

Report on Compliance for Each Major Federal Program

We have audited Bethel University's (the "University") compliance with the types of compliance requirements described in the *OMB Circular A-133 Compliance Supplement* that could have a direct and material effect on the University's major federal program for the year ended July 31, 2013. The University's major federal program is identified in the summary of auditor's results section of the accompanying schedule of findings and questioned costs.

Management's Responsibility

Management is responsible for compliance with the requirements of laws, regulations, contracts, and grants applicable to its federal programs.

Auditor's Responsibility

Our responsibility is to express an opinion on compliance for each of the University's major federal programs based on our audit of the types of compliance requirements referred to above. We conducted our audit of compliance in accordance with auditing standards generally accepted in the United States of America; the standards applicable to financial audits contained in *Government Auditing Standards*, issued by the Comptroller General of the United States; and OMB Circular A-133, *Audits of States, Local Governments, and Non-Profit Organizations*. Those standards and OMB Circular A-133 require that we plan and perform the audit to obtain reasonable assurance about whether noncompliance with the types of compliance requirements referred to above that could have a direct and material effect on a major federal program occurred. An audit includes examining, on a test basis, evidence about the University's compliance with those requirements and performing such other procedures as we considered necessary in the circumstances.

We believe that our audit provides a reasonable basis for our opinion on compliance for each major federal program. However, our audit does not provide a legal determination of the University's compliance.

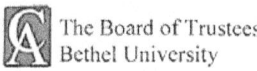
The Board of Trustees
Bethel University

Opinion on Each Major Federal Program

In our opinion, the University complied, in all material respects, with the types of compliance requirements referred to above that could have a direct and material effect on its major federal program for the year ended July 31, 2013.

Report on Internal Control Over Compliance

Management of the University is responsible for establishing and maintaining effective internal control over compliance with the types of compliance requirements referred to above. In planning and performing our audit of compliance, we considered the University's internal control over compliance with the types of requirements that could have a direct and material effect on its major federal program to determine the auditing procedures that is appropriate in the circumstances for the purpose of expressing an opinion on compliance for its major federal program and to test and report on internal control over compliance in accordance with OMB Circular A-133, but not for the purpose of expressing an opinion on the effectiveness of internal control over compliance. Accordingly, we do not express an opinion on the effectiveness of the University's internal control over compliance.

A *deficiency in internal control over compliance* exists when the design or operation of a control over compliance does not allow management or employees, in the normal course of performing their assigned functions, to prevent, or detect and correct, noncompliance with a type of compliance requirement of a federal program on a timely basis. A *material weakness in internal control over compliance* is a deficiency, or combination of deficiencies, in internal control over compliance, such that there is a reasonable possibility that material noncompliance with a type of compliance requirement of a federal program will not be prevented, or detected and corrected, on a timely basis. A *significant deficiency in internal control over compliance* is a deficiency, or a combination of deficiencies, in internal control over compliance with a type of compliance requirement of a federal program that is less severe than a material weakness in internal control over compliance, yet important enough to merit attention by those charged with governance.

Our consideration of internal control over compliance was for the limited purpose described in the first paragraph of this section and was not designed to identify all deficiencies in internal control over compliance that might be material weaknesses or significant deficiencies. We did not identify any deficiencies in internal control over compliance that we consider to be material weaknesses. However, material weaknesses may exist that have not been identified.

The purpose of this report on internal control over compliance is solely to describe the scope of our testing of internal control over compliance and the results of that testing based on the requirements of OMB Circular A-133. Accordingly, this report is not suitable for any other purpose.

Crosslin & Associates, P.C.
Nashville, Tennessee
December 8, 2013

BETHEL UNIVERSITY
SCHEDULE OF FINDINGS AND QUESTIONED COSTS
YEAR ENDED JULY 31, 2013

I. SUMMARY OF INDEPENDENT AUDITOR'S RESULTS

Financial Statements

Type of auditor's report issued:	Unmodified
Internal control over financial reporting:	
• Material weakness(es) identified?	___Yes _X_ No
• Significant deficiency(ies) identified?	___Yes _X_ None Reported
Noncompliance material to financial statements noted?	___Yes _X_ No

Federal Awards

Internal control over major program:	
• Material weakness(es) identified?	___Yes _X_ No
• Significant deficiency(ies) identified?	___Yes _X_ None Reported
Type of auditor's report issued on compliance for major program:	Unmodified
Any audit findings disclosed that are required to be reported in accordance with section 510(a) of Circular A-133?	___Yes _X_ No

BETHEL UNIVERSITY
SCHEDULE OF FINDINGS AND QUESTIONED COSTS
YEAR ENDED JULY 31, 2013

I. SUMMARY OF INDEPENDENT AUDITOR'S RESULTS - Continued

Major Program:

CFDA Number	Name of Federal Program	Amount Expended
SFA Cluster:		
84.063	Federal Pell Grant Program	$15,391,275
84.268	Federal Direct Student Loans Program (new loans processed)	62,870,520
84.038	Federal Perkins Loan Program	103,065
84.007	Federal Supplemental Educational Opportunity Grants Program	235,850
84.033	Federal Work Study Program	153,688
84.038	Perkins Loans ($490,034 outstanding balance of loans)	-
84.379	TEACHER Education Assistance for College and Higher Education Grant	43,000

Dollar threshold used to distinguish between type A
and type B programs $300,000

Auditee qualified as low-risk auditee   __Yes X No

II. FINANCIAL STATEMENT FINDINGS

None reported.

III. FINDINGS AND QUESTIONED COSTS FOR FEDERAL AWARDS

None reported.

- 39 -

BETHEL UNIVERSITY
SUMMARY SCHEDULE OF PRIOR AUDIT FINDINGS
YEAR ENDED JULY 31, 2013

ITEM #IC 12-1

ACCOUNTING SYSTEM, FISCAL MANAGEMENT AND ACCOUNTING DISCIPLINE

Criteria, Condition, Context, Cause and Effect

In general, an accounting and information system should provide management with accurate and timely financial information to enable well-informed business decisions to be made. The University's system did not function properly during fiscal 2012 and therefore, did not meet these expectations. This was due to various reasons including the lack of communication between senior management regarding major transactions, and the lack of application of generally accepted accounting principles to significant transactions throughout the year. Certain accounting functions, such as proper maintenance and review of the general ledger were not consistently performed during the year weakening internal controls and making interim financial information unavailable or possibly inaccurate. Problems in receiving timely and accurate financial information can significantly impact management's ability to effectively guide an organization. Critical areas such as financial analysis, budgetary control, and cash flow can all be impacted. Government funding, the obtaining of grants, contributions and banking relationships can also be jeopardized by the lack of timely and accurate financial information and the lack of communication. We noted instances where significant transactions were not communicated throughout the various levels of management, as well as the accounting function, in order to properly record these transactions within the general ledger and financial statements, and allow informed decisions to be made. There were also significant accounting areas which were not evaluated for adherence to generally accepted accounting principles through the year, where significant proposed audit adjustments resulted. These instances affected many major asset, liability and net asset accounts such as:

- Receivables (government receivables, student accounts and pledges)
- Property, buildings, and equipment
- Payables and accrued expenses
- Deferred revenue
- Endowment funds
- Recording of restrictions placed on revenues received
- Recording of various revenues and expenses to their proper accounts

BETHEL UNIVERSITY
SUMMARY SCHEDULE OF PRIOR AUDIT FINDINGS
YEAR ENDED JULY 31, 2013

ITEM #IC 12-1 - Continued

We understand that certain personnel changes and additions have been made by the University subsequent to the end of fiscal year 2013. These personnel are in the process of implementing changes to the system and assure existing processes are operating as designed by the University. We have not yet been able to test and evaluate the effectiveness of these accounting changes and procedures.

Recommendation and Benefit

We recommend that the University monitor and improve the accounting and information systems, implement proper accounting procedures and assure personnel are in place that will facilitate the production of accurate financial information, and provide for accountability of assets and the maintenance of an accurate historical record of operations. Accounting and financial information is the language of business and must be properly assessed and comprehended in a timely manner in order to allow management to guide and direct the University into the future. The following are recommendations, which if implemented, can help move the University toward these goals:

- Improvement of the current accounting policies and procedures manual to include processes to identify and adjust specific accounts and transactions that have not been properly recorded in accordance with generally accepted accounting principles.

- Properly train and supervise accounting staff and create a fiscal management team with the authority to assure that the proper procedures and internal controls are in place and are consistently followed.

- Develop clear lines of communication and required levels of approval throughout senior management in regards to significant transactions and events in order to ensure these items are appropriately recorded and reported within the accounting system.

Current Status

This item has been resolved in fiscal year ended July 31, 2013.

**CUMBERLAND PRESBYTERIAN
CHILDREN'S HOME**

FINANCIAL STATEMENTS
AND
AUDITORS' REPORT

DECEMBER 31, 2013

CUMBERLAND PRESBYTERIAN CHILDREN'S HOME

TABLE OF CONTENTS

	Page
Independent Auditors' Report	1
Statement of Financial Position	3
Statement of Activities	4
Statement of Cash Flows	5
Statement of Functional Expenses	6-7
Notes to the Financial Statements	8-14
Supplemental Information	
Schedule of Board of Stewardship Endowments	16-17

MEMBERS:
AMERICAN INSTITUTE OF
CERTIFIED PUBLIC
ACCOUNTANTS

TEXAS SOCIETY OF CERTIFIED
PUBLIC ACCOUNTANTS

HANKINS, EASTUP, DEATON, TONN & SEAY
A PROFESSIONAL CORPORATION

CERTIFIED PUBLIC ACCOUNTANTS

902 NORTH LOCUST
P.O. BOX 977
DENTON, TEXAS 76202-0977

TEL. (940) 387-8563
FAX (940) 383-4746

Independent Auditors' Report

Cumberland Presbyterian Children's Home
Denton, Texas

We have audited the accompanying financial statements of Cumberland Presbyterian Children's Home (a nonprofit organization), which comprise the statement of financial position as of December 31, 2013 and the related statements of activities and cash flows for the year then ended, and the related notes to the financial statements.

Management's Responsibility for the Financial Statements

Management is responsible for the preparation and fair presentation of these financial statements in accordance with accounting principles generally accepted in the United States of America; this includes the design, implementation, and maintenance of internal control relevant to the preparation and fair presentation of financial statements that are free from material misstatement, whether due to fraud or error.

Auditor's Responsibility

Our responsibility is to express an opinion on these financial statements based on our audit. We conducted our audit in accordance with auditing standards generally accepted in the United States of America. Those standards require that we plan and perform the audit to obtain reasonable assurance about whether the financial statements are free of material misstatement.

An audit involves performing procedures to obtain audit evidence about the amounts and disclosures in the financial statements. The procedures selected depend on the auditor's judgment, including the assessment of the risks of material misstatement of the financial statements, whether due to fraud or error. In making those risk assessments, the auditor considers internal control relevant to the entity's preparation and fair presentation of the financial statements in order to design audit procedures that are appropriate in the circumstances, but not for the purpose of expressing an opinion on the effectiveness of the entity's internal control. Accordingly, we express no such opinion. An audit also includes evaluating the appropriateness of accounting policies used and the reasonableness of significant accounting estimates made by management, as well as evaluating the overall presentation of the financial statements. We believe that the audit evidence we have obtained is sufficient and appropriate to provide a basis for our audit opinion.

Opinion

In our opinion, the financial statements referred to above present fairly, in all material respects, the financial position of Cumberland Presbyterian Children's Home as of December 31, 2013, and the changes in its net assets and its cash flows for the year then ended in accordance with accounting principles generally accepted in the United States of America.

Hankins, Eastup, Deaton, Tonn & Seay

Hankins, Eastup, Deaton, Tonn & Seay
Denton, Texas
May 29, 2014

CUMBERLAND PRESBYTERIAN CHILDREN'S HOME

STATEMENT OF FINANCIAL POSITION
DECEMBER 31, 2013

ASSETS:

Cash and cash equivalents	$ 2,428,124
Due from Board of Stewardship	74,689
Other receivables	57,551
Prepaid expenses	20,512
Land, buildings and equipment, net	4,122,229
Other long-term investments	9,105,467
TOTAL ASSETS	$15,808,572

LIABILITIES AND NET ASSETS:

Liabilities:	
Accounts payable and accrued liabilities	$ 48,001
Total Liabilities	48,001
Net Assets:	
Unrestricted	8,327,458
Temporarily restricted	56,060
Permanently restricted	7,377,053
Total Net Assets	15,760,571
TOTAL LIABILITIES AND NET ASSETS	$15,808,572

See Accompanying Notes to the Financial Statements.

CUMBERLAND PRESBYTERIAN CHILDREN'S HOME

STATEMENT OF ACTIVITIES
FOR THE YEAR ENDED DECEMBER 31, 2013

	Unrestricted	Temporarily Restricted	Permanently Restricted	Total
Revenues, Gains and Other Support:				
Contributions and grants	$ 727,318	$ 30,000	$ 83,051	$ 840,369
CPS revenue	537,380	-	-	537,380
Other program fees	32,773	-	-	32,773
Denominational support	74,386	-	-	74,386
Income on long-term investments	364,700	3	-	364,703
Oil and gas royalties	15,109	-	-	15,109
Realized gains on investments	-	-	510,693	510,693
Unrealized gains on investments	79,711	2,185	66,087	147,983
Special events	28,403	-	-	28,403
Rents	27,722	-	-	27,722
Other	11,233	-	-	11,233
Subtotal	1,898,735	32,188	659,831	2,590,754
Net assets released from Restrictions	-	-	-	-
Total Revenue, Gains and Other Support	1,898,735	32,188	659,831	2,590,754
Expenses:				
Program services:				
Children's residential program	1,064,043	-	-	1,064,043
Emergency shelter program	622,856	-	-	622,856
Single parent family program	311,429	-	-	311,429
Cumberland family services	181,665	-	-	181,665
Management and general	308,176	-	-	308,176
Fundraising	188,577	-	-	188,577
Total Expenses	2,676,746	-	-	2,676,746
Change in net assets	(778,011)	32,188	659,831	(85,992)
Net assets at beginning of year	9,105,469	23,872	6,717,222	15,846,563
Net assets at end of year	$ 8,327,458	$ 56,060	$ 7,377,053	$15,760,571

See Accompanying Notes to the Financial Statements.

CUMBERLAND PRESBYTERIAN CHILDREN'S HOME

STATEMENT OF CASH FLOWS
FOR THE YEAR ENDED DECEMBER 31, 2013

Cash Flows from Operating Activities:	
Change in net assets	$ (85,992)
Adjustments to reconcile change in net assets to net cash provided by operating activities:	
Depreciation	209,146
(Increase) Decrease in receivables	(70,585)
(Increase) Decrease in prepaid expenses	34,512
Increase (Decrease) in accounts payable/accrued liabilities	(8,591)
Realized gains on investments	(510,693)
Unrealized gains on investments	(147,983)
Contributions restricted for long-term investment	(83,051)
Net Cash Provided (Used) by Operating Activities	(663,237)
Cash Flows from Investing Activities:	
Redemption of investments (net)	1,381,171
Net (gains) losses on investments	658,676
Net Cash Provided (Used) by Investing Activities	2,039,847
Cash Flows from Financing Activities:	
Proceeds from contributions restricted for investment in endowment	83,051
Net Cash Provided by Financing Activities:	83,051
Net Increase in Cash and Cash Equivalents	1,459,661
Cash and Cash Equivalents at Beginning of Year	968,463
Cash and Cash Equivalents at End of Year	$ 2,428,124
Supplemental Data:	
Interest paid during the year	$ 1,723
Noncash investing activities:	
Gifts in kind	1,048
Unrealized gains on investments	147,983

See Accompanying Notes to the Financial Statements.

CUMBERLAND PRESBYTERIAN CHILDREN'S HOME

STATEMENT OF FUNCTIONAL EXPENSES
FOR THE YEAR ENDED DECEMBER 31, 2013

	Program Services			
	Children's Residential Program	Emergency Shelter Program	Single Parent Family Program	Cumberland Family Services
Salaries and Wages	$ 580,141	$ 339,595	$ 169,797	$ 99,049
Employee Benefits	76,588	44,832	22,416	13,076
Payroll Taxes	46,216	27,053	13,527	7,890
Total Salaries and Related Expenses	702,945	411,480	205,740	120,015
Activities and travel	40,724	23,838	11,919	6,953
Clothing and supplies	24,668	14,440	7,220	4,212
Food and dining out	31,584	18,488	9,244	5,392
Training and education	8,640	5,058	2,529	1,475
Medical and dental	3,234	1,893	947	552
Other program expenses	3,347	1,959	980	571
Utilities	52,635	30,811	15,405	8,986
Property, liability insurance	24,355	14,257	7,128	4,158
Repairs and maintenance	30,902	18,089	9,045	5,276
Supplies, postage, printing	17,318	10,138	5,069	2,957
Computer software, maintenance	8,280	4,847	2,424	1,414
Small furniture and equipment	12,203	7,143	3,572	2,083
Permits and fees	2,622	1,535	767	447
Special events expense	-	-	-	-
Vehicle expenses	9,667	5,659	2,829	1,651
Professional fees	5,169	3,026	1,513	883
Public relations/communications	-	-	-	-
Board expense	-	-	-	-
Interest	-	-	-	-
Total Expenses Before Depreciation	978,293	572,661	286,331	167,025
Depreciation	85,750	50,195	25,098	14,640
TOTAL EXPENSES	$ 1,064,043	$ 622,856	$ 311,429	$ 181,665

The accompanying notes are an integral part of this statement

| | Supporting Services | | | Total |
Total	Fundraising	Administration	Total	Expenses
$ 1,188,582	$ 70,749	$ 155,648	$ 226,397	$ 1,414,979
156,912	9,340	20,547	29,887	186,799
94,686	5,636	12,399	18,035	112,721
1,440,180	85,725	188,594	274,319	1,714,499
83,434	4,966	10,926	15,892	99,326
50,540	3,008	6,618	9,626	60,166
64,708	3,852	8,473	12,325	77,033
17,702	1,054	2,318	3,372	21,074
6,626	-	-	-	6,626
6,857	-	-	-	6,857
107,837	6,419	14,122	20,541	128,378
49,898	2,970	6,535	9,505	59,403
63,312	3,769	8,290	12,059	75,371
35,482	2,112	4,646	6,758	42,240
16,965	1,010	2,221	3,231	20,196
25,001	1,488	3,274	4,762	29,763
5,371	320	703	1,023	6,394
-	22,608	-	22,608	22,608
19,806	1,179	2,594	3,773	23,579
10,591	-	12,880	12,880	23,471
-	37,640	-	37,640	37,640
-	-	11,253	11,253	11,253
-	-	1,723	1,723	1,723
2,004,310	178,120	285,170	463,290	2,467,600
175,683	10,457	23,006	33,463	209,146
$ 2,179,993	$ 188,577	$ 308,176	$ 496,753	$ 2,676,746

CUMBERLAND PRESBYTERIAN CHILDREN'S HOME

NOTES TO FINANCIAL STATEMENTS
DECEMBER 31, 2013

NOTE A - SUMMARY OF SIGNIFICANT ACCOUNTING POLICIES

Organization

Cumberland Presbyterian Children's Home (CPCH) is a nonprofit organization originally chartered in Kentucky in 1904 and moved to Denton, Texas in 1932. Its purpose is to provide long-term residential basic child care for children between the ages of 3 and 17. CPCH is licensed to care for up to 40 children. CPCH's primary sources of revenue are income from child care, donations and income from long-term investments.

Basis of Presentation

The accompanying financial statements have been prepared on the accrual basis of accounting in accordance with accounting principles generally accepted in the United States of America. Net assets and revenues, expenses, gains, and losses are classified based on the existence or absence of donor-imposed restrictions. Accordingly, net assets of CPCH and changes therein are classified and reported as follows:

Unrestricted Net Assets – not subject to donor-imposed restrictions. Unrestricted net assets may be designated for specific purposes by action of the Board of Directors.

Temporarily Restricted Net Assets – subject to donor-imposed stipulations that may be fulfilled by actions of CPCH to meet the stipulations or that become unrestricted at the date specified by the donor.

Permanently Restricted Net Assets – subject to donor-imposed stipulations that they be retained and invested permanently by CPCH to use all or part of the investment return on these net assets for specified or unspecified purposes.

Income Taxes

CPCH is exempt from Federal income taxes under Section 501(c)(3) of the Internal Revenue Code. In addition, CPCH has been determined by the Internal Revenue Service not to be a private foundation within the meaning of Section 509(a)(1) and 170 (b)(1)(A)(vi) of the Code.

Fixed Assets

All acquisitions of property and equipment in excess of $5,000 and all expenditures for repairs, maintenance, or improvements that significantly prolong the useful lives of the assets are capitalized. Prior to 1/1/13 CPCH used an acquisition cost threshold of $1,000 but increased the threshold to $5,000 at that date in order to reduce the administrative costs of recording and tracking items of furniture and equipment. Purchases of property and equipment are recorded at cost. Donations of property and equipment are recorded as support at their estimated fair value at the date of gift. Such donations are reported as unrestricted support unless the donor has restricted the donated asset to a specific purpose. Assets donated with explicit restrictions regarding their use and contributions of cash that must be used to acquire property and equipment are reported as restricted support. Absent donor stipulations regarding how long those donated assets must be maintained, CPCH reports expirations of donor restrictions when the donated or acquired assets are placed in service as instructed by the donor. CPCH reclassifies temporarily restricted net assets to unrestricted net assets at that time. Property and equipment are depreciated using the straight-line method over the estimated useful life of assets.

CUMBERLAND PRESBYTERIAN CHILDREN'S HOME

NOTES TO FINANCIAL STATEMENTS
DECEMBER 31, 2013

The class lives of the more significant items within each property classification are as follows:

Vehicles	5 years
Equipment	5 to 10 years
Furniture and fixtures	5 to 10 years
Buildings	20 to 40 years

Investment Securities

Investments in marketable securities with readily determinable fair values and all investments in debt securities are valued at their fair values in the statement of financial position. Unrealized gains and losses are included in the change in net assets.

Estimates

The preparation of financial statements in conformity with generally accepted accounting principles requires management to make estimates and assumptions that affect the reported amounts of assets and liabilities at the date of the financial statements and the reported amounts of revenues and expenses during the reporting period. Accordingly, actual results could differ from those estimates.

FASB 116 and 117

In accordance with Statement of Financial Accounting Standards ("SFAS") No. 116, *Accounting for Contributions Received and Contributions Made*, contributions received are recorded as unrestricted, temporarily restricted, or permanently restricted support depending on the existence and/or nature of donor restrictions. CPCH reports gifts of cash and other assets as restricted support if they are received with donor stipulations that limit the use of the donated assets. When a donor restriction expires, that is, when a stipulated time restriction ends or purpose restriction is accomplished, temporarily restricted net assets are reclassified to unrestricted net assets and reported in the statement of activities as net assets released from restrictions. Contributions that are restricted by the donor are reported as increases in unrestricted net assets if the restrictions expire in the fiscal year in which the contributions are recognized.

Unconditional promises to give are recorded as revenue when received. Unconditional promises to give that are due within one year are recorded at the face amount of the commitment. Unconditional promises to give that are due beyond one year are not reflected at the face amount of the commitment, but when material are discounted to a present value, or net realizable value, using a 3% discount rate. Unconditional promises to give that are determined to be uncollectible are written off as an expense at that time. At December 31, 2013, CPCH had no outstanding unconditional promises to give.

CPCH reports gifts of land, buildings, and equipment as unrestricted support unless explicit donor stipulations specify how the donated assets must be used. Gifts of long-lived assets with explicit restrictions that specify how the assets are to be used and gifts of cash or other assets that must be used to acquire long-lived assets are reported as restricted support. Absent explicit donor stipulations about how long those long-lived assets must be maintained, CPCH reports expirations of donor restrictions when the donated or acquired long-lived assets are placed in service.

CUMBERLAND PRESBYTERIAN CHILDREN'S HOME

NOTES TO FINANCIAL STATEMENTS
DECEMBER 31, 2013

Contributed Services and Materials

In addition to receiving cash contributions, CPCH occasionally receives in-kind contributions from various donors. It is the policy of CPCH to record the estimated fair market value of certain in-kind donations as an asset or expense in its financial statements, and similarly increase donations by a like amount.

A substantial number of volunteers have donated significant amounts of time to CPCH's programs and supporting services. Contributions of donated services that create or enhance non-financial assets or that require specialized skills, are provided by individuals possessing these skills, and would typically need to be purchased if not provided by donation, are recorded at their fair values in the period received. For the year ended December 31, 2013, there were no amounts recorded for contributed services and materials.

Cash and Cash Equivalents

For purposes of the statement of cash flows, CPCH considers all highly liquid investments with a maturity of three months or less to be cash equivalents.

NOTE B – INVESTMENTS

Investments in equity securities with readily determinable fair values and all investments in debt securities are measured at fair value. All non cash contributions are recorded at fair value at the date of receipt. Stock is recorded at the average of the high and low selling price on the date received. Investments sold are recorded at amount received on the trade date.

Investment income and realized gains and losses are reported as increases in unrestricted net assets unless the donor placed restrictions on the income's use. The change in fair value between years along with realized gains or losses are reflected in the statement of activities in the year of the change.

Some investments are held and managed by the Board of Stewardship, Finance and Benefits of the Cumberland Presbyterian Church, while other investments are held in an investment brokerage account in the name of CPCH, and are managed by investment managers of the brokerage firm. No single investment exceeds five percent of CPCH's net assets.

NOTE C – ENDOWMENTS

CPCH's endowments consist of 86 individual donor-restricted funds established by individual donors for a variety of purposes. Net assets associated with endowments are classified and reported based on the existence or absence of donor-imposed restrictions.

A reconciliation of the beginning and ending balances of endowment funds is as follows:

	Permanently Restricted
Balance, 12/31/12	$6,260,012
Contributions	83,051
Investment gains	510,693
Balance, 12/31/13	$6,853,756

CUMBERLAND PRESBYTERIAN CHILDREN'S HOME

NOTES TO FINANCIAL STATEMENTS
DECEMBER 31, 2013

Funds with Deficiencies

From time to time, the fair value of assets associated with individual donor restricted endowment funds may fall below the level that the donor requires CPCH to retain as a fund of perpetual duration. CPCH did not have any net deficiencies of this nature as of December 31, 2013.

Return Objectives and Risk Parameters

CPCH has adopted investment and spending policies for endowment assets that attempt to provide a predictable stream of funding to programs supported by its endowment while seeking to maintain the purchasing power of the endowment assets. Under this policy, as approved by the board of trustees, the endowment assets are invested in equity securities, fixed-income securities and short-term reserves with asset allocation within defined acceptable ranges, while assuming a moderate level of investment risk. CPCH expects its endowment funds, over time, to provide an average rate of return sufficient to provide operating funds as needed. Actual returns in any given year may vary from this amount.

Strategies Employed for Achieving Objectives

To satisfy its long-term rate-of-return objectives, CPCH relies on a total return strategy in which investment returns are achieved through both capital appreciation (realized and unrealized) and current yield (interest and dividends). CPCH targets a diversified asset allocation that places a greater emphasis on equity-based investments to achieve its long-term return objectives within prudent risk constraints.

Spending Policy and How the Investment Objectives Relate to Spending Policy

CPCH has no written spending policy that commits it to annual distributions from any of the endowment's fund balances. CPCH normally appropriates for distribution each year sufficient earnings needed to fund its operating budget. Accordingly, over the long term, CPCH expects the current spending policy to allow its endowment to continue to grow. This is consistent with CPCH's objective to maintain the purchasing power of the endowment assets held in perpetuity or for a specified term as well as to provide additional real growth through new gifts and investment return.

NOTE D – FAIR VALUE OF FINANCIAL INSTRUMENTS

CPCH's financial instruments, none of which are held for trading purposes, include cash, securities and receivables. CPCH has estimated fair value of financial instruments in accordance with requirements of SFAS No. 157. The estimated fair value amounts have been determined by CPCH, using available market information and appropriate valuation methodologies. However, considerable judgment is necessarily required in interpreting market data to develop the estimates of fair value. Accordingly, the estimates presented herein are not necessarily indicative of the amounts that CPCH could realize in a current market exchange. The use of different market assumptions and estimation methodologies may have a material effect on the estimated fair value amounts. The carrying amount of cash and cash equivalents, and receivables approximated fair market value at December 31, 2013 because of their relatively short maturity and market terms. The fair value of long term investments at December 31, 2013 is determined based on quoted market values for U.S. government securities, fixed income securities and equity securities.

CUMBERLAND PRESBYTERIAN CHILDREN'S HOME

NOTES TO FINANCIAL STATEMENTS
DECEMBER 31, 2013

NOTE D – FAIR VALUE OF FINANCIAL INSTRUMENTS (CONT'D)

Financial instruments are considered Level 1 when their values are determined using quoted prices in active markets for identical assets that the reporting entity has the ability to access at the measurement date. Level 2 inputs are inputs other than quoted prices included within Level 1, such as quoted prices for similar assets in active or inactive markets, inputs other than quoted prices that are observable for the asset, or inputs that are derived principally from or corroborated by observable market data by correlation or other means.

Financial instruments are considered Level 3 when their values are determined using pricing models, discounted cash flow methodologies or similar techniques and at least one significant model assumption or input is unobservable. Level 3 financial instruments also include those for which the determination of fair value requires significant management judgment or estimation.

In accordance with these definitions, the following table represents CPCH's fair value hierarchy for its investments measured at fair value as of December 31, 2013:

	Quoted Prices for Active Markets for Identical Assets (Level 1)	Significant Other Observable Inputs (Level 2)	Total
U.S. Government securities	$1,237,333	$ -	$1,237,333
Equity securities	7,304,926	-	7,304,926
Fixed income securities	-	563,208	563,208
Total	$8,542,259	$ 563,208	$9,105,467

The estimated fair value of investments was determined by CPCH in accordance with its investment policy. Estimated fair value is determined by CPCH based on a number of factors, including: comparable publicly traded securities, the costs of investments to CPCH, as well as the current and projected operating performance. Changes in unrealized appreciation or depreciation of the investments are recognized as unrealized gains and losses in the statement of activities. Because of the inherent uncertainty of these valuations, the estimated values may differ from the actual fair values that may or may not be ultimately realized.

NOTE E - LAND, BUILDINGS AND EQUIPMENT

Land, buildings and equipment at December 31, 2013 consist of the following:

	Cost	Accumulated Depreciation	Book Value
Land	$ 23,477		$ 23,477
Buildings	5,774,167	$2,134,645	3,639,522
Campus infrastructure	574,766	182,951	391,815
Furniture & equipment	325,432	270,076	55,356
Vehicles	146,946	134,887	12,059
Total	$6,844,788	$2,722,559	$4,122,229

CUMBERLAND PRESBYTERIAN CHILDREN'S HOME

NOTES TO FINANCIAL STATEMENTS
DECEMBER 31, 2013

NOTE F - TEMPORARILY RESTRICTED NET ASSETS

Temporarily restricted net assets are available for the following purposes or periods:

Lena Hart Educational Fund	$ 3,510
Humphrey Scholarship Endowment	724
Walker Trimble Scholarship Fund	1,364
David Long Memorial Fund	194
Sybil V. Cockerham College Fund	1,027
Eleanor Sargeant Endowment	350
Medical clinic	26,000
New van	4,000
For periods after December 31, 2013 - term endowment to be received in a future year -- Naomi Locke Trust	18,891
Total	$ 56,060

NOTE G - PERMANENTLY RESTRICTED NET ASSETS

Permanently restricted net assets are restricted as follows:

Investments in perpetuity, the income from which is expendable to support any activities of CPCH	$7,377,053
Total	$7,377,053

NOTE H - OTHER LONG-TERM INVESTMENTS

	Total	Unrestricted	Temporarily Restricted	Permanently Restricted
Endowments held by the Board of Stewardship	$ 6,833,915	$ -	$ -	$6,833,915
Mutual funds held by Regions Bank -- Laura Harpole Trust	106,185	-	-	106,185
Mutual funds held by Fairfield Natl. Bank - Naomi Locke Trust	18,891	-	18,891	-
Funds held at Fidelity Investments:				
Lena Hart Educational Fund	6,010	-	3,510	2,500
Humphrey Scholarship Endowment	4,205	-	724	3,481
Walker Trimble Scholarship Fund	9,644	-	1,364	8,280
David Long Memorial Fund	1,194	-	194	1,000
Sibyl V. Cockerham College Fund	3,027	-	1,027	2,000
Eleanor Sargeant Endowment	2,930	-	350	2,580
Operating Reserve	1,714,666	1,684,666	30,000	-
4,000 shares Exxon-Mobil held by CPCH - Jessie DiCarlo Endowment	404,800	-	-	404,800
Total	$ 9,105,467	$1,684,666	$ 56,060	$7,364,741

CUMBERLAND PRESBYTERIAN CHILDREN'S HOME

NOTES TO FINANCIAL STATEMENTS
DECEMBER 31, 2013

NOTE I – SUBSEQUENT EVENTS

Management evaluates subsequent events through the date of the report, which is the date the financial statements were available to be issued.

NOTE J – COMPONENTS OF INVESTMENT RETURN

Investment return for the year ended December 31, 2013, including interest and dividends on investments and interest earned on cash balances is summarized as follows:

Unrestricted investment return:	
Interest and dividend income:	
Board of Stewardship investments	$ 292,456
Harlow Capital investments	61,634
Exxon Mobil stock investment	9,840
Fidelity investments	770
Unrealized gains on investments	79,711
Total unrestricted investment return	444,411
Restricted investment return:	
Interest income	3
Unrealized gains on investments	68,272
Realized gains on investments	510,693
Total restricted investment return	578,968
Total Investment Return	$1,023,379

SUPPLEMENTAL SCHEDULE

CUMBERLAND PRESBYTERIAN CHILDREN'S HOME

SCHEDULE OF BOARD OF STEWARDSHIP ENDOWMENTS
DECEMBER 31, 2013

Donor-established Endowments:

	Balance
Merlyn & Joann Kitterman Alexander	1,453
W.A. and Elizabeth Bearden Trust	16,547
Grace Johnson Beasley Memorial Endowment	38,528
Bethlehem CPC Memorial Endowment	6,297
Bridges Scholarship Fund	43,042
J.T. and Dorothy Britt Trust	11,652
Children's Home Endowment	336,117
Lavenia Campbell Cole Trust 20%	21,195
Lavenia Campbell Cole Annuity Endowment	86,077
Lavenia Cole Testamentary Trust 25%	617,512
Mrs. A.L. Colvin Memorial Fund	999
John W. and Eva Cox Trust Fund	32,261
Steve Curry Trust	566,294
Daniel Class, First Cumberland Presbyterian Church	33,317
Donnie Curry Davis Memorial	194,961
Mary Elberta Davis Memorial	20,804
Fred and Mattie Mae Dwiggins Memorial Trust	83,530
J.S. Eustis Memorial Trust Fund	13,187
Clester H. Evans, Sr., Trust	22,017
John M. Friedel Trust	22,774
Joyce C. Frisby Memorial Endowment	29,162
Vaughn and Mary Elizabeth Fults Trust	21,008
Garner-Miller Memorial Trust	12,960
James C. and Freda M. Gilbert Endowment	114,361
Henry and Jayne Glaspy Memorial Fund	8,597
Rev. W.J. Gregory Memorial	108,061
Glenn Griffin Endowment	46,068
Rev. and Mrs. Henry M. Guynn Memorial	4,787
Chad Harper Endowment	11,004
Newsome and Imogene Harvey Endowment	2,642
Clarence & Lula Herring Endowment	6,290
Kenneth and Clara Holsopple Trust	55,682
George and Lottie M. Hutchins Trust	1,184,216
Norma K. Johnson Memorial Library	11,884
P.F. Johnson Memorial Endowment	19,728
Robert and Genevie Johnson Endowment	5,005
Mr. and Mrs. Robert L. Johnson	12,431
Violet Louise Jolly Endowment	1,255
Eulava Joyce Memorial Trust	10,373
Ruth Cypert and Harlie Klugler Memorial Fund	20,889
Blanche R. Lake Endowment	15,054
Wade P. Lane/Maude Dorough Memorial Trust	9,908
Adolphus M. Latta Memorial Trust	53,463
Mr. and Mrs. Robert F. Little Endowment Fund	35,490
Charles E. and Addie Mae Lloyd Endowment Fund	23,549
Tony and Ann Martin Endowment	2,377
Mrs. Lucille (Lucy) Mast Endowment	2,416

CUMBERLAND PRESBYTERIAN CHILDREN'S HOME

SCHEDULE OF BOARD OF STEWARDSHIP ENDOWMENTS (CONT'D)
DECEMBER 31, 2013

Donor-established Endowments:

	Balance
W.B. and Azales McClurkan, Sr. Memorial	20,133
Williams J. McCall Memorial Trust	10,373
McEwen Church Trust	7,969
McKinley and Barnett Families Endowment	836,713
J.C. McKinley Endowment	19,642
Velma McKinley Trust	19,642
Mary McKnight Memorial Trust	10,486
Kenneth and Mae Moore Endowment Fund	7,335
Operational Trust Fund	154,337
Bert and Pat Owen Endowment	1,632
Hamilton & Merion Parks Family Trust #3	11,170
Joe Parr Trust Fund	81,558
Martha Sue Parr Endowment	1,665
Mary M. Poole Endowment Fund	997,790
Jack and Mary Proctor Memorial Trust Fund	66,529
SQ&K Maurine Proctor Trust	5,893
Mary Acena Prewitt Trust Fund	94,051
Rev. and Mrs. Joe Reed Memorial	2,716
Marguerite D. Richards Endowment	26,497
Agnes Durbin Richardson Trust	31,430
Pat N. & Essie H. Roberts Memorial	61,346
Frances Benefield Roberts Trust Fund	2,430
Rev. and Mrs. John A. Russell Memorial	4,745
John Ann and Mary Shimer	15,617
Rev. W.B. and Lydia Snipes Memorial Trust	18,815
Don M. & Nancy Tabor Endowment Trust	35,836
Townsend Trust Fund	40,038
Hattie A. Wheeless Fund	20,597
Whitfield Family Endowment	12,497
Porter and Hattie S. Williamson Memorial Trust	178,652
Helen Wynn Endowment Fund	10,431
Maxie and Will Young Memorial Endowment	21,625
Dixie Campbell Zinn Memorial Trust	6,501
Total	$ 6,833,915

MEMPHIS THEOLOGICAL SEMINARY OF THE
CUMBERLAND PRESBYTERIAN CHURCH

FINANCIAL STATEMENTS AND REPORT OF INDEPENDENT
CERTIFIED PUBLIC ACCOUNTANTS

JULY 31, 2013

TABLE OF CONTENTS

	PAGE
INDEPENDENT AUDITOR'S REPORT	3
FINANCIAL STATEMENTS	
Statements of Financial Position	6
Statement of Activities	7
Statement of Functional Expenses	9
Statements of Cash Flows	10
NOTES TO FINANCIAL STATEMENTS	11
SUPPLEMENTAL INFORMATION	
Schedule of Expenditures of Federal Awards	22
NON-FINANCIAL SECTION	
Independent Auditor's Report on Internal Control over Financial Reporting and on Compliance and Other Matters Based on an Audit of Financial Statements Performed in Accordance with *Government Auditing Standards*	24
Independent Auditor's Report on Compliance for Each Major Program and on Internal Control over Compliance Required by OMB Circular A-133	26
Schedule of Findings and Questioned Costs	28
Schedule of Prior Year Findings and Questioned Costs	29
Independent Auditors' General Comments	31

CERTIFIED PUBLIC ACCOUNTANTS
ATRIUM 1, 6800 POPLAR AVE., STE. 210
GERMANTOWN, TENNESSEE 38138
(901) 523-8283   (901) 523-8287 FAX
www.zkcpas.com

INDEPENDENT AUDITOR'S REPORT

Board of Trustees
Memphis Theological Seminary of the
    Cumberland Presbyterian Church
Memphis, Tennessee

Report on the Financial Statements

We have audited the accompanying financial statements of Memphis Theological Seminary of the Cumberland Presbyterian Church (the "Seminary", a nonprofit organization), which comprise the statement of financial position as of July 31, 2013, and the related statements of activities, functional expenses, and cash flows for the year then ended, and the related notes to the financial statements.

Management's Responsibility for the Financial Statements

Management is responsible for the preparation and fair presentation of these financial statements in accordance with accounting principles generally accepted in the United States of America; this includes the design, implementation, and maintenance of internal control relevant to the preparation and fair presentation of financial statements that are free from material misstatement, whether due to fraud or error.

Auditor's Responsibility

Our responsibility is to express an opinion on these financial statements based on our audit. We conducted our audit in accordance with auditing standards generally accepted in the United States of America and the standards applicable to financial audits contained in *Government Auditing Standards*, issued by the Comptroller General of the United States. Those standards require that we plan and perform the audit to obtain reasonable assurance about whether the financial statements are free from material misstatement.

An audit involves performing procedures to obtain audit evidence about the amounts and disclosures in the financial statements. The procedures selected depend on the auditor's judgment, including the assessment of the risks of material misstatement of the financial statements, whether due to fraud or error. In making those risk assessments, the auditor considers internal control relevant to the entity's preparation and fair presentation of the financial statements in order to design audit procedures that are appropriate in the circumstances, but not for the purpose of expressing an opinion on the effectiveness of the entity's internal control. Accordingly, we express no such opinion. An audit also includes evaluating the appropriateness of accounting policies used and the reasonableness of significant accounting estimates made by management, as well as evaluating the overall presentation of the financial statements.

We believe that the audit evidence we have obtained is sufficient and appropriate to provide a basis for our audit opinion.

Opinion

In our opinion, the financial statements referred to above present fairly, in all material respects, the financial position of the Seminary as of July 31, 2013, and the changes in its net assets and its cash flows for the year then ended in accordance with accounting principles generally accepted in the United States of America.

Other Matters

Other Information

Our audit was conducted for the purpose of forming an opinion on the financial statements as a whole. The accompanying schedule of expenditures of federal awards, as required by Office of Management and Budget Circular A-133, *Audits of States, Local Governments, and Non-Profit Organizations*, is presented for purposes of additional analysis and is not a required part of the financial statements. Such information is the responsibility of management and was derived from and relates directly to the underlying accounting and other records used to prepare the financial statements. The information has been subjected to the auditing procedures applied in the audit of the financial statements and certain additional procedures, including comparing and reconciling such information directly to the underlying accounting and other records used to prepare the financial statements or to the financial statements themselves, and other additional procedures in accordance with auditing standards generally accepted in the United States of America. In our opinion, the information is fairly stated, in all material respects, in relation to the financial statements as a whole.

Other Reporting Required by *Government Auditing Standards*

In accordance with *Government Auditing Standards*, we have also issued our report, dated December 16, 2013, on our consideration of the Seminary's internal control over financial reporting and on our tests of its compliance with certain provisions of laws, regulations, contracts, and grant agreements and other matters. The purpose of that report is to describe the scope of our testing of internal control over financial reporting and compliance and the results of that testing, and not to provide an opinion on internal control over financial reporting or on compliance. That report is an integral part of an audit performed in accordance with *Government Auditing Standards* in considering the Seminary's internal control over financial reporting and compliance.

Report on Summarized Comparative Information

We have previously audited the Seminary's 2012 financial statements and our report, dated May 10, 2013, expressed an unmodified opinion on those audited financial statements. In our opinion, the summarized comparative information presented herein as of and for the year ended June 30, 2012, is consistent, in all material respects, with the audited financial statements from which it has been derived.

Zoeola Kaplan, PLLC

Germantown, Tennessee
December 16, 2013

FINANCIAL STATEMENTS

MEMPHIS THEOLOGICAL SEMINARY
OF THE CUMBERLAND PRESBYTERIAN CHURCH
STATEMENTS OF FINANCIAL POSITION
July 31, 2013 and 2012

ASSETS

	2013	2012
Assets		
Cash and cash equivalents (Notes B5 and E)	$ 838,001	$ 200,006
Cash and cash equivalents, temporarily restricted	215,776	6,309
Total cash and cash equivalents	1,053,777	206,315
Investments, at fair value (Notes B3, C, D, and K)		
Unrestricted	1,510,028	1,515,220
Temporarily restricted	1,672,184	1,216,298
Permanently restricted	5,966,473	6,241,021
Total investments	9,148,685	8,972,539
Tuition and fees receivable, net of allowance of $234,747 in 2013 and $222,243 in 2012 (Note E)	213,992	161,393
Pledges receivable (Note F)	60,000	150,000
Other receivables	112,522	36,772
Capital assets, net of accumulated depreciation (Notes B4 and B8)	3,550,769	4,409,017
Cash value of life insurance	38,708	36,583
Land held for sale (Notes B8 and D)	81,851	74,343
Other assets	41,147	35,019
Total assets	$ 14,301,451	$ 14,081,981

LIABILITIES AND NET ASSETS

	2013	2012
Liabilities		
Accounts payable and accrued expenses (Note K)	$ 281,652	$ 342,171
Deferred revenue	204,919	-
Line of credit (Note G)	75,000	399,739
Notes payable (Notes H and K)	2,399,362	2,401,677
Total liabilities	2,960,933	3,143,587
Net Assets (Note B1)		
Unrestricted	3,426,085	3,324,766
Temporarily restricted	1,947,960	1,372,607
Permanently restricted	5,966,473	6,241,021
Total net assets	11,340,518	10,938,394
Total liabilities and net assets	$ 14,301,451	$ 14,081,981

The accompanying notes are an integral part of these financial statements.

MEMPHIS THEOLOGICAL SEMINARY
OF THE CUMBERLAND PRESBYTERIAN CHURCH
STATEMENT OF ACTIVITIES
For the Years Ended July 31, 2013 and 2012

	2013				2012
	Unrestricted	Temporarily Restricted	Permanently Restricted	Total	Total
Operating Revenues and Support					
Tuition and fees, net of scholarships of $429,993 and $441,283	$ 2,069,821	$ -	$ -	$ 2,069,821	$ 1,959,208
Contributions and grants (Note B2)	643,712	337,756	80,042	1,061,510	1,123,730
Other revenue and support	338,107	-	-	338,107	344,229
Net assets released from restrictions	484,628	(484,628)	-	-	-
Total operating revenues and support	**3,536,268**	**(146,872)**	**80,042**	**3,469,438**	**3,427,167**
Expenses (Note B9)					
Educational program services					
Instruction	1,356,786	-	-	1,356,786	1,289,549
Library	240,343	-	-	240,343	245,489
Student services	232,436	-	-	232,436	199,743
Program for alternative studies	118,169	-	-	118,169	119,466
Academic support	104,631	-	-	104,631	99,831
Supporting services					
Facilities operations	736,143	-	-	736,143	832,898
Institutional support	816,710	-	-	816,710	793,152
Security services	51,624	-	-	51,624	62,397
Development and fundraising	437,598	-	-	437,598	389,268
Total operating expenses	**4,094,440**	**-**	**-**	**4,094,440**	**4,031,793**
Increase (decrease) in net assets from operations	(558,172)	(146,872)	80,042	(625,002)	(604,626)
Non-operating revenues and expenses					
Investment income (loss) (Notes B3 and D)	539,691	472,364	15,071	1,027,126	(183,594)
Reduction in fair value of land held for sale	-	-	-	-	(80,161)
Increase (decrease) in net assets	(18,481)	325,492	95,113	402,124	(868,381)
Reclassifications of net assets (Note L)	119,800	249,861	(369,661)	-	-
Net Assets, beginning of year	3,324,766	1,372,607	6,241,021	10,938,394	11,806,775
Net Assets - end of year	$ 3,426,085	$ 1,947,960	$ 5,966,473	$ 11,340,518	$ 10,938,394

The accompanying notes are an integral part of these financial statements.

7

MEMPHIS THEOLOGICAL SEMINARY
OF THE CUMBERLAND PRESBYTERIAN CHURCH
STATEMENT OF ACTIVITIES (CONTINUED)
For the Year Ended July 31, 2012

	2012			
	Unrestricted	Temporarily Restricted	Permanently Restricted	Total
Operating Revenues and Support				
Tuition and fees, net of scholarships of $441,283	$ 1,959,208	$ -	$ -	$ 1,959,208
Contributions and grants (Note B2)	534,392	446,603	142,735	1,123,730
Other revenue and support	344,229	-	-	344,229
Net assets released from restrictions	750,542	(701,638)	(48,904)	-
Total operating revenues and support	3,588,371	(255,035)	93,831	3,427,167
Expenses (Note B9)				
Educational program services				
Instruction	1,289,549	-	-	1,289,549
Library	245,489	-	-	245,489
Student services	199,743	-	-	199,743
Sustaining pastoral excellence	-	-	-	-
Program for alternative studies	119,466	-	-	119,466
Academic support	99,831	-	-	99,831
Supporting services				
Facilities operations	832,898	-	-	832,898
Institutional support	793,152	-	-	793,152
Security services	62,397	-	-	62,397
Development and fundraising	389,268	-	-	389,268
Total operating expenses	4,031,793	-	-	4,031,793
Increase (decrease) in net assets from operations	(443,422)	(255,035)	93,831	(604,626)
Non-operating revenues and expenses				
Investment income (loss) (Note B3 and D)	(35,928)	(139,326)	(8,340)	(183,594)
Reduction in fair value of land held for sale	(80,161)	-	-	(80,161)
Increase (decrease) in net assets	(559,511)	(394,361)	85,491	(868,381)
Reclassification of net assets (Note L)	1,236,067	323,653	(1,559,720)	-
Net Assets, beginning of year	2,648,210	1,443,315	7,715,250	11,806,775
Net Assets - end of year	$ 3,324,766	$ 1,372,607	$ 6,241,021	$ 10,938,394

The accompanying notes are an integral part of these financial statements.

MEMPHIS THEOLOGICAL SEMINARY
OF THE CUMBERLAND PRESBYTERIAN CHURCH
STATEMENT OF FUNCTIONAL EXPENSES
For the Years Ended July 31, 2013 and 2012
(With Summarized Comparative Financial Information for the Year Ended July 31, 2012)

	Educational Program Services					Supporting Services					
	Instruction	Library	Student Services	Program for Alternative Studies	Academic Support	Facilities Operations	Institutional Support	Security Services	Development and Fundraising	2013 Total	2012 Total
Salaries and wages	$1,031,888	$141,619	$168,412	$68,092	$87,515	$159,309	$411,715	$ -	$239,521	$2,308,071	$2,183,245
Benefits	150,403	34,290	26,269	6,771	12,330	55,570	74,877	-	37,484	397,994	339,681
Professional Development	10,587	-	175	-	325	415	789	-	90	12,381	14,311
Travel/Auto Expense	5,267	185	5,152	4,087	2,110	2,966	8,048	-	10,719	38,534	38,458
Office Supplies and Expense	29,277	61,727	4,319	1,947	2,196	10,140	36,617	-	32,325	178,548	187,733
Consultants / Professional	-	-	-	-	-	-	71,635	51,624	-	123,259	100,857
Special Events	71,785	-	1,655	36,582	-	-	32,360	-	41,086	183,468	184,470
Student / Covenant Groups	44,021	-	-	-	-	-	-	-	-	44,021	109,638
Repairs and Maintenance	442	1,193	988	116	-	51,904	2,182	-	-	56,825	43,903
Utilities	-	-	18,409	-	-	68,191	-	-	-	86,600	83,219
Insurance Expense	-	-	-	-	-	89,348	-	-	5,000	94,348	92,939
Property Taxes	-	-	-	-	-	-	-	-	-	-	67,522
Other Expense	13,116	1,329	7,057	574	155	18,197	33,182	-	71,373	144,983	145,245
Interest Expense	-	-	-	-	-	-	145,305	-	-	145,305	156,652
Depreciation	-	-	-	-	-	280,103	-	-	-	280,103	283,920
	$1,356,786	$240,343	$232,436	$118,169	$104,631	$736,143	$816,710	$51,624	$437,598	$4,094,440	$4,031,793

The accompanying notes are an integral part of these financial statements.

MEMPHIS THEOLOGICAL SEMINARY
OF THE CUMBERLAND PRESBYTERIAN CHURCH
STATEMENTS OF CASH FLOWS
For the Years Ended July 31, 2013 and 2012

	2013	2012
Cash Flows from Operating Activities		
Change in net assets	$ 402,124	$ (868,381)
Adjustments to reconcile change in net assets to net cash provided by (used in) operating activities:		
Depreciation	280,103	283,920
Bad debt expense	12,779	18,145
Changes in operating assets and liabilities:		
(Increase) decrease in assets		
Tuition, fees and other receivables	(141,128)	40,422
Pledges receivable	90,000	15,000
Donations of property	-	-
Other assets	(6,128)	(20,019)
Increase in liabilities		
Accounts payable and accrued expenses	(60,519)	-
Deferred Revenue	204,919	(294,191)
Net cash provided by operating activities	782,150	(825,104)
Cash Flows from Investing Activities		
Withdrawals from investments	583,537	399,985
Investments of endowment gifts	(80,043)	(142,735)
Net earnings on investments-(reinvested)/distributed	217,072	82,431
Capital (gains) losses on investments	(896,712)	279,789
(Increase) decrease in value of land held for sale	(7,508)	80,161
(Increase) decrease in cash surrender value of life insurance	(2,125)	-
Sale of property	749,440	-
Purchases of property and equipment	(171,295)	(105,282)
Net cash used for investing activities	392,366	594,349
Cash Flows from Financing Activities		
Decrease in line of credit	(324,739)	-
Principal payments on long term debt	(2,315)	(10,410)
Net cash provided by financing activities	(327,054)	(10,410)
Net increase (decrease) in cash and cash equivalents	847,462	(241,165)
Cash and cash equivalents, beginning of year	206,315	447,480
Cash and cash equivalents, end of year	$ 1,053,777	$ 206,315
Supplemental Disclosure:		
Interest paid	$ 165,211	$ 285,108

The accompanying notes are an integral part of these financial statements.

MEMPHIS THEOLOGICAL SEMINARY
OF THE CUMBERLAND PRESBYTERIAN CHURCH
NOTES TO FINANCIAL STATEMENTS
For the Year Ended July 31, 2013

NOTE A – ORGANIZATION AND PURPOSE

The Memphis Theological Seminary of the Cumberland Presbyterian Church (the "Seminary") is an ecumenical Protestant seminary serving the mid-south region from its campus in Memphis, Tennessee. The Seminary provides postgraduate theological education to clergy and church leaders of the parent denomination and qualified students from other denominations. The Seminary is governed by a Board of Trustees elected by the General Assembly of the Cumberland Presbyterian Church.

NOTE B – SIGNIFICANT ACCOUNTING POLICIES

1. Financial Statement Presentation

   The Seminary prepares its financial statements in accordance with FASB ASC 958-205, *Not-For-Profit Entities Presentation of Financial Statements*. Under FASB ASC 958, the Seminary reports information regarding its financial position and activities according to three classes of net assets: unrestricted net assets, temporarily restricted net assets, and permanently restricted net assets.

   The financial statements are prepared using the accrual basis of accounting.

2. Contributions

   Contributions received by the Seminary are recorded as unrestricted, temporarily restricted, or permanently restricted support depending on the existence and/or nature of any donor restrictions. Temporarily restricted net assets are reclassified to unrestricted net assets upon satisfaction of the time or purpose restrictions.

3. Investment Valuation and Income Recognition

   Investments are reported at fair value. Fair value is the price that would be received to sell an asset or paid to transfer a liability in an orderly transaction between market participants at the measurement date. See Notes C and D for discussion and computation of fair value.

   Unrealized holding gains and losses are included in current year revenue and support as a component of investment income. Realized gains and losses are computed using the specific identification method.

4. Capital Assets

   All acquisitions of property and equipment and expenditures for repairs and maintenance that prolong the useful lives of assets in excess of $1,000 are capitalized at cost. Expenditures for normal repair and maintenance are expensed to operations as they occur. Depreciation is provided through the straight-line method over the assets estimated useful lives which range from three to ten years for equipment, fifteen years for library books and twenty-five to forty years for buildings. Depreciation expense for the years ended July 31, 2013 and 2012 was

MEMPHIS THEOLOGICAL SEMINARY
OF THE CUMBERLAND PRESBYTERIAN CHURCH
NOTES TO FINANCIAL STATEMENTS (CONTINUED)
For the Year Ended July 31, 2013

NOTE B – SIGNIFICANT ACCOUNTING POLICIES *(Continued)*

$280,103 and $283,920, respectively. Fixed assets are as follows:

	2013	2012
Building and improvements	$ 4,412,187	$ 5,154,128
Furniture and equipment	842,476	841,276
Library books	1,724,046	1,680,609
Vehicles	48,515	48,515
	7,027,224	7,724,528
Less accumulated depreciation	4,030,098	3,866,026
	2,997,126	3,858,502
Land	208,650	208,650
Construction in progress	344,993	341,865
Capital assets, net	$ 3,550,769	$ 4,409,017

5. Cash Equivalents

   Cash equivalents are defined as short term, highly liquid investments that are both readily convertible to known amounts of cash and are so near maturity that they present insignificant risk of changes in value because of changes in interest rates.

6. Use of Estimates in the Preparation of Financial Statements

   The preparation of financial statements in conformity with generally accepted accounting principles requires management to make estimates and assumptions that affect the amounts reported in the financial statements and accompanying notes. Actual results could differ from those estimates.

7. Income Taxes

   The Seminary is a not-for-profit organization that is exempt from income taxes under Internal Revenue Code Section 501 (c) (3) and is also exempt from state income taxes.

8. Donated Property, Equipment and Services

   Donations of property and use of property are recorded as support at their estimated fair value at the date of donation. Such donations are reported as unrestricted support unless the donor has restricted the donated asset to a specific purpose. The value of donated property was $0 in 2013 and 2012, respectively.

   Donated services are recognized as contributions if the services (a) create or enhance non-financial assets or (b) require specialized skills, are performed by people with those skills, and would otherwise be purchased by the Organization. There were no contributed services recorded for accounting and consulting in 2013 or 2012.

MEMPHIS THEOLOGICAL SEMINARY
OF THE CUMBERLAND PRESBYTERIAN CHURCH
NOTES TO FINANCIAL STATEMENTS (CONTINUED)
For the Year Ended July 31, 2013

NOTE B – SIGNIFICANT ACCOUNTING POLICIES *(Continued)*

9. Functional Allocation of Expenses

    The cost of providing the various educational programs and supporting services has been summarized on a functional basis in the statement of functional expenses. Accordingly, certain costs have been allocated among the programs and services benefited.

10. Subsequent Events

    The Seminary evaluated all events or transactions that occurred after July 31, 2013 and through December 16, 2013, the date the Seminary approved these financial statements for issuance.

NOTE C – FAIR VALUE MEASUREMENT

The FASB ASC Subtopic 820-10 *Fair Value Measurements,* (formerly SFAS No. 157), defines fair value as the exchange price that would be received for an asset or paid to transfer a liability in the principal or most advantageous market for the asset or liability in an orderly transaction between market participants at the measurement date. SFAS No. 157 established a three-level fair value hierarchy that prioritizes the inputs used to measure fair value. This hierarchy requires entities to maximize the use of observable inputs and minimize the use of unobservable inputs.

The three levels of inputs used to measure fair value are as follows:

- Level 1 – Quoted prices in active markets for identical assets or liabilities.
- Level 2 – Observable inputs other than quoted prices included in Level 1, such as quoted prices for similar assets and liabilities in active markets; quoted prices for identical or similar assets or liabilities in markets that are not active; or inputs that are observable or can be corroborated by observable market data.
- Level 3 – Unobservable inputs that are supported by little or no market activity and that are significant to the fair value of the assets or liabilities. This includes certain pricing models, discounted cash flow methodologies and similar techniques that use significant unobservable inputs.

The estimated fair value of the Seminary's financial instruments has been determined by management using available market information. However, considerable judgment is required in interpreting market data to develop the estimates of fair value. Accordingly, the fair values are not necessarily indicative of the amounts that the Seminary could realize in a current market exchange. The use of different market assumptions may have a material effect on the estimated fair value amounts.

The carrying amounts of cash and cash equivalents, net receivables, cash value of life insurance, payables, accrued liabilities, and debt are a reasonable estimate of their fair value, due to their short term nature, method of computation and interest rates for current debt.

All financial assets that are measured at fair value on a recurring basis (at least annually) have been segregated into the most appropriate level within the fair value hierarchy based on the inputs used to determine the fair value at the measurement date. These assets measured at fair value on a recurring basis are summarized in Note D.

MEMPHIS THEOLOGICAL SEMINARY
OF THE CUMBERLAND PRESBYTERIAN CHURCH
NOTES TO FINANCIAL STATEMENTS (CONTINUED)
For the Year Ended July 31, 2013

NOTE D – INVESTMENTS AND OTHER ASSETS

Nearly all of the Seminary's investments are managed by the Board of Stewardship, Foundation and Benefits of the Cumberland Presbyterian Church, Inc., and maintained in pooled investment accounts with other funds. The investments generally originate from gifts and contributions for which separate identifiable investment accounts are created that indicate the source of the funds and/or the purpose for which the funds are to be used. Many of these accounts are designated for monthly distributions to the Seminary based on one-twelfth of 5% of the rolling average value. The Board of Stewardship, Foundation and Benefits issues an aggregate amount to the Seminary and charges the applicable accounts for their proportionate share. In addition, the Seminary can request on an as needed basis, additional distributions that will be used for the purpose for which the account was created.

Accounts subjected to the fair values measurement process consist of the following:

	July 31, 2013			
	Total Fair Value	Quoted Prices in Active Markets for Identical Assets (Level 1)	Significant Other Observable Inputs (Level 2)	Unobservable Inputs (Level 3)
Investment securities				
Cash/Cash Equivalents	$ 1,627,077	$ 1,627,077	$ -	$ -
Money market funds	7,747	7,747	-	-
U. S. Treasuries	83,122	83,122	-	-
Mortgage - backed securities	1,112,265	-	1,112,265	-
Bonds and bond funds	1,196,920	10,213	1,186,707	-
Common and preferred stocks	107,152	107,152	-	-
Real estate investment funds	725,050	-	725,050	-
Private Investment entities	4,289,352	-	-	4,289,352
Total investments	$ 9,148,685	$ 1,835,311	$ 3,024,022	$ 4,289,352
Land held for sale	$ 81,851	$ -	$ -	$ 81,851

MEMPHIS THEOLOGICAL SEMINARY
OF THE CUMBERLAND PRESBYTERIAN CHURCH
NOTES TO FINANCIAL STATEMENTS (CONTINUED)
For the Year Ended July 31, 2013

NOTE D – INVESTMENTS AND OTHER ASSETS *(Continued)*

	July 31, 2012			
	Total Fair Value	Quoted Prices in Active Markets for Identical Assets (Level 1)	Significant Other Observable Inputs (Level 2)	Unobservable Inputs (Level 3)
Investment securities				
Cash/Cash Equivalents	$ 724,971	$ 724,971	$ -	$ -
Money market funds	3,583	3,583	-	-
U. S. Treasuries	128,987	128,987	-	-
Mortgage/asset - backed securities	888,556	-	888,556	-
Bonds and bond funds	1,408,069	9,544	1,398,525	-
Common and preferred stocks	97,128	97,128	-	-
Real estate investment funds	920,159	-	920,159	-
Mutual funds				
Private investment entities	4,801,086	-	-	4,801,086
Total investments	$ 8,972,539	$ 964,213	$ 3,207,240	$ 4,801,086
Land held for sale	$ 74,343	$ -	$ -	$ 74,343

The private investment entities for the years ended July 31, 2013 and 2012, are investments entered into by the Board of Stewardship to achieve greater rates of return. They include funds whose inputs used to determine fair value are considered unobservable and are therefore Level 3 inputs.

The carrying value of the above land held for sale is based on expected recoverability at the time of sale. The Seminary uses appraised values and other information available to determine the carrying value. At July 31, 2013, the carrying value was increased by $7,508 to reflect the expected recoverable amount (fair value). The inputs used to determine fair value are considered unobservable and are therefore Level 3 inputs.

MEMPHIS THEOLOGICAL SEMINARY
OF THE CUMBERLAND PRESBYTERIAN CHURCH
NOTES TO FINANCIAL STATEMENTS (CONTINUED)
For the Year Ended July 31, 2013

NOTE D – INVESTMENTS AND OTHER ASSETS *(Continued)*

Transactions in Level 3 assets for the years ended July 31, 2013 and 2012, were as follows:

	July 31, 2013	July 31, 2012
Private investment entities		
Beginning balance	$ 4,801,086	$ -
Investments/withdrawals, net	(993,601)	4,974,090
Realized/unrealized gains (losses)	481,867	(173,004)
Ending balance	$ 4,289,352	$ 4,801,086
Land held for sale		
Beginning balance	$ 74,343	$ 153,307
Improvements to land previously received	7,508	1,197
Reduction in fair value of land	-	(80,161)
Ending balance	$ 81,851	$ 74,343

Non-operating income (loss) from investments was as follows:

	July 31, 2013	July 31, 2012
Investment income	$ 130,414	$ 130,689
Realized investment gains (losses)	57,519	33,337
Unrealized investment gains (losses)	839,193	(347,620)
Net investment income (loss)	$ 1,027,126	$ (183,594)

MEMPHIS THEOLOGICAL SEMINARY
OF THE CUMBERLAND PRESBYTERIAN CHURCH
NOTES TO FINANCIAL STATEMENTS (CONTINUED)
For the Year Ended July 31, 2013

NOTE E – CONCENTRATION OF CREDIT RISK

The Seminary has cash equivalents invested by the Board of Stewardship, Foundation and Benefits. At July 31, 2013, these funds total $215,776 and are not insured by the Federal Deposit Insurance Corporation (FDIC).

In addition, the Seminary maintains cash balances in accounts at a well established financial institution located in Memphis, Tennessee. These balances are insured by the Federal Deposit Insurance Corporation up to $250,000. At July 31, 2013, the Seminary had substantial uninsured balances. Soon after July 31, 2013, disbursements were made to pay off loans and other payables reducing total cash balances; however, as of December 16, 2013, the Seminary's cash balances remained in excess of the insured limit.

The Seminary's tuition and fees receivable are from students for which the majority receive some form of financial assistance. Management maintains an allowance for uncollectible based on periodic reviews of each individual student's account.

NOTE F - PLEDGES RECEIVABLE

Pledges receivable represent pledges from several donors to be used for various programs of the Seminary. At July 31, 2013, pledges receivable totaled $60,000 of which all is due to be received during fiscal year ending July 31, 2014.

NOTE G – LINE OF CREDIT

The Seminary has a $400,000 revolving line of credit agreement with a local bank. Borrowings outstanding under the agreement ($75,000 at July 31, 2013) bear interest at the bank's prime rate (3.25 percent at July 31, 2013). The line is guaranteed by the Board of Stewardship, Foundation and Benefits.

MEMPHIS THEOLOGICAL SEMINARY
OF THE CUMBERLAND PRESBYTERIAN CHURCH
NOTES TO FINANCIAL STATEMENTS (CONTINUED)
For the Year Ended July 31, 2013

NOTE H – NOTES PAYABLE

Notes payable consist of the following at July 31, 2013 and 2012:

	2013	2012
Note payable, due in monthly installments at a variable interest (4.75% at July 31, 2013) through November	$ 62,536	$ 64,852
Note payable, due in monthly installments at a variable interest (4.75% at July 31, 2013) through March 2030.	80,153	80,153
Note payable, due in monthly installments at a variable interest (4.75% at July 31, 2013) through January 2031.	771,793	771,793
Note payable, due in monthly installments at a variable interest (4.75% at July 31, 2013) through April 2031.	108,699	108,699
Note payable, due in monthly installments at a variable interest (4.75% at July 31, 2013) through December 2031.	121,823	121,823
Note payable, due in monthly installments at a variable interest (4.75% at July 31, 2013) through April 2032.	118,920	118,920
Note payable, due in monthly installments at a variable interest (4.75% at July 31, 2013) through April 2032.	678,325	678,325
Note payable, due in monthly installments through April 2033 as follows: $1,597, including interest at 5%, for the period May 2008 through April 2011; thereafter amortizable at a various interest (4.75% at July 31, 2013).	261,046	261,046
Note payable, due in monthly installments through September 2033 as follows: $1,308, including interest at at 6%, for the period September 2008 through August 2011; thereafter amortizable at a various interest. (4.75% at July 31, 2013)	196,067	196,066
Total notes payable	$ 2,399,362	$ 2,401,677

The notes payable are collateralized by income earned from permanently restricted investments and are payable to the Board of Stewardship, Foundation and Benefits.

Scheduled principal payments and past due principal payments were not made during the year ended July 31, 2013 for $211,067 of the notes payable.

After July 31, 2013, the Seminary paid $565,551 to the Board of the Stewardship to liquidate 5 of the notes and partially pay another.

MEMPHIS THEOLOGICAL SEMINARY
OF THE CUMBERLAND PRESBYTERIAN CHURCH
NOTES TO FINANCIAL STATEMENTS (CONTINUED)
For the Year Ended July 31, 2013

NOTE H – NOTES PAYABLE *(Continued)*

Scheduled principal payments required for each of the next five fiscal years and thereafter are as follows:

Year Ending July 31,	Amount
2014	$ 285,683
2015	77,503
2016	82,737
2017	79,619
2018	80,567
Thereafter	1,793,253
Total notes payable	$ 2,399,362

NOTE I – RETIREMENT PLAN

The Seminary sponsors a qualified defined contribution retirement plan for eligible employees as defined by the plan under IRC Section 403(b). Employees are eligible to participate in the plan immediately upon hire and contributions to the plan are vested immediately. Each participant in the plan may make voluntary contributions to the plan of up to the lesser of twenty percent (20%) of annual compensation received by the participant during the plan year, or the maximum allowed by law. The Seminary matches participant's contributions to a maximum of 2.5%. Contributions to the plan by the Seminary for the years ended July 31, 2013 and 2012 were $42,406 and $41,841, respectively.

NOTE J - FINANCIAL STATEMENT PRESENTATION

Certain amounts in the July 31, 2012 financial statements have been reclassified to conform to the July 31, 2013 presentation.

MEMPHIS THEOLOGICAL SEMINARY
OF THE CUMBERLAND PRESBYTERIAN CHURCH
NOTES TO FINANCIAL STATEMENTS (CONTINUED)
For the Year Ended July 31, 2013

NOTE K – RELATED PARTY

The Seminary and the Board of Stewardship are separate corporations but both are affiliated with the Cumberland Presbyterian Church in that the governing board of the Church elects the members of the Board of Trustees of the Seminary and the Board of Stewardship. There are no common board members between the Seminary and the Board of Stewardship. Amounts due to and from the Board of Stewardship are as follows:

	July 31, 2013	July 31, 2012
Due the Board of Stewardship from the Seminary:		
Accounts Payable	$ -	$ 30,299
Notes Payable	$ 2,399,362	$ 2,401,677
Accrued Interest	$ 18,366	$ 38,272
Due to the Seminary from the Board of Stewardship:		
Seminary cash held	$ 215,776	$ 6,309
Seminary investments held	$ 9,023,572	$ 8,862,285

NOTE L – RECLASSIFICATIONS OF NET ASSETS

Management has determined that since 2007, state law has given charitable institutions the flexibility in management of endowment funds to move from traditional fiduciary accounting concepts to a total return concept without requiring a formal amendment to the governing instrument of the endowment fund. Under the statute, terms in a gift instrument designating a gift as an endowment or authorizing only the distribution of "income" or words of similar import do not limit the authority of the institution to determine how much to appropriate and how much to accumulate based on a wide variety of considerations listed in the statute, including expected total return from both income and the appreciation of investments. Based on the statute, management has determined that original gifts plus subsequent gifts to an endowment should be considered permanently restricted; while accumulated earnings plus appreciation of investments should be considered either unrestricted or temporarily restricted depending on the endowment's specification of the use of "income". In accordance with the adoption of this concept, with the flexibility allowed by state law, as of July 31, 2012, management has identified a reclassification of $1,559,720 from permanently restricted net assets, of which $323,653 is reclassified to temporarily restricted net assets and $1,236,067 is reclassified to unrestricted net assets. As of July 31, 2013, management has identified an additional reclassification of $369,661 from permanently restricted net assets, of which $249,861 is reclassified to temporarily restricted net assets and $119,800 is reclassified to unrestricted net assets. These amounts are reflected on the statement of activities.

SUPPLEMENTAL INFORMATION

MEMPHIS THEOLOGICAL SEMINARY
OF THE CUMBERLAND PRESBYTERIAN CHURCH
SCHEDULE OF EXPENDITURES OF FEDERAL AWARDS
For the Year Ended July 31, 2013

CFDA Number	Federal Grantor / Pass-Through Grantor	2013	2012
84.032	U.S. Department of Education Federal Family Education Loan Program	$ 2,501,924	$ 2,650,203

NON-FINANCIAL INFORMATION

CERTIFIED PUBLIC ACCOUNTANTS
ATRIUM 1, 6800 POPLAR AVE., STE. 210
GERMANTOWN, TENNESSEE 38138
(901) 523-8283 (901) 523-8287 FAX
www.zkcpas.com

INDEPENDENT AUDITOR'S REPORT ON INTERNAL CONTROL OVER FINANCIAL REPORTING AND ON COMPLIANCE AND OTHER MATTERS BASED ON AN AUDIT OF FINANCIAL STATEMENTS PERFORMED IN ACCORDANCE WITH *GOVERNMENT AUDITING STANDARDS*

Board of Trustees
Memphis Theological Seminary
 of the Cumberland Presbyterian Church
Memphis, Tennessee

We have audited, in accordance with the auditing standards generally accepted in the United States of America and the standards applicable to financial audits contained in Government Auditing Standards issued by the Comptroller General of the United States, the financial statements of Memphis Theological Seminary of the Cumberland Presbyterian Church (the "Seminary", a nonprofit organization), which comprise the statement of financial position as of July 31, 2013, and the related statements of activities, and cash flows for the year then ended, and the related notes to the financial statements, and have issued our report thereon dated December 16, 2013.

Internal Control over Financial Reporting

In planning and performing our audit of the financial statements, we considered the Seminary's internal control over financial reporting (internal control) to determine the audit procedures that are appropriate in the circumstances for the purpose of expressing our opinion on the financial statements, but not for the purpose of expressing an opinion on the effectiveness of the Seminary's internal control. Accordingly, we do not express an opinion on the effectiveness of the organization's internal control.

A *deficiency in internal control* exists when the design or operation of a control does not allow management or employees, in the normal course of performing their assigned functions, to prevent, or detect and correct, misstatements on a timely basis. A *material weakness* is a deficiency, or a combination of deficiencies, in internal control, such that there is a reasonable possibility that a material misstatement of the entity's financial statements will not be prevented, or detected and corrected on a timely basis. A *significant deficiency* is a deficiency, or a combination of deficiencies, in internal control that is less severe than a material weakness, yet important enough to merit attention by those charged with governance.

Our consideration of internal control was for the limited purpose described in the first paragraph of this section and was not designed to identify all deficiencies in internal control that might be material weaknesses or significant deficiencies. Given these limitations, during our audit we did not identify any deficiencies in internal control that we consider to be material weaknesses. However, material weaknesses may exist that have not been identified. We did identify certain deficiencies in internal control, described in the accompanying schedule of findings and questioned costs that we consider to be significant deficiencies (see Finding 2011-1).

Compliance and Other Matters

As part of obtaining reasonable assurance about whether the Seminary's financial statements are free from material misstatement, we performed tests of its compliance with certain provisions of laws, regulations, contracts, and grant agreements, noncompliance with which could have a direct and material effect on the determination of financial statement amounts. However, providing an opinion on compliance with those provisions was not an objective of our audit, and accordingly, we do not express such an opinion. The results of our tests disclosed no instances of noncompliance or other matters that are required to be reported under Government Auditing Standards.

The Seminary's Response to Findings

The Seminary's response to the findings identified in our audit is described in the accompanying schedule of findings and questioned costs. The Seminary's response was not subjected to the auditing procedures applied in the audit of the financial statements and, accordingly, we express no opinion on it.

Purpose of this Report

The purpose of this report is solely to describe the scope of our testing of internal control and compliance and the results of that testing, and not to provide an opinion on the effectiveness of the organization's internal control or on compliance. This report is an integral part of an audit performed in accordance with *Government Auditing Standards* in considering the organization's internal control and compliance. Accordingly, this communication is not suitable for any other purpose.

[signature]

Germantown, Tennessee
December 16, 2013

CERTIFIED PUBLIC ACCOUNTANTS
ATRIUM 1, 6800 POPLAR AVE., STE. 210
GERMANTOWN, TENNESSEE 38138
(901) 523-8283 (901) 523-8287 FAX
www.zkcpas.com

INDEPENDENT AUDITOR'S REPORT ON COMPLIANCE FOR A MAJOR PROGRAM AND ON INTERNAL CONTROL OVER COMPLIANCE REQUIRED BY OMB CIRCULAR A-133

Board of Trustees
Memphis Theological Seminary
 of the Cumberland Presbyterian Church
Memphis, Tennessee

Report on Compliance for a Major Federal Program

We have audited the Seminary's compliance with the types of compliance requirements described in the *OMB Circular A-133 Compliance Supplement* that could have a direct and material effect on the Memphis Theological Seminary of the Cumberland Presbyterian Church's (the "Seminary") major federal program for the year ended July 31, 2013. The Seminary's major federal program is identified in the summary of auditor's results section of the accompanying schedule of findings and questioned costs.

Management's Responsibility

Management is responsible for compliance with the requirements of laws, regulations, contracts, and grants applicable to its federal program.

Auditor's Responsibility

Our responsibility is to express an opinion on compliance for the Seminary's major federal program based on our audit of the types of compliance requirements referred to above. We conducted our audit of compliance in accordance with auditing standards generally accepted in the United States of America; the standards applicable to financial audits contained in *Government Auditing Standards*, issued by the Comptroller General of the United States; and OMB Circular A-133, *Audits of States, Local Governments, and Non-Profit Organizations*. Those standards and OMB Circular A-133 require that we plan and perform the audit to obtain reasonable assurance about whether noncompliance with the types of compliance requirements referred to above that could have a direct and material effect on a major federal program occurred. An audit includes examining, on a test basis, evidence about the Seminary's compliance with those requirements and performing such other procedures as we considered necessary in the circumstances.

We believe that our audit provides a reasonable basis for our opinion on compliance for each major federal program. However, our audit does not provide a legal determination of the Seminary's compliance.

Opinion on a Major Federal Program

In our opinion, the Seminary complied, in all material respects, with the types of compliance requirements referred to above that could have a direct and material effect on its major federal program for the year ended July 31, 2013.

Report on Internal Control over Compliance

Management of the Seminary is responsible for establishing and maintaining effective internal control over compliance with the types of compliance requirements referred to above. In planning and performing our audit of compliance, we considered the Seminary's internal control over compliance with the types of requirements that could have a direct and material effect on a major federal program to determine the auditing procedures that are appropriate in the circumstances for the purpose of expressing an opinion on compliance for a major federal program and to test and report on internal control over compliance in accordance with OMB Circular A-133, but not for the purpose of expressing an opinion on the effectiveness of internal control over compliance. Accordingly, we do not express an opinion on the effectiveness of the Seminary's internal control over compliance.

A *deficiency in internal control over compliance* exists when the design or operation of a control over compliance does not allow management or employees, in the normal course of performing their assigned functions, to prevent, or detect and correct, noncompliance with a type of compliance requirement of a federal program on a timely basis. A *material weakness in internal control over compliance* is a deficiency, or combination of deficiencies, in internal control over compliance, such that there is a reasonable possibility that material noncompliance with a type of compliance requirement of a federal program will not be prevented, or detected and corrected, on a timely basis. A *significant deficiency in internal control over compliance* is a deficiency, or a combination of deficiencies, in internal control over compliance with a type of compliance requirement of a federal program that is less severe than a material weakness in internal control over compliance, yet important enough to merit attention by those charged with governance.

Our consideration of internal control over compliance was for the limited purpose described in the first paragraph of this section and was not designed to identify all deficiencies in internal control over compliance that might be material weaknesses or significant deficiencies. We did not identify any deficiencies in internal control over compliance that we consider to be material weaknesses. However, material weaknesses may exist that have not been identified.

The purpose of this report on internal control over compliance is solely to describe the scope of our testing of internal control over compliance and the results of that testing based on the requirements of OMB Circular A-133. Accordingly, this report is not suitable for any other purpose.

Boccola Kaplan, PLLC

Germantown, Tennessee
December 16, 2013

MEMPHIS THEOLOGICAL SEMINARY
OF THE CUMBERLAND PRESBYTERIAN CHURCH
SCHEDULE OF FINDINGS AND QUESTIONED COSTS
For the Year Ended July 31, 2013

SECTION I - SUMMARY OF AUDITOR'S RESULTS

Financial Statements

Type of auditor's report issued:	*Unqualified*
Internal control over financial reporting:	
- Material weakness(es) identified?	____ yes ✓ no
- Significant deficiencies identified that are not considered to be material weaknesses?	✓ yes ____ none noted
- Noncompliance material to financial statements noted?	____ yes ✓ no

Federal Awards:

Internal control over major programs:	
- Material weakness(es) identified?	____ yes ✓ no
- Significant deficiencies identified that are not considered to be material weaknesses?	____ yes ✓ none noted
Type of auditor's report issued on compliance for major program:	*Unqualified*
Any audit findings disclosed that are required to be reported in accordance with section 510(a) of OMB Circular A-133?	____ yes ✓ no

Identification of major programs:

CFDA 84.032	U. S. Department of Education Federal Family Education Loan Program
Threshold for distinguishing type A and B programs:	*$300,000*
Auditee qualified as low risk auditee:	✓ yes ____ no

SECTION II - FINANCIAL STATEMENT FINDINGS

Finding 2011-1

SECTION III - FEDERAL AWARD FINDINGS AND QUESTIONED COSTS

There were no federal award findings or questioned costs for the year ended July 31, 2013.

MEMPHIS THEOLOGICAL SEMINARY
OF THE CUMBERLAND PRESBYTERIAN CHURCH
SCHEDULE OF PRIOR YEAR FINDINGS AND QUESTIONED COSTS
For the Year Ended July 31, 2013

Prior year findings and the current status of these findings is as follows:

Finding 2011-1

Condition: During our review of endowment activity, it was noted that requests for withdrawals from certain endowment funds were made by the Seminary. In several instances, the requests were made from individual endowments where funds were not available. The requests for distribution were granted by the Board of Stewardship causing several individual endowments to have negative balances in temporarily restricted or unrestricted categories. In the aggregate, the amount of temporarily restricted and unrestricted funds is positive; however, the balances in all individual funds should remain positive.

Current Status: Test work for the year ended July 31, 2013 revealed that the Seminary has continued to withdraw from individual endowments in a manner that caused new or increased negative balances in either the temporarily restricted or the unrestricted category. The Seminary should monitor withdrawals to allow these individual endowments to eliminate negative balances through the accumulation of contributions, capital gains, or interest/dividend income. This finding cannot be considered cleared as of July 31, 2013.

Management's Response: Management will increase its efforts to eliminate withdrawals from endowments where a negative balance in either a temporarily restricted or unrestricted category will result from the withdrawal.

Finding 2010-4

During our review of payroll related liabilities, we noted that the amounts due to Pacific Life for employee retirement have not been paid consistently. Amounts have been withheld from employee wages, but not remitted to the insurance company.

Current Status: Payment of the full amount due to Pacific Life for past years was made during the current year. The Seminary appears to be current on its payments of employee retirement as of July 31, 2013. This finding is considered cleared.

MEMPHIS THEOLOGICAL SEMINARY
OF THE CUMBERLAND PRESBYTERIAN CHURCH
INDEPENDENT AUDITOR'S GENERAL COMMENTS
For the Year Ended July 31, 2013

Required disclosures related to the auditor:

Name of Lead Auditor:	W. Marcus Rountree, CPA
Firm:	Zoccola Kaplan, PLLC
Firm Address:	6800 Poplar Avenue, Suite 210, Germantown, TN 38138
Firm Telephone Number:	(901) 523-8283
Firm Federal I.D. Number:	62-1152935

The
Proceedings
of the

**ONE HUNDRED EIGHTY-FOURTH
GENERAL ASSEMBLY**

of the

CUMBERLAND PRESBYTERIAN CHURCH

session held in

CHATTANOOGA, TENNESSEE
June 16 - 20, 2014

At Chattanooga, Tennessee and within the facilities of the Chattanooga Choo Choo Hotel, there the sixteenth day of June in the year of our Lord, Two Thousand Fourteen, at the appointed hour of two o'clock in the afternoon, Minister and Elder Commissioners from the various presbyteries, youth advisory delegates and visitors assembled.

FIRST DAY – MONDAY – JUNE 16, 2014

PRE-ASSEMBLY WORKSHOPS

Commissioners, Youth Advisory Delegates, and visitors were invited to attend the following workshops:

"Step Out: Creating Church Hospitality" led by T.J. Malinoski.
"Women in Ministry: Bible, Denomination, and Reality" led by Andy and Tiffany McClung
"Behavior, Identity, and Re-Envisioning Individual and Community Ministry" led by Troy Green.
"Safe Sanctuary" led by Susan Groce and Elinor Brown.
"Heading to Colombia, South America in 2015" led by the Colombian Host Committee & the GA Office.
"Our United Outreach" led by Cliff Hudson and Ron Gardner.

OPENING WORSHIP

In the Chattanooga Choo Choo, the one hundred eighty-fourth General Assembly, the Convention of Cumberland Presbyterian Women's Ministry, and visitors shared in worship. The Worship Director was the Reverend Abby Cole Keller, Presbytery of East Tennessee. The Worship Leader was Ms. Melody Dierking, President of Cumberland Presbyterian Women's Ministry. The Music Director was Mr. Gerald Peel, First Cumberland Presbyterian Church, Chattanooga, Tennessee. The pianist was Mr. Bruce Clark, First Cumberland Presbyterian Church, Chattanooga, Tennessee. The Anthem was presented by the Korean Pastors Choir with Special Music by the Hiawassee Presbytery Choir. Andra Felix, Janet Black and Kristy Miller from First Cumberland Presbyterian Church, Chattanooga and Lee Armstrong from Bartow Cumberland Presbyterian Church served as ushers. The Reverend Forest Prosser, Retiring Moderator of the General Assembly, delivered the sermon, *"What is Wrong with the Middle?...Nothing!"* which was based on the Scripture readings which were incorporated into the sermon: Genesis 2:7, Exodus 19:20, John 19:18, John 3:16 and I John 3:18. Following the Blessing and Benediction pronounced by the Reverend Abby Cole Keller, the Moderator announced a 15 minute break to allow the delegates to come to the front of the auditorium in preparation for the business session.

THE ASSEMBLY IS CONSTITUTED

The Moderator, the Reverend Forest Prosser, called the assembly to order at 3:15pm. The Reverend Clinton Buck, West Tennessee Presbytery, prayed the constituting prayer. On motion, the program was adopted.

The Reverend Bill Middleton, Presbytery of East Tennessee, presented the Report of the Credentials Committee. There were forty-seven (47) ministers, thirty-nine (39) elders, making a total of eighty-six (86) commissioners and twenty-five (25) Youth Advisory Delegates present at 2:00 p.m. On motion the report was concurred in, marked appendix "A" and filed.

ASSEMBLY BUSINESS

Moderator Forest Prosser declared the floor open for nominations for the office of Moderator of the one hundred eighty-fourth General Assembly. The following nominations, previously endorsed by their presbytery were presented: Elder Herb Dewees, Nashville Presbytery, nominated the Reverend Paula Louder, Nashville Presbytery. The Reverend Clinton Buck, West Tennessee Presbytery, nominated the Reverend Lisa Anderson, West Tennessee Presbytery.

The Moderator asked if there were further nominations. On Motion, the Moderator declared that nominations cease and the body proceeded to hear the nomination speeches. The Reverend Stephen Louder, Nashville Presbytery, gave the nominating speech in favor of the Reverend Paula Louder and the Reverend Frank Ward, West Tennessee Presbytery, spoke in favor of the Reverend Lisa Anderson.

The Moderator asked Pastor Host, Reverend Jennifer Newell, Tennessee-Georgia Presbytery, to come forward to bring greetings to the Assembly. The Pastor Host gave details about the Joint Evening Worship Service at First Cumberland Presbyterian Church, Chattanooga, Tennessee. She reported that all should visit the displays and Resource Center located at Track 29. The Pastor Host announced that tours of the Chattanooga area were arranged for Wednesday and that tickets for the Memphis Theological Seminary/ Program of Alternante Studies luncheon are available at the host table.

Pastor Host Newell introduced Mr. Andy Berke, mayor of Chattanooga. Mayor Berke brought greetings on behalf of the city to those assembled and told of highlights of the city of Chattanooga.

Moderator Prosser informed the delegates that it was time to cast their ballots for Moderator of the one hundred eighty-fourth General Assembly. The Engrossing Clerk and members of the Credentials Committee collected the ballots. The Credentials Committee and the Stated Clerk exited the assembly hall to count the ballots.

While the ballots were being counted, the Moderator asked the Reverend Richard Brown, President of the Cumberland Presbyterian Children's Home to come forward. Reverend Brown gave some history of the Children's Home citing some of the people whose lives had been touched by the Children's Home as well as those who left a lasting influence on the Children's Home. One whom he wanted to honor was the Reverend Doctor James C. Gilbert. A video presentation portraying Doctor Gilbert's legacy at the Children's Home was shown. Following the video, a standing ovation was given honoring the life of Doctor Gilbert before members of his family who were in attendance.

Reverend Brown introduced staff and current Children's Home Trustees as well as those who had served in the past. The presentation ended with the Reverend Alfonso Marquez offering a prayer for the ministry of the Cumberland Presbyterian Children's Home.

ELECTION OF MODERATOR AND VICE MODERATOR

Ms. Lana Moore, Missouri Presbytery, reported the results of the Election of the Moderator. Forty-eight (48) votes cast for Reverend Lisa Anderson and thirty-nine (39) votes for Reverend Louder. Moderator Prosser declared the Reverend Lisa Anderson, Moderator, of the one hundred eighty-fourth General Assembly of the Cumberland Presbyterian Church.

Retiring Moderator, Forest Prosser, placed the Moderator's cross on Reverend Anderson and presented her the gavel. Moderator Anderson introduced her family: husband, Reverend Doctor Barry Anderson; mother, Patricia Hall; daughter, Sarah Anderson Edward; grandson, Oliver Edward; granddaughter, Lily Anderson; sister, Tammy Hall Pennington; sister, Reverend Doctor Tiffany Hall McClung; brother-in-law, Reverend Doctor Andy McClung; nephew, Ian McClung; and niece, Maggie McClung to the Assembly.

Moderator Anderson opened the floor for nominations for Vice Moderator. The Reverend Paula Louder was nominated. On Motion, nominations ceased and the Reverend Paula Louder was elected Vice Moderator of the one hundred eighty- fourth General Assembly of the Cumberland Presbyterian Church.

Vice Moderator Louder introduced her family to the Assembly: her husband, Reverend Stephen Louder; mother-in-law, Ms. Ruth Louder; and granddaughter, Jessica.

PRESENTATION BY STATED CLERK

The Stated Clerk, Reverend Michael Sharpe, invited the retiring Moderator, Reverend Forest Prosser, to the podium and presented him with a replica of the Moderator's cross and a gavel representing the one used in the one hundred eighty-third General Assembly. Reverend Prosser thanked the assembly for allowing him to serve as moderator.

CORRESPONDENCE

The Stated Clerk announced that the only correspondence was a resolution from Commissioner Sherrlyn Frost, Grace Presbytery, which was referred to Theology and Social Concerns.

INTRODUCTION OF BOARD/AGENCY REPRESENTATIVES

Bethel University	Eugene Leslie
Commission on Chaplains	Lowell Roddy
Children's Home	Alfonso Marquez
Historical Foundation	Tommy Jobe
Judiciary	Kimberly Sillvus
Memphis Theological Seminary	Sondra Roddy
Ministry Council	Troy Green
Our United Outreach	Ron Gardner
Stewardship	Debbie Shanks
Theology and Social Concerns	Lezlie Daniel (CPC)
Unification Task Force	Leon Cole (CPCA) and Gloria Villa-Diaz (CPC)

REFERRALS TO COMMITTEES

Referrals to the Committee on Children's Home and Historical Foundation
Page   Report
- 71   The Report of the Board of Trustees of the Historical Foundation
- 116   The Report of the Board of Trustees of the Cumberland Presbyterian Children's Home

Referrals to the Committee on Higher Education
Page   Report
- 81   The Report of the Board of Trustees of Memphis Theological Seminary
- 115   The Report of the Board of Trustees of Bethel University

Referrals to the Committee on Judiciary
Page   Report
- 42   The Report Number One of the Ministry Council, Section I.C.2
- 100   The Report of the Permanent Committee on Judiciary

Referrals to the Committee on Chaplains/Missions/Pastoral Development
Page   Report
- 40   The Report Number One of the Ministry Council (shaded sections only)
- 98   The Report of the Commission on Military Chaplains and Personnel

Referrals to the Committee on Ministry Council/Communication/Discipleship
Page   Report
- 40   The Report Number One of the Ministry Council, except shaded sections which are referred to Chaplains/Missions/Pastoral Development and Section I.C.2 which is referred to Judiciary
- 57   The Report Number Two of the Ministry Council

Referrals to the Committee on Stewardship/Elected Officers
Page   Report
- 32   The Report of the Moderator
- 34   The Report of the Stated Clerk
- 44   The Report Number One of the Ministry Council, Section II. d
- 59   The Report of the Board of Stewardship, Foundation and Benefits
- 96   The Report of the Our United Outreach Committee
- 104 The Report of the Place of Meeting Committee
- 121 Line Item Budgets Submitted by General Assembly Agencies

Referrals to the Committee on Theology and Social Concerns
Page   Report
- 106 The Report of the Unified Committee on Theology and Social Concerns
- 108 The Report of the Unification Task Force
       Resolution from Commissioner Sherrlyn Frost, Grace Presbytery

ADJOURNMENT

At 4:30 p.m. recess was declared by Moderator Anderson until Thursday Morning at 9:00 a.m. Committees met briefly following the adjournment to organize.

THE EVENING PROGRAM

The General Assembly of the Cumberland Presbyterian Church, the Convention of Cumberland Presbyterian Women's Ministry, visitors and the Cumberland Presbyterian Church in America met at 7:00 p.m. at the First Cumberland Presbyterian Church for a Joint Communion Service under the direction of General Assembly Worship Director, Reverend Abby Cole Keller, Presbytery of East Tennessee, who served as Worship Leader for the night. The Music Director was Mr. Gerald Peel, First Cumberland Presbyterian Church, Chattanooga, Tennessee. The Organist was Mr. Bruce Clark, First Cumberland Presbyterian Church, Chattanooga, Tennessee.

Service Music was provided by the Male Choir, inspirit with Special Music by the Hiwassee Presbytery Choir. The Scripture, Luke 22:31-32, was read by the Worship Leader. The Reverend Roosevelt Baugh, Red River Presbytery, preached the sermon, *"When Jesus Prays For Us."*

The Sacrament of Communion was served by Co-Celebrants, the Reverend Abby Cole Keller, Presbytery of East Tennessee and the Reverend Anthony Hollis, Hiwassee Presbytery. Serving Communion were: Jimmy Johnson, Ed Reeves, Allan Carpenter, Courtney Lewis, Les Spencer, Sandra Felix. Ronni Stone, Mark Stone, Sam Quattrochi, Sam Jones, Myron Hughes, Emily Howard, Mary Alice Cotter, John Bergen, Mike Ricketts and Sara Faires from First Chattanooga CPC and Mark Craven and Vickie Stone from the Red Bank CPC. The seven elders from the CPCA that helped to serve communion were: Thomas Ward, Michael Cooper, Jeff Johnson, James Abkins, Leon Cole, Jr., Theo Collier and William Page. The ushers for the service were Marshall Watson, Sharon Turner, Claire Broome, John Brammer, Mike Zelokovic, M K Cole, Linda Boran, Delmas Rigsby, Jerry Cotter and Christie Miller from First Chattanooga Church, Chattanooga, Tennessee.

Following the service, the First Cumberland Presbyterian Church sponsored a reception to honor the past Moderator, the Reverend Forest Prosser; the newly elected Moderator, the Reverend Lisa Anderson; the newly elected Vice-Moderator, the Reverend Paula Louder; Sally Sain, the President of the Cumberland Presbyterian Women's Ministry; Athala Jaramillo, the President-elect of the Cumberland Presbyterian Women's Ministry; and the Moderator-elect of the CPCA, Elder Leon Cole, Jr.

SECOND DAY – TUESDAY – JUNE 17, 2014

The General Assembly and visitors began their day with a joint devotional with the Cumberland Presbyterian Church in America. An opening prayer was offered by Reverend Iwao Satoh, Japan Presbytery, pastor of Louisville Japanese Christian Fellowship.

Reverend Lynn Thomas, Director of Global Cross Culture Missions, announced a special recognition honoring the 50th anniversary of the commissioning of Beverly and Buddy Stott as missionaries to Japan. In honor of the Stotts, the gathering sang "Here I am." The scripture reading for the morning was Matthew 13:33 which was read by Reverend Luz Guerrero Gutierrez. The message was given by Reverend Juan

Blandon and translated by Reverend Lynn Thomas.

Stated Clerk, Michael Sharpe, addressed the body with announcements. The Chattanooga Choo Choo campus is large, but should be explored. Located at Track 29 are the Cumberland Presbyterian Book Store, the Memphis Theological Seminary Silent Auction, and other vendors as well as the Memphis Theological Seminary/Program of Alternate Studies Luncheon. The hotel offers shuttle service to all points of the hotel campus.

The Unification Task Force introduced its members that were present. Copies of a Proposed Plan for Union of Cumberland Presbyterian Church and Cumberland Presbyterian Church in America (with Reflective Questions) were made available to everyone in attendance. Sections of the proposal were read to those in attendance and each table was asked to discuss the reflection questions and report the discussion on provided tablets. After moving through the 12 sections and Time Line for Unification, Reverend William Robinson gave the closing prayer.

Following the closing prayer, General Assembly Committees were dismissed to their meetings. Forty-four (44) ministers, thirty-nine (39) elders and twenty three (23) Youth Advisory Delegates were in attendance in committees.

THE EVENING PROGRAM

At 7:00 p.m. on Tuesday evening, the Cumberland Presbyterian Church and the Cumberland Presbyterian Church in America Youth sponsored a joint worship service at Track 29. The worship consisted of a combination of music, dramatic reading, interpretive dance and messages by Youth Advisory Delegate, Mariah Jones, Missouri Presbytery; Youth Advisory Delegate, Michael Keenan, West Tennessee Presbytery; and Reverend A'Yonnika Rogers, Huntsville Presbytery. The Reverend Dwight Lyles, Columbia Presbytery, introduced his new song, "God Make Us One."

At 8:00 p.m. Fun Night for everyone.

THIRD DAY – WEDNESDAY – JUNE 18, 2014

The third day began with joint devotionals led by the Women Ministries. The service opened with the Joint Women's Ministry Choir singing "Here I Am Lord" featuring Steve and Faye Delashmit. The Reverend Joy Warren, Murfreesboro Presbytery, brought the devotional, *"Called to Incarnational Justice Work."* The scripture reading was Luke 4:14-21. Following announcements, the Missionary Choir of the Cumberland Presbyterian Church in America sang "I'll Fly Away."

Following the closing prayer, the committees were dismissed to meet. There were thirty-four (34) ministers, twenty-nine (29) elders for a total of 63 commissioners, and seventeen (17) youth advisory registration cards turned in. The day was devoted to committee work.

THE EVENING PROGRAM

At 7:00 p.m., the Assembly gathered for a joint service of worship celebrating the history of ordaining women in the Cumberland Presbyterian Church in America and the Cumberland Presbyterian Church. An overflow crowd gathered for the service which was opened with Prelude/Time of Praise by the Louisa Woosley Celebration Choir under the direction of Minister S.J. Moore. Leading the worship were Licentiate Anna Sweet Brockman, Reverend Elinor S. Brown, Candidate Whitney Brown, Archivist Susan Knight Gore, Reverend Abby Cole Keller, Reverend Doctor Debra Matthews, Reverend Doctor Tiffany Hall McClung, Minister S.J. Moore, Reverend Doctor Milton Ortiz, Reverend Doctor Pam Phillips-Burk, and Reverend Michael Sharpe.

All women ministers were invited to join in the processional hymn, "Joyful, Joyful, We Adore Thee." Highlights of the service included the introduction of members of Louisa Woosley's descendants in attendance as well as a dramatic reading from Louisa Woosley's pen. Susan Knight Gore and Michael Sharpe introduced a new song, "Shall Women Preach" with music and lyrics by Reverend J. Geoffrey Knight.

A special presentation was made by Doctor Pam Phillips-Burk and Doctor Milton Ortiz honoring the Reverend Betty Shirley who was ordained 64 years ago.

Following an inspiring sermon by the Reverend Doctor Debra Matthews, *"Where Do We Go Now?"* from Acts 1:3-8, a reception was held to honor women ministers and those who support them.

FOURTH DAY – THURSDAY – JUNE 19, 2014

The General Assembly and visitors began their day in worship. Worship was led by Children's CONNECT under the direction of Jodi Rush. The children shared songs, scripture readings, prayers and a dramatization on bullying. The theme was *"Unity: Perfectly and Wonderfully Made."*

CALL TO ORDER

The Moderator, Reverend Lisa Anderson, called the assembly to order. The constituting prayer was offered by the Moderator. There were forty-three (43) ministers, thirty-six (36) elders for a total of 79 commissioners, and seventeen (17) youth advisory delegates present as of 9:00 a.m.

PARLIMENTARIAN APPOINTED

Moderator Anderson explained the decorum for committees making reports and for speakers at the microphone. She appointed the Reverend Andy McClung, West Tennessee Presbytery, as Parliamentarian.

ANNOUNCEMENT

Reverend Troy Greene, representing the Ministry Council, introduced Reverend Milton Ortiz, Missions Ministry Team Leader.

ASSEMBLY BUSINESS

Reverend Don Nunn presented the Nomination Committee report. A motion was made to consider Sections I-X separately. Motion passed. On motion, the names listed in the report were placed into nomination. The Moderator asked for other nominations. There being none, on motion, those nominated were elected by acclamation.

On motion, Section XI was concurred in and the three recommendations were adopted.

STEWARDSHIP/ELECTED OFFICERS

The Report of the Committee on Stewardship/Elected Officers. Motion made by Reverend Mindy Acton to concur in the report and adopt the recommendations. The report was read by Youth Advisory Delegates Dakota Harris, Kennedy McKreaigg, and Mindy Jones. On motion, the report was divided to consider Recommendation 11 separately. On vote, Recommendation 11 was adopted. By vote, the report was concurred in and its recommendations adopted. The report was marked Appendix "C" and filed.

REPORT OF THE COMMITTEE ON THEOLOGY AND SOCIAL CONCERNS

The Report of the Committee on Theology and Social Concerns was presented by Reverend Darren Kennemer, who made the motion that the report be concurred in and its recommendations adopted. The report was read by Youth Advisory Delegates McKenzie Bybee and Hailey Russell and Reverend Cynthia Maddux.

An editorial change was made. The resolution in Recommendation 8 was submitted by Commissioner Sherrylynn Frost of Grace Presbytery, not by Grace Presbytery.

On motion the question was divided to consider Recommendations 8 and 9 separately. On vote, Recommendations 8 and 9 were adopted. On motion, the report was concurred in and its recommendations adopted. The report was marked Appendix "D" and filed.

RECESS DECLARED

The Moderator declared a recess until 10:30 a.m.

BUSINESS RESUMES

The Moderator called the meeting back to order at 10:30 a.m.

Parliamentarian, Reverend Doctor Andy McClung, gave a brief explanation of the parliamentary procedure that would be used during the meeting.

REPORT OF THE COMMITTEE ON JUDICIARY

The Report of the Committee on Judiciary was presented by Elder Ladd Daniel who made the motion that the report be concurred in and its recommendations adopted. The report was read by Youth Advisory Delegate A'an Para, Choctaw Presbytery. On Motion, the report was concurred in and its recommendations adopted. The report was marked Appendix "E" and filed.

REPORT OF THE COMMITTEE ON
MINISTRY COUNCIL/COMMUNICATIONS/DISCIPLESHIP

The Report of the Committee on Ministry Council/Communications/Discipleship was presented by Commissioner Sherrlynn Frost who made the motion to concur in the report and its recommendations adopted. Youth Advisory Delegate Mandy Jones read the report. A Motion was made to divide the question to consider Recommendation 2 separately. By vote of 55 to 24, Recommendation 2 adopted. On Motion, the report was concurred in and its recommendations adopted. The report was marked Appendix "F" and filed.

REPORT OF THE COMMITTEE ON
CHAPLAINS/MISSIONS/PASTORAL DEVELOPMENT

The Report of the Committee on Chaplains/Missions/Pastoral Development was presented by Reverend James Messer, North Central Presbytery, who made the motion to concur in the report and adopt its recommendations. The report was read by Youth Advisory Delegate, Jay Truitt, Murfreesboro Presbytery. On motion, the report was concurred in and its recommendations adopted. The report was marked Appendix "G" and filed.

ASSEMBLY BUSINESS

Moderator Anderson asked the Vice-Moderator, Reverend Paula Louder to preside over business in her absence.

REPORT OF THE COMMITTEE ON HIGHER EDUCATION

The Report of the Committee on Higher Education was introduced by Reverend Sam Wayman, Trinity Presbytery, who called upon Elder Judy Franco, Red River Presbytery, to read the report. Elder Franco made the motion that the report be concurred in and its recommendations be adopted. A Motion was made to divide the question to consider Recommendation 6 separately. A motion was made to amend Recommendation 6 which failed. On motion, the report was concurred in and its recommendations adopted. The report was marked Appendix "H" and filed.

RECESS DECLARED

Vice-Moderator Louder declared a recess for lunch until 1:30 p.m.

ASSEMBLY CALLED TO ORDER

Vice-Moderator Louder called the meeting to order at 1:30 p.m.

REPORT OF THE COMMITTEE ON
CHILDREN'S HOME/HISTORICAL FOUNDATION

The Report of the Committee on Children's Home/Historical Foundation was introduced by Reverend Rhonda McGowan who made the motion that the report be concurred in and its recommendations adopted. The report was read by Youth Advisory Delegates Michael Keenen, Nicole Franco, and Craig Barkley. On motion, the report was concurred in and its recommendations adopted. The report was marked Appendix "I" and filed.

ASSEMBLY BUSINESS

Moderator Anderson resumed her duties as Moderator of the General Assembly.

The Moderator recognized Reverend Troy Green of the Ministry Council. Reverend Green spoke of the change of the nature of our church's leadership to a Ministry model and encouraged going further.

Reverend Green re-introduced Reverend Milton Ortiz and asked Reverend Ortiz to stand and be recognized.

Reverend Green spoke about the position that is open for Pastoral Development Ministry Team Leader, asking to have possible candidates for the position identified.

A presentation was made by the Colombian Host Committee. A video was shown which told what delegates could expect when they go to Colombia in 2015. Angelica Proveda, Cauca Valley Presbytery and Colegio Americano representative, welcomed the Assembly to attend General Assembly in 2015 in Cali, Colombia, South America.

Sally Sain, Cumberland Presbyterian Women's Ministry Convention President, announced the new three year program on domestic violence. She explained that this new program would especially be promoted in Guatemala.

RESOLUTION OF THANKS

Commissioner Reverend Jo Warren, Arkansas Presbytery, presented the following resolution of thanks.

The 184th General Assembly of the Cumberland Presbyterian Church wishes to express its thanks and gratitude to God for the opportunity to assembly and to serve our Lord and Savior, Jesus Christ, in the power of the Holy Spirit, through the ministries and work of the Cumberland Presbyterian Church.

The body of this 184th General Assembly, meeting in Chattanooga, Tennessee, wishes to thank Tennessee-Georgia Presbytery (Cumberland Presbyterian Church) and Hiwassee Presbytery (Cumberland Presbyterian Church in America) for their hard work and warm hospitality in hosting this unique assembly; to pastor host, the Reverend Jennifer Newell; and to all the local Cumberland Presbyterian churches and Cumberland Presbyterian Church in America churches who helped organize and plan this assembly. You have our gratitude and appreciation. We also wish to thank Mayor Andy Berke and the city of Chattanooga, Tennessee for graciously welcoming us to this city.

The 184th General Assembly was truly blessed by well prepared, unified, and varied worship services and inspiring messages. Therefore, we wish to express our gratitude to Reverend Abby Cole Keller, Worship Director, and to Mr. Gerald Peel, Music Director, for their planning and leadership of the worship services.

The body wishes to thank Moderator, Reverend Lisa Anderson, for her leadership and guidance provided during deliberations and to Vice Moderator, Reverend Paula Louder. Our prayers go with you both as you represent our church through this coming year. To retiring Moderator, Reverend Forest Prosser, and retiring Vice-Moderator, Reverend Jamie Lively, thank you for your wonderful service throughout this past year. In addition, we wish to thank the staff of the General Assembly Office: Reverend Michael Sharpe, Stated Clerk; Reverend Vernon Sansom, Engrossing Clerk; and Mrs. Elizabeth Vaughn, Assistant to the Stated Clerk; for their tireless leadership and support. We also give thanks for each committee chairperson and for each commissioner and youth advisory delegate who has participated in the deliberations of the Assembly.

Special thanks are also extended to the Reverend Michael Sharpe, Stated Clerk of the Cumberland Presbyterian Church and to the Reverend Doctor Lynne Herring, Administrative Director of the Cumberland Presbyterian Church in America for their hard work organizing the gathering of these two great Presbyterian bodies.

May God be with each of us as we come to understand our uniqueness; as we work toward unification of these two great denominations; as we go about God's work in a world that truly needs to hear His message of love and salvation, through Jesus Christ.

On motion, the resolution was adopted, marked Appendix "J" and filed.

ASSEMBLY BUSINESS

Reverend Nathan Scott, Choctaw Presbytery, and Elder Erin Smith, Red River Presbytery, were excused by consent

READING OF THE MINUTES

The printed minutes were corrected and the minutes for Wednesday and Thursday were read. On motion, the minutes were accepted as corrected.

RECESS DECLARED

A recess was declared to prepare for Closing Worship.

CLOSING WORSHIP

The Closing Worship for the 184th General Assembly meeting in Chattanooga, Tennessee was a wonderful ending to a great and historic General Assembly. The Worship Leader was the Reverend Abby Cole Keller, Presbytery of East Tennessee. The music was led by Mr. Gerald Peel, First Cumberland Presbyterian Church, Chattanooga, Tennessee and the pianist was Mr. Bruce Clark, also of First Cumberland Presbyterian Church, Chattanooga, Tennessee. The Pastor Host, the Reverend Jennifer Newell, Tennessee-Georgia Presbytery, brought the sermon, *"The Next Step Is a Doozie."* The scripture reading was Matthew 14:13-18. A memorial roll of Ministers and Elders who have died in the past year was read and prayer was offered by Reverend Abby Cole Keller.

ADJOURMENT

Moderator Anderson thanked the Assembly for the honor of serving the Assembly as Moderator. A Motion was made and seconded to adjourn. Motion passed. Moderator Anderson proclaimed that the 184th General Assembly of the Cumberland Presbyterian Church stands adjourned until we meet in Cali, Colombia, South America on June 19-26, 2015.

APPENDICES

REPORT OF THE CREDENTIALS COMMITTEE
(Appendix A)

The Credentials Committee certifies the list of commissioners on pages 6 and 7 of the Preliminary Minutes with the following changes:

On the part of the Minister Commissioners: Reverend Gordon Warren and Reverend Jo Warren, Arkansas Presbytery; Reverend Wendall Ordway, Covenant Presbytery; Reverend Douglas Park, Cumberland East Coast Presbytery; Reverend Terry Herston, Hope Presbytery; and Reverend Stewart Salyer, Nashville Presbytery are not present.

On the part of the Elder Commissioners: Elder Kathy McGrew and Elder Steve Shaw, Cumberland Presbytery; Elder Gerald McGee, Hope Presbytery; Elder Charles Carr and Elder Doug Newman, Nashville Presbytery are not present.

Enrollment as of 2:00 p.m. is certified as forty-three (43) ministers, thirty-nine (39) elders and twenty-four (24) youth advisory delegates.

Respectfully submitted,
Bill Middleton, Chair
Wendell Ordway
Lana Moore
Mandy Jones

REPORT OF THE COMMITTEE ON STEWARDSHIP/ELECTED OFFICERS
(Appendix B)

I. REFERRALS

Referrals to this committee are as follows: The Report of the Moderator, The Report of the Stated Clerk; The Report Number One of the Ministry Council, Section II.d, The Report of the Board of Stewardship, Foundation and Benefits; The Report of the Our United Outreach Committee; The Report of the Place of Meeting Committee; and The Line Item Budgets submitted by General Assembly Agencies.

II. PERSONS OF COUNSEL

Appearing before this committee were: Reverend Robert Heflin, Executive Secretary, Mr. Mark Duck, Coordinator of Benefits: Ms. Debbie Shanks; representative from the Board of Stewardship, Foundation and Benefits; Mr. Ron Gardner, Chair of the Our United Outreach Committee; Reverend Cliff Hudson, Fund Development Coordinator of Our United Outreach; and Reverend Michael Sharpe, Stated Clerk.

We wish to express our appreciation to the persons of counsel for their presentations.

III. CONSIDERATION OF REFERRALS

A. REPORT OF THE MODERATOR

We commend the Moderator for his leadership and the thoughtfulness of his suggestions.

RECOMMENDATION 1: That the Report of the Moderator be concurred in.

B. REPORT OF THE STATED CLERK

We commend the excellent work of the Stated Clerk, Reverend Michael Sharpe. The Report of the Stated Clerk was received and the following recommendations are made:

RECOMMENDATION 2: That Recommendation 1 of the Report of the Stated Clerk, "that the 184th General Assembly approve the following dates for the 2014-2015 Church Calendar:

CHURCH CALENDAR 2014-2015

July-2014
6-11	Cumberland Presbyterian Youth Conference, Bethel, McKenzie, TN
12	Program of Alternate Studies Graduation
12-26	PAS Summer Extension School, Bethel, McKenzie, TN
19	Children's Fest, Bethel, McKenzie, TN
22-26	Ministers Retreat, Bethel, McKenzie, TN

August-2014
23	MTS Fall Semester Begins
31-Sept 28	Christian Education Season

September-2014
10	MTS Opening convocation
14	Senior Adult Sunday
21	Christian Service Recognition Sunday
28	International Day of Prayer and Action for Human Habitat

October-2014
	Clergy Appreciation Month
5	Worldwide Communion Sunday
12	Pastor Appreciation Sunday
26	Native American Sunday

November-2014
	Any Sunday Loaves and Fishes Program
1	All Saints Day
2	Stewardship Sunday
9	World Community Day (Church Women United)
9	Day of Prayer for People with Aids and Other Life-Threatening Illnesses
16	Bible Sunday
23	Christ the King Sunday
30-Dec 25	Advent in Church and Home

December-2014
	Any Sunday Gift to the King Offering
24	Christmas Eve
25	Christmas Day

January-2015
6	Epiphany
11	Human Trafficking Awareness Day
12-13	Stated Clerks' Conference
15	Deadline for receipt of 2014 Our United Outreach Contributions

February-2015
1-28	Black History Month
1	Annual congregational reports due in GA office
1	Denomination Day
1	Historical Foundation Offering

1	Souper Bowl Sunday
8	Our United Outreach Sunday
15	Youth Sunday
18	Ash Wednesday, the beginning of Lent
18–Apr 5	Lent to Easter

March-2015

	Women's History Month (USA)
22-28	National Farm Workers Awareness Week
29	Palm/Passion Sunday
29	One Great Hour of Sharing

April-2015

2	Maundy Thursday
3	Good Friday
5	Easter
12	CPCH Sunday
12-18	Family Week
25-26	30-Hour Famine

May-2015

1	Friendship Day (Church Women United)
10	MTS Closing Convocation & Graduation
24	Memorial Day Offering for Military Chaplains & Personnel for USA churches
24	Pentecost
24	World Mission Sunday

June-2015

19-26	General Assembly, Colombia, South America
19-26	CPWM Convention, Colombia, South America

July-2015

6-11	Cumberland Presbyterian Youth Conference, Bethel, McKenzie, TN
11	Program of Alternate Studies Graduation
11-25	PAS Summer Extension School, Bethel, McKenzie, TN
22-26	Ministers Retreat, Bethel, McKenzie, TN

August-2015

22	MTS Fall Semester Begins
30-Sept 27	Christian Education Season

September-2015

2	MTS Opening convocation
13	Senior Adult Sunday
20	Christian Service Recognition Sunday
20	International Day of Prayer and Action for Human Habitat

October-2015

	Clergy Appreciation Month
4	Worldwide Communion Sunday
11	Pastor Appreciation Sunday
25	Native American Sunday

November-2015

	Any Sunday Loaves and Fishes Program
1	All Saints Day
1	Stewardship Sunday
6	World Community Day (Church Women United)

8	Day of Prayer for People with Aids and Other Life-Threatening Illnesses
15	Bible Sunday
22	Christ the King Sunday
29-Dec 25	Advent in Church and Home

December-2015

	Any Sunday Gift to the King Offering
24	Christmas Eve
25	Christmas Day,"

be denied.

The committee substituted the following recommendation:

RECOMMENDATION 3: That General Assembly adopt the following calendar with the addition of the last Sunday of September (September 28, 2014, September 27, 2015) Seminary/PAS Sunday; delete from the calendar July 6-11 dates for CPYC, as this will have already occurred June 22-27, 2014.

CHURCH CALENDAR 2014-2015

July-2014

12	Program of Alternate Studies Graduation
12-26	PAS Summer Extension School, Bethel, McKenzie, TN
19	Children's Fest, Bethel, McKenzie, TN
22-26	Ministers Retreat, Bethel, McKenzie, TN

August-2014

23	MTS Fall Semester Begins
31-Sept 28	Christian Education Season

September-2014

10	MTS Opening convocation
14	Senior Adult Sunday
21	Christian Service Recognition Sunday
28	International Day of Prayer and Action for Human Habitat
28	Seminary/PAS Sunday

October-2014

	Clergy Appreciation Month
5	Worldwide Communion Sunday
12	Pastor Appreciation Sunday
26	Native American Sunday

November-2014

	Any Sunday Loaves and Fishes Program
1	All Saints Day
2	Stewardship Sunday
9	World Community Day (Church Women United)
9	Day of Prayer for People with Aids and Other Life-Threatening Illnesses
16	Bible Sunday
23	Christ the King Sunday
30-Dec 25	Advent in Church and Home

December-2014

	Any Sunday Gift to the King Offering
24	Christmas Eve
25	Christmas Day

January-2015
6	Epiphany
11	Human Trafficking Awareness Day
12-13	Stated Clerks' Conference
15	Deadline for receipt of 2014 Our United Outreach Contributions

February-2015
1-28	Black History Month
1	Annual congregational reports due in GA office
1	Denomination Day
1	Historical Foundation Offering
1	Souper Bowl Sunday
8	Our United Outreach Sunday
15	Youth Sunday
18	Ash Wednesday, the beginning of Lent
18–Apr 5	Lent to Easter

March-2015
	Women's History Month (USA)
22-28	National Farm Workers Awareness Week
29	Palm/Passion Sunday
29	One Great Hour of Sharing

April-2015
2	Maundy Thursday
3	Good Friday
5	Easter
12	CPCH Sunday
12-18	Family Week
25-26	30-Hour Famine

May-2015
1	Friendship Day (Church Women United)
10	MTS Closing Convocation & Graduation
24	Memorial Day Offering for Military Chaplains & Personnel for USA churches
24	Pentecost
24	World Mission Sunday

June-2015
19-26	General Assembly, Colombia, South America
19-26	CPWM Convention, Colombia, South America

July-2015
6-11	Cumberland Presbyterian Youth Conference, Bethel, McKenzie, TN
11	Program of Alternate Studies Graduation
11-25	PAS Summer Extension School, Bethel, McKenzie, TN
22-26	Ministers Retreat, Bethel, McKenzie, TN

August-2015
22	MTS Fall Semester Begins
30-Sept 27	Christian Education Season

September-2015
2	MTS Opening convocation
13	Senior Adult Sunday
20	Christian Service Recognition Sunday
20	International Day of Prayer and Action for Human Habitat
27	Seminary/PAS Sunday

October-2015

	Clergy Appreciation Month
4	Worldwide Communion Sunday
11	Pastor Appreciation Sunday
25	Native American Sunday

November-2015

	Any Sunday Loaves and Fishes Program
1	All Saints Day
1	Stewardship Sunday
6	World Community Day (Church Women United)
8	Day of Prayer for People with Aids and Other Life-Threatening Illnesses
15	Bible Sunday
22	Christ the King Sunday
29-Dec 25	Advent in Church and Home

December-2015

	Any Sunday Gift to the King Offering
24	Christmas Eve
25	Christmas Day.

C. REPORT OF THE BOARD OF STEWARDSHIP, FOUNDATION AND BENEFITS

We commend the Board of Stewardship, Foundation, and Benefits for their diligent work. The Report of the Board of Stewardship, Foundation, and Benefits was received and the following recommendations were made:

RECOMMENDATION 4: That Recommendation 1 of the Report of the Board of Stewardship, Foundation and Benefits, "that the General Assembly encourage congregations, presbyteries, synods and individual Cumberland Presbyterians to consider establishing an endowment as their legacy to further the local or worldwide ministry of the Cumberland Presbyterian Church, be adopted.

RECOMMENDATION 5: That Recommendation 2 of the Report of the Board of Stewardship, Foundation and Benefits, "that the General Assembly encourage congregations, presbyteries and synods to consider the Cumberland Presbyterian Investment Loan Program when they desire to save money for a special project or other need," be adopted.

RECOMMENDATION 6: That Recommendation 3 of the Report of the Board of Stewardship, Foundation and Benefits, "that the General Assembly encourage individual Cumberland Presbyterians who live in the states of Kentucky, Missouri, New Mexico, Tennessee and Texas to consider opening Investment Loan Program accounts to help Cumberland Presbyterian churches to build or expand their facilities," be adopted.

RECOMMENDATION 7: That Recommendation 4 of the Report of the Board of Stewardship, Foundation and Benefits, "that the General Assembly encourage churches to work with their pastor or other church staff to see that they have a retirement account and are saving on a regular basis for their retirement. It is important for a congregation to see that their pastor or other church staff are taken care of during their retirement years," be adopted.

RECOMMENDATION 8: That Recommendation 5 of the Report of the Board of Stewardship, Foundation and Benefits, "that the General Assembly encourage presbyteries to identify retired pastors who may need some financial assistance and provide the Board of Stewardship, Foundation and Benefits with the name and contact information of those pastors," be denied.

The committee substitutes the following recommendation to protect the privacy of individual retired pastors:

RECOMMENDATION 9: That the General Assembly encourage presbyteries to identify retired pastors who may need some financial assistance and with the retired pastors' permission provide the Board of Stewardship, Foundation, and Benefits with the name and contact information of said pastor(s).

The committee recognizes the importance of relating information about benefits to participants and non-participants who are eligible for the benefits; therefore, we make the following recommendation:

RECOMMENDATION 10: That the General Assembly encourage the Board of Stewardship, Foundation, and Benefits to electronically mail all ministers and church related employees, including non-participants, about benefit options available and open enrollment once a year.

The committee recognizes the importance in stewardship of knowing how monies are being utilized; the importance is further emphasized with the mandate to be salt and light in our culture; therefore, we make the following recommendation:

RECOMMENDATION 11: That the General Assembly ask the Board of Stewardship, Foundation, and Benefits to investigate what is being covered by the health insurance benefits offered and to clarify anything that might conflict with our Confession of Faith and previous General Assembly rulings regarding sanctity of life; if conflicts are found that they be referred to the Unified Committee on Theology and Social Concerns and that it be reported to the 185th General Assembly.

The committee recognizes the importance of educating local churches and presbyteries regarding planned giving; therefore, we make the following recommendation:

RECOMMENDATION 12: That the General Assembly encourage Presbyteries and Sessions of local churches to invite representatives from the Board of Stewardship, Foundation, and Benefits to educate laity and presbyters on planned giving.

D. REPORT OF THE OUR UNITED OUTREACH COMMITTEE

We commend the work of the Our United Outreach Committee and the Development Director. We especially commend their work toward debt retirement. We are excited about the prospect of the denomination being debt free by March 2015 and that $120,000 dollars will be available for ministry rather than debt retirement.

RECOMMENDATION 13: That Recommendation 1 of the Report of the Our United Outreach Committee, "that we ask General Assembly that the following allocation for incoming 2015 for Our United Outreach funds,

The allocation is to be as follows:	$2,900,000.00	
Development Coordinator	79,000.00	
Debt Retirement	119,993.00	
Legal Expenses—Insurance Deductible	25,000.00	
Evaluation Committee	3,500.00	
Unification Task Force	20,000.00	
Sub-total	$ 247,403.00	
Ministry Council	$1,326,254.00	50%
Bethel University	132,625.00	5%
Children's Home	79,575.00	3%
Stewardship	159,150.00	6%
General Assembly Office	212,201.00	8%
Memphis Theological Seminary/ Program of Alternate Studies	185,676.00	7%
Historical Foundation	79,575.00	3%
Shared Services	450,926.00	17%

(next 5 items total 1%)
Comm. on Chaplains	9,284.00	.350%
Judiciary Committee	8,753.00	.330%
Theology/Social Concerns	3,249.00	.123%
Nominating Committee	2,719.00	.103%
Contingency Fund	2,520.00	.095%
	$2,652,507.00	

Our United Outreach Goal $2,900,000.00," be adopted:

RECOMMENDATION 14: That Recommendation 2 of the Report of the Our United Outreach Committee, "that congregations and individuals consider the use of electronic giving when making contributions to Our United Outreach," be adopted.

RECOMMENDATION 15: That Recommendation 3 of the Report of the Our United Outreach Committee, "that we ask General Assembly to encourage Presbyterian Boards of Missions and other appropriate agencies to cooperate with Our United Outreach Director of Development to educate ministers of other denominations who are serving as Stated Supplies on the significance of Our United Outreach," be adopted.

The committee recognizes the need for further education of local churches and Presbyteries on the work supported by Our United Outreach; therefore, we make the following recommendation:

RECOMMENDATION 16: That General Assembly encourage Sessions and Presbyteries to invite Reverend Cliff Hudson to speak at events or to fill pulpits speaking on Our United Outreach.

E. REPORT OF THE PLACE OF MEETING COMMITTEE

We commend the work of the Place of Meeting Committee. The Report of the Place of Meeting Committee was received and the following recommendation is made:

RECOMMENDATION 17: That Recommendation 1 of the Report of the Place of Meeting Committee, "that the 184th General Assembly accept the invitation of Nashville Presbytery to host the concurrent meetings of the 186th General Assembly (CPC) and the General Assembly of the Cumberland Presbyterian Church in America (CPCA), June 17-21, 2016," be adopted.

F. LINE ITEM BUDGETS SUBMITTED BY GENERAL ASSEMBLY AGENCIES

The committee reviewed the line item budgetary items. No actions were required of this committee.

Respectfully submitted:
The Committee on Stewardship

REPORT OF THE COMMITTEE ON THEOLOGY AND SOCIAL CONCERNS
(Appendix C)

I. REFERRALS

Referrals to this committee are as follows: The Report of the Unified Committee on Theology and Social Concerns, The Report of the Unificaition Task Force and the Resolution from Commissioner Reverend Sherrlyn Frost, Grace Presbytery.

II. PERSONS OF COUNSEL

Appearing before this committee were: Reverend Lezlie Daniel, representative from the Unified Committee on Theology and Social Concerns: Reverend Michael Sharpe, Stated Clerk: and Reverend Gloria Villa-Diaz, representative from the Unification Task Force.

III. CONSIDERATION OF REFERRALS

A. REPORT OF THE UNIFIED COMMITTEE OF THEOLOGY AND SOCIAL CONCERNS

We commend the work of the Unified Committee on Theology and Social Concerns.

RECOMMENDATION 1: We recommend that the Report of the Unified Committee on Theology and Social Concerns be concurred in.

B. REPORT OF THE UNIFICATION TASK FORCE

We commend the work of the Unification Task Force. We recognize that this document is a working document designed for study and discussion over the next year. We encourage every commissioner of the 184th General Assembly to go back to her or his home congregation and presbytery, resolve to study this document and provide feedback to the Unification Task Force. We applaud their efforts to develop a plan that would allow for "buy in" at the grass roots level. This can be better accomplished if we all commit to study and discussion concerning this document.

RECOMMENDATION 2: That Recommendation 1 of the Report of the Unification Task Force, "that the Unification Task Force be given time at Summer and Fall 2014 and Spring 2015 presbytery and synod meetings to present updates on unification and to get feedback on the plan for union," be adopted.

RECOMMENDATION 3: That Recommendation 2 of the Report of the Unification Task Force, "that joint clusters of churches also schedule a time for a presentation on unification by a member of the task force, unification advocates, and/or other leaders within both denominations," be adopted.

RECOMMENDATION 4: That Recommendation 3 of the Report of the Unification Task Force, "that the General Assembly continue its funding for the programming and travel of the Unification Task Force," be adopted.

RECOMMENDATION 5: That Recommendation 4 of the Report of the Unification Task Force, "that the proposed plan of union and reflection questions be received by General Assembly and circulated widely among the people, and that feedback be provided to the Office of General Assembly by July 1, 2015," be adopted.

RECOMMENDATION 6: That Recommendation 5 of the Report of the Unification Task Force, "that this timeline for unification be approved," be denied.

RECOMMENDATION 7: That this proposed timeline for unification be approved.

C. RESOLUTION FROM REVEREND SHERRLYN FROST, GRACE PRESBYTERY, CONCERNING THE EXCLUSIVITY OF SAVING FAITH IN JESUS CHRIST

The Committee discussed the Resolution submitted by Commissioner Reverend Sherrlyn Frost. The committee affirms the Sovereignty of God, the Authority of Scriptures, and the strength of statements

3.08 and 4.08 of the Confession of Faith, which clearly states that (3.08) *"Jesus Christ, ... is the only hope of reconciliation between God and sinful persons"* and (4.08) *"that persons rely solely upon God's grace in Jesus Christ for salvation."*

RECOMMENDATION 8: That the Resolution from Commissioner Sherrlyn Frost, Grace Presbytery, Concerning the Exclusivity of Saving Faith in Jesus Christ, which states:
"With the acceptance of our 1984 Confession of Faith, the General Assembly confirmed verbally that Jesus is the only way to salvation. However, this declaration was never added to the General Assembly minutes as directed and agreed upon at that meeting of General Assembly. Therefore, we submit to you, the 184th General Assembly meeting in Chattanooga, Tennessee in 2014, this resolution:

WHEREAS, we acknowledge the ambiguity that may be found in the 1984 Confession of Faith as it relates to our doctrine of the exclusivity of Jesus as Lord and Savior, and that the stated doctrinal position of the Cumberland Presbyterian denomination was not documented in the minutes of the General Assembly upon adoption of our 1984 Confession, and that it seems now there are many and various beliefs pervading our denomination, including a universalist perspective which we believe contradicts the message of Scripture. and

WHEREAS, we acknowledge the integrity of Scripture as the infallible rule of faith and practice as spelled out in our 1984 Confession of Faith (Introduction to the 1984 Confession, page xv and Section 1.05), and

WHEREAS scripture clearly indicates that there will be eternal separation from God for those who choose the path of destruction by not living in righteousness before God, and that because of the inherent sinful, nature of man due to the fall of Adam we are all bound for destruction and are only to find true righteousness before God through the atoning work of Jesus Christ, and

WHEREAS, we are seeing a trend toward monism and the unity of all faiths and an increased intolerance toward Biblical Christianity, and

WHEREAS, the eschatological view of scripture points to the Ruler of Darkness behind the formation of a one-world religion which requires the diminishing of Christ as Lord and Savior.

BE IT RESOLVED that the 184th General Assembly meeting in Chattanooga, Tennessee in 2014 would officially rule that the Cumberland Presbyterian Confession of Faith affirms the exclusivity of saving faith in Jesus Christ as an essential doctrine of the Cumberland Presbyterian Church and that this ruling be recorded and passed to presbyteries to uphold," be denied.

RECOMMENDATION 9: That the Unified Committee on Theology and Social Concerns be directed to study the scripture references for Section 3.08 of the 1984 Confession of Faith to see if it could be further clarified or strengthened by the addition of John 14:6 or other scripture references.

Respectfully submitted,
Committee on Theology and Social Concerns

REPORT OF THE COMMITTEE ON JUDICIARY
(Appendix D)

I. REFERRALS

Referrals to this committee are as follows: The Report Number One of the Ministry Council, Section I.C.2 and The Report of the Permanent Committee on Judiciary.

II. PERSONS OF COUNSEL

Appearing before this committee were: Reverend Michael Sharpe, Stated Clerk ; Ms. Kimberly Silvus and Reverend Andy McClung, Permanent Committee on the Judiciary; Reverend Milton Ortiz and

Reverend Lynn Thomas, Missions Ministry Team, and Reverend Troy Green, representative for the Ministry Council.

III. CONSIDERATION OF REFERRALS

A. REPORT NUMBER ONE OF THE MINISTRY COUNCIL, SETION I.C.2

The committee reviewed the action of 183rd General Assembly, pertaining to adoption of the recommendation to establish "the Missions Ministry Team as the agency responsible for oversight, guidance and authority for mission work and mission fields that cannot have a meaningful relationship with a presbytery due to distance and/or language."

B. REPORT OF THE PERMANENT COMMITTEE ON JUDICIARY

The committee reviewed and discussed at length the Report of the Permanent Committee on Judiciary, in consultation with its committee representative(s). The committee also received and reviewed supplemental study information from The Permanent Judiciary Committee and others.

RECOMMENDATION 1: That Recommendation 1 of the Report of the Permanent Committee on Judiciary, "that the unconstitutional action of the 183rd General Assembly, which authorized the Missions Ministry Team to conduct all actions typical of a presbytery in oversight of non-USA mission work, be rescinded," be denied.

RECOMMENDATION 2: That Recommendation 2 of the Report of the Permanent Committee on Judiciary, "that the 184th General Assembly direct Mission Synod of the Cumberland Presbyterian Church to establish immediately a non-geographic presbytery called New Missions Presbytery of the Cumberland Presbyterian Church to serve as a transitional presbytery which will facilitate new mission work and provisional congregations outside the United States until membership in an existing or new geographic presbytery has been established," be denied.

The Committee affirms the actions of the 183rd General Assembly, regarding Recommendation 8 pertaining to the authority of the Missions Ministry Team to conduct its work.

RECOMMENDATION 3: That the Permanent Committee on Judiciary work in concert with the Missions Ministry Team, in development of amendment(s) to the constitution, empowering the Missions Ministry Team (or its successor) to develop new churches outside of the United States.

Respectfully submitted,
The Committee on Judiciary

REPORT OF THE COMMITTEE ON
MINISTRY COUNCIL/COMMUNICATIONS/DISCIPLESHIP
(Appendix E)

Referrals to this committee are as follows: The Report Number One of the Ministry Council, except shaded sections which are referred to Champlains/Missions/Pastoral Development and Section I.C.2 which is referred to Judiciary and The Report Number Two of the Ministry Council.

II. PERSONS OF COUNSEL

Appearing before this committee were: Ms. Edith Old, Director of Ministries; Reverend Troy Green, Representive from Ministry Council; Reverend Elinor Brown, Discipleship Ministry Team; and Mr. Mark Davis, Communications Ministry Team.

III. CONSIDERATION OF REFERRALS

A. REPORT NUMBER ONE OF THE MINISTRY COUNCIL EXCEPT SHADED SECTIONS AND SECTION I.C.2

We commend the Ministry Council and other teams for incorporating the use of technology into our denomination, and make the following recommendations:

RECOMMENDATION 1: We concur in Sections I. A., B.; C. 1., 3-5; II. A., C. 2- 5., 9;, D. 1-2., 4- 5;, G. 1- 2., 4- 6;, H. 1., 4., 5., 7;, I.; K. 3., 9-10;, M.; N;, O, 1-2.; III. A., B. 1-2., 4., 6., and IV of Report Number One of the Ministry Council.

1. Section H of the Report One of the Ministry Council

RECOMMENDATION 2: Regarding In view of the theological direction and decisions of the Presbyterian Church USA, it is imperative for the Ministry Council to evaluate our association with the Presbyterian Church USA to re-determine the boundaries of that association, pending the actions of the meeting of the Presbyterian Church USA 2014 General Assembly.

2. Section K.9. of the Report One of the Ministry Council

RECOMMENDATION 3: Regarding we recommend that the present deadline be deleted and require the Stated Clerk of General Assembly and the Discipleship Ministry Team to resend all Safe Sanctuary information directly to pastors and Stated Clerks of Presbyteries by the 2015 Spring Presbytery meetings.

B. REPORT NUMBER TWO OF THE MINISTRY COUNCIL

RECOMMENDATION 4: That the report be concurred in.

Respectfully submitted:
The Committee on Ministry Council/Communication/Discipleship

REPORT OF THE COMMITTEE ON CHAPLAINS/MISSIONS/PASTORAL DEVELOPMENT
(Appendix F)

I. REFERRALS

Referrals to this committee are as follows: The Report Number One of the Ministry Council (shaded sections only) and the Report of the Commission on Military Chaplains and Personnel.

II. PERSONS OF COUNSEL

Appearing before this committee were: Reverend Larry Greenslit, Director Presbyterian Council for Chaplains and Military Personnel; Reverend Lowell Roddy, representative; Reverend Lynn Thomas, Director of Global Missions; and Reverend Milton Ortiz, Missions Ministry Team Leader;

III. CONSIDERATION OF REFERRALS

A. REPORT NUMBER ONE OF THE MINISTRY COUNCIL (SHADED SECTIONS ONLY)

The committee reviewed the Report Number One of the Ministry Council Section II. B.; C. 1, 6-8; D. 6-7; E.; G. 3, 7; H. 2-3, 6, 8; J.; K. 1-2, 4-8, 11-12; L.; O. 3 and Section III B. 3, 5; and discussed it with the representatives.

RECOMMENDATION 1: That the referred sections of the Report Number One of the Ministry Council be concurred in.

The committee discussed the growth and expansion of the Cumberland Presbyterian Church, the governing of new churches, the Asian Mission Forum and shared events that are being planned, the Central American Adelante evangelism program, and the Stott-Wallace Missionary Offering and Fund.

After discussion and comments from those on the committee most directly affected, the committee wishes to concur with Section E 11 of the Report One of the Ministry Council page 46 and affirm the General Assembly action of 2013 that allows the Missions Ministry Team to be judicatory host for our mission work where there are no presbyteries, as it has been evidenced that this model is effective.

While we recognize that our current system which requires missionaries to raise their own support has provided opportunity for exponential expansion of our missionary staff, we also recognize that this system adds instability, stress, and distraction to those missionaries. We believe that in some ways we have abdicated our responsibility to collectively participate in the work of global Gospel expansion. We affirm our responsibility as a denomination to commission, coordinate, and provide primary financial support for those answering the call to provide cross-cultural missionary service for our denomination.

The committee strongly encourages that each congregation participates in the Stott-Wallace Offering and set a minimum 2015 goal of at least $5.00 per active member.

B. REPORT OF THE COMMISSION ON MILITARY CHAPLAINS AND PERSONNEL

The committee reviewed the Report of the Commission on the Military Chaplains and Personnel and discussed it with the representatives of the Presbyterian Council for Chaplains and Military Personnel. The representatives explained the duty of the council in regards to recruiting, assessment, and readiness of candidates for chaplaincy. Discussion included the ministry of chaplains and the practical aspects of chaplaincy.

RECOMMENDATION 2: That the Report of the Commission on the Military Chaplains and Personnel be concurred in. The committee encourages churches and presbyteries to invite representatives from the Presbyterian Council for Chaplains and Military Personnel to speak to churches, presbyteries, Committees on Ministry, or other gatherings of those interested in chaplaincy.

We commend Reverend Lowell Roddy and Reverend Larry Greenslit for their ministry and their service. The committee strongly encourages that the churches in the United States support our military Chaplains by participating in the previously established annual offering on the Sunday closest to Memorial Day, Veteran's Day or Independence Day. Last year the total offering for the entire United States member churches was approximately $2200.00. The committee would like to challenge churches to reach a goal of at least one dollar per member. The proceeds of the offering will go to support the missions, outreach, and maintenance of the Presbyterian Council for Chaplains and Military Personnel.

In the course of discussion the subject of the increased suicide rate among military service men and women was raised and affirmed by our representatives. The committee urges local presbyteries and churches to seek out educational programs for pastors and lay leaders that can increase their awareness and ability to recognize the signs and symptoms of depression and suicide to help combat this increased epidemic not just in our returning service men and women but in all people in our communities.

As our denomination grows and expands in many countries, we acknowledge that United States Military chaplains are not the only Cumberland Presbyterian men and women serving in the role of chaplain around the world.

RECOMMENDATION 3: That the denomination seek new ways to minister to and support those who are serving as chaplains in hospitals, hospices, schools, non-United States military service, first responders, and other such chaplaincy roles around the world.

Respectfully submitted:
The Committee on Chaplains/Missions/Pastoral Development

REPORT OF THE COMMITTEE ON HIGHER EDUCATION
(Appendix G)

I. REFERRALS

Referrals to this committee are as follows: The Report of the Board of Trustees of Memphis Theological Seminary and The Report of the Board of Trustees of Bethel University.

II. PERSONS OF COUNSEL

Appearing before this committee were: Reverend Jay Earheart-Brown, President Memphis Theological Seminary; Ms. Sondra Roddy, Member of the Board of Trustees for Memphis Theological Seminary; and Reverend Michael Qualls, Director of Program of Alternate Studies; Dr. Walter Butler President of Bethel University; Ms. Nancy Bean, Vice President of the College of Arts and Sciences of Bethel University, and Reverend Eugene Leslie, Member of the Board of Trustees of Bethel Univeristy.

We want to thank all those who provided counsel to our committee. They made our work easier and we appreciate all they do.

III. CONSIDERATION OF REPORTS

A. BOARD OF TRUSTEES OF MEMPHIS THEOLOGICAL SEMINARY

RECOMMENDATION 1: That Recommendation 1 of the Board of Trustees of Memphis Theological Seminary, "that the General Assembly express its gratitude to Reverend Dr. Tom Bell for his faithful service to Memphis Theological Seminary and the Cumberland Presbyterian Church," be adopted.

Dr. Jay Earhart-Brown reported to the committee that Dr. Doy Daniels had decided not to be nominated for re-election to the Board of Trustees of Memphis Theological Seminary. Dr. Daniels has served the Board of Trustees well for six years and gratitude should be expressed to him for his faithful service to the seminary.

RECOMMENDATION 2: That the General Assembly express its gratitude to Reverend Dr. Doy Daniels for his faithful service to Memphis Theological Seminary and the Cumberland Presbyterian Church.

The seminary is celebrating 50 years since their move from their location on Bethel's campus to their current location in Memphis, Tennessee. Dr. Earhart-Brown gave an update on the capital campaign which includes plans for a new chapel. Since local churches put such strong emphasis on able worship leadership and strong preaching the following recommendation is made.

RECOMMENDATION 3: The 184th General Assembly emphasize the importance of constructing a new chapel at MTS.

We encourage the General Assembly to read "Ministry for the Real World: Scholarship, Piety, Justice" as it provides an excellent picture of the ecumenical ministry of Memphis Theological Seminary. The committee noted the construction of a Methodist House of Studies. Methodists will be funding that building in its entirety. Recognizing the need for a chair for Cumberland Presbyterian Studies the following recommendation is made.

RECOMMENDATION 4: That the 184th General Assembly encourage churches and members to give to the capital campaign, which will work toward fully funding the Baird-Buck Chair of Cumberland Presbyterian Studies which has a goal of $1.5 million.

RECOMMENDATION 5: That Recommendation 2 of the Board of Trustees of Memphis Theological Semianry, "that the General Assembly urge all probationers to consider Memphis Theological Seminary and the Program of Alternate Studies as their first options for meeting educational requirements for ordained ministry," be adopted.

The committee discussed the role of the director of the Program of Alternate Studies, the PAS Advisory Council, the Academic Review Committee, and Presbyterial Committees on Preparation for Ministry in the ordination process and makes the following recommendation.

RECOMMENDATION 6: We recommend that the 184th General Assembly affirm the constitutional role of the Presbytery to confer or acknowledge ordination within constitutional boundaries, and that the 184th General Assembly affirm the role of the Program of Alternate Studies to evaluate and determine the precise course requirements for all students sent to them by a presbytery.
Completion of these course will result in PAS certifying to the presbytery that the student has met the educational standard for ordination. PAS certification is one of the considerations and Presbytery should wait for this certification before ordaining candidates.

The committee discussed the offering of the online courses through the Program of Alternate Studies. The seminary is working on developing new courses each year and patience is encouraged and appreciation expressed for the work of the faculty in developing these online courses and working on developing the Colombia Program of Alternate Studies.

The committee discussed the plan to retire the debt to the Board of Stewardship. Part of the plan in place included the sale of certain properties to retire portions of the debt and a line item in the capital campaign will be used to retire the rest. The Chief Financial Officer has done a significant job in bringing the seminary's budget in line and managing the finances in such a way as to retire the debt and continue to provide the academic programs currently offered. As the financial condition of the seminary improves we want to encourage the Board of Trustees to look forward to the possibility of purchasing additional properties and to continue to develop and maintain a plan for this expansion.

The committee wants to express appreciation to the faculty and staff of the seminary for being willing to work in the ministry of Memphis Theological Seminary despite not receiving raises or at times even accepting reduced compensation. Appreciation is also extended to those in leadership who have navigated these difficult financial times with wisdom. The committee is pleased to hear that there are plans for a compensation increase in the upcoming year's budget.

The committee discussed the issue of Estate Gifts. The committee wants to emphasize the importance of estate giving, which will be of great benefit to the future of the seminary. MTS has resources available to assist individuals who want to give in this way. Inquirers are directed to call (901) 458-8232.

RECOMMENDATION 7: That Recommendation 3 of the Report of the Board of Trustees of Memphis Theological Seminary, "that the General Assembly encourage all churches to recognize and support Seminary Sunday," be adopted.

RECOMMENDATION 8: That Seminary/PAS Sunday be designated for September 28, 2014 and that on this Sunday an emphasis be given to estate giving and planning for the future ministry of Memphis Theological Seminary.

The committee discussed the importance of Our United Outreach (OUO) in funding the ministry of MTS. The role of OUO in all the ministries of the Cumberland Presbyterian Church is very important and the committee wants to encourage all congregations to give at least 10% annually to OUO not only to support the ministry of MTS but also to continue to support the ministries of our entire denomination.

As a committee we want to commend the Board of Trustees for their hard work and dedication. Be assured of our prayers as you move into the future preparing leaders for the global ecumenical church to teach, preach, and serve in the church of tomorrow.

B. BOARD OF TRUSTEES OF BETHEL UNIVERSITY

We recognize the covenant relationship between Bethel University and the Cumberland Presbyterian Church and the continuing financial support given to the University through Our United Outreach and we appreciate the annual reporting of the University to General Assembly.

We want to commend the Board of Trustees for their hard work and the committee is pleased with the progress Bethel is making and has plans to make in the future. We want to encourage the congregations and members of the Cumberland Presbyterian Church to continue to remember the University in its prayers and ongoing support and make the following recommendation:

RECOMMENDATION 9: Recognizing the importance of a free standing chapel to expose the student body to Cumberland Presbyterian Faith and Values, we recommend that the General Assembly encourage congregations and members of the Cumberland Presbyterian Church to support the building of the Cumberland Chapel with their prayers and offerings.

Respectfully submitted,
Committee on Higher Education

REPORT OF THE COMMITTEE ON
CHILDREN'S HOME/HISTORICAL FOUNDATION

(Appendix H)

I. REFERRALS

Referrals to this committee are as follows: The Report of the Board of Trustees of the Cumberland Presbyterian Children's Home and The Report of the Board of Trustees of the Historical Foundation.

II. PERSONS OF COUNSEL

Appearing before this committee were: Reverend Richard Brown, President, CEO and General Counsel; Dr. Jennifer Livings, Vice President Programs, and Reverend Stephanie Brown of the Cumberland Presbyterian Children's Home; Reverend Alfonso Marquez, member of the Board of Trustees of the Cumberland Presbyterian Children's Home; Ms. Susan Knight Gore, Executive Director of the Historical Foundation; and Reverend Tommy Jobe, member of the Board of Trustees of the Historical Foundation.

III. THE REPORT OF THE BOARD OF TRUSTEES
OF THE CUMBERLAND PRESBYTERIAN CHILDREN'S HOME

Their heart for the Children's Home and professionalism was apparent. We appreciated their commitment to their call. We affirm the work they are doing and the "Pyramid of Care" structure they have established to care for the children and families that God brings to them. They are changing lives for generations to come. We believe that the Children's Home will continue to flourish under their leadership and care.

RECOMMENDATION 1: That the Report of the Board of Trustees of the Cumberland Presbyterian Children's Home be concurred in.

IV. REPORT OF THE BOARD OF TRUSTEES OF THE HISTORICAL FOUNDATION

A. HISTORY INTERPRETATION AND PROMOTIONAL ACTIVITIES

1. 1810 Circle

RECOMMENDATION 2: That Recommendation 1 of the Report of the Board of Trustees of the Historical Foundation, "that the General Assembly make congregations and presbyteries aware of the 1810 Circle and encourage new members to support this endeavor annually," be adopted.

2. Denomination Day Offering

RECOMMENDATION 3: That Recommendation 2 of the Report of the Board of Trustees of the Historical Foundation, "that congregations be encouraged to have a special offering on the Sunday designated as Denomination Day to help support the special project designated for that year," be adopted.

B. PUBLICATIONS

1. Publication Series

RECOMMENDATION 4: That Recommendation 3 of the Report of the Board of Trustees of the Historical Foundation, "that the General Assembly make presbyteries, congregations, and individuals aware that the Historical Foundation is interested and has funds to publish books on topics concerning the Cumberland Presbyterian Church and Cumberland Presbyterian Church in America," be adopted.

2. Online Promotions

RECOMMENDATION 5: That Recommendation 4 of the Report of the Board of Trustees of the Historical Foundation, "that the General Assembly encourage presbyteries, congregations, and individuals active on the internet to join the Historical Foundation of the CPC & CPCA Facebook group," be adopted.

C. ACQUISITIONS

RECOMMENDATION 6: That Recommendation 5 of the Report of the Board of Trustees of the Historical Foundation, "that the General Assembly encourage all congregations to preserve their session records by depositing them in the Historical Foundation," be adopted.

RECOMMENDATION 7: That Recommendation 6 of the Report of the Board of Trustees of the Historical Foundation, "that the General Assembly instruct each synod and presbytery to deposit their minutes in a timely fashion with the Historical Foundation," be adopted.

RECOMMENDATION 8: That Recommendation 7 of the Report of the Board of Trustees of the Historical Foundation, "that the General Assembly instruct presbyteries to locate the session records when closing a church and then deposit them in the Historical Foundation," be adopted.

V. RESOLUTION HONORING THE REVEREND DOCTOR JAMES CAYCE GILBERT LEGACY

RECOMMENDATION 9: That the resolution honoring the Reverend Doctor James Cayce Gilbert, which reads:

WHEREAS, James C. Gilbert participated in the sale of Easter eggs to benefit the Cumberland Presbyterian Children's Home during the Great Depression, and

WHEREAS, Reverend James C. Gilbert joined the Board of Trustees of the Cumberland Presbyterian Children's Home in 1959; and

WHEREAS, Reverend James C. Gilbert was elected to the Executive Board of Trustees of the Cumberland Presbyterian Children's Home as Secretary in 1960; and

WHEREAS, Reverend James C. Gilbert began his service as Executive Director of the Cumberland Presbyterian Children's Home in 1964; and

WHEREAS, Reverend Doctor James C. Gilbert's 26 year tenure as Executive Director stabilized the Cumberland Presbyterian Children's Home; and

WHEREAS, Reverend Doctor James C. Gilbert innovated new child care programs; and

WHEREAS, Reverend Doctor James C. Gilbert enlisted ecumenical partners; and

WHEREAS, Reverend Doctor James C. Gilbert promoted a sustaining endowment; and

WHEREAS, Reverend Doctor James C. Gilbert restored Cumberland Presbyterian confidence and pride in the Cumberland Presbyterian Children's Home;

NOW, THEREFORE, BE IT RESOLVED that the Cumberland Presbyterian Children's Home hereby recognizes the legacy of Reverend Doctor James C. Gilbert and the benefit that legacy continues to bring children and families; and

BE IT FURTHER RESOLVED that copies of this Resolution be framed and presented to Reverend Doctor James C. Gilbert's four daughters: Elizabeth Gilbert Horsley, Suzanne Gilbert Dougherty, Kathryn Gilbert Craig and Rosalie Gilbert Nelson, who themselves have no small part in the legacy of Reverend Doctor James C. Gilbert; and

BE IT FURTHER RESOLVED that a copy be framed and presented to Mrs. Freda Mitchell Gilbert in honor of the work, ministry and family they shared.
be adopted.

Respectfully Submitted,
The Committee on the Children's Home and the Historical Foundation

CHURCH CALENDAR 2014-2015

JULY 2014

6-11	CPYC, Bethel University, McKenzie, TN
12	Program of Alternate Studies Graduation
12-26	PAS Summer Extension School, Bethel University, McKenzie, TN
19	Children's Fest, Bethel University, McKenzie, TN
22-26	Ministers Retreat, Bethel University, McKenzie, TN

AUGUST 2014

23	MTS Fall classes begin
31-Sept 28	Christian Education Season

SEPTEMBER 2014

3	MTS Opening Convocation
14	Senior Adult Sunday
21	Christian Service Recognition Sunday
28	International Day of Prayer and Action for Human Habitat

OCTOBER 2014

1-31	Clergy Appreciation Month
5	Worldwide Communion Day
12	Pastor Appreciation Sunday
26	Native American Sunday

NOVEMBER 2014

Any Sunday in November Loaves and Fishes Program

1	All Saints Day
2	Stewardship Sunday
3-6	The Forum
9	World Community Day (Church Women United)
9	Day of Prayer for People with AIDS and Other Life-Threatening Illnesses
16	Bible Sunday
23	Christ the King Sunday
30-Dec 25	Advent in Church and Home

DECEMBER 2014

Any Sunday in December Gift to the King Offering

24	Christmas Eve
25	Christmas Day

JANUARY 2015

6	Epiphany
11	Human Trafficking Awareness Day
12-13	Stated Clerk's Conference
15	Deadline for receipt of 2014 Our United Outreach contributions

FEBRUARY 2015

1-28	Black History Month
1	Annual congregational reports due in GA office
1	Denomination Day
1	Historical Foundation Offering
1	Souper Bowl Sunday
8	Our United Outreach Sunday
15	Youth Sunday
18	Ash Wednesday, the beginning of Lent
18-Apr 5	Lent to Easter

MARCH 2015

1-31	Women's History Month (USA)
22-28	National Farm Workers Awareness Week
29	Palm/Passion Sunday
29	One Great Hour of Sharing

APRIL 2015

2	Maundy Thursday
3	Good Friday
5	Easter
12	CP Children's Home Sunday
12-18	Family Week
25-26	30-Hour Famine

MAY 2015

1	Friendship Day (Church Women United)
16	MTS Closing Convocation & Graduation
24	Memorial Day Offering for Military Chaplains & Personnel for USA churches
24	Pentecost
24	World Mission Sunday

JUNE 2015

7	Children's Fest, CPCH, Denton, TX
19-26	General Assembly, Colombia, South America
19-26	CPWM Convention, Colombia, South America